Tour Design, Marketing, and Management

James M. Poynter

REGENTS/PRENTICE HALL
Englewood Cliffs, New Jersey 07632

Library of Congress Cataloging-in-Publication Data

Poynter, James M.
    Tour design, marketing, and management / James M. Poynter.
        p.   cm.
    Includes bibliographical references and index.
    ISBN 0-13-205345-4
    1. Tour guides (Persons)—Vocational guidance.   I. Title.
G154.7.P69 1993
338.4'791023—dc20   92–15906
                                                        CIP

Acquisition Editor: Robin Baliszewski
Production Editors: Fred Dahl and Rose Kernan
Copy Editor: Rose Kernan
Designers: Fred Dahl and Rose Kernan
Prepress Buyer: Ilene Levy
Manufacturing Buyer: Ed O'Dougherty
Supplements Editor: Judy Casillo

© 1993 by REGENTS/PRENTICE HALL
A Division of Simon & Schuster
Englewood Cliffs, New Jersey 07632

Printed in the United States of America
10 9 8 7 6 5 4 3 2 1

ISBN 0-13-205345-4

Prentice-Hall International (UK) Limited, London
Prentice-Hall of Australia Pty. Limited, Sydney
Prentice-Hall Canada Inc., Toronto
Prentice-Hall Hispanoamericana, S.A., Mexico
Prentice-Hall of India Private Limited, New Delhi
Prentice-Hall of Japan, Inc., Tokyo
Simon & Schuster Asia Pte. Ltd, Singapore
Editora Prentice-Hall do Brasil, Ltda., Rio de Janeiro

To
Bill Poynter,
The Intrepid Traveler

Contents

CHAPTER 2

Costing and Pricing a Tour, 23

CHAPTER 3

One-Day Domestic Tours, 44

CHAPTER 4

Tour Marketing, 81

CHAPTER 5

Established Tour Operator's Initial Tour Development, 117

CHAPTER 6

Itinerary Development, 136

CHAPTER 7

Pre-Tour Management and Processing Considerations, 167

CHAPTER 8
Tour Manuals, 188

CHAPTER 13

The Vendor Booking Process, 280

CHAPTER 14

Client Reservations, 291

About the Author

Jim Poynter has worked in the travel industry for nearly 30 years. He has worked in almost every segment of the industry, in ten countries, and on four continents. Mr. Poynter received both his B.A. and his M.A. from The George Washington University in Washington, D.C. He has taught with the Florida State University Hotel School, National College, Tallahassee Community College, and Metropolitan State College of Denver, where he currently directs the Travel Administration Program in the Hospitality, Meeting, and Travel Administration Department of the School of Professional Studies. Mr. Poynter was the first Director of the Institute of Certified Travel Agents and served as a TransWorld Airlines' Educational Consultant to Saudi Arabian Airlines for five years.

He has conducted seminars for five national travel associations, at 12 universities and colleges, and for a wide range of private institutions. He has owned or co-owned five travel agencies (including one devoted primarily to running tours), designed and marketed over 60 tours, personally guided more than 40 tours, and has been a consultant to a large number of tour companies.

Mr. Poynter was a founding board member of the Rocky Mountain Chapter of the Professional Guides Association of America and has served on the board of five other national and regional associations. He is the only honorary member ever selected by the Institute of Certified Travel Agents and the Rocky Mountain Business Travel Association. He has been selected for inclusion in several "Who's Whos," most recently the Marquis Who's Who In The West. Mr. Poynter has authored more than 60 articles and four travel-industry related textbooks.

Preface

Tour Design, Marketing, and Management is the first comprehensive book on how to develop, design, and market tours and how to set up and run a tour company. Therefore, the book meets several needs. It is designed to provide travel educators with a text for a standard one-semester or one-quarter course devoted to tour development, design, and marketing. It also is designed to meet the needs of a new tour company practitioner, be that person a tour company executive, a reservationist, a planner, or a guide. It allows this person to understand the basics of his job, but equally important, it gives the new practitioner an opportunity to gain a more global view and to understand how his job interfaces with others working for the company. Finally, the book is designed to meet the needs of experienced tour executives who are undertaking new or different aspects of tour operations and who seek a reference publication to guide them as they take on these new tasks.

Since the late 1970s, the approaches used in this book have been used to teach college and university students how to design and market tours and how to develop and run a tour company. These approaches work. Many graduates of this system have established successful tour companies. Their companies are of all sizes—mostly small, but some are the largest in their geographic areas and in their fields of specialization. Their companies offer tours of all types—mostly local and regional bus tours, but many are international air tours.

The book begins with the premise that you should start small. It then presents tour design and development processes which break down learning (a few basic concepts are presented in each chapter), building continuously on previously learned concepts. In class, students work in small teams to design all aspects of a short, one-day local tour. Components of the program from which this book was written move the student from the one-day local tour to two-day, weekend more-distant tours, multi-day domestic tours, and, finally, to lengthy international tours.

This is a "hands-on" practical approach to learning tour development, design, and marketing. Although the tours developed by students may never "go," students are always encouraged to treat them as "real" rather than "made-up-for-educational-purposes" tours.

The chapter organization helps both the student and the teacher. Each chapter starts with a list of objectives, followed by the chapter text. End-of-chapter materials include a summary, a set of discussion questions (the answers are in the *Instructor's Manual*), three role-play exercises, a group discussion situation, and one or more practical application exercises that can either be completed by a "team" of students or by each student individually. The role plays reinforce the learning concepts presented in the chapter. The group discussion situations allow students to discuss often controversial tour issues in a frequently humorous format. The practical application exercises allow students to build a tour and a simulated tour company over the several weeks of the quarter or the semester with the exercises of one chapter building and adding to those that came in previous chapters.

Experienced tour executives will find several chapters of special interest if they elect to use the book as a reference publication. The costing and pricing section in Chapter 2 provides a comprehensive approach toward including all costs, yet keeping pricing at a competitive level. The editorial copy is supplemented by a schematic formula identifying a step-by-step costing and pricing process. This process is circular in effect and the circular dynamic is diagrammed for easy reference.

One of the major areas of altercations in the tour business is between those who work in the home office operation and those who lead or "guide" tours. The chapter dealing with the tour operator—tour manager relationship helps to identify where the potential "pressure" points are in the relationship, suggesting processes for developing a smooth, easy-flowing relationship.

The marketing of tours is one of the major problem areas of many tour companies. In the section on marketing, several major marketing approaches successfully used by tour company executives are identified and discussed in detail. Analyzing potential marketing strategies and selecting those that will be most beneficial for an individual tour company is made easier through the use of the approaches discussed in this chapter.

One reviewer commented that the chapter on tour buses and tour bus drivers is so comprehensive that it could be a "mini-book" itself. The selection of an appropriate bus, the contracting process, and the interrelationships between the tour company and the bus company, on the one hand, and between tour guides and bus drivers, on the other, are all frought with potential problems. This section guides the tour executive through the selection and negotiation process and provides guidelines for tour leaders and tour managers in their interrelationships with tour bus drivers. Although not all potential problems are addressed, this set of guidelines provides both the tour executive and the tour guide with a set of procedures and processes which should be helpful in reducing, if not eliminating the major problems.

For the student or the new tour company employee, it is suggested that this book be read in the normal manner—progressing from Chapter 1 through

Chapter 17. After reading each chapter, stop and consider the main points. Review the end-of-chapter summaries and answer the end-of-chapter discussion questions. Then complete the exercise(s). This summary and series of questions combine to provide an excellent review for the entire chapter. The completion of the exercise(s) allows you to "apply" much of the learning which was presented in the chapter. Next, read the role plays and attempt to pick up each role play either in your own mind, or even better, through a discussion with another student or someone else working in the tour field. This will provide yet another opportunity to review major points in the chapter. Finally, turn to the case situation. After reading the case situation, give some thought as to how you would handle the situation and what recommendations you would make. You may even wish to detail these in writing.

An alternative approach for the student or the new tour company employee is to start each chapter with a review of the summary and the end-of-chapter questions. This will provide an overview of the major points in the chapter and some of the most important questions that are answered in the chapter. After using the review and end-of-chapter questions as an introduction to the chapter, read the chapter looking for the answers to the questions as you go. This is not to suggest that this is the only purpose of reading the chapter, but it is suggested that you consciously think about the questions and perhaps even write down the answers to questions as you come to them in your reading of the chapter. After the chapter reading, again go back over the summary and the questions before moving on to the role plays, the case situation, and the exercise(s).

For the experienced tour executive, this book presents an excellent resource. The experienced executive may not wish to read the book from cover to cover, but may want to delve into specific chapters on an "as needed" basis. It is suggested that you use the table of contents and the index to identify those sections of the book that meet your specific needs. You may wish to go directly to those sections when the need arises.

This book is the result of the input and concerns of literally scores of those working in the tour industry. It is the outgrowth of industry tour management seminars, college tour classes, and a multitude of other industry and student educational programs. It was reviewed by and bears the strong imprint of travel and tour educators. It is designed to bring together the contributions of all to provide professional development for the practitioner, and rudimentary tour development and marketing expertise for the novice. It will be updated on a regular basis.

If you have suggestions or recommendations that will make the book better, please do not hesitate to write to me, the author, at the following address: 6994 East Heritage Place, North, Englewood, Colorado 80111. There is a strong probability that your suggestions will be included in the next revision and I thank you in advance for your contributions.

Acknowledgments

The contributors to this book are many. I am deeply indebted to all of them. Both Bill Poynter and Pat Poynter were inspirations for the book, and their contributions in the form of antecdotes from their many tours can be found in several of the chapters.

Unfortunately many of the historical contributions of tour industry leaders have not been salvaged and retained for those who have come after them. I will forever be grateful for the contributions of three tour industry leaders who have passed on but who provided me with a wealth of tour industry knowledge before they left us. They are R. W. "Bert" Hemphill (often called the Dean of the travel industry) of Helphill Tours (later merged and renamed Hemphill Harris Tours), George Brownell, of Brownell Tours, and Thomas Donovan of Cartan Tours.

The National Tour Association and especially its National Tour Foundation was of considerable assistance. They provided a listing of certification papers and copies of those that were of special value. This provided considerable help in preparing many chapters—especially the one on tour manuals. I was also given a listing of members. Contacts with many of the members provided a wealth of material contributions. Those whose contributions were utilized to the largest extent include Jim Devlin with Trentway Tours, Ltd., Isabel Rojo of Rojo Tours and Services, Inc., Barbara Osman, CTP with Four Seasons Tours, Patricia Barnett, CTP, with Barnett Tour and Travel, and Paul Weldin, CTP of Pressley Tours, Inc.

Special thanks go to Mark Holland and Bill Teasdale. Mark encouraged the writing of the book, contributed a large number of ideas for material that "should" be included, provided several good photos of adventure tour activities, his specialty, and solicited the many documents so kindly provided by Rojo Tours, the primary company for which Mark works as a guide/tour manager. Bill provided insights from running his own tour company, Premier Tours of Colorado, and the contributions he has made to other tour companies. He also undertook a study of tour manuals and in this way contributed to the tour manual chapter.

Officers in and members of the Professional Guides Association of America, especially those who are members of the Rocky Mountain Chapter, were of considerable help. Primary among these are Edd Farrell, Executive Director with PGAA; Jo Ann Fitch, CPG, (Past President of PGAA); Ruby Ellen Hale; and Lynette Hinings-Marshall.

Travel educators contributed, sometimes with sharp criticism, sometimes with quiet encouragement, and sometimes with "You ought to includes". Thanks for these contributions go to: Elisabeth Van Dyke, Ph.D., CTC of the University of New Haven, who provided information beneficial to end of chapter exercise development; Marc Mancini, Ph.D., whose experience in and whose contributions to the tour industry are legendary; Marilyn Kern-Ladner, CTC, whose tour program at Miami-Dade Community College is perhaps the most comprehensive of any in the country; Donald Vagell of Metropolitan State College of Denver; and Marci Butler, CTC, DS of the Community College of Denver.

Those who have sponsored my continuing education tour seminars in cities throughout the country have been special contributors. Their precise knowledge of short seminar education for those interested in starting tour companies or interested in entering the guiding field has helped to make the seminars more relevant and the book more precisely targeted to the needs of readers. These educators include John Hand of the Colorado Free University; Bill Hogue and Sue Glenn with FunEd in Dallas; Bob Wagner with The Chicago, New York City, and Cincinati divisions of The Discovery Center; Andrea Driessen of Open U. in Minneapolis; Lois Colson of the Jefferson County Public Schools' Adult and Continuing Education Center in Golden, Colorado; Gary Swenson with Global Insight; Tom Gorman of Mid-Plains Community College in North Platte, Nebraska; Debra Leopold of First Class, Inc. in Washington, D.C.; and Derek Selbo and Paul Picone of The Knowledge Shop in Orlando, Florida.

Considerable thanks go to those in my academic department at Metropolitan State College of Denver who so strongly support my writing efforts. Primary among these is the the Department Chair, Ray Langbenh; the Director of the Meetings Management Program, Yvonne Spaulding, and the secretary of the Hospitality, Meeting, and Travel Administration Department, who is far more than a secretary, Alma Anguiano.

Current and past students, especially those who have started, manage, or work with tour companies are thanked for their contributions, which have been many. These include: Brad Swartzwelter and Hugh Wilson of Main Line Tours; Nancy Adams of Travel To Music Tours; Dawn Morris with Rainbow Tours; Natali Olander with the Tour Division of James Travel Points International; and Kevin and Marsha Vaughn of Earth Tours Ltd.

Tour company owners and executives with whom I have worked over many years contributed substantially by providing examples of tour management problems and resolutions to those problems. These individuals include Nancy Richardson with Western Wanderers, Tom Stimson with Intertreck, Penny Pritchett with TimeFlight, Beth Narva with S. W. Tours; Janet Griffith, owner and developer of the Incentive Travel Division of Tabor Travel Professionals International; and Miles Hoover with Maritz Travel.

Others who contributed in significant ways include Andy Alpine with the *Specialty Travel Index,* United Airlines, Wight Mixon with Presenting Atlanta; Dan

Bicker with Classic World Travel; Dan Goodyear with Panorama Coaches; Vern West with the Private Rail Car Owners' Association; Nick Jones with Gray Line; Sandy Whistler with Airport Services; and Dave Wiggins with American Wilderness Experience, Inc.

Robin Baliszewski, Senior Editor with Prentice Hall, led the development of this book from the germ of an idea to the finished hardback product. Working with an editor with Robin's professionalism is indeed a pleasure. Guiding the manuscript through its many manufacturing stages and making the multitude of small changes that "polish" a publication was Rose Kernan. Thank you, Rose. And what are books without marketing? I have Dan Bowers, Regional Editor of the Prentice Hall College Sales and Marketing Division, to thank for pushing me to contract for this and other travel books and for promoting the cause of travel and tourism books in general among his peers and among his clients. Alice Price, President of the Colorado Authors League, is thanked for her review of contracts.

I am deeply indebted to Tom Salas, Graphic Designer with the Auraria Media Center. Tom has developed the original design work for the graphics used in many of my courses for a number of years. Several of the figures in this book were first developed from Tom's sophistication of my sometimes very rough sketches. He not only made sense out of them, but in addition he has helped me to fine tune several of the graphics as I have worked with them in classes and seminars.

Book reviewers make a substantial difference in the quality of textbooks. Their contributions make the book far more practical. I am, therefore, especially grateful to the following travel educators who lent their expertise to a review of the manuscript for this book: Roberta Sebo of Johnson & Wales University and Edmund Grey Metzold of the Spencer Business School. Patricia Altwegg, Ph.D. of Cloud County Community College not only reviewed the manuscript, but strongly encouraged the development and writing of the manuscript. Russell Nauta of Colorado Mountain College, reviewed an early copy of the manuscript and gave a number of suggestions for inclusions and alterations.

Special thanks go to my wife, Sorore, and my sons, Lewis, Robert, and Michael. It is probably never easy to live in the same house with a writer. The patience of my family with typing at all hours, the several years of research, and all the other inconveniences they have had to bear is very much appreciated.

CHAPTER 1

The Tour Operator–Tour Manager Relationship

OBJECTIVES

Upon completion of this chapter, the student will be able to:

1. Identify a realistic match between tour guide characteristics and tour company types by completing a tour company/guide matching chart.

2. Fill in the guide semantics continuum, identifying titles of those working in the guiding industry and placing those titles on appropriate points along the continuum.

3. Compare the most sought-after characteristics of tour managers as identified by tour operators with the characteristics of the most professional tour managers identified by the International Association of Tour Managers and to explain the differences.

4. Provide an explanation of the statement that, "More tour guides and managers have been fired for ethics violations than for any other reason."

Introduction

The relationship between the tour operator and the tour manager is crucial to the tour experience. The tour industry in America has grown substantially in recent years. However, with the growth have come misunderstandings and misconceptions about the industry. This chapter will introduce the tour concept. It will provide a brief background of the industry, and it will explore both inbound and outbound tours. Next, the reader will be brought up-to-date with an overview of tour operations today. Because many confuse tour operators with tour managers and are not sure of who does what in the industry, an introduction to tour guides and tour managers will be presented along with a comparison of the roles and types of tour operators and tour managers. Finally, the chapter will discuss the continuing struggle to come up with the perfect match between tour manager and tour operator.

Inbound Tours Versus Outbound Tours

Tours are two-directional. The most familiar type of tour in the industry is organized in a community. A group of people from the community go to another location for a trip that may last from one to several days. This is an *outbound tour*. In other words, it leaves from a home town, a home state, or a home country to a location away from that home location.

The other type of tour is less familiar. The *inbound tour* consists of a group of people coming into one's home town or home state. It can be a tour group of people from some other place in the United States or from another country. Many tour operators handle only outbound tours. However, increasingly in America we have begun to model the European tour industry by handling inbound tours as well.

The tour operator who specializes in inbound tours is frequently called either a *reception operator* or a *destination management specialist/company*. Although in the United States we have reception operators who handle nothing but inbound tours, increasingly tour operators are handling both outbound tours and inbound tours and are performing the role of reception operator/destination management specialist as well as outbound tour operator. The inbound reception operator/outbound tour operator works with the tour organizer and offers services that can consist of meeting an inbound tour group at the airport, transferring the tour group from the airport to its in-town hotel, arranging for short local sightseeing trips, and arranging for one day sightseeing or multiday tours of the home state or area. If local (step-on) guides are provided, they are usually experts in the specific area being traveled by the tour, and they will frequently work with the inbound tour group's full-time tour manager.

The outbound tour operator sells a tour to residents of the local community, a state, or a home country. The tour operator then may or may not:

- Arrange transportation to a central point where the tour starts.
- Provide a tour guide/manager to go with the tour from the point of origin to each destination.
- Contract with inbound tour operators or reception operators to provide buses and local sightseeing or local guide specialists.
- Make arrangements with other vendors such as hotel vendors, restaurants, and so forth to provide for their services as needed throughout the tour.

An Overview of Tour Management Today

The story of expansion applies to both tour managers and the tour industry. Tour managers or tour guides, those professionals who lead tours, have increased in number dramatically. In the early 1980s one of the major international associations for those working in the guiding field classified the United States as an "underdeveloped country" in terms of the "guiding" profession. America had so few professional tour guides/managers and so few who worked in the guiding field at all, that those evaluating the field in America wrote it off as both nonexistent and unprofessional. Today, the field is so big that when the Professional Guides Association of America started in 1988, it became the world's largest guide association in two years.

The Guide/Tour Manager Semantics and Hierarchy

Much in the industry is unwritten practice. Part of what is confusing to the person new to the industry, however, is the semantics. Terms are bantered about in such a way that it can be very confusing for the person who is not familiar with them. Probably the most confusing terms are those applying to the person who leads tours. Read the job description in Figure 1-1. This was routinely provided by one tour company to those applying for a guiding position. Note the several terms used for the person who would perform/provide guiding services for the tour company.

The most professional of the tour leaders is usually called a *tour manager*. This term itself can be confusing. Hearing this term, one might logically think the tour manager is the person who is the manager of a tour company. Because tour companies themselves are called tour operations (the person who owns and runs one is called a tour operator), many who encounter this term are also confused. Practically speaking, within the industry, terms are frequently used interchangeably and incorrectly. There are, for example, some in the industry who say "guide" and mean a step-on guide (normally an entry-level position), and there are those who say "guide" and mean tour manager (the most professional and experienced guide). Others use the term *guide* or *escort* for any of the positions on the continuum from entry-level position to the most professional position. Still others utilize terms that are totally foreign to most in the industry. For example, the term *interpreter* is becoming popular in some parts of America. Those who use this term justify it by saying the "interpreter" is "interpreting" what is seen and experienced by the tour members for the tour members and that this job of interpretation is the most important job undertaken by the tour leader. So many people who have associated themselves with this line of reasoning that there is a national association of interpreters along with an association of tour managers and an association of tour guides. All consider themselves professionals and all represent the industry.

The following guide to titles/terms will help to set aside the confusion, but the terms (and their descriptors) should not at all be treated as a "bible" (see Figure 1-2). The following are the more commonly used terms for those in the guiding field.

Step-On Guide

The step-on guide position is the most commonly found entry-level position. This person normally works for a ground operator, a sightseeing company, or an inbound tour operator. Step-on guides are experienced in specific tours. Normally they are experts for those short tours in and around the guide's home

FIGURE 1-1 SAMPLE TOUR GUIDE JOB DESCRIPTION.

The tour guide, step-on guide, or tour manager is responsible for the management of the entire tour or that portion of the tour for which he has been contracted. He is responsible for the safety and enjoyment of each and every tour member and of the tour as a group. He is responsible for all vendor interaction while on the tour. The tour guide/manager, while on tour, is usually the only personal contact the tour members have with our company. Therefore, he is our "PR Man" on-the-spot.

The tour guide/manager is expected to know all technical arrangements which have been made for the tour before departing on the tour. Minor adjustments may be made if the tour guide/manager deems them necessary. Before making any change, however, it is expected that one will consider possible ramifications to our company, vendors, and individual tour members and all changes should be reported in the daily tour report.

Interaction with vendors should be diplomatic, professional, and polite. Tips should be offered discretely and in sealed envelopes.

In dealing with tour members, lead by example and with a quiet, nonregimented calmness. Be attentive and act as an escort, not as a guard. Be available to all members equally, but avoid anything that might be considered as sexual in intent or in contact. Never touch a tour member unless that tour member asks you for physical assistance. Even then, use judgment before providing physical assistance.

The tour guide/manager is expected to set an example at all times. The image guidelines in the tour manual must be followed. Smoking and drinking are discouraged, but the company wil accept both in extreme moderation.

All reconfirmations should be made when scheduled and reconfirmation call reports should be prepared as soon as possible (no later than the same day they are made). The guide/manager is responsible for the smooth flow of the tour from beginning to end. All time and expense records are to be updated daily and all final documentation should be turned in within three business days of the completion of the tour.

The tour guide/manager is expected to read, know, and follow the guidelines and rules contained in the tour manual. Any question reguarding these should be brought up with the guide's/manager's immediate supervisor, the Guide Director, prior to the departure of the tour, if possible.

town. The step-on guide usually works on either a per-hour or a per-trip basis. The guide receives a phone call shortly before the tour is to depart asking that the guide arrive at the point where tour members will board a tour bus. They greet the tour members, run the tour, and handle debarkation or end-of-tour activities/paperwork. Many work as step-on guides on a part-time basis. They may be employed in some other full-time position and work as step-on guides in the evening or over the weekend. They may be housewives working short day trips two or three days a week while their children are in school. Many are retirees working as step-on guides whenever they are called. Typically they work a heavy schedule, perhaps almost every day, during the summer "peak" tour season and work either not at all or only a few days a week in the fall, winter, and spring.

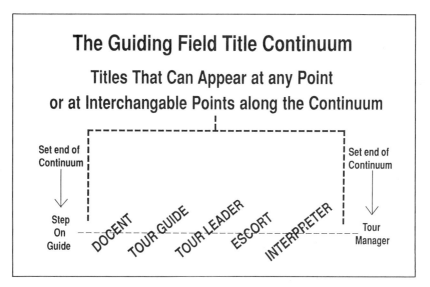

FIGURE 1-2 THE GUIDING FIELD TITLE CONTINUUM.

Guide/Escort

The guide or the escort (both terms are used interchangeably in the industry) has more authority and responsibility. The guide/escort often contracts for a multiday tour and usually is responsible for all aspects of the tour for its entire duration (from hometown departure to hometown return). He/she accompanies the tour at all times (except free time). This person usually works on a tour-by-tour basis, but the more professional guide/escort may be employed by a tour company throughout that company's season. Many guides and escorts start as step-on guides, and, as they become more professional, they move into a full-time guide/escort position during the season. Usually these people are employed full-time throughout the season. Rarely is a guide/escort employed full-time throughout the year. In some cases, especially when working for a large tour operator, the guide/escort may be employed in a marketing role in the off season, complementing the guide/escort role during the season. In this way they can be profitably employed on a full-time basis, benefiting both the tour operator and the guide/escort.

Tour Manager

The term *tour manager* is normally reserved for those who are considered to be the most professional in the guiding field. Most companies expect them to have at least five years of full-time experience in leading tours. Some companies require additional qualifications (such as membership in the International Association of Tour Managers).

Other terms, such as "tour leader" and "docent," are used to some degree in the industry.

The Roles of Tour Operator and Tour Management Professionals

The *tour manager* is a key person working for the tour operator. Typically, the tour manager is responsible for a tour from the time that the tour starts to the time that it is finished. The tour manager is the tour company as far as the client is concerned. In most cases, the client never sees another person other than the tour manager, who is a representative of the tour operator. Therefore, the tour manager's role is not only to conduct and direct the tour, but to represent the tour operator to tour members as well. In this role, tour managers are expected to abide by the policies and procedures specified by the tour operator and to handle themselves with professional decorum.

The tour manager also acts as the tour operator's representative in relationships with vendors. The tour manager is the tour operator's front-line quality control specialist. It is the tour manager's responsibility to make certain that the quality of the vendor-provided services and products is that which has been negotiated for, agreed upon, and contracted. If a vendor offers a service or product less than that which was agreed upon, the tour manager is expected to evaluate the inferior service or product and insist upon receiving the product or service that was agreed upon.

The tour manager also acts in an arbitrator role. When there is confusion regarding the quality of a service or product to be provided, it is normally expected that the tour manager will make decisions on behalf of the tour operator and arbitrate any differences so that tour members receive the quality of service contracted.

The *tour operator,* on the other hand, has the responsibility of putting the tour together, marketing it, taking reservations, handling all financial and accounting aspects, and selecting and managing tour managers. Some tour operators believe that they need to provide tour managers with detailed guidelines and specifications so that all decisions, including all minor decisions are made by the tour operator rather than the tour manager. Other tour operators believe that the tour manager needs to have flexibility. They provide the tour manager with general guidelines, but leave decisions enroute to the tour manager.

The degree to which the tour operator guides and directs the tour manager is a major source of contention between tour operators and tour managers. Some tour managers work very well with a considerable degree of management and guidance. Many others, however, expect and wish to receive considerable flexibility. Matching the tour company's styles and approaches with those which a tour guide or tour manager brings to a tour operator is difficult. Finding a good match is a continuing struggle. This struggle is often times more difficult with large tour companies since the guide/tour manager must interface to some

Typical Organization Chart of a Small Tour Company

FIGURE 1-3 TYPICAL ORGANIZATION
CHART OF A SMALL TOUR COMPANY.

Typical Organization Chart of a Large Tour Company

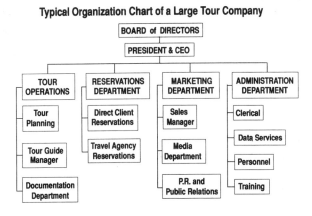

FIGURE 1-4 TYPICAL ORGANIZATION CHART OF A
LARGE TOUR COMPANY.

extent with more persons in a wider variety of position titles than the guide/tour manager in a small tour company. Figures 1-3 and 1-4 reflect this difference in numbers of employees/titles found in small versus large tour companies.

Relations between the Operations Department and the Tour Manager

In many tour companies it is the operations department that is charged with the responsibility of preparing all aspects of a tour prior to the departure. They oversee the tour during the time that it is running, and follow up on the tour after it is over. Although this series of responsibilities will be organized differ-ently ently from company to company, the tour operator typically will assign one person or one department the responsibility for all aspects of a tour.

This responsibility includes developing the tour in the beginning, mak-ing certain that all contracts with vendors are completed, working with the marketing department to make certain that the tour meets client needs, work-ing with the reservations department in obtaining the names of tour clients, developing rooming lists and other documents relating to the tour, briefing the tour manager prior to departure, staying in touch with the tour manager while the tour is being conducted, and handling all end-of-tour wrap-up and paperwork activities. Because it is the operations department with which the tour manager interfaces most and because it is the operations department that is responsible for the tour from the beginning to the end, the mainte-nance of a good relationship between the tour manager and the operations department is essential. To make this relationship work well, it is necessary for both the tour manager and the manager of the operations department to understand the importance of the relationship. Ideally, adequate discus-sion whenever a problem or a potential problem arises and a mechanism set up in advance to resolve problems easily and comfortably guarantee maxi-mum results.

Much of the success of this relationship depends upon personalities. Typi-cally, the personalities required to do each of the jobs are very different. Tour managers need to be outgoing, gregarious individuals. Some are less detail ori-ented than others. The tour operations department, however, must be con-cerned with details. Therefore, the operations department is usually headed by a person who is very detail oriented. Because of the different types of person-alities involved, the potential for misconceptions, misunderstandings, and diffi-culties is high. When the tour manager reports to someone other than the manager of the operations department (this is rare, but it does happen), prob-lems can be enhanced if neither has authority over the other. Both can view their roles as being superior in importance and both can make strained rela-tionships uncomfortable, even to the point of resulting in a bad tour for the clients.

Most tour operators, however, structure the organization so that the tour manager reports to the operations manager. This produces a clear line of au-thority. Tour managers then follow the policies and procedures established by operations managers. A potential difficulty under these circumstances is that operations managers may not be aware of the practical problems on tour and may be less marketing conscious than executives in the company would like them to be. This can result in policies and procedures that may result in clients being concerned or upset about some aspect of the tour. Ideally, an operations manager will have some experience in managing tours. Some companies require their operations managers to have tour management experience. Some even re-quire them to lead one or more tours per year so that they can stay aware of the practical concerns and problems faced by a tour manager.

What the Tour Operator Looks For in Tour Managers

Many consider leading tours to be a glamorous job and, in many ways, it is. It is also hard work. The hard work is what tour operators think about when selecting tour guides and tour managers.

The results of a recent survey of tour operators asking what they consider to be of greatest importance in hiring tour guides and tour managers prove very interesting when compared with the listing of criteria developed by the International Association of Tour Managers for the professional tour manager. None indicated a requirement for the completion of a specified number of years of education, but several indicated a preference for such specialized training as first-aid and CPR. As a group, employers listed the following as important characteristics:

- image
- an outgoing personality
- a sense of humor
- organizational skills
- a strong sense of ethics
- the ability to make decisions and
- a love of people, places, and travel

The International Association of Tour Managers, on the other hand, has identified the following eight comprehensive tour manager travel skills:

1. Overseeing the whole tour
2. Dealing with problems
3. Cultural and language guidance
4. Sales representation
5. Providing information
6. General organization
7. Quality control
8. Business generation

"Image" heads the list of characteristics sought by tour operators. Just as airlines consider inflight services (stewards and stewardesses) to be the most important public contact job for the air carrier (the client sees the stewardess or steward for more hours than the client sees any other airline employee), so tour operators consider tour guides and tour managers to be their most important public contact persons. The image that is being sought, however, varies with type of tour and type of tour operator.

An important part of the criteria is to have a professional image. It is vital that the tour guide/manager handle himself as a professional. Having a good "spoken" image is also important. The guide/manager must be able to speak loudly enough and strongly enough to be heard by the entire group, even without a microphone. The voice should be pleasing (not grating) and words should be enunciated both clearly and precisely.

Age is also important. Although there are some exceptions, wealthy seniors usually prefer tour guide/managers who are at or near the same age that they are. Although it can be done, a guide or a tour manager who is in his/her early twenties will struggle to obtain the respect of a group comprised of wealthy 60- and 70-year-old retirees. On the other hand, college-age adventurers biking across Switzerland will usually prefer to have a tour guide/manager who is at or near their age rather than a senior citizen. The well-conditioned 50- or 60-year-old tour guide may be physically able to lead the tour, but will usually have difficulty obtaining the respect of the physically fit younger tour members. Although adults of all ages are generally able to lead most tours, these examples show that age is a consideration in leading some tours.

Part of the image is also the physical condition of the tour guide/manager. Although an elderly person with some degree of physical impairment may still be able to go on a tour as a tour member, the guide/manager, who may be of a similar age, needs to be in good health and good physical condition. The guide should still have good mental acuity, little or no difficulty in walking, good speaking ability, and reasonably good hearing. For many tours, being in top physical shape is a definite requirement.

This is especially true of "adventure" tours. For most tours, however, being in peak physical condition, while beneficial, is not a requirement. Nevertheless, there is no question but that many tour operators prefer not to hire guides who are either very fat or very thin.

Special types of tours require special physical condition. A young guide who had good experience in working with travel agencies leading tours in the Himalayan mountains experienced considerable difficulty getting a position with an adventure tour company leading similar adventure tours. His experience, documented on his resume, got him interviews, but he continually failed in the interview process. Finally, one tour operator told him that he simply did not look the part. According to the tour operator, he was far too thin to inspire confidence in tour members in spite of the fact that he had some experience leading tours for these same types of clients. After following the tour operator's advice to, "Put some meat on your bones," he had no difficulty obtaining the position he sought. Tour companies depend upon repeat business. They tend to select conservative, dignified, well-mannered, and generally good-looking tour guides/managers.

In addition to having a good image, tour operators look for tour guide/managers with outgoing personalities and a sense of humor. A successful guide/manager must have an extroverted personality, not being at all shy to speak before a group, and having the ability to both organize the group and control the group without having tour members feel that they are being controlled.

Some people are born with a terrific sense of humor and this serves the tour guide/manager very well. However, a sense of humor can be developed if

FIGURE 1-5. A tour guide/manager should both look and act the part. (Printed with permission from Mr. Mark Holland, Professional Guide.)

one is unfortunate enough to be, as most people are, born without a natural ability to make people laugh. The goal is to have the kind of personality where tour members at the end of the tour will say, "I would follow him/her anywhere," and mean it.

Organizational skills are also vital. It is difficult to find a person who has a gregarious, outgoing, extroverted personality and who is also detail oriented. Nevertheless, all documents need to be maintained in a proper order and the tour guide/manager must be able to move through each and every one of the various job tasks, accomplishing a wide range of jobs throughout the day while still giving the impression of being relaxed and having everything under control. This requires considerable ability to organize one's activities and to organize paperwork.

A sense of ethics is also very important. It has been said that more tour guides and managers have been fired for ethics violations than for any other reason. This may or may not be true, but the temptation to lie, steal, cheat, accuse, and perform activities in an unethical manner is considerable. Some companies report that the biggest reason for turnover in tour managers is the loss of these seasoned professionals to marriage (to wealthy tour members). One tour operator actually advises tour managers employed by her company, "Don't have sex with your clients, but if you do, marry the client right after the tour. You had better find a rich one, because you will no longer have a job with our company." Stealing tip monies and getting high (or drunk) are the next "most common" ethics problems. It is difficult to screen for ethics, but tour operators make a concerted effort to do so for their own protection and for the protection of their clients.

The ability to make quick and correct decisions is also important. The tour guide/manager is an isolated representative of the tour company. Experienced tour operators know that on almost any tour something will go wrong. It can be one minor thing or it can be a range of major problems. The tour guide/manager must be the type of person who has faced problems in the past and can overcome problems as they occur. This cannot be done if the guide/manager cannot make decisions and make them rapidly.

Maintaining the respect of the tour group is essential. Although the tour guide/manager attempts to resolve problems before the group is even aware that there is a problem, there are many times when a problem occurs which the group is immediately aware of. They will expect the tour guide/manager to make a good decision right away. The right decision must be made to maintain respect for the guide/manager and for the tour company.

Another characteristic tour operators look for when selecting tour guides/ managers is a love of people, places, and travel. There are those who believe that without these loves, the tour manager cannot be successful. Being a guide/manager is a full-time job that occupies one from early in the morning until late at night every day. Without a desire to be with interesting people, to see exciting places, and to travel, it is unlikely anyone could be successful.

However, tour companies must be careful to avoid hiring tour guides/managers who have a tendency to be biased toward specific tour members. There are guides who take positions leading tours simply to have the opportunity of meeting and marrying a wealthy tour member. That does little to enamor the rest of the tour members to the tour guide or to the tour company. Tour operators make every effort to avoid hiring guides whose motivation in leading tours is strictly matrimonial.

What Tour Managers Look For from Tour Operators

Because the tour guide/manager is crucial to the tour experience, and because tour operators rely heavily on repeat business, there is strong competition in the industry to hire the best guides/managers available. Obviously, there is only so much money to be spent on tour guides/managers. Therefore, the competition to obtain guides/managers often centers around nonmonetary benefits as well as financial benefits. To be able to obtain top quality guides/managers, it is essential to understand what tour managers look for from tour operators. The employment interview is a two-way street with the professional tour guide/manager evaluating the tour operator at the same time the tour operator is evaluating the guide/manager applicant.

The associations representing guides and tour managers are clear in their lobbying efforts with the employers in identifying those factors of greatest importance to guides and managers. With most guides/managers, monetary compensation heads the list. Although tour operators usually have a written schedule specifying the salary/benefits in the compensation package, it is not at all unusual for a guide/manager to say that they simply will not work for the compensation being offered.

Some companies will not deviate from their written compensation packages. However, many companies will evaluate the guide/manager, determine what it will take to have that guide/manager work for them, and make an effort to meet the requirements of the more professional guides/managers. Negotiation is the key. Remember, some of the best tour managers have a personal following that can ensure filled tours. With top quality professional tour managers, it is not at all unusual for clients at the end of the trip to say that they want to go with that tour manager next year or for their next trip. Many tour members do not select a trip on the basis of destination or date of departure. They select their trip on the basis of who the tour guide/manager will be. They often go with a particular guide/manager year after year. When one recognizes that such a guide/manager can often fill a tour that otherwise may be unprofitable or canceled, the negotiated compensation package can be considerable. Some monies that would otherwise be spent on marketing activities can be diverted to guide/manager compensation if the guide/manager helps to fill the tour with his personal following.

Usually the second most important consideration for a professional guide/manager is having full-time employment. Many companies compensate guides/managers on a per-diem salary basis as independent contractors rather than on a straight salary basis as full-time, long-term employees. Some of the more professional guide/managers accept this type of compensation (it can be more beneficial to both the tour operator and the tour guide/manager from the standpoint of taxes). Many, however, are concerned with what they will do during the winter "off" season. Some make so much money during the summer "high" season, that they do not want to work during the winter. Others, however, want full-time employment. To obtain top-quality professional tour managers, some companies employ tour managers in the off-season as marketing executives. They go from city to city working with local travel agencies or they hold tour reunions of those people who have gone on one or more of the company's tours selling tours scheduled for the following season. This marketing strategy works well. Therefore, tour operators find it a good way to employ tour managers in the off-season and to be able to offer the full-time, long-term employment sought by professional tour managers.

Other benefits sought by the more professional tour guides/managers are insurance and retirement. An increasing number of tour operators have found ways of developing health, life, disability, and other insurance benefit programs for their professional tour guide/managers. The Professional Guides Association of America is working on insurance programs for guides who work as independent contractors. Fewer companies, however, have developed and offer retirement programs. Nevertheless, this appears to be a growing concern, especially on the part of middle-aged tour guide/managers. Therefore, more tour companies can be expected to develop retirement programs.

Working conditions and working relationships are also important to tour guide/managers. Frictions can and do occur especially when the tour guide/manager reports to a person who has never led tours and who does not understand the concerns of guides and managers. Tour guides and tour managers can be critical of operation departments which provide sloppy documentation and/or do not confirm vendor arrangements. It can be embarrassing and difficult for a guide/manager to show up at a restaurant or a hotel only to find that the arrangements specified in the guide/manager copies of the documentation are different than the arrangements specified in the vendor contract. It is even worse to show up when the vendor has not been contacted at all. Even professional tour companies slip up once in a while, especially during the rush season. Slip-ups which do occur usually relate to individual tour members. For example, a last minute tour member may be added to a tour, but the count is not changed with vendor restaurants and sightseeing companies. Usually this kind of problem can be easily taken care of enroute. But it could be disastrous if the slip-up includes not notifying hotels that an extra hotel room will be needed. Professional tour managers should make confirmation calls one or two days prior to their arrival at a hotel, restaurant, or sightseeing destination so that any problems are identified in advance. They can usually be resolved over the phone. But even though the problems can almost always be resolved easily, the respect of the tour manager for the operations department can be seriously diminished—especially if the tour guide/manager repeatedly encounters this type of problem.

Guides/managers wish to be treated with respect and consideration when tour changes are contemplated. Many tour companies ask tour guides/managers to evaluate vendors at the end of each trip. At the end of the season, some will pay guide/managers to attend debriefing (evaluation) sessions where next-season changes in vendors are being considered. Tour guides/managers tend to like being considered professional enough to be paid for their participation in evaluation sessions. This factor alone can endear a guide/manager to a tour company sometimes more than additional wages.

Tour Company Differences and the Keys for Success

Tour companies tend to differ in two major areas and in several minor ones. The major areas are *destination* and *specialization*. Minor areas are numerous but two of the more important ones are *marketing approach* and *organizational structure*.

Most tour companies select specific parts of the world in which to offer their tours. They may be domestic only, specializing in a particular region of the country. Or, they may be international only, specializing in a continent, multi-country area, single country, or region. A few tour operators will serve both domestic and international destinations. Only a very few operate all over the world.

until that person has a minimum of five years of full-time experience leading tours. Some feel that the award of the Silver Badge of Tour Management or the Gold Badge of Tour Management (at least 10 years of full-time experience) is the only industry differentiation factor used to identify the professional, successful tour manager.

But this criteria may not adequately consider guides who specialize. A successful tour manager who specializes in wind surfing tours marketed to doctors notes that by the time he gets 10 years of experience and earns the Silver Badge of Tour Management, he believes the tour operator will be looking for someone younger. Whether or not he is correct, experience alone should not be the only criteria utilized by tour operators in selecting tour managers.

Expertise in the area of the tour's specialization is frequently more important. It can be expected that as tour associations become more established, a pattern identified in other travel professions (i.e., the participation and the involvement of the professional in the industry and in the industry's associations) will become an increasingly important mark of success. Several tour operators are already sending representatives to the annual convention of the Professional Guides Association of America to identify guide/managers who they wish to recruit.

How the Tour Guide/Manager Fits In—or Does Not Fit In

The tour guide/manager can make or break a tour. Most tour operators believe the most important factor is how the guide/manager is perceived by tour participants and how smoothly the tour "goes." No matter what their credentials, the guide/manager must fit with the tour operator and its tours. Only experience can determine if a guide/manager fits well or not. All of these points need to be considered during the selection process but the continuous struggle for the perfect match goes on with many tour operators constantly endeavoring to find a cadre of tour guide/managers who will best fit their company.

Summary

Few relationships are as important in the tour business as the relationship between the tour manager and the operator. The tour guide/manager can make or break the tour operator. However, the type of tour guide/manager which will best fit the tour company varies considerably from one type of company to another.

This is largely due to the growth of inbound travel which the field of tour management has developed so rapidly in America. From having few employed in the guiding industry in the early 1980s, the United States has seen a large increase in the number of guides employed and has enjoyed this growth on a continuing basis during the past five years.

To understand the guiding profession better, it is important to understand the semantics relating to what a guide can be called. There is general agreement that those who are new to the industry and working on a part-time basis at a local level are usually called *step-on guides*. There is also general agreement that the most professional persons employed in the industry are called *tour managers*. In between these two extremes come terms such as *guide, escort, tour leader,* and even *interpreter*.

Guides perform a range of duties. Their roles include manager (conducting and directing all aspects of the tour), tour company representation, and quality control specialist. Guides work closely with the operations department of a tour company and a smooth interrelationship between the tour operations department staff and tour managers or guides is essential to the success of any tour. To make the interrelationship work well, both need to understand the importance of the other. Typically, the personalities required to do each job are different and it is not at all unusual to find a clash in personalities. Many tour companies, therefore, have detailed procedures and policies and a direct reporting relationship which clearly identifies the operations executive as being the superior manager within the guide/operations department relationship.

Tour operators are usually clear about what they want when selecting a tour guide or tour manager. Image is usually the most important factor, but employers also seek persons with outgoing personalities, organizational skills, good humor, a sense of ethics, the ability to make decisions, and a love of people, places, and travel. Tour managers see themselves in much the same way, but they also consider it important to oversee the whole tour, deal with problems, guide tour members in the culture and language, and generate business.

To attract the best possible tour guides and tour managers, tour operators identify factors which are important for tour managers (i.e., what they look for when considering employment offers). Compensation is one of the most important factors. The compensation package, therefore, needs to be spelled out in detail. Recognizing that the best tour managers will have a following, some companies modify their compensation packages based on the business that a tour manager can bring to the company. Usually full-time, year-round employment is also important. Some companies have found ways of being able to offer this, but the majority still employ guides and managers on a part-time basis for "the season." Both insurance and retirement benefits are also important to many tour managers. Some companies, as well as the PGAA, are developing and offering such programs. Working conditions and working relationships are also important. If a company is to retain professional tour managers, it is essential that coworkers in the operations department and in other departments be professional.

Those characteristics about tour companies that make them different from one another and successful tend to be oriented toward the destinations served, the specialization of the company, its marketing approaches, and its organizational structure. Some of these same factors can be used to characterize successful tour managers. Many tour managers specialize in both the type of tour that they conduct and in a particular geographical area. Experience, however, is usually the most crucial factor in identifying the most professional of tour managers. Age is another factor that can be important, but the "best age" for the tour is often correlated to the type of tour itself.

Because of the crucial importance of the tour manager, many companies continuously work hard to identify and hire the "best" tour managers for their company. It is hard, however, to come up with a perfect match. Therefore, the search for many companies is an ongoing and continuous one.

DISCUSSION QUESTIONS

These questions may be discussed by two or more students outside of class as a fun way of reviewing this chapter or they may be discussed by everyone during class for a more wide-ranging discussion.

1. What are some of the reasons why a tour guide or a tour manager might "make or break" a tour?
2. What is meant by the statement, "Tours are two-directional?"
3. Why is the "image" of a tour guide/manager considered so important by tour operators?
4. What is an "interpreter" in the tour industry?
5. Why might a tour guide or a tour manager be considered a "quality control" specialist?
6. With which department in a tour company do tour managers interface to the greatest degree?
7. In addition to image, what other characteristics do tour operators look for in selecting tour managers?
8. What types of tours require special physical condition?
9. What do tour managers look for from tour operators?
10. In what ways do successful tour company differences parallel successful tour manager differences?

ROLE PLAY EXERCISE

1. Two students may participate in this role play either out of class as a fun way to review the chapter or as an in-class exercise. One plays the role of the first tour operator and the other plays the role of the second tour operator. Please read the script and then pick up the conversation in your own words.

   FIRST TOUR OPERATOR: I'm continually changing tour guides. I just don't seem to be able to find guides that have the combination of ethics and willingness to work hard needed to do the job.

SECOND TOUR OPERATOR: That's a problem for all of us. We get lots of applications in, but it's very difficult to identify which ones meet our specifications. We've done pretty good by using telephone call screening and very lengthy interviewing of those few applicants who we bring in for a face-to-face interview.

FIRST TOUR OPERATOR: What kinds of questions and evaluation characteristics do you use to make your screening effective?

SECOND TOUR OPERATOR: We start in our telephone interview by asking . . .

CONTINUE ON YOUR OWN

2. Two students may participate in this role play either out of class as a fun way to review the chapter or as an in-class exercise. One plays the role of the first tour guide and the other plays the role of the second tour guide. Please read the script and then pick up the conversation in your own words.

FIRST TOUR GUIDE: You are a model for the guiding industry. I'm continually amazed at the number of tour companies that are constantly trying to get you to work for them. Most of us have to work hard just to get tour companies to notice us while you seem to attract tour companies like flies on an elephant.

SECOND TOUR GUIDE: I can think of more flattering comparisons, but you are right. I'm fortunate enough to get a large number of job offers. I think it's because of the many past tour members who have been on my trips and who ask for me when they book their next trips with their travel agencies. Tour companies are always anxious to get tour managers who have a strong following.

FIRST TOUR GUIDE: I think the tour members on my trips are pleased with my work. They tip me well and I sometimes even get letters of thanks. But, with rare exceptions, I'm not aware of their going back to their travel agencies and saying they want to go on a trip with me next year. What do you do differently that makes your clients so anxious to travel with you again?

SECOND TOUR GUIDE: That's a good question. I've spent some time analyzing what I can do to build up client loyalty and repeat trip requests. There are a number of things I do which are probably no different than what other tour managers do, but perhaps my actions are different in the degree of effort and enthusiasm I put into them. For example, I . . .

CONTINUE ON YOUR OWN

3. Two students may participate in this role play either out of class as a fun way to review the chapter or as an in-class exercise. One plays the role of a travel agent and the other plays the role of a tour operator. Please read the script and then pick up the conversation in your own words.

TRAVEL AGENT: I never get a complaint about your tours and I'm constantly having clients come back and sign up for another one just a few days after they return. They say that your guides are exceptionally professional, all share outstanding images, and they offer both knowledge and continuous assistance. But what they say most often is that the job looks so easy. There seem to be no problems. I sure don't get that kind of comment about most tour guides or in regards to most tour companies.

TOUR OPERATOR: Thanks for your compliments. We work very hard to match the tour managers assigned to tours with the tours they are most qualified to lead. The matching is important. However, obviously having a cadre of professional guides as a pool from which to assign tours is very important. Our ability to make it look easy and to get the best guides in the industry is something I give credit to our operations department for. They are very selective, but equally important, they have continuous training for our guides. We run training programs on . . .

CONTINUE ON YOUR OWN

GROUP DISCUSSION SITUATION: STRETCH STRINGLY AND THE NONEMPLOYING ADVENTURE TOUR COMPANIES

Stretch Stringly is frustrated. He has been very active in sports since grade school and was always an avid outdoorsman. He prides himself on his camping, rafting, and mountain climbing skills. While in high school, Stretch seemed to spend every free day in the outdoors camping, hunting, and fishing. His abilities kept the family freezer so full of fish and game that he started having to give away some of his take. Stretch prides himself on his constant good tan and his enthusiastic excitement about outdoor activities. He has an outgoing personality and seems to be in command during even the most bizzare or dangerous experiences in either the forest or the mountains.

At six foot four, Stretch towers over his friends and since he is as thin as a rail, he seems even taller. Stretch credits his height and his natural skills along with his radiant personality for the ability to "naturally" lead any group that accompanies him on his outings. Stretch excels at many sports. He has won prizes in running, swimming, and high jumping. He has won more Explorer Scout badges than anyone he knows, including badges for mountain climbing, hiking, camping, canoeing, rafting, bow and arrow hunting, and swimming.

Throughout his high school and college years, Stretch found himself leading groups ranging from three or four persons up to 30 or 40 almost every weekend when he went into the nearby forests to camp. He did such a good job of putting these groups together and creating memorable weekend outdoor experiences that Stretch started charging people to accompany him on tours. He did so well with this that in his senior year he was able to pay for all of his costs, including tuition, from the profits.

Stretch had little difficulty in getting local travel agencies to let him lead their tours. His reputation in the community was easy to track as many of the local travel agencies heard about him first from clients who, having been on an outdoor trip with Stretch, booked much longer adventure tours through the agency. Stretch was easily able to obtain tour guide assignments from travel agencies in the community almost any weekend he was available during the last semester of his senior year in college.

However, when Stretch graduated and wanted to pursue a full-time career in tour management, he found himself unable to obtain a position with any of the adventure tour companies with which he applied. His resume was so good that he got a large number of interviews. However, he just did not seem to do well in the interviewing phase. No matter what he said, the tour companies never offered him a position.

As Stretch has interviewed with one company after another, he has become increasingly frustrated. A number of times he has called companies and asked if they would tell him why he was not selected. In each case, they have either said that it is their policy not to discuss nonselection reasons or they have given him very general reasons that don't help. The only pattern he has been able to identify among the reasons given is that he doesn't fit the company's "image."

This morning, when Stretch was talking to an executive with a fairly new adventure tour company, he again got the response that he did not fit their "image." However, this time he pushed for greater clarification. Hesitatingly, the adventure tour company executive explained that while Stretch has all the qualifications and experience needed and while adventure tour companies would normally be anxious to hire him as a guide, the executive and his associates felt that Stretch simply did not look sufficiently capable of instilling confidence in tour members. The executive stated, "While you may be able to lead people up and down mountains on mountain climbing trips or across the trails of Switzerland on mountain bikes, and while your resume proves that you can do this, you simply don't look like you can. One of our recruiters commented that you look like you would 'blow away' with a high gust of wind. We must have guides whose image instills confidence in our tour members right away."

Stretch felt both insulted and pleased. He expected his experience to speak for itself, but he was pleased with the honesty of the tour executive. Stretch has asked several of the travel agents who have given him employment in the past if they will meet with him and help him identify the exact kind of image adventure tour companies look for as well as helping him develop a plan that he can follow in changing his image to meet the requirements of outdoor tour companies.

You are the travel agents he has asked to meet with. What do you recommend that Stretch do? Discuss the situation among yourselves. You are expected to reach agreement. Be prepared to present your suggestion to the entire class by a spokesperson from your group.

EXERCISE

Fill in the blanks on the tour company/tour guide matching chart by listing types of tour companies along the left-hand column and guide characteristics along the top column. Where there is a characteristic that is applicable, simply

Specialization also differentiates tour companies. Well over half of all tour companies specialize in offering tours that center around a specific activity or a specific area of interest. Specialization helps to target markets and to reduce the range of potential competitors. (Chapter 3 discusses both geographic and product specialization in detail.)

Companies also differ when it comes to marketing approach. There is no single marketing approach which appears to be the "best" for all tour companies. Perhaps the most popular marketing approach is to work through travel agencies, paying a commission for each and every tour member they book. While this approach works for many tour operators, it does not work well for others. These tend to be those tour operators which specialize in specific products or activities. For example, a company that runs buying tours only for professional jewelers solicits through trade publications, booths at trade shows, and presentations at trade meetings. Adventure tour operators often find that many of the people who take their tours buy as a result of reading advertisements in adventure-oriented magazines and/or trade publications.

Another major difference in tour companies is the size of the company itself. There are many "mom and pop" or one and two person owned and operated tour companies that tend to operate on a local level only. Other tour companies are quite large, employing over 100 staff members. And, of course, there are tour companies ranging in size between both of these extremes.

Documentation suggests that the more successful tour companies are those that have been in business for several years (three or more), that employ five or more staff persons, that have clearly defined market targets, and those that have found consistently profitable, highly effective, return-on-investment marketing strategies. When professional tour guides/managers evaluate the companies with which they wish to become associated, they frequently look for companies that bear these marks of success. Of course, generally the unsophisticated new guide/manager, who may not yet have built up a reputation, will be less particular about the company with which he/she wishes to work. However, the experienced guide/manager with a substantial following will often investigate thoroughly being careful about the company with which he associates.

Tour Manager Differences and the Keys for Success

Just as tour companies differ, exhibiting qualities that tend to be correlated with success, so too do tour managers differ. Probably the most important characteristic regarding a tour manager's success directly relates to his/her number of years of experience and his/her areas of specialization. In addition, professionalism exhibited in terms of industry involvement, association participation, and contributions to the industry frequently differentiate the successful tour manager from the guide/manager who is less successful.

Experience is perhaps most crucial. The International Association of Tour Managers does not consider a person for the Silver Badge of Tour Management

TOUR COMPANY/TOUR GUIDE MATCHING CHART

No.	Type of Tour Co.	Guide Characteristics
01	Adventure	
02		
03		
04		
05		
06		
07		
08		
09		
10		

INSTRUCTIONS: Adventure tours are one type of tour company. This one type has been listed. Fill in nine other types of tour companies down the left-hand column and the characteristics of tour managers along the top. Fill in an "X" where the characteristic matches the needs of the tour company and a descriptor of the variable relating to the characteristic where appropriate.

put a check in the cross-block unless that characteristic is variable. If it is a variable characteristic, such as age, enter the appropriate characteristic identifiers. For example, with age, the appropriate characteristic identifier would be an age range. It is recognized that you are not yet an expert at matching tour guide types to tour companies. However, the completion of this exercise should give you an understanding of the type of company you may want to work for if you decide to follow a career as a guide in the industry. And it may give you an understanding of the type of guide(s) you may want to hire if you decide to make your career one in which you will be working in the operations department of a tour company.

CHAPTER 2

Costing and Pricing a Tour

OBJECTIVES

Upon completion of this chapter, the student will be able to:

1. List the major categories of expense encountered by tour operators in running two-day domestic bus tours.
2. Calculate a price per tour when all costs are provided and when a percentage of profit is provided.
3. Divide all major tour costs of a sample two-day bus tour into fixed costs and variable costs.
4. Identify the customary range of tour company profit percentages on domestic bus tour.

Introduction

Costing and pricing tours is one of the most difficult tasks a tour executive can face. To effectively cost and price a tour, it's necessary to project prices so that they cover costs, but not so that they go over expected costs by a wide margin or a considerable percentage. For clients to buy the tour, the total cost must be perceived by the client to be reasonable. However, tour companies are in business to make a profit. Managing this task of getting prices close enough that the tour company will earn a reasonable profit and that the client will consider the tour to be a reasonable enough bargain to be motivated to purchase it is a challenge tour company executives face every day. The person who has developed a skill in pricing so that these two contradictory tasks are accomplished on a consistent basis is a person who will probably never be out of a job.

Unfortunately, this costing and pricing skill is not one that is gained overnight. It is garnered only through practice. To develop such a skill, it is best to start costing and pricing tours on a continuing basis, identifying errors and correcting them for future tours. Be careful not to make serious errors as they can be very expensive for the tour company. If the tour is priced too low, the tour company will have to cancel the tour or try to make up the difference itself. If the tour is priced too high, few tour participants will sign up and the tour company will either cancel or operate the tour at a loss.

This chapter will emphasize the key factors that need to be considered in costing and pricing a tour. It will stress the importance of profit and how to determine appropriate levels of profit.

Considerable attention will be given to budgeting. The reasons why one should establish a budget will be provided and a sample one-day budget will be presented. The chapter will discuss the categories of cost encountered in offering a two-day (weekend) domestic bus tour. These will include the following 10 ingredients:

1. bus (and other transportation)

2. hotel

3. personnel (including the tour manager) and research

4. marketing

5. food and beverage (meals)

6. sightseeing and activity fees

7. tips (and a tip plan)

8. tour member packets (and optional tour member gifts)

9. miscellaneous costs

10. profits

Costs will be classified by type: *variable costs* or *fixed costs.* The importance of a breakeven point will be identified. In addition, the reader will learn how to establish or set a breakeven point. The final part of the chapter will discuss the costing process. In this section, the reader will be taken on a step-by-step basis through the costing of a sample tour.

The Importance of Profit

It is important to build a reasonable profit into the cost of any tour. Those new to the tour business frequently price their tours so that little or no profits result. Although this is oftentimes the result of a fear of pricing for a profit, it is frequently a result of all cost factors not being considered in advance. Many times profit may have been priced into the tour, but after paying for unexpected costs, little or no profit results. By utilizing the costing process described in this chapter and adding profit as the last factor in the process, all costs are included and a reasonable profit for the town should be realized. Of course, there are no guarantees. Profit depends on an accurately priced tour, including all costs, and one which has been marketed well enough to fill it beyond breakeven (ideally to capacity).

How Much Profit?

Obtaining the "right" amount of profit is a challenge. As noted earlier, it is important to price the tour low enough that the client will buy, but it is also important to price it high enough to realize a profit. Tour companies vary considerably in the amount of profit that they include. Frequently, the profit percentage will vary from one tour to the next within the menu of tours offered by a single company. It is recommended that the new tour operator include a profit level that is no lower than 10 percent and no higher than 15 percent. Many start with 15 percent and work down from there, if necessary.

Establishing a Budget

Establish a budget before costing and pricing a tour. If there are similar tours offered by competitors, one of the best ways of developing a budget framework is to review the brochures and tour costs of your competitors. In doing so, identify tours that have the same type of offerings, utilize the same type of hotels, and go to the same destinations at the same time of the year. If you find competitor brochures that meet these criteria, a review of the tour costs should provide a start in determining your budget framework.

If the tour is being prepared for a club or an organization and tailor-designed for its members, and if that club/organization has a history of offering tours to its members, often the club or organization will have a framework cost built into the tour. This cost will determine guidelines for the overall tour budget.

Many times, however, neither of these options are available. The tour is unique and no competitor offers a similar tour. In addition, it is either being prepared for an organization that has not offered tours in the past or it is being prepared to be sold to the general public. Under such circumstances, you should undertake market research to determine the cost of similar duration tours (if it is a domestic tour) and/or similar destination and duration tours (if it is an international tour). For example, if a one-day tour is being offered to the general public, you might get copies of brochures from continuing education or recreation centers to find out what these institutions charge for a one-day tour. Often the same approach can be used in determining a ball park figure for a two-day or a weekend tour.

Whatever approach is used, however, it is better to start the costing and pricing process with a budget and to start the budget with a determination of a per person estimated cost figure. This per person estimated cost becomes a guideline, framework, or limitation for the tour. Although you may go over that figure to a slight degree, it is recommended that you not plan to exceed the figure by more than 5 to 10 percent.

FIGURE 2-1 BUDGET PROJECTED EXPENSES VS. ACTUAL EXPENSES
ONE-DAY TOUR TO ESTES PARK

	Projected Expenses		*Actual Expenses*	
1.	Bandanas	$19.28	Bandanas &	
	Doughnuts	20.00	Breakfast Items	$33.76
	O.J., Cups, Misc.	10.00		
2.	Bus	$272.00	Bus	$272.00
3.	Driver Gratuity	$39.00	Driver Gratuity	$10.00
4.	Lazy H Brunch	$130.00	Lazy H Brunch	
	Gratuity	20.00	and Gratuity	$147.22
5.	Aerial Tramway	$60.00	Aerial Tramway	$46.75
6.	Stanley Hotel Snack	$155.00	Stanley Hotel Snack	$155.35
7.	Stanley Hotel Guide		Stanley Hotel Guide	
	Bob Hellis—		Bob Hellis—	
	Gratuity	$20.00	Gratuity	$20.00
8.	Brochures	$25.00	Brochures	$25.00
9.	Name Tags	$9.00	Name Tags	$9.00
10.			Folders	$25.17
11.			Kazoo (Gifts)	$26.67
12.			Beverages at the	
			Lazy H Dude Ranch	$11.50
Total		$779.28		$782.42

One-Day Tour Budget Example

Figure 2-1 shows budgeted to "projected" expenses for a one-day tour run by a tour management class in the early 1990s. This one-day tour went from Denver into the Rocky Mountains, up to Estes Park, stopping at a Dude Ranch for lunch. Tour participants were given a tour of the Stanley Hotel, including a view of the room that is said to be haunted (the inspiration of the book and the movie, *The Shining*). They then drove to the Aerial Tramway which they took from Estes Park up into the mountains. After a brief hike in the mountain area they returned to Estes Park where they were given a slide presentation on the history and the development of Estes Park. They then had one and a half hours to shop before returning to Denver. The tour included a light breakfast of coffee, orange juice, and doughnuts, brunch at a Dude Ranch, and a light snack at the Stanley Hotel. There were 20 participants on the tour. The projected (budgeted) expenses came very close to the actual expenses. However, there were costs that were either overbudgeted or underbudgeted. There were no personnel, research, or profit figures projected or spent since this was a tour class and the research was conducted by the team of students which also constituted the tour management team.

The $49.28 budgeted for bandanas, for the breakfast which consisted of doughnuts and orange juice, for cups and miscellaneous expenses (including coffee) actually turned out to be $33.76. The driver's gratuity was reduced substantially from the budgeted gratuity since the driver was rude and purposely took a different route than on his map in returning so that he would accumulate overtime. The $150 budget for brunch at the Lazy H Ranch (including gratuity) came very close to the real figure, $147.22.

The aerial tramway cost was reduced from the budgeted cost since two free tickets were obtained (the tramway had a policy of one free for each 10 paid tour members). The Stanley Hotel costs and the gratuity for the guide were both almost the same as projected. Tour brochures were less expensive than projected, but normally would be considerably greater than the cost indicated here. Name tags were exactly the same cost as that which was budgeted. Three unforeseen costs were incurred. These were for folders, kazoos (provided as tour member gifts in the tour packets), and beverages at the Dude Ranch. Planning for the meal at the Dude Ranch was in error because the researchers had missed the contract notation that the meal was provided with beverages, but that beverages would be available at an additional cost. This is the type of cost you should always look out for in a contract. It provided a valuable lesson for those who conducted the tour. They will scrutinize restaurant contracts much more carefully on future tours.

Weekend Bus Tour Cost Categories

Since many who are new to the tour industry will start their tour offerings by running bus tours and since many of these will be one-day and two-day bus tours, let's look at a typical two-day or weekend bus tour budgeting process. The budgeting process starts with identifying, categorizing, and projecting all costs. In dealing with costs, it is usually better to treat each cost in a hierarchical order based upon their relative percentages or total amounts. As costs are categorized, they should also be prioritized and ranked. By doing this, the tour planner will be in a better position to consider potential trade-offs to make the tour cost effective. The tour planner should consider and work with potential costs and services until he is able to develop a tour that is reasonably priced and meets the needs of most of the tour's target audience.

When negotiating with a bus company to lease a bus, you'll find that buses are normally leased on either a time basis, a mileage basis, or both. For short duration trips, bus companies often quote a mileage-based cost. For lengthy tours (usually multi-day tours), it is not uncommon to find a time-based cost. This will normally be by the day and by the hour. Most companies will quote on both a mileage basis and a time basis, however. These quotes are based on a specified number of hours of bus usage with a pre-determined number of free miles and an additional cost per mile beyond the specified amount in the contract. If the bus is used beyond the contracted time, there is usually a per hour (sometimes broken down to per minute) additional cost. Since it may mean that a bus driver will have to be paid overtime (often at the rate of one and a half hours of pay for each hour worked), the additional time cost can be substantial.

In contracting for a bus it is important to determine whether or not the bid includes the following:

1. all driver costs except tips (including driver's salary, meals, and accommodations—not including admission to sightseeing points);
2. fuel charges;
3. maintenance fees;
4. a bathroom on board the bus;
5. a working microphone on the bus (preferably with a long cord—at no additional charge);
6. any toll or road fees that may apply;
7. bus luggage facility useage at no additional cost; and
8. on-board video playback units.

Although you can normally get along quite well without the video playback units, for a bus tour of any length, a bathroom is essential. When there will be presentations on board the bus by tour guides/managers, a microphone is essential. For one-day tours, the use of luggage facilities is seldom needed, but on multi day tours it is essential. You should also check to determine what deposits are required, when they are required, and whether or not they are refundable. Finally, it is essential to determine the type of bus that will be utilized.

One of the main considerations in determining the cost of the bus is bus size. Rates will normally be quoted on the basis of the number of passenger seats. For example, a 25-seat bus will be far less expensive than a 39 seat bus. This seat size cost is important to keep in mind in determining breakeven factors and overall tour budget cost projections.

Hotel Costs

In negotiating hotel costs, it is wise to obtain a rate quote for double rooms (two people to a room and two beds in the room) and single rooms. Most tours are sold on the basis of two people to a room (double occupancy) with a surcharge added for a single room. It is customary to offer a single room to an individual who wishes one at the supplement charged by the hotel without adding anything additional for the tour company. In negotiating, contract for rooms that are as identical as possible and make certain they have similar views. It is usually best if they can all be on the same floor. Often in the contract, the hotel agrees to provide rooms in the same section and on the same floor. This makes it easier for the tour manager to control the tour, for the bell staff to deliver and pick up bags, and for tour members to visit with one another.

In negotiating for hotel rooms, obtain as late a date and as small an amount as possible for deposits. Of course, the rate per room is the major factor that needs to be negotiated, but you should also consider the type of room, the amenities provided, whether or not there are any lodging taxes, tourist taxes, other special taxes or fees that would be levied, and whether or not gratuities will be automatically added. Add-ons can increase the per night room price by as much as 50 percent. Hotels in resort areas sometimes have restrictions applying to guests. Determine whether or not any will apply, especially if there is a penalty charge applied. If a cocktail party, reception, or other function is planned, food and beverage costs need to be determined and any required gratuity costs need to be identified. Sometimes room rental can be waived for function rooms based upon the number of sleeping rooms rented. This should be considered if some type of get together is planned.

Personnel/Research Costs

Personnel and research costs frequently are underestimated. Research expenses include such costs as familiarization trips, contract negotiation expenses, and so forth. When research costs are projected, there is a tendency to assign all such costs to the first tour and not to spread them over several tours. On many tours, the personnel/research costs constitute the third largest tour expense. Personnel costs include the cost of the tour planner and any other staff members who are involved in tour planning. They also include the cost of reservationists, the tour guide or tour manager, step-on guides (if utilized), and others in the company who are involved with the tour. The compensation of tour company executives and administrative staff persons, such as the corporate accountant, are normally allocated to one-time tours by totalling all of their monthly compensation and dividing that by the number of hours of tours run during the month. This figure is multiplied times the number of hours each tour is conducted. Of course, these figures are projected figures rather than actual figures, since tour prices must be determined and announced in advance of marketing the tour. This approach, most believe, clearly distributes the administrative and executive costs of the company to all one-time tours in an accurate and appropriate fashion.

The same concept is used in allocating executives/administrative costs for multi-run tours (those that are repeated or run several times during a season or a year). For these tours, you should work with annual (instead of monthly) executive/administrative staff compensation and the total hours of all projected tour runs. The resulting figure is then divided by the number of tour runs projected for the season or the year.

The personnel cost of the tour planner is calculated in a similar way. The tour planner may work on several tours each month, but the planner's compensation is allocated to tours based on two types of cost. One is long-term planning and research and the other is the next tour preparation cost. The cost of preparing for each tour in sequence is far less than the cost of long-term planning and initial tour development. The average cost of next tour planning is calculated and projected into the overall cost of the tour each time the tour is run.

The long-term planning and research cost, however, is projected and divided into a minimum of 10 runs. Usually the long-term planning and research cost is divided into all sections of the tour which are offered for the tour's first two years.

The cost of the tour guide, tour planner, and/or local step-on guides is projected. This figure is added to the total cost of each section or run of the tour. Tour personnel costs are considered fixed costs. They are added to determine a total personnel cost. This personnel cost is divided by the total number of tour participants determined to be the breakeven number in order to calculate the cost per person for personnel costs. This process is detailed later in this chapter in the section on "The Costing and Pricing Process."

Marketing Costs

Marketing costs can be substantial. An appropriate amount should be budgeted to cover them. The reservations cost alone (normally considered a marketing cost) can run 10 percent or more of the total cost of the tour. This is especially true when the reservations function is contracted to a travel agency.

For the small tour company that is just starting out, marketing costs normally are allocated to each tour and an individual tour marketing plan is developed. The process of developing individual tour marketing plans is detailed in the chapter on marketing. When one adds up all projected marketing expenses, the total becomes the marketing cost for the tour.

When a tour company becomes larger, however, all tours tend to be marketed together and any additional individual tour marketing costs tend to be minimal. The marketing that is conducted by the company is designed to promote all or most of the tours offered by the company. In this case, you simply add up the total number of days of all tours being offered during the year and divide the total number of projected tour days into the total projected marketing cost. This daily tour marketing cost is then multiplied times the total number of days during the year the planned tour is projected to be run. This figure becomes the annual marketing cost for the tour being planned.

To calculate the marketing cost per run of the tour, simply divide the number of annual tour runs into the annual marketing cost for the planned tour. This is the marketing cost that is applied to each tour run. Add to this marketing cost per run any additional individual tour marketing costs (also divided by the number of runs of the tour) to come up with a total per run cost for marketing the tour. This is a fixed cost. It is added to all other fixed costs to calculate the total which is then divided by the breakeven number of participants in the tour costing calculation process.

Food and Beverage Costs

Food and beverage costs can be either considerable or quite reasonable. Although you would normally think that the major food and beverage cost variable would be the ingredients (i.e., the type of food or beverage consumed), quite often a more important variable is the formality of the function. Meals served in formal hotel dining rooms tend to be quite expensive. Meals consumed in informal settings, such as the dude ranch picnic in the example provided earlier (see Figure 2-1) tend to be far less expensive. Catered meals can run from moderately expensive to very expensive, but can provide an opportunity to get in more sightseeing during short tours. They can also provide quality meal functions in rural areas where it is difficult to find a high-quality, full-service restaurant.

Usually buffet type meals will be less expensive than those that are served on a table d'hote or ala carte basis. Cafeteria dining is generally inexpensive. Often, cafeteria provides an opportunity for tour members to eat all they wish and allows a full tour bus to get fed and back on the road rapidly. Some tours, however, require quality dining because that is what is expected by tour members.

In negotiating for meals, it is customary to request a menu in advance and to work with a contract. Make certain that beverages (preferably a choice of beverages) are included in food and beverage contracts, that automatic gratuities are not included, and that all taxes and fees are identified. If a private dining room can be made available at little or no additional cost, this should be considered. The wait staff/tour member ratio needs to be spelled out in the contract and tipping requirements/policies need to be clarified. Some tour companies also specify the number of bus persons to be utilized. If wine is to be served, the cost of the wine and any special fees for the sommelier need to be listed.

Sightseeing/Activity Fees

On most tours, sightseeing/activity fees constitute a high expenditure area. These fees will vary with the tour. Sightseeing costs are calculated by taking the per person cost for all sightseeing and activity admissions and adding them up. Most sightseeing destination vendors have established group fees which are substantially below general public admission costs. Also, destination vendors usually provide some free admissions. Usually the best ratio is one free for every 10 paid, but some vendors will have a far less generous ratio. This can and should be negotiated. Remember to request free admissions for the tour guide/manager and for the bus driver.

Tips

Tips are discussed in detail in a later chapter. They constitute a significant cost and they need to be budgeted. The tip plan constitutes a tip budget becoming the total for all tips. This is a variable cost since the amount of many of the tips will depend upon the number of persons who are provided with a service.

Tour Member Packets/Gift

Many tour companies provide packets of material to tour participants at the beginning of the tour. Also a small gift is frequently provided for each tour member. The cost of the packet, packet inserts, and the gift are determined by adding up the per person cost of each item. This is a variable cost since the total packet/gift cost will vary depending upon the number of people taking the tour.

Miscellaneous Expenses

Some tour companies include insurance premiums in the miscellaneous expense category since the per person cost of insurance premiums tends to be low. This approach works well for an established tour company which offers a large number of tours. However, the per person premium for insurance can be substantially greater for the tour company that is just getting started, does not have a history with the insurance company, does not have a large number of tours (and tour members to share the annual insurance premium cost), and frequently purchases tour insurance on a per tour basis rather than on an annual basis for all tours.

For the smaller tour company running very few tours each year, and especially for the tour company which purchases liability and sometimes errors and omissions insurance on a tour-by-tour basis, insurance should be considered as a separate line item in the budget. This is especially true if the insurance company does not charge insurance premiums based on the number of actual tour participants going on the tour (variable cost). Many do not. Large tour companies pay an annual premium. This is either a set fee or a fee based on the number of the previous year's tour participants (with projections of the total number the company will serve during the next year). For many established tour companies, therefore, insurance is treated as a fixed cost.

Miscellaneous expenses are usually budgeted on a percentage of tour cost. For the tour company that runs tours on a regular basis and has a substantial history, it is possible to identify the nonallocated costs on each tour, average that cost and add a small (one or two percent or less) additional amount to calculate a per tour miscellaneous cost budget figure that, spread over several tours, should be very close to exact on an annual basis.

For the new tour company, this approach will not work since a substantial tour history has not yet been developed. In this case, an arbitrary miscellaneous expense figure should be allocated. For the first tour run by a new tour operator, a miscellaneous expense figure of between 12 and 15 percent of the total cost of the tour is suggested. Since learning can be expected, other first year tours might be allocated an average miscellaneous expense of between seven and 10 percent of the total tour cost (not including profit). It is presumed that these will all be one-time, single run tours. These figures do not include insurance premium costs.

The more experienced tour companies which have an opportunity to calculate and budget miscellaneous expenses based on a solid history usually find that the necessary miscellaneous cost expense does not exceed four percent (including insurance premium costs). The miscellaneous expense cost is treated as a fixed cost since miscellaneous expenses often occur no matter how many people are on the tour.

Profit

The calculation of a profit budget is an issue with which many struggle. It is recommended that the budget for profits be somewhere on a range of from a low of 10 percent to a high of 15 percent of the total cost of the tour. The per person dollar amount of profit is added to the total per person cost of the tour after all other expenses are calculated.

Variable Versus Fixed Costs

Several references have been made to the terms fixed costs and variable costs. All tour costs are either fixed costs or variable costs. The *fixed costs* are those which will be incurred whether one person or a large number of people go on the tour. One of the best examples of a fixed cost is the cost of a tour bus. The bus cost will be the same whether one person takes the tour, 10 people take the tour, or every seat on the tour bus is filled.

Variable costs are those costs which vary with the actual number of participants on the tour. They are costs which will be incurred by and for each person on the tour. Although there are a number of true variable costs (such as meals, which are normally not charged to the tour if the tour member does not consume the item), in calculating a price for the tour, all costs must be ultimately reduced to a per person cost. Initially, every cost should be labeled either a fixed cost or a variable cost. The costing process cannot proceed until every cost has been categorized as either "fixed" or "variable."

Setting a Breakeven Point

When developing a tour, it is necessary to determine a breakeven point. The *breakeven point* is exactly that. It is that point at which the income derived from the sale of a tour is exactly equal to the expenditures incurred in running the tour. This is the point at which the tour operator neither makes nor loses money.

The breakeven point can be identified in terms of the number of dollars of sales required or it can be identified in terms of the number of passengers required in order to obtain the income needed to break even. In the tour industry, it is common to quote the number of persons needed to fill a tour in order for that tour to break even rather than the dollar amount of sales.

The traditional way of calculating the breakeven point is to identify the amount of sales that will cover all fixed costs plus any variable costs incurred to that point (but not any profits). One approach that is used in working with bus tours is to determine a breakeven point that will coincide with filling most of the seats on a small bus (for example, a 25 seat bus), but signing a contract with the bus company for an option to run the tour on a larger bus (for example, a 39 seat bus) and including the cost of the larger bus in the tour budget. The tour is then cancelled if the smaller bus is not filled, but if enough tour members are sold to move to the larger bus, a profit will be earned and the larger bus will provide clients with more comfort. If it is also filled, a substantial profit will be made. By determining a breakeven point based on bus size, the tour company is in a position to hedge its bets. When a tour sells extremely well, it has the additional bus seats available and, therefore, it is not limited to a small degree of profit.

Remember, the smaller the number of tour members constituting the breakeven point, the larger the per passenger cost will be. The reverse is also true. The larger the number of tour members constituting the breakeven point, the smaller the per passenger cost will be. This can be seen by comparing the breakeven price example for 20 persons shown in the "Costing and Pricing" section of this chapter with the breakeven price example for the same tour for 25 persons shown in the second and third exercises for this chapter.

The Costing and Pricing Process

The costing and pricing process is composed of several steps (see Figures 2-3 and 2-4). The first and second steps have already been accomplished, namely to identify all costs and to place them into identifiable categories. The second step is to divide all cost categories into those that are fixed costs and those that are variable costs.

The third step is to calculate a breakeven point. The process for determining a breakeven point has been outlined in the previous section. The next step is to total all fixed costs. This total should be divided by the breakeven point (number of client sales) and the resulting dollar figure becomes the per person fixed cost. In step five, you add each per person variable cost to the per person fixed cost. The result will be the base cost of the tour, not including profit.

Step six is the calculation of a profit projection. To determine this, multiply the base tour cost times the percentage of profit projected. The resulting figure will be the profit dollar figure. This profit dollar figure should be added to the projected base tour cost to determine the sales price of the tour.

The sample one-day tour shown in Figure 2-1 on page 26 provides a good example. The budget in Figure 2-1 does not include hotel costs (it is for a one-day tour), it includes only limited (unrealistic) marketing costs and there are no personnel costs (since it was a learning tour run by and for students). Nevertheless, a base tour cost exists. It is a budgeted cost of $779.28. To calculate a 12 percent profit, multiply 12 percent times $779.28. The resulting figure ($93.51) is added to the $779.28 for a total price of $872.79.

Step seven is the determination of a calculated per person breakeven tour price. To determine this, divide the breakeven number of tour participants into the total price (not including profit). In this case, the breakeven is 20 tour members. Dividing 20 into $779.28 provides a per person breakeven price of $38.694 or, rounded upwards, $38.97. For reference purposes, this is labeled the Calculated Per Person Breakeven Tour Price.

The last step is to compare the Calculated Per Person Breakeven Tour Price to the Budgeted (ball park) Projected Per Person Tour Price (discussed in the first few pages of this chapter), modify the per person price to be charged for the tour and the breakeven number of tour participants accordingly and add the calculated per person profit.

This approach used in determining a per person price to be charged for a tour is only one approach. Tour companies work with several standard, as well as a large number of individualized, approaches in developing tour prices. For example, Figure 2-2 is the Cost and Pricing Sheet used by Rojo Tours to develop a per person tour cost. It is suggested that, in the beginning, the new tour operator use the approach discussed in this chapter. It can and should be modified to meet the individual needs of the tour company.

Summary

The costing and pricing of tours is a task with which many in the tour business are uncomfortable. It is difficult. You must develop a price that is high enough to include a profit, but low enough to attract a sufficient number of clients to take the tour so that the tour will fill to a point beyond breakeven.

This chapter introduces the importance of including a profit in the budget and it provides recommendations for determining profit levels. The chapter then discussed the development of a budget. Several budget guideline options are presented and a one-day tour budget example is provided. The bulk of the chapter is devoted to analyzing weekend bus tour cost categories. Approaches toward developing realistic costs in each area are provided. The division of these costs into fixed and variable costs is also discussed.

In the last part of the chapter, the reader learns how to set a breakeven point. Working with the budgeting and breakeven information provided, an eight-step costing and pricing process is detailed. Learning these eight-steps in the costing and pricing process will be reinforced through the completion of the exercises that accompany this chapter.

DISCUSSION QUESTIONS

These questions may be discussed by two or more students outside of class as a fun way of reviewing this chapter or they may be discussed by everyone during class for a more wide-ranging discussion.

FIGURE 2-2 ROJO TOURS, INC.
COST AND PRICING SHEET

Name: _____ Telephone: _____
Address: _____ Contact: _____
City/State: _____ No. of Pax: _____
Zip Code: _____ Tour Dates: _____
Hotel/Motel: _____

Day/Date	Tour/Activity	Trans.	Guide	B.k.	L	D	Ent	Fees	Comm	S/T	Tax	Total	Cost Per Person

FIGURE 2-3 THE TOUR
COSTING AND PRICING FORMULA AND STEP BY STEP PROCESS

Formula	Steps	Process
$TC = \begin{matrix}A+B+\\D+E+G+\\H+I+K\end{matrix}$	1	Identify and Categorize Costs
$\begin{matrix}F = A+B+D+E\\V = G+H+I+K\\\therefore TC = F+V\end{matrix}$	2	Divide Costs into "Fixed" and "Variable"
Determine BEP	3	Determine Breakeven Point
$\dfrac{F}{BEP}$	4	Total All Fixed Costs and Divide by Breakeven Point
$\begin{matrix}PPV+PPF =\\BC\ (NIP)\end{matrix}$	5	Add the Per Person Variable Cost to the Per Person Fixed Cost to get the the Base Cost, Not Including Profit
$\begin{matrix}BTC \times PPP = PDF\\PDF + PBTC = TSP\end{matrix}$	6	Calculate the Tour Sales Price by Multiplying the Base Tour Cost, Times the Projected Percentage of Profit and Adding the Resulting Figure (Profit Dollar Figure) to the Projected Base Tour Cost
$\dfrac{TTP(NIP)}{BEN} = CPPBETP$	7	Determine the Calculated Per Person Breakeven Tour Price by Dividing the Breakeven Number of Tour Participants into the Total Tour Price (Not Including Profit) of the Tour
$CPPBETP + PPR \overset{\wedge}{\underset{\vee}{\ }} BPPPTP$	8	Compare the Calculated Per Person Breakeven Tour Price (After Adding the Per Person Profit) to the Bugeted Projected Per Person Tour Price and Modify Accordingly

TC: Tour Costs
A,B,D,E,G,H,I,K: Individual and Unique Tour Costs
F: Fixed Costs
V: Variable Costs
BEP: Breakeven Point
PPV: Per Person Variable Costs
PPF: Per Person Fixed Costs
BC: Base Cost
NIP: Not Including Profit
BTC: Base Tour Cost
PPR: Per Person Profit

PPP: Projected Percentage of Profit
PDF: Profit Dollar Figure
PBTC: Projected Base Tour Cost
TSP: Tour Sales Price
TTP: Total Tour Price
BEN: Breakeven Number of Tour Participants
CPPBETP: Calculated Per Person Breakeven Tour Price
BPPPTP: Bugeted Projected Per Person Tour Price
$\therefore$: Therefore
$\overset{\wedge}{\vee}$: Compare to/with

1. According to this chapter, what will a tour company have to do if one of its tours is priced too low?

2. What do you do in the last step (step number eight) of the costing and pricing process?

3. Two reasons are given in this chapter for pricing tours in such a way that little or no profits result. One of these reasons is the fear to price high enough to include a profit. What is the other reason?

4. What do you do in step five of the costing and pricing process and what will be the result?

5. What is the profit level range recommended for a new tour operator?

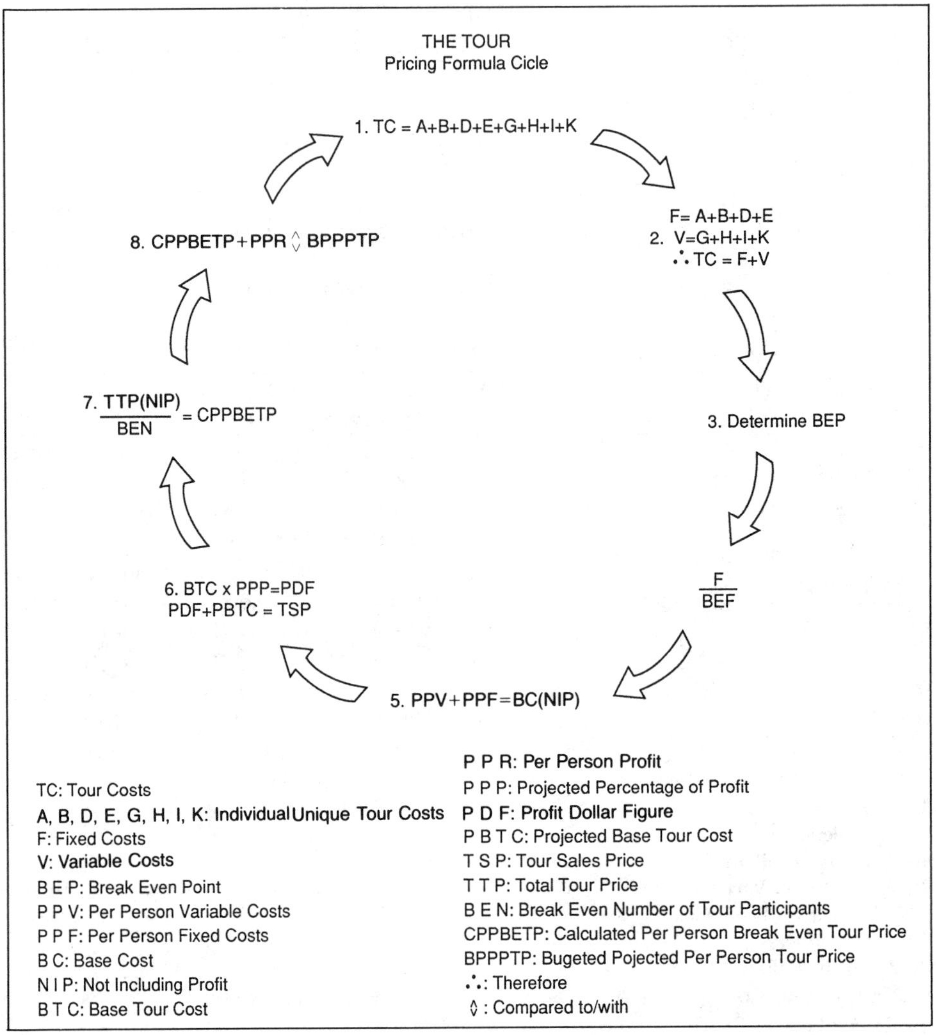
THE TOUR
Pricing Formula Cicle
1. TC = A+B+D+E+G+H+I+K
F= A+B+D+E
2. V=G+H+I+K
∴ TC = F+V
3. Determine BEP
F / BEF
5. PPV+PPF=BC(NIP)
6. BTC x PPP=PDF
PDF+PBTC = TSP
7. TTP(NIP) / BEN = CPPBETP
8. CPPBETP+PPR ◊ BPPPTP
TC: Tour Costs
A, B, D, E, G, H, I, K: Individual Unique Tour Costs
F: Fixed Costs
V: Variable Costs
B E P: Break Even Point
P P V: Per Person Variable Costs
P P F: Per Person Fixed Costs
B C: Base Cost
N I P: Not Including Profit
B T C: Base Tour Cost
P P R: Per Person Profit
P P P: Projected Percentage of Profit
P D F: Profit Dollar Figure
P B T C: Projected Base Tour Cost
T S P: Tour Sales Price
T T P: Total Tour Price
B E N: Break Even Number of Tour Participants
CPPBETP: Calculated Per Person Break Even Tour Price
BPPPTP: Bugeted Pojected Per Person Tour Price
∴: Therefore
◊ : Compared to/with

FIGURE 2-4 THE TOUR-PRICING FORMULA CIRCLE.

6. Will the per tour member cost become larger or smaller as the tour member breakeven point (the number of tour members needed to break even) becomes smaller?
7. It is recommended that you not plan to exceed the budgeted ball park projected per person tour price by more than what percent?
8. The "breakeven" point is the point at which what two factors are exactly even?
9. Tour buses are leased on one of two different bases or on a combination of both. What are these two bases?

10. All tour costs can be classified into two categories of costs and all tour costs will fit into one of these two categories. What are the two categories?

ROLE PLAY EXERCISES

1. Two students may participate in this role play either out of class as a fun way to review the chapter or as an in-class exercise. One plays the role of a new tour planner and the other plays the role of an experienced tour planner. Please read the script and then pick up the conversation in your own words.

NEW TOUR PLANNER: I don't understand how this eight-step costing and pricing process works. I have attempted to work with it, but I must be leaving something out since it simply doesn't seem to work for me.

EXPERIENCED TOUR PLANNER: The costing and pricing process is really fairly simple once you get the hang of it. Let me go through each of the steps with you and that should give you a good feel for it. The first thing we do is to start by . . .

CONTINUE ON YOUR OWN

2. Two students may participate in this role play either out of class as a fun way to review the chapter or as an in-class exercise. One plays the role of a new tour planner and the other plays the role of an experienced tour planner. Please read the script and then pick up the conversation in your own words.

NEW TOUR PLANNER: In the last step of the costing and pricing process you mentioned the budgeted or ball park projected per person tour price.

EXPERIENCED TOUR PLANNER: That's right. In that step you compare it to the calculated per person tour price (after adding the profit) and then you modify the actual price charged for each person based on that comparison. Of course, your breakeven number of tour participants may have to change as well. You may have to look hard at that factor.

NEW TOUR PLANNER: I think I understand that. But I really don't understand how one gets to or figures out the budgeted or ball park projected per person tour price. How is that done?

EXPERIENCED TOUR PLANNER: That's a separate procedure from that followed in the costing and pricing process used to determine the calculated per person breakeven tour price. To come up with the budgeted or ball park projected per person tour price, it is necessary for you to . . .

CONTINUE ON YOUR OWN

3. Two students may participate in this role play either out of class as a fun way to review the chapter or as an in-class exercise. One plays the role of a new tour planner and the other plays the role of an experienced tour planner. Please read the script and then pick up the conversation in your own words.

NEW TOUR PLANNER: I'm really not sure I understand the difference between what a fixed cost is and what a variable cost is. Will you explain the difference?

EXPERIENCED TOUR PLANNER: In concept, they are very different kinds of costs. Let's start with the fixed cost. This is a cost that . . .

CONTINUE ON YOUR OWN

GROUP DISCUSSION SITUATION: FANTASTIK'S BUDGET GAP

Florence Fantastick feels fortunate. But Florence also feels frustrated. Last month she graduated at the top of her class (of three graduates) from the Nome University Graduate School of Tour Planning. Upon graduation, she had 12 job offers and took one as a new tour planner with Single Saleswomen's Adventure Tours. Although the tour company already had two experienced tour planners, their expansion rate has become so considerable and their tours have become so popular that they needed to add a new tour planner. Kari Kares, the Chief Executive Officer of Single Saleswomen's Adventure Tours had interviewed 14 other candidates for the position as well as Florence. Kari was very impressed with Florence and made an attractive offer.

The first day on the job, Kari confided to Florence that the company was now in a position to put together a tour that Kari had wanted to run for many years, but because it was not the traditional adventure tour, she had had to put it on the back burner for some time. It would be Florence's first assignment. This tour is to the annual Kurdistan Camel Race in Krakaloa, Kurdistan. It will be for single saleswomen, the target audience to which Single Saleswomen's Adventure Tours markets.

Florence has worked hard on the tour, reviewing its development during three weekly meetings with Kari. Since the beginning, however, Kari has expressed concerns about the cost of the tour. At each meeting these concerns have been discussed at greater and greater length. Kari has stressed the fact that she wants this tour to sell out the very first time that it is offered. She expects Florence to do an outstanding job in offering all tour ingredients discussed at each of the meetings yet still keep the price of the tour low enough to attract enough single saleswomen to sell all openings on the tour within the first three weeks of its announcement. "I know it's a challenge," reflected Kari, "but I expect you to meet the challenge."

Florence believes her job is on the line. However, today as she has finalized preliminary costing figures, she has discovered what she suspected for over a week. This is that there is a major problem.

At the beginning, when Florence first started work on this tour, she developed a budgeted projected per person tour price based upon tours of similar duration to somewhat similar destinations. There were no camel tours and there were no other tours of the same duration to Kurdistan. In fact, there were no other adventure tours to Kurdistan period. However, she felt fairly comfortable that she was able to come up with figures that adequately reflected what could be considered the only competition which existed. Kari agreed when Florence presented her research and her conclusions during the second of Florence's weekly meetings with Kari.

Today, Florence completed the calculated per person breakeven tour price. There is a $562 per person difference between the budgeted projected price and the calculated breakeven price (including profit). Try as she may, no matter what she does, Florence has been unable to substantially reduce the difference without eliminating some of the features that she knows Kari considers to be critical to the tour's success. Florence has been able to get the difference down to $473 by reducing some of the "fluff" in the tour. She knows, however, that if she goes to Kari with this much of a difference in price between the budgeted projected per person tour price and the calculated per person breakeven tour price, Kari will become very upset and Florence is convinced Kari will fire her.

Florence has asked for advice from the other tour planners in the company. You are meeting with her to review the situation. Florence's next meeting with Kari is scheduled for the day after tomorrow. Consider the situation. What should Florence do? Decide among yourselves how you would handle the situation. Be prepared to present your suggestions in a paper that will be no longer than three pages in length. Also make sure the paper is double spaced and typed. Be prepared to also present your suggestions verbally in class if your instructor suggests that you do so.

EXERCISES

1. Working with the projected expenses in Figure 2-1, break out the fixed costs from the variable costs and list each in a column by type of cost and amount. Once this has been done, calculate the total of the fixed costs and the total of the variable costs.

Fixed Costs

1. _____ $ _____
2. _____ $ _____
3. _____ $ _____
4. _____ $ _____
5. _____ $ _____
6. _____ $ _____
7. _____ $ _____
TOTAL $ _____

Variable Costs

1. _____ $ _____
2. _____ $ _____

3. _____ $ _____
4. _____ $ _____
5. _____ $ _____
6. _____ $ _____
7. _____ $ _____
TOTAL $ _____

2. Working with the figures calculated in exercise number one, consider a breakeven figure of 25 tour members and identify a per person fixed cost.

Total Fixed Cost		*Per*
Divided By	*equals*	*Person*
Breakeven Number of Tour Members		*Fixed Cost*

$$\frac{\$ \rule{2cm}{0.4pt}}{25} = \$ \rule{1cm}{0.4pt}$$

3. Review step five of the costing and pricing process (covered in this chapter). Based upon the per person fixed cost identified in Exercise 2 and the per person variable costs, calculate a per person base cost for the tour (not including profit).

Per Person Fixed Cost
1st Per Person Variable Cost   (   )$
2nd Per Person Variable Cost   (   )$
3rd Per Person Variable Cost   (   )$
4th Per Person Variable Cost   (   )$
5th Per Person Variable Cost   (   )$
6th Per Person Variable Cost   (   )$
7th Per Person Variable Cost   (   )$
                                                    _____

Per Person Base Cost (Not Including Profit) $

4. Review step six of the costing and pricing process and the example shown immediately after the presentation of step six in this chapter. Based on the Per Person Base Cost calculated in exercise number three and a profit projection of 15 percent, calculate the dollar amount of profit per person to be budgeted for this tour.

Per Person	*Multiplied*	*The Percentage*		*The Dollar Amount*
			Equals	*of Profit*
Base Cost	*by*	*of Profits*		*Per Person*
$_____	×	.15	=	$_____

5. Review step seven of the costing and pricing process and the example shown in that paragraph of this chapter. Based on the Per Person Base Cost calculated in Exercise 3 and the Per Person Dollar Profit Projection calculated in Exercise 4, determine the Calculated Per Person Breakeven Tour Price which might be charged by the tour company for this tour.

Per Person Base Cost	Plus	Per Person Dollar Profit Projection	Equals	Calculated Per Person Breakeven Tour Price
$_____	+	$_____	=	$_____

CHAPTER 3
One-Day Domestic Tours

OBJECTIVES

Upon completion of this chapter, the student will be able to:

1. Identify the interrelationship between tour market and tour product.
2. Select product and geographical specializations in the *Specialty Travel Index* appropriate to a specialized tour product.
3. Explain how a tour operator might develop expertise in a selected area of specialization by progressively offering more lengthy and more destination encompassing tours.
4. Explain the combination of sightseeing, food and beverage, on-bus activity, shopping, and other one-day tour ingredient mix that best fulfills the needs and expectations of single-day, single-destination tour members.

Developing the First One-Day Tour

"I can't do it!" That is the reaction of many people who want to run tours, set up their own tour companies, and be tour operators. Many feel they simply cannot run tours because they do not have enough knowledge, enough skill, or enough "something" to accomplish it. However, almost everyone who decides that he or she can and wants to put together a tour, if they approach it in a systematic, businesslike manner, can plan, design, and operate/manage tours. Those who say they can't do it often provide themselves with a self-fulfilling prophecy that need not be so.

Planning and designing tours, working with vendors, establishing effective marketing programs, running and managing a tour, handling the finances, and following up on the tour are all jobs that are not easy. But, they are jobs mature people can learn. Motivation, which comes from within, and the determination that you "can do it" are key. Once a person makes up his mind that he can and will do it, much of the battle is won.

One key that helps is to start with a one-day tour. Your goal may be to run multi-week tours around the world, but most people will become discouraged if they start with such a big project. Even though your goal may be to run an around-the-world tour, start easily and work your way up from a one-day local tour. You should take it step by step, slowly increasing the tours that you run from a one-day, to a weekend, to a long weekend (Friday through Sunday) to a partial or a full week tour. Start with an easy local city tour and then develop tours that are further and further away from home. By starting with the basics and working your way up, your chances of ultimately being successful in running multi-week round-the-world tours (or whatever your goal) will be considerably better. Instead of having to learn everything for your international tour all at once, you will have taken your learning process a step at a time. As you obtain greater knowledge and skill and as you add the new learning elements which come from longer, more wide-ranging tours, you will start feeling comfortable with the basics and more able to concentrate your attention on the new aspects.

This does not mean that if a person fails to take it step by step they will automatically fail. A nurse in Cincinnati put together three-week tours of China for people in the medical profession as her first tour undertaking and she was successful. Her first tour went out full, she made a profit, and she continued to run similar tours to similar international destinations and remarked, "Why does everybody have so much trouble with putting together profitable international tours?" However, for every nurse from Cincinnati who develops a successful multi-week international tour as her first tour, there are hundreds of others who fail when taking this grandiose approach.

Tour Development and Sales

Which comes first: the design or the marketing of the tour? It is not exactly a chicken or the egg riddle, but it comes close. Many people decide in advance exactly what kind of tour(s) they wish to run and then they set out to research and develop that tour. Some spend years researching a destination and putting together what they believe to be an ideal tour. Then they turn to marketing. Occasionally, this approach works, but often it does not. The mistake that many make when they choose to proceed in this manner is that they believe that "everyone" will want to take their tour once the "public" has found out about it. This is usually naive. It ignores marketplace realities. People who take this approach frequently do not identify the "everyone" or the "public". Frequently, they do not have any idea how the "public" will find out about the tour so that they can come running to sign up for it.

For example, in 1988, a microbiologist working in the Mid West decided that he would put together a tour for microbiologists. He spent time identifying destinations in Europe which he felt would be of special interest to his group. He signed contracts and made nonrefundable hotel, airline, and other vendor deposits for a group of 30 persons. He paid for half-page Sunday newspaper advertisements and contracted for these ads to run three Sundays in a row in the travel section of his hometown newspaper. The advertisement headlined in big bold letters, "Germ Tours!" Unfortunately, neither the general public nor microbiologists were interested in taking a tour of Europe to study germs. Not a single person signed up for his tour. He lost a considerable amount of money in paying the newspaper for contracted advertising, as well as the airline and hotel nonrefundable deposits.

Several mistakes were made. The major one was to pre-suppose that "everyone" wanted to take a germ tour. Therefore, the newcomer to the tour industry should consider researching the market before researching the product. If possible, identify a buying nucleus that is a real market. Survey a sample of the market to find out what the buyers want. Then design the tour to meet the needs of the buying target market.

This "better" approach is one that is taken by too few. It calls for you to identify a market, usually a specific group, and to determine the kind of tour which that market or group desires. The tour is then designed to meet the target market/group's specifications. This approach has a greater chance of success, since one is starting with an identifiable group. The chances of success are even greater if before undertaking any research, you've approached a club, organization, business entity, or association first, sold a key person associated with that group on the concept, and obtained both an agreement of interest and a plan to move forward in running the tour(s) if they are researched, designed, and priced appropriately.

However, this approach has a singular disadvantage. If you decided to enter the tour operations and tour development field because you wanted to run a specific type of tour or tours to a specific destination, you may find that many of the groups you work with may select tour types and destinations that are different than the type of tour you wanted to put together. A second potential disadvantage of this approach is that beginners in the field may believe that they have a target market or group and not really have that market or group sold.

The Interrelationship between Market and Tour Product

Each person has a distinctive background. This background usually includes the attainment of special interests and often the attainment of special expertise. Many, when they decide to enter the tour field, make the decision based upon a desire to capitalize on their special interests and expertise. Unless that interest and expertise is germs, the concept usually has merit.

Rail tours, for example, are often designed, developed, and run by rail buffs. Some of the best ski tours are run by ski enthusiasts. Even knitting tours run by experts in knitting have been successful. However, markets are fickle. Sometimes they do not react the way the tour operator expects. Therefore, it is essential to combine factors to make them work together so that the probability of success will become greater.

One factor of importance, recognized by many but ignored by many more, is numbers. When the target market is small, the tour operator must obtain a large percentage of the market to make a tour successful. However, when the target market is large, a smaller percentage needs to be captured.

For example, if you decide to market a high school seniors tour to those who are graduating from a single high school, you must obtain a significant percentage of high school graduates if the tour is to be successful. If there are 100 graduates and the tour bus has 39 seats, you'll need to capture approximately one-third of the target market (i.e., about 33 or 34 persons). This is a fairly large percentage of the target market. However, if you run a tour for a large group of retirees (one tour company specializes in marketing tours to a retirement group which consists of several million people), you can fill a single tour with a small percentage of the target market.

Therefore, the chances of success are greater when you work with a large target market. However, with a large target, it is essential to reach all or at least a significant percentage of those in that market. Sometimes, you must effectively get the attention of potential participants several times before a significant number of the target market will start booking the tour. Sheer numbers, however, are important.

A second factor in this interrelationship is to start to make the tour meet the exact needs of the target market. A tour operator who specializes in tours to China for acupuncturists, for example, found that in initially researching the market, the acupuncturists wanted to have a significant part of the tour written off as a business expense. The tour operator contacted the Internal Revenue Service, determined what would be needed to qualify the tour for at least a portion of business expense write-off. He made certain that the tour met the IRS guidelines. He got an IRS ruling and put the IRS exemption number on his brochure. He would not have known, he said, that this was such an important consideration to potential tour members if he had not communicated with them prior to developing the tour.

Sometimes people put together tours because they want to use the tour as an opportunity to travel to a destination they have always wanted to visit. Sometimes this works. Most of the time it does not. If your justification for developing and running a tour is to be able to travel, it is usually less expensive to sign up for somebody else's tour and go as a tour member than to run the tour yourself.

If your real delight is leading tours, then it is usually much better to pursue a career as a tour guide or tour manager and not as a tour operator. The tour operator should be concerned with finding a guide or a tour manager who is either an expert in guiding or an expert with the organization. Because of his expertise and recognition within the target market, being the guide or tour manager will, in itself, attract a substantial number of tour members. For example, many national sports figures have substantial numbers of loyal fans.

When a tour operator announces that a top national football quarterback will be the tour manager for a tour, many fans will sign up without caring about the destination or the qualifications of the quarterback in terms of leading a tour. They will go on the tour so that you can meet and associate with the player.

To perhaps a lesser extent, the same concept applies for tours marketed to many identifiable target markets. For example, business people have signed up for financial management tours of Switzerland (and Swiss banks) led by internationally renowned financial wizards. Several of these "financial wizards," however, have been terrible tour managers. With tours of this type, tour operators provide a professional tour manager to go along to actually run the tour even though the person with the name is presumably in charge of the tour. In some cases, it does not matter how bad the name person is in running the tour, tour participants simply want to have an opportunity to meet with, be with, associate with, and quite frequently have pictures taken with the famous personality.

The more you can tie in interrelationships between the target market group and the tour itself, the better the chances are of you selling enough people for the tour to break even and make a profit.

While many of the examples presented are of multi-day, international tours, the concepts apply equally well to one-day, domestic tours. Even for the one-day tour, you should consider working with a large target audience, determine and meet the exact needs of that audience, and include a key figure of importance as the guide (or in some other role). Figure 3-1 shows how Rojo Tours gathers group information from organizations, travel agents, and companies so they can tailor a one-day (or longer) tour for the group.

Tailoring a Tour to the Market

Some people specialize in a single market and tailor a single tour to that market, running that tour over and over again. This approach is one taken by most sightseeing companies which market to people who are visiting the destination area. However, it is also an approach taken by many who are specialists in both an interest area and a geographical area. For example, a New York tour operator only runs music tours to Austria. The woman who started and heads the company received her doctorate degree in music history and is a native of Austria. She not only knows Austrian music history (her Ph.D. dissertation was on the history of music in Austria), but she has developed and maintained the contacts to provide special musical experiences for those who take her trips. She is able to get top name musical artists to perform individually for her tour members and to meet with them at cocktail receptions. She obtains good seats at internationally renowned performances, a feat duplicated by few even in Austria. Because of her knowledge, experience, and contacts, her tours are filled with little small touches that make the tours especially memorable. These small touches not only constitute the most memorable aspects of the tour, but they also create something which cannot be duplicated by competing tour operators.

FIGURE 3-1 ROJO TOURS AND SERVICES—GROUP PLANNING WORKSHEET

DATE OF INQUIRY _____   RESPOND BY _____

ORGANIZATION
TRAVEL AGENT
COMPANY NAME   _____

CONTACT NAME   _____

ADDRESS   _____

ZIP CODE   _____

TELEPHONE   (_____) _____

FAX NUMBER   (_____) _____

TOUR DATES   _____

NO. OF PAX   _____ MIN _____

HOTEL/MOTEL   _____

(Notes)

_____ ALB. AIR. P/U _____

_____ TURQUOISE TRAIL _____

_____ SANTA FE CITY TOUR _____

_____ BANDELIER TOUR _____

_____ TAOS TOUR _____

_____ O'KEEFFE TOUR _____

_____ ARTISANS TOUR _____

_____ OTHER TOURS _____

_____

_____

MEALS/RESTAURANTS _____

_____

_____

ENTERTAINMENT   _____
SPECIAL ACTIVITIES _____
OPERA/CHAMBER   _____

REFERRED BY: _____

-- NOTES --

_____

_____

_____

_____

_____

A tour operator in Florida specializes in tours for high school, college, and university performing bands. The company has developed an expertise in obtaining performance contracts for bands and then arranging for the band to be flown to the performance site, to take a tour of the area, to perform, and then return home. The tour operator gets client bands into some of the top parades, sporting event break periods, and other good exposure opportunities both in America and overseas. No fees are charged for developing the contracts, but because the tour operator is able to work out arrangements for performance contracts, having the tour operator handle all aspects of the travel is a natural and expected add-on to the contracting responsibility. As tour operators tailor specific touches designed to meet the special needs of their market(s), they are finding that their market(s) become more and more captured.

Finding a Market for the Tour

Some tour operators start with a tour and then seek a market for it. Frequently, this is the only way inbound tour operators can work. Their tour product is the destination area consisting of their home town and the area around it. Tour members are people coming to that home town. The inbound tour operator designs one or more tours in the local community or within a one- or two-day drive from the area's major airport.

Although some tour operators find that other vehicles are more beneficial (usually because of the specialized nature of their tours), many who run repeat offerings of specialized tours in specific areas depend upon travel agents to sell their tours. More tours are sold through travel agents than through any other marketing vehicle. Tour companies reach travel agents through a multitude of approaches. The direct mail marketing of brochures is an approach that gets the tour into agencies. Seldom are brochures thrown away until they are outdated. However, this may not get the travel counselor's attention. Therefore, tour companies list their tours in specialized indexes used by travel agents. Perhaps the most utilized is the *Specialty Travel Index*. The *Consolidated Air Tour Manual* and other tour directories also offer opportunities for listing tours in publications that are referenced by travel agents.

Tour operators also use full-time, contract, and multi-line sales representatives to call on travel agencies. Although this can be expensive, many tour operators have found these reps get travel agents familiar with and selling their tours fast.

Specialized publications constitute another vehicle for reaching a tour market. Many adventure travel tour companies find that they receive more bookings as a result of advertising in publications directed toward those who are interested in outdoor activities than they do from travel agents. It sometimes takes experimenting with advertising to find the publications that will produce the best results, but increasingly tour operators are finding that specialized publications can bring in a substantial number of tour clients.

Using the *Specialty Travel Index* to Identify a Geographical Specialization and a Product Specialization

The *Specialty Travel Index* is a publication designed for use by travel agents and tour operators. It is a listing of tours by type of specialization and by geographical destination. Tour operators who elect to have their tours listed in the *Specialty Travel Index* pay a fee for a one-eighth page description of their tours. The publication is used by travel agents to help match tours to client trip preferences. The agent looks up a key word related to the type of tour the client wants and finds tour operators who run that type of tour. If the client has identified a destination area, the travel agent can turn to the destination section of the *Index,* look up the tour operators offering tours to that destination, and determine which ones offer both the speciality type of tour the client wishes and operate that tour to the destination the client wishes to visit. The *Index* helps agents to narrow down the tour operators which provide tours that would most probably meet the needs of each client. Tour operators are coded in the listings with a numerical code. When a travel agent looks up a tour specialty, the agent has only to write down the numbers of all tour operators which operate that type of specialty tour. When moving to the geographical index, the travel agent then need only identify matching numbers. Once the numbers have been matched and the travel agent has one or more numbers providing the type of tour and destination the client desires, the agent can then turn to the listing of tour operators and read a several line description of those tours meeting his client's interest/geography specifications.

If brochures on these tours are not currently on file in the travel agency, the agent can call or write the tour operator and receive information. If the client is at the agent's desk and wishes to book the tour right away, phone calls to the tour operator(s) can offer substantial information about upcoming tours of possible interest to the client.

Since the *Specialty Travel Index* benefits travel agents, a large number of tour operators advertise in it. However, some tour companies will not advertise. They consider their tours too general in nature for such a listing.

A newcomer to the tour industry can obtain a number of ideas for specialization by turning to the *Specialty Travel Index* listing of tour specialty types. This helps to determine the types of tour with which he/she may wish to specialize. Figure 3-2 shows a listing of tour specializations identified in a recent issue of the *Specialty Travel Index.* One might note that "Germ" tours are not listed. Figure 3-3 identifies destinations.

Let's say, for example, that the tour operator decides to run tours for those who are interested in cut or uncut germs. The tours will be to Southeast Asia and Latin America concentrating on countries that have high exports of specific germs. The tours will go to the mining locations as well as to the centers of polishing and finishing gems, providing opportunities for tour participants to visit show rooms in almost every location and where the tour participant may buy uncut gems, cut but not mounted gems, or cut and mounted gems. The tour

FIGURE 3-2 *SPECIALTY TRAVEL INDEX*
INTEREST/ACTIVITY CATEGORIES*

Aerobics	Air Safari
Agriculture	Air Show
Airline Company	America's Cup
Anthropology	Antiques
Antiques	Archeology/History
Architecture	Art History
Artists Workshops	Art/Architecture
Astrology	Astronomy
Auto Racing	Backpacking
Ballooning	Barge/Canal Cruising
Bed and Breakfast	Biblical Tours
Bicentennial French Revolution	Birdwatching
Bicycle Touring	Brewery/BeerFestival
Botany	Businessmen Tours
Broadcasting TV/Radio	Campervan
Camel Safaris	Canoeing/Kayaking
Camping	Cattle Breeding
Castles	Caving
Cave Art	Chateau Rental
Character Tours	Children Permitted
Chauffeured Tours	Christian Church Tours
Chocolate Tours	Clans
Christmas Tours	Condo/Apartment Rental
Computer Sciences	Cooking School
Conservation	Country House/Cottage Rent
Cooking Tours	Covered Wagons
Country Inn/Guest Ranch	Cruises
CraftsTours	Dance
Cultural Expeditions	Disabled
Design Tours	Doctors Tours
Diving	Driver Guide
Dogsledding	Ecology
Dude ranch/Farmstay	Equestrian Tours
Elephant Ride	FIT's
Exposition	Farmstay
Family Groups	Festival Tours
Fashion Tours	Fishing
Film/Film History	Flightseeing
Flat Rental	Four-wheel Drive
Foliage Tours	Game Viewing
Gambling	Garden Tours
Gangland Tours	Gem Collecting
Gay Tours	Geology
Genealogy	Gold Panning
Goat Packing	Gourmet/Cooking Tours
Golf	

*Compiled and reproduced with permission from *Specialty Travel Index.*

FIGURE 3-2   (*continued*)

Group Tours	Gymnastics
Guest Ranch	Hang Gliding/Soaring
Health and Fitness	Helicopter Tours
Hiking	Historic Houses
History Tours	History
Holistic Health	Home Stay/Exchange
Honeymoon Adventures	Horse Breeding
Horse Carriage Tours	Horse Racing
Horse Riding/Packing	Horticulture
Hostels	Houseboating
Hunting	Ice Climbing
Investment	Island Vacation
Jeep Safari	Jet Boat Expeditions
Jogging	Jungle Expeditions
Kayaking	Kosher Tours
Language Study	Legend
Literary Tours	Llama Packing
Marine Biology	Martial Arts
Meditation	Military History
Miniatures	Motorcamping/Campervan
Motorcycle Touring	Motorhome Tours/Farmstay
Mountain BicycleTours	Mountaineering/Rock Climb
Museum Tours	Music/Dance
Mystery Tours	National Parks
Native Americans	Natural History
Nature Trips	Newsletter
Non-smoker Tours	Nudist
Nurses	Olympic Games
Opera	Outdoor Skills School
Overlanding	Painting
Paleontology	Photographic Tours
Photography	Pilgrimage/Mythology
Pioneer Skills	Politics
Polo Instruction	Porcelain/China Pottery
Professional Study	Psychology/Psychiatry
Public Affairs	Railway Trips
Ranching	Religion Spirituality
Research Expeditions	Restoration
River Lore	River Rafting/River Exp
Rock Climbing	Rowing
Running/Jogging	Safari/Game Viewing
Sailing Schools	Sailing
School Visits	Scuba/Snorkeling
Sculling	Seaplane Services
Seminars	Seniors/Retired
Shopping	Single Travelers
Skiing/Cross Country/Tour	

FIGURE 3-2   *(continued)*

Skiing/Downhill and Heli	Snorkeling
Snowmobiling	Snowshoeing
Soccer	Solar/Alternative Energy
Spectator Sports	Sports Tours
Stress Management	Student Tours
Study Tours	Summer Camps
Surfing	Swimming
Teachers Tours	Tennis
Textile Arts	Theatre
Tourist Guides	Treasure Hunting
Trekking	University Tours
Vegetarian Tours	Veterans
Villa/Chateau Rental	Vintage Aeroplanes
Vintage Cars	VISA Services
Volcano Tours	Wagon Trains
Walking Tours	Waterskiing
Weekend Escapes	Whalewatching
Wild Horse Watching	Wilderness Courses
Wilderness Lodge	Windjamming
Windsurfing	Winery Tours/Wine Tasting
Womens' Tours	Yacht Charter, Power
Yacht Charter, Sailing	Yoga/Meditation
Youth	

operator makes certain that certificates of authenticity and receipts for monies paid for the items are provided when gems are purchased.

Take a glance at the categories in Figure 3-2 and identify those in which you feel this tour operator would wish to be listed. Jot these down and then go to the destination index. Again decide which geographical listings you would request if you were the operator of these tours. Jot these down. Now go to Figure 3-4 and see what categories others have identified for this tour operator. If you identified the categories in the *Specialty Travel Index* section and the *Geographical* section which are shown in Figure 3-4, your selections will match those of many others.

Annual subscriptions to the *Specialty Travel Index* run approximately $10. Orders can be placed by phone (415-459-4900) or by mail: 305 San Anselmo Avenue, San Anselmo, California 94960.

The Gem Tour Growth Example

Now, of course, you will no doubt say that these are tours that would have to be more than one day in length and this chapter has cautioned any beginning tour operator to start with one-day tours. The newcomer to the travel industry who wishes to run the gem tours to Southeast Asia and Latin America may, therefore, decide to experiment by identifying a one-day tour that would be appropriate

FIGURE 3-3 *SPECIALTY TRAVEL INDEX*
GEOGRAPHICAL INDEX*

Index categories are broken down into the following categories with United States categories first, followed by international categories.

Domestic Regions
Midwest, New England, Western U.S.

States
All states and the District of Columbia are listed alphabetically

Africa
There is a category called "Africa" followed by country listings for twenty-seven African countries. There are also categories for East Africa, North Africa, and West Africa.

Antarctica

Arctic

Asia
There is a category called "Asia" followed by country listings for thirty-two Asian countries (Tibet is listed separately, the same as a country and not as a part of China)

Canada

Canadian Arctic

Caribbean
Thirty-four Caribbean countries are listed alphabetically. Also listed in the alphabetical list are categories labeled "Caribbean," and "West Indies"

Europe
Thirty-three European countries are listed alphabetically. Also listed in the alphabetical list are categories labeled "Eastern Europe," "Europe," "Scandinavia," and "United Kingdom"

Mediterranean
Categories for Cyprus, Mediterranean, and Sardinia

Mexico and Central America
Categories as follows: Baja California, Belize, Central America, Costa Rica, El Salvador, Guatemala, Honduras, Mexico, Nicaragua, and Panama

Middle East
Categories as follows: Egypt, Israel, Jordan, Middle East, Oman, Syria, and Yemen

South America
Ten countries are listed alphabetically. There are also listing categories as follows: Amazon, Falkland Islands, and the Galapagos Islands

South Pacific
Listings are: Australia, Cocos Islands, Cook Islands, Easter Islands, Fiji, French Polynesia, Guam, Irian Jaya, Marianas, Micronesia, New Zealand, Papua/New Guinea, Rarotonga, Saipan, Samoa, Solomon Islands, South Pacific, Tahiti, Tasmania, Tonga, and Vanuatu.

*Compiled and reproduced with permission from *Specialty Travel Index*.

FIGURE 3-4

SPECIALTY AREA LISTINGS SELECTED BY STUDENTS
Gem Collecting, Geology, Gold Panning, Investment, Shopping

GEOGRAPHICAL LISTINGS SELECTED BY STUDENTS
Asia, Burma, China, Hong Kong, India, Indonesia, Malaysia, Sri Lanka, Thailand, Turkey

Mexico and Central America, Central America, Mexico, Panama

South America, Amazon, Argentina, Bolivia, Brazil, Chile, Colombia, Ecuador, Latin America, Paraguay, Peru, South America, Venezuela

and closely tied in to the interest area. In many parts of the United States, this is a distinct possibility.

For example, if the newcomer is located in Denver, he/she may decide to run a one-day gold panning tour. He/she then would decide to identify where gold panning can be undertaken and after some research will soon discover that there are at least 10 sights in Colorado where tourists may pan for gold. He/she may decide to include in the one-day trip a tour of a recently (within the last 50 years) operating gold mine. After research, he/she will find that there are at least three of these which offer daily sightseeing during the summer high season and periodic sightseeing opportunities at other times. Some of these one or two hour (or less) mine visits will also operate on an "on request" basis, but the cost for this is high and probably impractical for a one-day tour. He/she will discover that the sites where one can pan for gold and the sites where one can visit gold mines are not always the same. Some, however, are close enough to one another to combine into a one-day tour.

Next, the would-be gem tour operator identifies locations where unpolished gold nuggets, polished gold nuggets, and gold nugget jewelry or finished gold jewelry can be purchased. Again, his/her research will uncover the fact that there are several Colorado locations where such purchases can be made. Some are located right at the mines while others are in both small towns and in Denver itself. Most provide certificates of authenticity. Many tour members like to have these when they purchase gold items.

Now that the would-be gem tour operator has identified the skeleton ingredients for a domestic one-day tour that shadows to some degree, the type of tour he wishes to run internationally, he will need to put together the balance of sightseeing activities, combine interesting food and beverage functions into the one-day tour menu, identify a bus company from which buses can be leased, and cost out all ingredients.

Having a rough one-day tour put together and a good idea of what the costs will be as well as the minimum number of participants needed to make the tour break even or be profitable, the gem tour operator starts to look for a market. One logical market consists of those residents of the greater Denver area who are interested in gems. These people will probably belong to gem clubs and associations. For example, Denver lapidary and gemologist associations would provide one marketing direction. Another possibility might be high school or even junior high (middle school) science classes, especially those that specialize in geology. A third, may be those who belong to travel or outdoor oriented social organizations or clubs. The range of options is large.

The would-be gem tour operator might next decide to approach key persons in these various organizations. By approaching enough of these organizations and individuals, he/she will find that some will express a very real interest while most will not be interested at all. For those who are interested, a series of marketing activities can be planned. Ideally, the club or organization will take on the responsibility of filling the bus tour in exchange for a percentage of the cost or a flat fee. The gem tour operator takes all costs, including his profit and adds a figure of perhaps $10 or $15 per person for the club or organization. He comes up with a total, publishable cost for the one-day tour.

After successfully running one or two tours of this type, the gem tour operator may decide to go to a more regular schedule of tours and enter the inbound travel market, the sightseeing travel market, or a market dedicated to working with education, continuing education, and/or recreation center founded clients. Generally, these tours are either contracted to incoming groups or establishing clubs and organizations for set dates or they are announced in continuing education or recreation center catalogs for specific dates. By working with these organizations and running the same basic one-day tour for each of them, the gem tour operator will rapidly discover which ones will provide continuing profits and which ones will not fill or lose money. Sometimes those that do not fill will have a steady production of tour clients, but not enough production to create a profit. In some cases, two or three of these can be combined in order to offer profitable one-day tours.

At some point after running a number of successful one-day tours, the gem tour operator may decide that a two-day or a weekend tour should be tried. Essentially, the same process will be undertaken. Again, a basic tour will be put together and marketed on a one-time experimental basis first. When this has been developed into a steady, profitable tour for the gem tour operator, then the tour operator can expand to perhaps a five-day or seven-day tour. Finally, the gem tour operator will be ready to expand to a multi-day international tour.

One of the benefits of this approach is that not only has the gem tour operator learned the pitfalls and how to overcome them on a gradual basis as the length of the tour has been increased and the destination has grown from being local to international, but if he/she was diligent enough to keep a listing of individual and organizational clients, when the tours to Asia and Latin America are introduced, the gem tour operator has a solid base on which to market these tours. In fact, if the one-day, two-day, five-day, and longer domestic tours are continued and run on a profitable basis regularly, either in season or throughout the year, the gem tour operator will continue to develop a solid flow of potential clients to feed into the international tours. If this foundation base is combined with other marketing activities, (including listings in the *Specialty Travel Index* and other approaches used to draw on travel agency clients), the tour operator may find that there will be a large and growing foundation for a steady flow of international tours. All of this should contribute to continuous profitability.

The Importance of Research and Finding a Niche

Many have found that it is very difficult to be all things to all people. If the person desiring to enter the tour field will concentrate on identifying his areas of interest and specialization, if that person will research not only the tours that seem to fit those areas of interest and specialization, but also the potential market relating to those areas of interest and specialization, his/her tours should be successful. If that person will honestly look at the results of his/her research and say "no" if it appears that the market does not exist and "yes", being prepared to act on that "yes" if the market does exist, then the chances of success will be considerably greater.

The examples seen thus far show both the positive progressive approach (successfully based upon researching both the tour and its ingredients) and the market. They have also shown what happens when that research is not undertaken. Theoretically (though it is hard to believe), even the germ tour might have sold had sufficient research into the market and ways to capture that market been undertaken prior to actually contracting for the newspaper advertising. This is certainly not to suggest that one enter the germ tour market (if there is a germ tour market), but rather to stress the importance of undertaking marketing research prior to spending money and time on a tour that that research would have shown to be unprofitable.

The One-Day, Single Destination Tour

The one-day, single destination tour is the easiest of all tours to run. It typically leaves in the morning, goes to a single city or activity destination, and returns in the evening. One-day, single destination tours are frequently built around going to a location to participate in or view highlights and features of that, often well-known destination. For example, many in the major cities of the Northeast (New York City, Newark, and Philadelphia, for example) will take a Saturday bus tour to Atlantic City for the gambling and, in the Summer, for the beach. Other examples include Annapolis and the Naval Academy as a one-day destination for those from Baltimore or Washington, D.C. Disney World is a one-day tour destination from Tampa and Saint Petersburg. Los Angeles residents may go to Long Beach to see the Spruce Goose (the largest commercial airplane ever built) and the Queen Mary.

Other one-day, single destination tours are built around a short-term specific activity or event. For example, tour buses from throughout the West take visitors to rodeos. And one-day bus tours are organized from many cities in Florida to go to the Strawberry Festival held each year in the early days of Spring.

The advantages of a one-day, single destination tour are many. There are no hotel accommodation arrangements. Frequently, breakfast can be just coffee and doughnuts or something light provided at the time tour participants check in for the tour. Most tours return by 6:00 P.M., so dinner is normally not included. The only meal function that needs to be considered on many one-day tours is lunch and frequently it is both logical and expected by tour participants that this will be an "on your own" activity. For example, most tour members going to Atlantic City to gamble do not want to get back together with the group for lunch. They would prefer to have lunch on their own. Those attending the Strawberry Festival (and other food theme-oriented day tours) usually eat so many strawberries (or other theme food) that they do not want to have lunch.

Even when a lunch meal function is included, it often can be an easy meal to organize. Frequently, it will consist of a box lunch prepared by a caterer and either cold or hot drinks carried in coolers or large thermoses in the luggage compartment of the bus. These picnic-type lunches are often not only easy to arrange (the caterers will provide everything in the box), but many tourists enjoy stopping at off-highway picnic grounds and seeing the scenery while getting off of the bus for awhile for lunch.

The essential elements for a one-day tour, therefore, will be arrangements for the lease of a bus and driver, admission fees for the events, tour packets (including a map of the destination area), and the contracted services of a knowledgeable step-on guide.

For some destinations, little is needed in terms of destination arrangements. For example, when a bus full of senior citizens arrives in Atlantic City, typically they are given a tour cost-included roll of quarters, a map of the casinos, and instructions indicating where to meet in order to come back to the tour bus (usually with an appropriately marked map). They are left on their own to gamble, shop, or enjoy the beach. No destination vendor contract is needed.

Frequently, the same is true when visiting a public site. Those going to Annapolis do not have to sign a contract with the Naval Academy. However, it is better to coordinate with the facility so that you know where to park the buses and when special events may be occurring.

However, when the one-day tour is centered around an activity, it is essential to contract with that activity or function director in order to arrange sightseeing activities that will, perhaps, give tour participants an edge over those who may simply drive to the event or function. For example, the tours going to the rodeo will probably want to coordinate with that rodeo to make certain that tour participants get good seats. Blocks of seats are booked well in advance so that tour participants will have seats with excellent views. The same is true with the Strawberry Festival and the Strawberry Parade. Most tour companies pay for grandstand seats so that tour participants will have not only a place to sit down, but also seats in the same area where the judges are seated; thus ensuring that they will have the best views of the floats.

However, the number of contracts that need to be signed and the number of vendors with which the tour operator needs to work are few for the one-day, single destination tour as compared to single-day, multi-destination or multi-day and multi-destination tours. Frequently, because the single-day, single destination tour involves so little that is needed from the tour company, it can wind up being a far more profitable tour in addition to being a far easier tour to run.

A single disadvantage sometimes cited by those who run one-day, single destination tours is that the tour is not nearly as exciting or interesting to put together or to run as an international multi-day, multi-destination tour. Nevertheless, a large number of tour companies throughout the United States have founded their success on one-day, single destination tours. It is the easiest type of tour for the newcomer to start with because there are fewer things to go wrong. The chances of being able to run such a tour profitably are greater for the newcomer to the industry than any other type of tour.

The One-Day, Multi-Destination Tour

Only slightly more difficult (in many cases) is a one-day, multi-destination tour. Because it is a one-day tour, only a limited number of destinations can be included. When destinations and activities are close to one another, often in the same city or community, the major difference between the multi-destination tour and the single destination tour will be that since more contractors are worked with the tour timing needs to be watched so that tour participants do not feel rushed.

Colorado Springs is a good example of a one-day, multi-destination tour. If a tour bus originates in Denver, it is possible to go through the Air Force Academy, a few miles later to drive through the Garden of the Gods, and a few miles later take tour participants to the top of Pikes Peak on the Incline Railroad. Although there are many sites in Colorado Springs that could be added to the tour, if you include lunch and time to do some shopping, this will provide members with a full day. It is a multi-destination tour in that even though the tour goes to only a single city and its environs, tour participants move from place to place via the tour bus, requiring them to get off of the bus and back on the bus several times throughout the day. This type of one-day, multi-destination tour, therefore, involves only slightly more work than the one-day, single destination tour.

Researching and Designing a One-Day Tour

In researching and designing any tour, it's good to start with local resources. Most will contact the Chamber of Commerce in the community and often the state division of tourism can be of assistance. Every city of any size has a convention and visitor bureau, often called by its initials (CVB). The help they offer tour planners is considerable. Obtain as much information as possible about the widest variety of possible points of interest in the destination area. Sometimes, even though it is just a one-day tour, that will mean contacting the Chamber of Commerce and the convention and visitors bureaux of several cities. Local and state historical societies may also provide beneficial information. Even when the tour is in your own state, it can be beneficial to contact your Division of Tourism. Chambers of Commerce, CVBs, historical societies, and tourism divisions have information on points of interest that are open year-round as well as special, one-time or periodical activities. They provide information on who to contact and on activity dates.

Though much of the information received from historical societies, CVBs, Divisions of Tourism, and Chambers of Commerce has considerable detail, it is usually insufficient for detailed tour planning purposes. Therefore, the next step is to telephone the contact people working with the sightseeing points of interest you are considering for your tour. Do not exclude a large number of options. Explore all options in some detail before excluding. Having said this, for some groups and target audiences there are points of interest that would logically be immediately excluded. For example, not a lot of senior citizens will want to go through Guerrilla Warfare Land when each participant going through is required to enter into simulated combat at each stage. And, tours for high school football players will probably not include visits to the Knitting Museum. After telephoning contact persons with each of the sightseeing points of interest, you will be able to determine hours of operation, admission costs, bus parking arrangements, and other mechanical details of importance if you ultimately decide to include that point on your tour. However, you will also be able to find out information about closing dates/times (the point of interest may not be open during the time of your tour), admission restrictions (there may be a dress code or it may have other limited access restrictions), or it may be that you will decide that it just would not be of as much interest to your tour participants as other potential options.

For those sites that are of interest and where everything you confirm via phone seems to be something that could work out for your tour, schedule a meeting with a person of as much authority as possible. Take a personal tour and discuss details appropriate for your group both with destination coordinators and your guide. Schedule your personal trip together with a visit of other potential sites so that you will maximize the economies involved. Allocate enough time to not only see the points of interest in detail, but to plan to spend time talking with the executives of the site. Many problems have occurred because during the research trip the tour planner did not spend a sufficient amount of time investigating a point of interest because of pressure to make another appointment. Sometimes more than one visit with the vendor is necessary. Some planners routinely schedule two trips to visit with all tour vendors. When this is not possible, telephone follow up should be planned. During the time of your visit(s), check out all aspects of the site. Even if it seems apparent what the person will experience at the sightseeing point, go over every detail yourself. If possible, experience the sightseeing point exactly as your tour participant would experience it. This may not always be possible, especially if you are visiting during the off-season when the site is officially closed. However, do your best. If you can reach the person who will actually be in charge the day your tour arrives, it is wise to meet that person and to discuss arrangements for handling your group.

It is not unusual for vendors to provide group facilities and arrangements that are different than those designed for individuals who may be touring the site. However, in the United States, many sightseeing points have been especially designed for individuals and families rather than for groups. For example, there are many sites that have recorded messages in each room which play when a person pushes a button to hear the message. This works fine for an individual or a family, but when a group of 35 people arrives in a very small waiting room area with some backed up into the hallway, they will be shuffling around and talking among themselves. The chances are probable that at least 50 percent will not hear the message, nor will they be able to view what is being talked about.

As you gather data, make copious notes. Come back to your office and put together the skeleton of a tour. Keep in mind that the mistake most newcomers to the tour industry make is trying to include too much. Balance the activities. Avoid keeping tour participants on the tour bus for lengthy periods of time. Try to schedule one-day tours so that tour participants are not on the bus for more than one hour at a time. This is not always possible. However, when long bus trips are required, consider breaking the time by including a snack or a meal at some place where the bus can stop. City parks and highway roadside picnic areas are often good options. Remember to visit the park or the highway stop in advance. Walk through it to evaluate how well it will work for your group.

The last part of the research is to actually go on at least one simulated run of the tour by yourself. Simulate the activities and flow of your tour participants on a step-by-step basis. Time the activity. Make sure the timing works out as you have planned it.

The Single-Day Tour Designer's Familiarization Trip

As with any tour of any length, the designer/planner needs to visit each area covered by the tour and undertake or participate in each activity scheduled for tour members. Tour planners may be tempted to take short cuts by either phoning the destination vendor and working out arrangements by phone or by going to the site and simply looking around, not undertaking the activity personally. Even the most experienced tour designer/planner finds that when taking such short cuts, unpleasant surprises frequently result. What may have been viewed as an interesting experience may wind up being more challenging than expected or less interesting than expected. Remember to visit all sites on days similar to the day when the tour will be there. If the destination is visited during the off-season and the tour is scheduled during the in season, the crowds one will not see during the planning visit may make the experience less enjoyable than expected for tour members who are there during high season.

Remember to obtain the names of those people at the destination who will actually be working "on site" at the time that the tour arrives during each of the one-day trips. The names should be given to the tour manager. The tour manager will then know who to interface with at each destination and for each activity.

The Single-Day Tour Manager's Familiarization Trip

Tour guides and tour managers who will be accompanying the tour should also undertake a familiarization trip which should be designed to be as close to the actual tour trip in all aspects as possible. The tour manager should make copious notes. Many find that bringing a tape recorder with them is beneficial. Recordings can be transcribed when they return and the notes can assist in developing the tour manager's ongoing dialog throughout the tour as tour participants progress from point to point. During the tour manager's familiarization trip, an effort should be made for the tour manager to meet vendor contact persons so that each will recognize the other person's face at the time of the actual tour.

Although the familiarization tour for the tour manager should be undertaken close to the time when the tour actually is conducted, a few days should be left between the familiarization trip and the actual tour so that the tour manager can digest all aspects of the familiarization tour and can contact key vendor personnel by phone if there are any questions or concerns that develop as a result of the initial trip.

Costing and Pricing a One-Day Tour

Over the years, single-day tour operators have attempted to come up with a maximum one-day tour cost figure. This, they maintain, is a cost beyond which no tour member would pay for a one-day tour. Therefore, they have consistently kept their tours below the "maximum" figure. Today, there are one-day tours that are filling despite being priced at more than each of the figures that "they say" cannot be exceeded. There really never has been and probably never will be a magical figure that one must stay within on a one-day or on a multi-day tour.

Nevertheless, tour operators must constantly keep in mind that with every dollar increase in the price of their tour, a percentage of the potential target population may be excluded from being able to afford the tour. This is especially true for people who are living on a limited budget. That frequently applies to senior citizen groups and young people up to and through college age. These two groups constitute major target populations for one-day bus tours. Therefore, for these target populations, costing and pricing a tour at the lowest possible price will make a considerable difference in terms of the number of tour participants who can afford to take the tour.

Having recognized this, however, you should also note that one of the biggest problems newcomers to the tour industry have is pricing tours so that all costs are covered (including those of the guide), so that a per person unforseen expense cost is included (frequently referred to as a miscellaneous expenses fee), so that the step-on guide is paid a good income, and so that a profit is made. Often tour planners are simply afraid to price a tour at a cost which will result in their covering all costs and earning a reasonable profit.

However, professional tour operators believe a tour should not be operated unless it can be run profitably. It is important for the newcomer to the tour industry to overcome the price obstacle on the very first tour so that the newcomer will not be underpricing himself consistently. Avoid running tours at below cost, making do with inferior quality and giving yourself too little remuneration. Avoid unrealistic overpricing fears.

It is important to recognize the severity of the problem while also factoring in inflation and cost of living differences throughout the country. To do so, use the following ball park guidelines. Try to cost the one-day single destination tour between $65 and $100. Consider costing the one-day, multi-destination tour at between $75 and $100. Remember, however, these are only ball park figures. In some parts of the country, much higher prices will need to be levied. In some sections of the country lower amounts can be charged. Maximum figures may vary, but be careful about going below the minimums indicated here.

Start pricing by dividing all costs into variable costs and fixed costs. Fixed costs are those prices which apply no matter how many tour members participate. The cost of the tour bus, for example, is a fixed cost. This cost will remain the same whether one person goes on the tour or if all seats on the bus are occupied. The cost of the step-on guide is also a fixed cost. The guide normally works for a daily or an hourly fee whether there is one person on the tour or there are a large number of people on the tour. Examples of variable prices include name badges, tour member gifts, and meals. Identify all costs and place those costs in columns of fixed costs and variable costs. Add up the fixed costs, determining a minimum number of participants that you will accept for breakeven. Usually this is 50 percent or less of the number of seats on the tour bus.

After determining a total of the fixed costs, add up the variable costs, which are costs per person. Multiply the variable costs times the minimum number of tour participants for breakeven. Add the total of the fixed costs plus the variable cost total that has already been calculated. To this total, add 10 percent for miscellaneous expenses and 15 percent for profit. Now that you have a grand total, divide this grand total by the minimum number of tour participants for breakeven. (see the chapter on costing and pricing for a step-by-step breakdown of this process). This will give you a cost per person. Show this cost on your brochures and other literature and indicate that unless the minimum registration is received, the tour will be cancelled. In a later section in the book, marketing literature is discussed and appropriate wording for this is provided. However, unless there is some reason not to do so, the tour should be cancelled if a sufficient number of people fail to sign up and pay the calculated tour cost.

Make sure that all costs are covered. They should include marketing expenses, reservations expenses, a portion of the expenses involved in researching the tour (usually this is spread over between ten and twenty tours), administrative expenses (telephone, paper, cost of letters, and so forth), and remuneration to you for your time spent in researching and administering the development of the tour.

If the tour is being run for a sponsoring organization, that organization may very well have contracted with you to pay them a fee for each participant taken on the tour. This should be considered a marketing cost. It is also a variable cost. Sometimes such organizations require a flat fee. If that is the case, then the fee should be included in the fixed costs.

Special Considerations in Costing Food and Beverages

Food and beverage costs can escalate rapidly. Many who are new to the tour industry tend to either underestimate or to overestimate the food and beverage requirements for a tour. This is especially true for tours where food and beverages are carried on the tour bus or adventure tours where meals are provided in the open, catered by the tour company.

When ala carte dining is provided for tour members, newcomers to the tour industry tend to overestimate what tour members will consume (this determines what the cost of the meal will be). They, therefore, overestimate the budget for ala carte meals. To avoid these problems, newcomers to the industry are encouraged to avoid including food and beverage functions on board the tour bus. When restaurants are utilized, try to find the all-you-can-eat variety of buffets. Be careful, however, to make sure that the quality of the buffet is in keeping with the tour group. Many buffets provide only inexpensive foods. These will not be appreciated by most tour members. Some full-service cafeterias also provide all-you-can-eat meal prices. Often upscale cafeterias are good choices since they usually feature a wide variety of entrees, side dishes, salads, and desserts ranging from inexpensive to fairly expensive selections. In addition, because of the nature of cafeteria serving, a full bus load of passengers can be served, eat leisurely, and be back on the bus within an hour to an hour and a half. Usually for one and two day trips (also for longer trips) top quality full-service cafeterias are a good choice for included meals.

Of special concern should be food and beverage functions at check-in time and on the bus. Many who offer one-day tours will schedule an early morning departure. It is appropriate to have light food and beverages at these early departures. Some will feature an inexpensive champagne mixed with orange juice. If alcohol is planned, however, check to see if local laws require a liquor license. If so, do not serve it—even if it is just an orange juice/champagne mix. And never serve anything alcoholic to minors. Coffee and tea are more customery. Offer an assortment of danish, doughnuts, and perhaps some type of appropriate roll for those who are on a low-fat or low-cholestoral diet (for example, oat bran muffins). For an adult group, this is usually all that is needed. Most adults eat and drink very little early in the morning. The newcomer to offering one-day and two-day tours almost always overspends on morning food and beverage functions. It is important to calculate as closely as possible, not just because of the cost (though this is an important reason), but also because of the waste and leftovers that must be disposed of. If you want to make the morning pre-departure food and beverage function especially nice, consider having decorations such as a few flowers and paper table cloths. However, both the set up and the tearing down of check-in facilities needs to be rapid.

Everything should be self-contained. One tour, for example, used a school as a meeting place for their Saturday tour. They were given keys for the outside doors so that they would have access to the restrooms which were located between the outside doors and the main part of the building. However, they did not have access to the main school building. There was a small area near the doors with picnic benches so that the school's students could eat their lunches outside on nice days. The tour company planned to have the check-in arrangements completed at the picnic tables and include food and beverage on a help-yourself type arrangement with coffee urns and trays of danish. There was an electrical outlet from the main building which they planned to use for their coffee. Unfortunately, they did not check out how to get electricity to the outlet, since all the electricity in the main building was turned off. As a result, they had neither coffee nor tea since the plug-ins to the electrical outlets produced no electricity.

You should also consider the fact that outdoor pre-departure check in food and beverage functions may be disrupted by weather. Rain is always a possibility, so having a covered check-in area is important. Wind is also a factor to be considered as well. Having name tags, paper cups, and paper plates all blowing around is a nuisance.

Serving food and beverages on board the tour bus can be appreciated by the tour members, but it can present definite problems. If the trip is going to be a long one, having food and beverages on the tour bus can help to break up the time. But, be careful about what is served. Although coffee and tea are usually appreciated, most tour companies are not prepared with the proper serving facilities to deal with the heat and the potential problems of spillage. When hot coffee or tea is spilled, it burns. Therefore, you should consider alternative beverages. A choice of juices is usually a good morning alternative—especially if it is served in tumblers that are only filled half full. It is usually better to serve food first and then serve beverages. If one holds a beverage very long, it will probably spill. By offering passengers danish or some other light food first and then serving juice, passengers will probably be thirsty enough to consume the juice rapidly. But if juice and danish are served at the same time, passengers will have problems balancing them. Spills will be likely.

Food and beverages served on board the tour bus should be stored on the back seat of the bus. If the bus is equipped with a bar, both food and beverage storing facilities are often built into the bar. These facilities, of course, should be utilized. Food and beverage service should start from the back of the bus and proceed toward the front of the bus until all passengers are served. Each person should be supplied with napkins and, if needed, eating utensils in addition to the food and beverage. Expect spillage and have absorbant paper towels, spot remover, and a sponge on hand. Bring a large thermos of water as well. This is the preferred drink for many passengers and water is beneficial in cleaning up spillage.

A good, but more expensive, morning tour bus alternative is a boxed snack prepared by a catering service. Individual boxes should include a napkin, danish, or other food snack, and a sealed container of juice or other beverage. Request wide-bottomed juice containers. When they are kept in the box and held on one's lap, the chance of spillage is reduced.

On-board beverage choices should be severely limited. Avoid soft drinks and alcoholic beverages. If soft drinks are served on the bus, everyone will want a different kind and some will not want a soft drink at all, but will want something else. Soft drinks are easy to spill and frequently the undrunk, partially filled can is placed on the floor of the bus. If the driver swerves or stops suddenly, many partially drunk soft drink cans can spill, creating a mess no one likes to clean up, but also soaking any carry-on bags passengers may have placed on the floor.

Always have trash bags available. Once food and beverages are served, make several trips up and down the aisle collecting trash until it all has been collected. Then make certain that bags are tied securely and placed in the rear of the bus.

If all of this sounds like a great deal of trouble, it is. If you can avoid serving food and beverages on board the tour bus, it is much easier for the guide and far less messy. However, when food and beverages are served, tour members appreciate it. Having a food and beverage function on the bus is a nice touch. It helps to make the one- or two-day tour special.

Frequently, in the evening, when tour members are often "on their own," an optional cocktail reception can be scheduled. Consider using the hotel's bar facilities. Price out the costs. This will be more expensive than having beer and/ or cocktails in a reception suite, but it has several advantages. The primary advantage is that the bar can be closed at a specified time and the reception can be concluded on time. In addition, there will be hotel staff members available to serve. The guide is free to mix with tour members. In addition, if there is a tour participant who is under 21 years of age, the responsibility for not serving that person or those persons will be the responsibility of the hotel. No tour company employee should ever serve liquor to a person who is below the legal drinking age.

Single-Day Tour Vendors and Vendor Relationships

Vendor performance for those on single-day tours is frequently considered more important than for those on tours of multiple days. If a vendor provides poor service on a one-day tour, tour participants are more likely to remember and to be upset since there are very few activities and programs involved in the one-day tour and each aspect of that tour stands out. Each one is potentially memorable. However, if you are taking a 21 day tour and one of the meals is served late or perhaps the service is not as good as it could be, tour members tend to forget about it if all other meals and services have been good. They consider it the exception, which it is.

On a one-day tour, however, there may be only one meal. Therefore, if it is served late or the service is bad, it is remembered more distinctly and the entire tour may well be judged badly because of it. Therefore, it is essential to work closely with vendors. Frequently, the one-day tour is repeated several times throughout the year. If vendors are made aware of the fact that they will be used repeatedly if their service is good and if the facilities provided are those which were contracted, the chances of receiving both quality and good service is usually better. This is not to suggest that you should lie to a vendor, promising tours that you never expect to run, but rather to recognize that when you run multiple tours, it provides greater negotiating ability as well as greater incentive on the part of the vendor to provide quality contracted services.

Sometimes tour planners are tempted to skip contracts for one-day tours simply because they are short tours. This is especially true if it is a one-time, one-day tour. The tour will not be repeated. Detailed contracts for one-day tours, however, are even more important for one-time tours than for multi-day tours or for tours that are run on a repeated basis since the vendor may be tempted not to provide good service.

Realistically speaking, however, most will not be able to justify the time or the expense to prepare lawyer-approved, multi-page legal documents for a one-day, one-time tour. However, letters of agreement or a standard contract can be utilized. If one is presented with a vendor contract, it will probably have been written by the vendor's lawyer. It probably will not provide the kinds of guarantees or penalties for nonperformance that the tour planner would prefer. Therefore, although the vendor may require the signing of its own contract, that contract should be read. If the sections that would protect the tour planner are not in the contract, then either they should be written in as an addendum requiring the signatures of both parties (usually better) or they should be agreed to by either a separate contract or an attached letter of agreement.

Single-Day Tour Sightseeing and Sightseeing Mix

On a single-day tour, it is very easy to overdo the sightseeing that is scheduled. Although tour participants want a complete tour, there is a limit to how much can be comfortably scheduled on a one-day tour. It is usually best not to include more than four hours of sightseeing broken into two hours in the morning and two hours in the afternoon. With a lunch in between and getting from the origin point to the point of sightseeing as well as from the point of sightseeing back in time to be able to drop off passengers so that they can make it home in time for dinner, it is seldom possible to schedule more than two hours in the morning and two in the afternoon. This, of course, should be treated as a guideline, not as a hard, fast rule.

Mix sightseeing with other activities. Most one-day tours include a meal function. Free time is often valued by tour participants, especially when shopping is available. If tour members will be able to buy things of a unique or of a different nature, consider including a presentation on shopping tips.

Single-Day Tour On-Bus Activities

Consider mixing on-bus activities. Include presentations regarding the flora, fauna, and historical buildings and/or other sights being passed by the tour bus along with information about what the person will be able to see at the next destination. This is a good time to include the shopping tip presentation. Age-appropriate on-bus games may be planned. If bus trips last one hour or more, include some time for tour participants to be able to rest and relax and to talk among themselves. Also, as noted earlier, consider serving some type of food and beverage on board the bus.

At the beginning of the tour, welcome participants, introduce yourself and other key persons (especially if this is for a dedicated group), and introduce the bus driver. Indicate the qualifications and speak about the background of the bus driver. After you have introduced yourself and the driver, this is a good time to introduce tour members to one another. Short self-introductions are usually best.

If the tour company has gathered advanced information on tour members (see Figure 3-5), you may want to review these in advance and interject such comments as, "Mr. and Mrs. Jones are celebrating a wedding anniversary today. Congratulations! May you celebrate many more." This shows you care. People like to be recognized and they like this kind of "personal" touch. As the tour bus gets underway, provide tour members with an overview of the day's schedule. Even though they will probably have literature, it is important to discuss it. Any rules and regulations that need to be followed should also be clarified. Tour bus time enroute to the destination is a good time to pass out brochures and other literature and to review appropriate information contained in the brochures and literature. Always ask if anyone has questions and address the questions as best possible.

At the end of the tour, thank tour participants for coming on the tour and make any last-minute announcements. Frequently, guides make a pitch to sell any future tours that may be scheduled.

Single-Day Tour Food and Beverage Menus

On most single-day tours, some type of meal function will be included. If this is at a full-service restaurant, obtain copies of the restaurant's menu in advance

trentway tours ltd.

LETS GET ACQUAINTED

* Please do not feel under any obligation to fill out all areas of this questionaire *

NAME:

ADDRESS: CITY:

PROVINCE OR STATE: COUNTRY:

POSTAL OR ZIP CODE: PHONE:

TRENTWAY BROCHURES: If you would like to have your name put on our mailing
                        list to have a brochure sent to you directly from our office,
                        please mark "YES". If you are already receiving the
                        brochure, it is not necessary to have your name on again.

                        YES _____   NO _____

ARE YOU CELEBRATING ANY SPECIAL EVENT WHILE ON THIS TOUR?   YES _____

                                                             NO _____

IF SO, WOULD YOU CONSIDER SHARING THE NATURE OF THIS EVENT WITH US?

DO YOU HAVE ANY HOBBIES OR SPECIAL INTERESTS?

IS THIS YOUR FIRST TRENTWAY TOUR?   YES _____   NO _____

IF NO, HOW MANY OTHER TRENTWAY TOURS HAVE YOU TAKEN?

OTHER COMMENTS ABOUT YOURSELF:

ARE THERE ANY NEW AREAS YOU WOULD LIKE TO SEE ON OUR TOURS?

TT 04

FIGURE 3-5 TRENTWAY TOURS LET'S GET ACQUAINTED SHEET
Reproduced with permission from Trentway Tours, Peterborough, Ontario, Canada.

and provide copies to participants. Some restaurants have mini-menus which are
ideal for this. They easily fit into tour member packets. In other cases, you may
want to reproduce the menu on a single sheet of paper and include it in the tour
participants' packets. If the meal will be in a cafeteria, sometimes it is possible to

find out from the cafeteria what the options will be for the day. Reproduce these in the same way so that tour participants can give consideration to what they want to order in advance. Even when the food function is a help-yourself buffet, it is sometimes possible to find out what the ingredients are on the buffet and to produce a menu. This is normally appreciated by tour participants and it is usually an easy addition to the packet of materials put together for tour members.

Single-Day Tour Bus Considerations

For a one-day tour, some will be tempted to contract for a bus of lesser quality than they might use for a multi-day tour. However, the single-day tour, especially if it is to a destination where there will be one or more hours of driving each way, still presents an opportunity to provide tour clients with a quality tour product. In most cases, a tour bus with both bathroom facilities and a microphone on board will be needed. If the one-day tour is all "in-town" (i.e., if it is from one place to another within a metropolitan city), a wider variety of buses will often be preferred. If no bus trip is more than 15 or 20 minutes in length, and if each of the locations being toured has bathroom facilities, no on-board restroom will be needed. Therefore, consider the more unique and interesting buses on the market. For example, British double-decker buses are often available. Many groups enjoy the novelty of this type of bus. Some bus companies offer theme designed buses. These too might be appropriate. By exploring the buses available through various companies, a unique and often less-expensive bus can be leased, providing tour members with an opportunity to experience an usual mode of transportation while saving money compared to traditional buses.

It is still important, even on a one-day tour, to establish criteria for the selection of a bus driver and to make certain that the driver is one who is very qualified. Always demand top quality driver services.

Summary

Developing and running one-day domestic tours assists the new tour planner in overcoming the fear of starting and running a first tour. In developing tours, there's a close relationship between tour development and sales. Research must be undertaken to make certain that there is a market for the tour being developed. There must be substantial numbers of people who can afford to take the tour, who have an interest in the tour product, and who have the time available to take the tour. Find out what the needs of the market are and plan the tour to meet those needs. Once tours are successfully designed and offered to a market, repeat them over and over again. Examples provided include musical tours, tours for performing bands, and tours for specific audiences, such as acupuncturists. Inbound tour operators work with a local tour product and market this product to groups originating in other parts of the country or in other countries.

Successful marketing approaches used in selling tours include direct mail marketing, sales representatives, advertisements in specialized publications, and listings in the *Specialty Travel Index.*

Start with short half-day local tours and build expertise as tours are extended in terms of both duration and geography. A gem tour example of this developmental process is provided. The recommended approach took the gem tour operator from offering a short half-day local trip to an extensive multi-day, multi-country gem tour. The importance of developing specialized tours which may result from extensive research and finding a niche through that research was stressed.

The components of a one-day, single destination tour were also discussed. Success examples were provided. Only slightly more complicated and difficult to run are one-day, multi-destination tours. This is usually the next step in the development phase.

In developing the components of a one-day tour, start with research and design. Obtain research information from divisions of tourism, CVBs, historical societies, Chambers of Commerce, and other sources. Initiate contact by phone or by letter. Personal visits are undertaken next. Work out verbal agreements. After the tour has been put together in semi-finished format, the tour designer and later the tour manager undertake familiarization trips, going through each aspect of the tour and working out any bugs that may still be in it.

As the tour is developed, costing and pricing concerns should be addressed. There is no magic price figure within which to stay for a one-day tour, but it is important to cover all costs plus a profit and to include some funds for unforseen expenses. Ball park guidelines for costing run from $65 to $100 for a one-day, single destination tour and from $75 to $100 for a one-day, multi-destination tour. Actual prices vary, but one should be careful about pricing below the $65 suggested minimum.

Identify both fixed and variable costs working with the formula provided in this chapter. Research costs should be spread over several tours. Food and beverage costs may be especially tricky. Wherever possible, offer either ala carte or buffet dining. Determine maximum price levels in advance. Maintain food and beverage quality. Upscale restaurants and cafeterias should sometimes be considered. Avoid alcoholic beverages and include menu items for those who are on low-fat or cholesterol-free diets.

Having some type of food and beverage available at the time of check in is convenient, but if it is provided, it should be simple and self-contained. You should prepare for rain, wind, and other weather conditions.

Serving food and beverages on the tour bus, while appreciated by tour members, can be messy. Hot "burning" beverages and messy food should be avoided. Simple, pre-packaged food and a beverage obtained from caterers, often works best.

When a tour will be arriving late and when tour members are on their own for dinner, an evening cocktail reception prior to the tour bus return home is often appreciated. Try to schedule these in hotels or restaurants.

Vendor service is especially important on single-day tours since, if service is less than what was expected, it will be remembered by those who are on the tour. Therefore, it is critical to have close ties with vendors and to have either letters of agreement or contracts. Ideally, contracts with financial penalties when services are provided that are less than expected will be agreed to. This helps to ensure a high quality level of vendor services.

Provide a good mix of sightseeing and other activities for your single-day tour. Usually no more than two hours of sightseeing in the morning and two hours in the afternoon is best. This should be mixed in with fun bus activities, shopping opportunities, meals, and major destination visits.

Bus trips should include an on-bus introduction to activities that will come later, a presentation on the flora and fauna being passed enroute, limited planned and spontaneous activity (bus games, etc.), and time for tour participants to have for themselves. Some will want to sleep, engage in conversation with seat-mates, or read. They will want the free time to engage in these activities.

It is recommended that menus be provided for food and beverage functions so that tour participants will have an opportunity to select their meal choices well in advance. Careful consideration should also be given to the selection of a tour bus so that tour participants will be comfortable. For trips that are out of town, a bus equipped with a restroom is essential, but for in-town tours where no bus transfer will exceed more than fifteen or twenty-minutes, more innovative, unique buses might be used.

DISCUSSION QUESTIONS

These questions may be discussed by two or more students outside of class as a fun way of reviewing this chapter or they may be discussed by everyone during class for a more wide-ranging discussion.

1. Why should a person who is new to the tour industry develop and offer a single-destination, one-day tour prior to offering a multi-destination, multi-day tour?

2. Why is it suggested that the newcomer to the tour industry consider researching the market before researching the product?

3. What two types of specialization are identified in the *Specialty Travel Index*?

4. Which type of tour is the easiest of all tours to run?

5. In researching and designing any tour it's good to start with what resources?

6. Why should both the tour designer and the tour manager take familiarization trips?

7. What ball park range of cost figures are recommended for consideration for one-day, single-destination tours and for one-day, multi-destination tours?

8. Why are upscale full-service cafeterias considered good choices for scheduling single-day tour meals?

9. What are the advantages of including a boxed snack as an alternative for morning food and beverage service on a tour bus?

10. As a general guideline, approximately how many hours of sightseeing should be scheduled in the morning and how many hours of sightseeing should be scheduled in the afternoon on a one-day tour?

ROLE PLAY EXERCISES

1. Two students may participate in this role play either out of class as a fun way to review the chapter or as an in-class exercise. One plays the role of a tour student and the other plays the role of an experienced tour company owner. Please read the script and then pick up the conversation in your own words.

   TOUR STUDENT: I can't do it! I've studied everything and I've put together a good tour. I've convinced a group of people to go with me on a one-day tour. I've done everything right and according to the book. But, I still can't do it.

   EXPERIENCED TOUR COMPANY OWNER: You never will run a tour until you decide that you are going to. The hardest part of putting together and running one's first tour is the psychological part. It is simply convincing yourself that you can do it.

   TOUR STUDENT: Do you think I can?

   EXPERIENCED TOUR COMPANY OWNER: Yes, you can do it if . . .

   CONTINUE ON YOUR OWN

2. Two students may participate in this role play either out of class as a fun way to review the chapter or as an in-class exercise. One plays the role of a new tour planner and the other plays the role of an experienced tour planner. Please read the script and then pick up the conversation in your own words.

   NEW TOUR PLANNER: I think I've put together a great tour. There is so much to do on this one-day tour, however, that I have had to time things to the exact minute so that we can get it all in. Even with very close timing, we are going to be leaving at six in the morning and getting back at nine thirty in the evening. It will be an unforgetable tour.

   EXPERIENCED TOUR PLANNER (AFTER REVIEWING THE ITINERARY): Your tour members will certainly have a full day's experience. Aren't you concerned that you might be trying to include just a little too much in the itinerary?

NEW TOUR PLANNER: We only have three meals, six sightseeing visits, and two multi-media presentations of about two hours each. I know it is tight and that there is no time left for shopping or for tour members to do things on their own, but look at all the features we can put on the brochure.

EXPERIENCED TOUR PLANNER: You may very well be able to sell it, but will the tour participants feel like they have had a good time at the end of the tour or will they finish it exhausted and feeling like they were just rushed from place to place?

NEW TOUR PLANNER: You have a point. Perhaps I should cut out one of the . . .

CONTINUE ON YOUR OWN

3. Two students may participate in this role play either out of class as a fun way to review the chapter or as an in-class exercise. One plays the role of a new tour planner and the other plays the role of an experienced tour planner. Please read the script and then pick up the conversation in your own words.

NEW TOUR PLANNER: I just got back from an exciting familiarization trip to India. The highlight of the trip was when we were visiting a small village and visited a place where elephants are breeded. A new baby elephant was being delivered and we were able to witness the entire birthing process. It was exciting and unforgetable.

EXPERIENCED TOUR PLANNER: I'm sure that was an unusual experience. One of the nice things about traveling is that we can experience the unusual from time to time.

NEW TOUR PLANNER: Yes, and they told me that new baby elephants are born in this breeding facility at least once a week. I'm going to put together an elephant birthing tour and sell it to all those people who like me get really excited about witnessing the birth of an elephant.

EXPERIENCED TOUR PLANNER: That sounds interesting. However, are you sure there is a market for such a tour.

NEW TOUR PLANNER: I'm certain of it. In fact, I . . .

CONTINUE ON YOUR OWN

GROUP DISCUSSION SITUATION: THE HOLLYWOOD GARBAGE TOUR

"Star Garbage!" "That's what I will call it! The Star Garbage Tour." With those comments, Grungee Mudd was off to develop her first single-day, single destination tour. She stressed to everyone she came into contact with that she was totally convinced she had a totally new tour for which there was no competition.

Grungee set out to discover the final burial grounds of the garbage thrown out by Hollywood's greatest stars. It wasn't easy. She had to sit outside the homes of the major stars whose garbage she wanted to feature, waiting for their garbage trucks to come by. She spent days waiting. But with each star selected, she was ultimately able to identify the garbage company that picked up their trash and to follow the truck to its garbage dump.

Grungee did note, however, that star garbage was mixed in with a lot of other people's garbage when it was dumped in the dump mound. But by searching through it, she was convinced that she had identified the relics of several feasts written about in the Hollywood Star gossip columns. Grungee was certain that she would be able to discover star feast remnants when taking tour members to garbage dumps. It was very convenient, she thought. There are three major star garbage dumping mounds. And they are within a reasonable distance. "I can run a five-hour tour visiting each of the garbage dumps and include a buffet snack at Cicero's on Rodeo Drive between the second and third dump and still have a good solid half-day tour," she thought to herself.

Now that Grungee has developed her exciting new Hollywood Garbage Tour, she has turned to you, her public relations and marketing specialists for advice on how to market the tours. She wants to make sure that each tour is filled to capacity and makes her a substantial profit in a very short period of time. Grungee has asked you to come up with your best ideas on how to effectively market the tour and how to price it so that it will still be reasonable in cost, but so that sufficient marketing can be undertaken and a substantial profit will still result.

Discuss among yourselves marketing possibilities and develop a one page marketing strategy for Grungee. You are expected to reach agreement. Be prepared to present your strategy to the entire class by a spokesperson from your group.

EXERCISES

1. Break into groups of no more than three students working together. Develop a one-day tour itinerary draft on the itinerary worksheet provided. Your group will take on the role of tour planner and you will be planning the tour for the other students in your class. The tour should depart from the parking lot nearest the building in which you are holding classes and should return to the same parking lot. The tour will leave at 8:30 A.M. and will return at 6:00 P.M. Tour members will pay no more than $60 per person for the tour. This will cover the cost of the tour bus, sightseeing, meals, and all other activities. Break the day into half-hour or quarter-hour segments.

The tour that you are developing for this exercise will continue to be developed throughout the course. In almost every chapter, your group will have an opportunity to apply some new learning to your one-day tour. Therefore, consider carefully the destination and activity schedule you are planning.

DRAFT ITINERARY PREPARATION FORM

ITINERARY FOR: _____

DAY ONE - EARLY MORNING

0600 _____

0630 _____

0700 _____

0730 _____

0800 _____

0830 _____

0900 _____

DRAFT ITINERARY PREPARATION FORM

ITINERARY FOR: _____

DAY ONE - LATE MORNING & EARLY AFTERNOON

0930 _____

1000 _____

1030 _____

1100 _____

1130 _____

1200 _____

1230 _____

DRAFT ITINERARY PREPARATION FORM

ITINERARY FOR: _____

DAY ONE - MID AFTERNOON

1300 _____

1330 _____

1400 _____

1430 _____

1500 _____

1530 _____

1600 _____

DRAFT ITINERARY PREPARATION FORM

ITINERARY FOR: _____

DAY ONE - LATE AFTERNOON - EARLY EVENING

1630 _____

1700 _____

1730 _____

1800 _____

1830 _____

1900 _____

1930 _____

DRAFT ITINERARY PREPARATION FORM

ITINERARY FOR: _____

DAY ONE - LATE NIGHT

2000 _____

2030 _____

2100 _____

2130 _____

2200 _____

2230 _____

2300 _____

DRAFT ITINERARY PREPARATION FORM

ITINERARY FOR: _____

DAY ONE - EARLY MORNING

0600 _____
_____
0630 _____
_____
0700 _____
_____

0730 _____
_____
_____
0800 _____
_____
0830 _____
_____
0900 _____
_____

DRAFT ITINERARY PREPARATION FORM

ITINERARY FOR: _____

DAY ONE - LATE MORNING & EARLY AFTERNOON

0930 _____
_____
1000 _____
_____
1030 _____
_____
1100 _____
_____
1130 _____
_____
1200 _____
_____
1230 _____
_____

DRAFT ITINERARY PREPARATION FORM

ITINERARY FOR: _____

DAY ONE - MID AFTERNOON

1300 _____
_____
1330 _____
_____
1400 _____
_____
1430 _____
_____
1500 _____
_____
1530 _____
_____
1600 _____
_____

DRAFT ITINERARY PREPARATION FORM

ITINERARY FOR: _____

DAY ONE - LATE AFTERNOON - EARLY EVENING

1630 _____
_____
1700 _____
_____
1730 _____
_____
1800 _____
_____
1830 _____
_____
1900 _____
_____
1930 _____
_____

DRAFT ITINERARY PREPARATION FORM

ITINERARY FOR: _____

DAY ONE - LATE NIGHT

2000 _____
_____
2030 _____
_____
2100 _____
_____
2130 _____
_____
2200 _____
_____
2230 _____
_____
2300 _____
_____

DRAFT ITINERARY PREPARATION FORM

ITINERARY FOR: _____

DAY ONE - EARLY MORNING

0600 _____
_____
0630 _____
_____
0700 _____
_____

0730 _____
_____
0800 _____
_____
0830 _____
_____
0900 _____
_____
_____

DRAFT ITINERARY PREPARATION FORM

ITINERARY FOR: _____

DAY ONE - LATE MORNING & EARLY AFTERNOON

0930 _____
_____
1000 _____
_____
1030 _____
_____
1100 _____
_____
1130 _____
_____
1200 _____
_____
1230 _____
_____

DRAFT ITINERARY PREPARATION FORM

ITINERARY FOR: _____

DAY ONE - MID AFTERNOON

1300 _____
_____
1330 _____
_____
1400 _____
_____
1430 _____
_____
1500 _____
_____
1530 _____
_____
1600 _____
_____

DRAFT ITINERARY PREPARATION FORM

ITINERARY FOR: _____

DAY ONE - LATE AFTERNOON - EARLY EVENING

1630 _____
_____
1700 _____
_____
1730 _____
_____
1800 _____
_____
1830 _____
_____
1900 _____
_____
1930 _____
_____

DRAFT ITINERARY PREPARATION FORM

ITINERARY FOR: _____

DAY ONE - LATE NIGHT

2000 _____
_____
2030 _____
_____
2100 _____
_____
2130 _____
_____
2200 _____
_____
2230 _____
_____
2300 _____
_____

DRAFT ITINERARY PREPARATION FORM

ITINERARY FOR: _____

DAY ONE - EARLY MORNING

0600 _____
_____

0630 _____
_____

0700 _____
_____

0730 _____
_____

0800 _____
_____

0830 _____
_____

0900 _____
_____

DRAFT ITINERARY PREPARATION FORM

ITINERARY FOR: _____

DAY ONE - LATE MORNING & EARLY AFTERNOON

0930 _____

1000 _____

1030 _____

1100 _____

1130 _____

1200 _____

1230 _____

DRAFT ITINERARY PREPARATION FORM

ITINERARY FOR: _____

DAY ONE - MID AFTERNOON

1300 _____

1330 _____

1400 _____

1430 _____

1500 _____

1530 _____

1600 _____

DRAFT ITINERARY PREPARATION FORM

ITINERARY FOR: _____

DAY ONE - LATE AFTERNOON - EARLY EVENING

1630 _____

1700 _____

1730 _____

1800 _____

1830 _____

1900 _____

1930 _____

DRAFT ITINERARY PREPARATION FORM

ITINERARY FOR: _____

DAY ONE - LATE NIGHT

2000 _____

2030 _____

2100 _____

2130 _____

2200 _____

2230 _____

2300 _____

CHAPTER 4
Tour Marketing

OBJECTIVES

Upon completion of this chapter, the student will be able to:

1. Review the major parts of a tour company's annual marketing plan and to explain how these components work together in the successful implementation of a tour company's annual marketing plan.

2. Prepare a "mock up" of a one-day tour brochure.

3. Explain the differences between the marketing of inbound tours compared to the marketing of outbound tours.

4. Explain the important points to consider in list purchasing and list development.

Developing a Tour Company Annual Marketing Plan

The marketing of tours is substantially different than the marketing of other travel products. One of the main characteristics relating to this difference is the fact that successful tour company marketing strategies vary considerably from one tour company to another and from one type of tour specialization to another. No other travel industry component has such a wide range of marketing specialization emphases with the possible exception of retail, leisure-oriented travel agencies.

For example, airline marketing strategies are very similar from one airline company to another. Cruise lines also market in a very similar manner. Even corporate travel-oriented travel agencies tend to have the same types of marketing strategies in their annual marketing plans.

However, in the tour industry the combination of marketing strategies that is effective and profitable for a small, high-end adventure tour operator, for example, will often be substantially different than the marketing strategies utilized by a tour company which specializes in offering from one-day to three-day local tours directed toward residents of a metropolitan area. And the marketing strategies which are effective and profitable for such a local tour company offering single or multi-day trips to a local market will usually be substantially different than those of the tour company which specializes in offering a grand tour of Europe. Therefore, to be effective in marketing it is beneficial for a tour operator to analyze what has been effective for others in the same tour specialization area.

Developing a Tour Marketing Plan

Recognizing the importance of researching the effectiveness of marketing strategies for specialized types of tours, you must also recognize that the building of an effective *tour marketing plan* requires developing the required mechanics of the plan as well. One of Webster's two definitions of "marketing" is, "an aggregate of functions involved in moving goods from producer to consumer" (*Webster's New Collegiate Dictionary,* p. 704). Although travel agencies are involved in services rather than goods, the 'aggregate of functions' referred to still applies. Most consider this to be the marketing plan. The plan's 'mechanics' are composed of several components including:

1. developing an annual marketing plan budget;
2. identifying annual marketing plan strategies;
3. preparing an annual marketing plan schedule;
4. deciding whether or not an annual media plan is needed (and developing it if it is);
5. developing an annual advertising plan (if appropriate);
6. developing an annual public relations plan; and
7. preparing an annual sales plan.

Optional elements which are vitally needed in some annual marketing plans, but will not appear at all in others, include a direct mail plan and a telemarketing plan. If these do appear, you should develop the interrelationship between the direct mail plan, the telemarketing plan, and the sales plan.

All marketing plan ingredients need to mesh so they fit together easily and comfortably and can be implemented economically. Each marketing plan element needs to be considered separately before addressing the ways in which they are integrated. Larger tour companies develop marketing plans for all of the company's tours (i.e., for the company as a whole). Smaller companies, those which run only a few different tours (but often run several sections of each tour) usually develop marketing plans for each tour. In this chapter, the corporate marketing plan (dealing with all of the company's tours) will be addressed first and individual tour marketing plans will be addressed next. Both require analyzing each of the marketing plan's components.

The Annual Marketing Plan Budget

For many companies, the first component of an annual marketing plan to be considered is the *budget* and the first part of the budget to be considered is the total amount of money that will be allocated for marketing expenditures for the next fiscal year. This figure is based on data from previous years. Start by identifying a percentage of projected income for the next fiscal year which will be applied to marketing. For example, if the company has found in the past that a budget of six percent of annual revenues is sufficient to generate the needed revenues, then it is probable that a similar percentage will work during the next fiscal year. If, however, the company is expanding its range of tours or introducing a number of new tours, it may be that the six percent which worked in the past will be insufficient for the next fiscal year. Therefore, while companies often project a marketing budget based upon the effectiveness of a percentage of sales for previous years, these projections must consider alterations to the tour product, new marketing innovations that will be utilized, and other factors before adopting the same percentage which worked last year.

Many travel companies work with a marketing budget of from five percent to several percent of total projected sales and find this is sufficient to develop needed sales. However, for new tour companies and for some specialized tour companies a higher budget will be needed. On the other hand, for tour companies which have a substantial amount of repeat clients (70 percent and above), a five or six percent allocation may be too high. Some new companies will budget as much as 20 to 30 percent of projected costs allocated to marketing as will some companies which specialize in hard-to-reach, high-end, and highly competitive markets.

The Annual Marketing Plan Strategies

Perhaps the most difficult part of developing an annual marketing plan is identifying marketing strategies which provide the highest return on investment possible. Adventure tour companies tend to plan advertisements in magazines targeted to outdoor, adventure, activity-oriented readers. This is the only marketing strategy many utilize because it is so effective. Tour operators which offer a range of fully escorted, partially escorted, and unescorted air tours to Europe, Hawaii, Latin America, and other international destinations frequently target travel agencies via a combination of strategies. These include advertising in agency media publications, distributing four-color brochures to all travel agencies or to a large number of agencies within a selected range of type, and either employing sales persons to call on travel agencies or contracting with multi-line sales persons (those sales persons representing many different travel industry vendors) who call on a large percentage of all travel agencies in the country. This combination appears to be effective for these tour operators.

Small local tour operators may work through recreation centers, continuing education centers, clubs, and organizations within the community paying a commission or an add-on fee per participant signing up for tours based on the marketing efforts of these organizations. For many this approach is not only cost-effective, but it often fills tours to capacity. Specialized tour operators often advertise in the *Specialty Travel Index* or an electronic tour specialization program. Some list themselves in the CTM (the *Consolidated Tour Manual*). Tour operators tend to measure the return on investment realized from marketing strategies at the end of each year. Those that produce the highest return on investment are retained. Those producing a lower return on investment are dropped. Many companies will add a few new strategies each year on an experimental basis while dropping one, two, or more of the strategies which have been least effective. This continuous effort maximizes return on investment from the marketing strategies utilized.

The Annual Marketing Plan Schedule

While some marketing strategies will be undertaken on a regular basis (every day or every week); other strategies will be undertaken only during a few days or a few weeks. These are treated as marketing projects and need to be scheduled for appropriate dates. In establishing the annual marketing schedule, include all marketing strategies, but time strategies so that they both maximize return on investment and minimize peak workload interruption. Schedule planning starts by identifying those times of the year which are heavy client buying periods. For most leisure travel-oriented agencies, the peak buying period runs from March through June. August and early September tend to be light while buying usually picks up and reaches another peak toward the end of November and early December. The lowest period of the year will usually be the last two weeks of December and the first two weeks of January.

For business travel-oriented agencies, the peak periods are more spread out, but Spring and Fall tend to be heavy. The entire month of December is usually very slow, but, for many business travel-oriented agencies, the first week of January is a strong booking week. Business picks up rapidly after the holidays. Summer for many business travel-oriented travel agencies is light and those which depend upon government business tend to have less in the months of September and June since government budgets often run through the end of June or the end of September.

Some nongovernmental businesses follow government fiscal year travel patterns and when they do, their travel often reflects the budgeting year that they select. There is less travel for many of these companies during the last month of their fiscal year.

Avoid scheduling marketing strategies that are heavily dependent upon travel agency personnel for either assisting the tour operator in the activities required to carry out the marketing strategy or in handling increasing bookings for agency clients that may result in the short run as a result of the marketing strategy during customarily heavy agency booking periods. It benefits neither the leisure oriented-travel agency nor the tour company to design a marketing strategy that requires agency staff to take an active role (such as making presentations to local groups or getting out local mailings promoting the tour) during the busiest booking months of the year (usually April and May).

Marketing strategies should be designed to spread out new business for client travel agencies so that the bulk of agency tour clients who book tours as a result of the tour operator's marketing strategies do so at a time when client travel agencies are least busy. Ideally, this should be during the last two weeks of December and, for leisure travel-oriented agencies, during the first two weeks of January.

A second consideration relates to timing marketing strategies for maximum effectiveness. For example, research has shown that the prime time for college students to buy Spring Break trips is at the same time that they register and buy books for their courses. At most universities and colleges this will be in January. Many college students returning for a new term after the holidays will bring money to pay college costs. For many, it is only at this time that they have the money to pay for Spring Break trips. Therefore, marketing for Spring Break trip tours must be in place in January. Many retirees who live all year in the northern states of the United States prefer to take their vacation trips during cold Winter months. Therefore, you should market to these people shortly before the Winter season or, at the latest, in the early weeks of Winter.

A *marketing schedule* is a chart identifying marketing strategies as they are planned throughout the year. Remember, marketing needs to come at or near appropriate times when target clients will buy, but staffing limitations should be considered as well. Reservations and other staff members will not be available to assist in running marketing programs during peak booking periods. Even when marketing strategies are scheduled for light booking periods, usually only a few marketing strategies can be undertaken at one time. If five or six marketing strategies are scheduled simultaneously, there may well be a lack of resources available, especially staff members, to implement them effectively. Therefore, the schedule of marketing strategies should be prioritized on the basis of expected return on investment and expected total sales income. If marketing strategies are ranked on a Return on Investment (ROI) hierarchy or on a hierarchy of greatest dollar sales expected down to least dollar sales expected, the marketing schedule can be planned to include those strategies which will be financially most beneficial to the tour company.

The Annual Media Plan

The *annual media plan* is developed in conjunction with the annual advertising plan. This plan includes strategies, budget, and, schedule. It is coordinated with all other marketing. The media plan is broken down into types of media with sections for radio, television, and print (if all three media are to be used). In most cases, only radio and print will be used, however, because of the high cost of television advertising.

The media plan budget should also include the costs of advertising development. However, some companies only show these costs in the advertising plan. The media plan includes media run schedules for each print medium (newspaper, magazine, newsletter, etc.) and for each radio or television station used. The schedule should not only show the day of run, but it should show the times when broadcast spots will be run for the broadcast schedule (unless run of station advertising is scheduled, but this is rare).

The Annual Advertising Plan

Most marketing strategies, will include advertising, public relations, or sales. Whenever advertising is included in the marketing strategies, that advertising needs to be reflected in the *annual advertising plan*. This plan consists of the media plan (media selection and run schedules) and the advertising budget.

The advertising plan also includes the selection criteria or the names of agencies which will develop advertising (if it is not done in house—and most advertising is not). It suggests media placement. It addresses tie or co-op ads that may be offered to travel agencies (agency advertising which is placed next to and in conjunction with the tour company's ads—often reducing the cost of both ads—telling the reader or listener that they may purchase the tour at the travel agency).

The advertising plan should also include a personnel staffing time schedule as well as a budget for both the preparation of advertising and the running of the ads themselves. Finally, feedback systems should be identified in conjunction with every advertising project so that the tour company will have a way of measuring the effectiveness of the ad based upon the dollar volume of sales generated either directly or partially from the advertising.

The Annual PR Plan

Many consider public relations to be only those activities which cost the company nothing or very little. Most in the tour industry, however, consider public relations to be all programs or strategies which involve a heavy element of public contact, usually with consumers or travel industry buyers (travel agents, travel brokers, and consolidators). However, public relations normally also includes those strategies which are made available to the tour company either on a *gratis* or an almost free basis. These will include guest speaking activities at travel agency conventions or seminars, television or radio interviews, and articles about individual tours or about the tour company which are run in newspaper and magazines at no cost to the tour operator.

The *PR plan* is normally developed based upon a review of the public relations plans in previous years, repeating, wherever possible, those strategies which were most successful. To this foundation are added other strategies usually based upon time availability and the probability of sales results. Remember, nothing (or very little) is really free. Even a speech takes time to prepare and deliver and this means personnel time—salary is spent.

The Annual Sales Plan

Direct sales provided by tour company salespersons, usually calling on travel agencies, constitutes the primary marketing strategy for some tour companies. Larger tour companies may employ a sales force consisting of regional sales managers, district sales persons, and local sales personnel. Smaller tour companies work with multi-line sales representatives while the smallest tour companies who use direct sales as a marketing strategy frequently find that the sales efforts are conducted by principles of the company, frequently the owner of the small tour company.

Whatever the size of the tour company, if sales is a primary marketing strategy, an *annual sales plan* can assist in maximizing return on investment. The sales plan essentially will match tour clients with tour products. If the tour company runs a variety of tours to many destinations, the sales plan may start by recognizing tour products that sell best during specific months of the year and focus sales on those tour products during the appropriate months.

In addition, the plan will identify travel agency specializations and match tours that are promoted by the sales persons with the specializations offered by agencies called on. If the structure includes regional managers, these executives are normally expected to maintain client information files and to find ways to work with district and local sales personnel in order to encourage greater sales.

District salespersons work with major clients in undertaking large promotional programs developed by or for the agencies. For example, if an agency is running a television or a radio campaign, district managers may assist in making available appropriate scripts and tapes which can be aired on radio or television. They may work with agencies in manning a booth during a customer-based travel show or make presentations during a travel lecture series sponsored by travel retailers. District sales managers frequently back up local sales personnel on major local marketing projects.

Local salespersons are provided with monthly or quarterly campaign sales materials pushing specific tour products. These salespersons are expected to make a large number of calls on travel agency retailers. Some salespersons have quotas to call on between 10 and 20 travel agencies per day, frequently making presentations on totally different tour products at each specialized agency visited. They file reports at the end of each day and at the end of each week they identify sales opportunities and any needed follow-up. If a local agency is undertaking a marketing campaign and the tour company can participate in such a way that there would probably be a good return on investment in sales, the local sales representative is expected to identify this opportunity and make participation recommendations. The local sales representative may return to the agency, providing the needed special assistance. Alternatively, either the district or the regional sales manager may be brought in.

The maintenance of a large marketing staff consisting of regional sales managers, district sales executives, and local sales personnel is expensive. Only the largest tour operators can afford such a marketing and sales structure. However, having a national sales effort with regional, district, and local sales personnel can provide a substantial flow of sales resulting in all or most tours being booked to full capacity.

Because of the expense, less costly sales structures are more prevalent. These may include the appointment of salespersons in high-density markets with full-time sales personnel expected to produce a sales level in their territory which will be sufficient to more than compensate the salespersons and still provide a profit for the tour company. Sales quotes tend to be high, but those who meet quotas are often rewarded with bonuses designed to motivate them to sell even more.

Because of the cost of maintaining a full-time sales force, most tour companies find that the expense is prohibitive. Some elect to work with *multi-line sales representatives.* These are independent contractors who represent several noncompeting travel firms. Typically, they represent one or more air carriers, a hotel chain, one or more cruise lines, a car rental company, and one or more noncompeting tour companies. When multi-line sales representatives call on travel agencies, they distribute literature for each of the firms they represent. Usually they make an extra effort to push two or three of the firms during each sales call.

Multi-line sales representatives cover a territory which may be as small as a portion of a city or as big as several states. Many make an effort to call on every travel agency in their territory each month, but some will call on only the most productive agencies, bypassing others. Multi-line sales representatives are compensated in one of two ways: Either they are paid a flat fee for each travel agency on which they make a sales call or they are paid a commission based on the total sales generated in their assigned sales territory. Most prefer the flat fee per sales call compensation arrangement and the most effective multi-line sales reps usually negotiate this type of compensation.

Tour companies, however, prefer to pay a commission based on actual sales. Better multi-line sales representatives find that they can make a good living under this compensation arrangement as well. Although the territory coverage may be spotty (the company is sometimes unable to find qualified multi-line representatives for all parts of the country), the tour operator is often able to budget marketing so that compensation is not paid out until an increase in business is actually realized. For many tour companies, this provides the best possible return on sales expense investment.

The Direct Mail Plan

Many tour companies undertake extensive *direct mail programs.* Tour brochures, newsletters, and other direct mail pieces are mailed to former and prospective tour clients and to travel agencies. The annual direct mail plan considers the cost of mailing per mailing piece, mailing list costs, sample study return on investment figures (the dollar amount of bookings resulting from a sample mailing to a purchased or compiled list with projections for similar return on investment when the same mailings go to the entire list), and the cost of personnel who undertake direct mail programs. Some tour companies realize a considerable return on investment through direct mail.

Working with a top quality list company can be beneficial in obtaining the names of client prospects. Some tour companies farm out all direct mail responsibilities to companies which specialize in developing lists and conducting direct mail campaigns. Although the cost per mailing may be greater by contracting such marketing, list and direct mail specialists frequently provide tour companies with a better return on investment for their direct mail expenditures than if the tour firm undertook the direct mail efforts itself. These companies are specialists. they have the knowledge and the experience needed to provide a high percentage of bookings from recipients of direct mail pieces. However, the tour company must select vendors with care. Contracted direct mail costs tend to be high. And, there is the risk that the number of needed bookings will not result or the return on investment will be too low.

The Telemarketing Plan

Some tour companies use telemarketing to follow up on inquiries generated through direct mail or media advertising. *Telemarketing programs* can stand-alone, constituting the major marketing effort, or they can be complementary (run in conjunction with direct mail or broadcast). When telemarketing is used in conjunction with direct mail, the direct mail piece is sent to the potential client based upon an inquiry. Between two and five business days later a telemarketer follows up the direct mail piece with a telephone sales call designed to obtain a commitment and either a deposit or a full payment.

When telemarketing is used as a stand-alone program, cold calls are made to names from purchased lists. Sometimes a phone call is the first contact made to a potential client. Following the telemarketing call, brochures and/or literature are mailed to those who are interested in a tour. Another telephone sales call can follow receipt of the direct mail piece. The company may contact the potential client three or more times by mixing this combination of telemarketing and direct mail.

Telemarketing should be tested to determine return-on-investment percentages in order to ensure that profits are realized. Without keeping a record of the number of bookings resulting from telemarketing, it is seldom possible to obtain a good feel for the profits or losses realized from telemarketing efforts.

The Interrelationship of Direct Mail, Telemarketing, and Sales

Tour companies using all three types of programs (i.e., direct mail, telemarketing, and salespersons) have the potential of maximizing the synergistic effect realized when combining all three forms of marketing. However, this is only a potential until the combination is worked in such a way that maximum benefits result. Frequently, it takes some experimentation to determine the best combination of direct mail, telemarketing, and sales.

Usually when a tour company markets directly to tour clients, bypassing travel agencies, combining direct mail and telemarketing will work well, but employing a sales force to make calls is impractical since potential clients may reside throughout the country. However, if the tour company is marketing through travel agencies, the combination frequently is most beneficial when it includes salespersons employed by the tour company to work with travel agencies in following up on leads. By working with the owners and managers of the agencies which have provided the largest number of tour clients to the company and asking the agencies to identify highly qualified prospects from their client lists, direct mail and telemarketing follow up to these potential clients can result in mutually profitable business.

Another form of combining direct mail, telemarketing, and sales is to work with leads provided as a result of magazine or other print advertisements. Material is sent to the individuals who request a brochure or further information and a follow-up telemarketing call is made by the tour company telemarketing staff. Since these prospective clients often reside in areas of the country quite distant from the tour company, telemarketers attempt to close the sale on the phone.

There are many combinations of direct mail, telemarketing, and sales which work for tour companies. Through experimentation, a tour company is often able to find an effective combination.

Meshing the Annual Marketing Plan Ingredients

Just as direct mail, telemarketing, and sales must be combined to produce customers for a company's tours, so also the other strategies of the marketing plan must be combined so that all elements synergistically produce a substantially greater number of clients than the total of all marketing strategies might produce by themselves. Logic dictates some of these combinations, but experimentation together with accurate record keeping will show tour company executives which marketing strategy combinations consistently produce the best results.

However, what works for one company frequently does not work for another. Each company brings to the market its own tour products and its own unique combinations of marketing strategies. What may be most effective for a tour company specializing in one-day, domestic local bus tours will very likely be quite different than the combination of marketing strategies that is most effective for a company which specializes in multi-day, multi-country fully escorted European tours.

Therefore, following someone else's "magic marketing formula" is a panacea which the tour marketing executive should avoid. This does not mean that you should not consider what has been effective for others and think about adopting similar strategies. There are strong correlations which work in the tour industry. However, you should proceed with caution and not invest an entire marketing budget in following a strategy that worked for someone else before testing it to find out if it will be effective for your own tour company.

Marketing Inbound Tours

For the first time since World War II, more money was spent by tourists coming to the United States in 1989 than by Americans traveling to other countries. In the late 1980s and early 1990s, the United States saw a phenomenal growth in inbound tourism primarily due to the exchange rate. As the United States dollar has bought less in other countries, the German mark, the British pound, and the Japanese yen have bought more in America. A Scandinavian tour operator noted that he could sell a two-week tour package to Scandinavians with Miami Beach being the destination for a lesser cost than a similar two-week package could be sold to the beaches of Spain. As hard to believe as this seems, there is no question that the United States has begun receiving many inbound tourists. This provides an unparalleled opportunity for inbound tour specialists.

Offering Off-The-Shelf Local Tours

Some inbound tour operators prepare standard (off-the-shelf) local tours which are offered to tour operators in other countries as well as domestic tour operators as components of their tours. These are usually similar to short duration sightseeing trips. They are usually four hours or less in duration, but can run a full day and occasionally will run more than one day. They are referred to as *off-the-shelf* because they are standard pre-packaged local tours offered in the same way and at the same price to all outbound tour companies, conventions, and other buyers.

Frequently, the local tour operator offers these tours with a wide variety of options. This allows the outbound tour operator (a major purchaser of local tours) to mesh these off-the-shelf local tours into their total tour program in such a way that there is a seemingly very natural "fit" for them. In offering off-the-shelf local tours as well as tailor-designed local tours, the local tour operator frequently functions as an "inbound" operator and markets these products as a local ground operator, a local sightseeing company, or a local travel "agent."

In marketing as a local travel "agent," the term "travel agent" is used more in its internationally recognized context than the form that is normally thought of as "travel agent" in the United States. The tour company is working as an "agent" for the out-of-country international tour company, not a domestic travel agent.

Offering Tailor-Designed Local Tours

The inbound tour operator may function as a destination management company. In this capacity, it offers tailor-designed local tours as well as off-the-shelf local tours. These are put together in response to a request for proposal received as a result of response to request lists circulated by state tourist bureaus, convention centers, and chambers of commerce.

When an association or a group of any type plans a meeting or a trip to the city in which the inbound tour operator is located, a request will be channeled through that city's chamber of commerce, convention center, or the state's tourist bureau to identify local vendors who will respond to an RFP (request for proposal) to provide local tours. Inbound tour companies subscribe to the inquiry lists. Through follow-up, they determine those organizations which require tailor-designed tours and which let requests for proposals. A letter is then sent asking for the request for proposal. Upon receipt, all local tours required by the association or organization are designed and a proposal is prepared. This is submitted for consideration to be evaluated along with other submitted proposals.

The Domestic Inbound Tour Market

The domestic inbound tour market is different than the international inbound tour market. For tour companies offering local tours and sightseeing, the inbound tour market from the United States is based primarily in handling ground operations for tour operators based in other parts of the United States. These ground operations include meet-and-assist services at local airport(s), transfers, and sightseeing trips or short one- or two-day trips. These are provided by the local tour operator for members of the tour which is organized and run by the tour company based in the other part of America. A second part of this market consists of clubs, organizations, and associations which wish to come to the destination for meetings, for organization-based activities, or for touring. These clubs, organizations, and associations are based in other parts of the United States. Sometimes they just want short trips, while other times all travel arrangements to the destination city and short trips from the destination city and back are desired.

For example, a Symphony Orchestra Guild in the Northwest wished to visit the Aspen Music Festival. A request for proposal was developed and released to Colorado-based inbound tour companies (acting as destination management companies). These companies were expected to provide meet-and-assist services at the Denver airport, transfers from the airport to a downtown Denver hotel, Denver area sightseeing, transportation to Aspen, tours in the Denver-Aspen corridor, tickets to performances of the Aspen Music Festival, a few contracted meals, and other arrangements. Several tour companies and other destination management firms bid for the tour. The end product was one with which the symphony orchestra guild was so pleased that the guild went back to the same Colorado inbound tour operator in following years asking for tours to other destinations in America and to international destinations.

The International Inbound Tour Market

The international inbound tour market is composed primarily of tours organized in other countries and coming to the United States. As an inbound tour operator handling these tours, the United States based tour operator is expected to provide similar services as those provided for the domestic inbound tour market. These include meet-and-assist services, transfers, sightseeing, and short-duration tours in the vicinity of the tour operator's headquarters.

In some cases, however, the U.S.-based tour operator handling inbound international tours will be expected to provide tour buses, guides, and full tour services for tours that may cover a distance of as much as several states and a period of time that can last one week or longer.

Tour components are expected to be those which are appreciated by the natives of the country of origin. These components may be different than those which might be expected to appeal to U.S. tourists. For example, a tour composed of French doctors and French medical laboratory directors was designed based upon the requirements of the French tour members. One of the major sites these tourists wished to include was listed as the "wide open spaces." The French doctors and laboratory managers had never viewed expansive countryside vistas where wilderness, mountain areas, or desert were as far as they could see. Those who reside in Western states of the United States are sometimes surprised to find that it is often aspects of daily life which are taken for granted that can be most appealing to people from other countries.

Marketing Strategies for Inbound Tours

Frequently, obtaining contracts to handle inbound tours is quite different than handling outbound tours. Selling outbound tours, the tour operator is usually selling to each and every tour member, possibly through the media and often through travel agencies. In fact, unless a tour operator undertakes substantial contracting with groups and organizations for outbound tours, the familiar way to market is to provide strategies which will reach individual potential clients. Inbound tours, however, are marketed to outbound tour companies in other countries, and to clubs, organizations, and associations in the United States.

In marketing inbound tours, therefore, you obtain lists of those organizations and tour companies which are interested in travel to the destinations served by the inbound tour operator. On a domestic basis, this includes membership in chambers of commerce, local and regional tourism development organizations, and state travel departments. In addition to the inquiry lists sold by these organizations, personal contacts can be important. On a domestic basis, requests for proposals are obtained and responded to with an expectation that a reasonable percentage of the proposals will be accepted, creating a steady flow of business. On an international basis, however, contacts need to be more substantial. The state tourist bureau and the U.S. Travel Service are organizations with which the inbound tour operator may want to work closely.

The Travel Industry Association of American (TIAA) provides substantial contact with those international travel agencies and tour companies which wish to bring groups to the United States. Each year the TIAA conference (called a "Pow Wow") is held in a major city in the United States. U.S. inbound tour suppliers meet in a series of 15-minute scheduled meetings each with international travel agency and tour company representatives (buyers). These meetings are planned so that the international travel agencies and tour companies may purchase from the U.S.-based inbound tour firms those travel and tour components required in order to operate their tours to the United States during the following year. These meetings have been so successful that many inbound tour operators find they need no other marketing in order to sell all of their inbound tour components.

Developing an Individual Tour Marketing Plan

Recognizing that small tour companies are new to the development of tours, it becomes important to understand the approaches needed in developing an individual tour marketing plan. Though most medium-size and large tour companies do not market individual tours, many small tour companies develop marketing plans for each and every tour they offer. Sometimes, these tours are developed under a contract for a target organization, association, or company. In other cases, they are marketed by the tour company to the general public or to a specific target audience selected from the general public. In either case, the marketing plan is centered around a single tour product. The tour company may run the tour one time or on a repeated basis. Whether or not it is a one-time run or a multiple run, the marketing plan is centered around the tour itself.

The Importance of a Brochure

When developing the marketing plan for an individual tour, most consider a brochure essential. The *brochure* is a point of sale product provided to potential clients. It usually constitutes the most important print piece in the marketing process. Potential clients obtain brochures from several companies for comparison. A selection will often be made based on the brochure alone.

Because so many of the final purchase decisions are made on the basis of the study of brochures, the brochure must be a marketing piece of high quality. In must sell the tour rather than just present the tour. All essential ingredients need to be included in the brochure if it is to accomplish this purpose.

Targeting Sales

In developing the marketing for a tour, many tour operators find that the only economical way in which to sell is to target sales efforts. Two *sales targets* include pre-formed groups and individuals. Pre-formed groups are usually easier to sell and frequently take less effort. For marketing purposes, pre-formed groups can be divided into outbound groups and inbound groups.

Frequently, the approach used in selling to outbound groups is to identify local and regional groups which either currently offer tours to their members or are potential organizations for the marketing of tours. Once these groups are identified, research should be combined with telemarketing calls to identify key decision makers in each group. Calls to decision makers by telemarketers can screen the decision makers who have an interest in and the capability of forming an outbound tour group.

Strong potentials should be contacted by salespersons. They should work with key contact individuals to design and market a tour to executive committees, boards of directors, and others which need to approve the tour before it can be offered to employees, club members, or other potential tour participants. Once an organization agrees to have a tour offered to its employees or members, the tour company marketing staff designs a tailored marketing plan designed to encourage full participation in the tour, to not only fill the tour, but to fill a wait list as well. The marketing strategies may include direct sales, mail pieces, telemarketing, company or internal media marketing, and other strategies.

Targeting sales in an effort to sell to individuals is more difficult. These efforts often focus on travel agencies, magazines or other print media, and/or other organizations through which an approach can be channeled to interested individuals. This approach, discussed earlier, is often more difficult, more time-consuming, and more expensive.

The Reunion as a Sales Strategy

Some tour companies will use a reunion of past clients and their associates as a sales strategy. Travel agencies which have a history of selling a large number of the tour operator's tours host the reunions. A tour manager from the tour company will fly into the city and make a presentation to invited guests, tour participants, their friends, and any invited potential clients. Often the format includes a cocktail party and a film or slide presentation which is followed by a question/answer session. The travel agency will have brochures available and will be prepared to take deposits from invited guests for tours which will be operated during the next season.

Tour guides may be scheduled to hold *reunions* in different cities almost every night of the week during the off-season. A reunion is a low key sales mechanism. It can result in a large number of repeat and new client tour enrollments.

List Development

Successful tour companies develop lists composed of the names and addresses of previous clients and the names and addresses of those who in some way have expressed interest in taking one or more tours offered by the company. Lists are usually maintained based upon the probability of the person(s) taking future tours. The list of those who have taken tours in the past will often identify not only the dates of the tours taken, but also the destinations. In this way, clients who take frequent trips to specific parts of the world can be targeted for upcoming trips to the same general geographical area. Many will have a system for purging lists so that those who either have not taken a trip for a long period of time (usually several years) or who respond indicating that they no longer wish to receive information on tours are deleted from the list.

Most tour companies also maintain a list developed from telephone inquiries. When a call comes in to the reservations office, the caller's name, address, phone number, and either the tour or the geographical area of interest are noted. If a booking results, then the name is recorded as a booking for the tour. However, if a booking does not result, the name, address, and phone number are placed on a follow-up list. As noted, names also come from media advertisements. Lists should be purged periodically to make certain that they do not include those who are unlikely to take a future tour.

List Purchasing and Direct Mail Programs

List companies abound in the United States. You have only to turn to the list section in the Yellow Pages to find a multitude of companies which offer lists for sale. Most list companies provide two services. They will either find a list for a client company and charge a fee (normally a percentage) for the service or they will compile a list for a client company themselves. As noted earlier, some provide turn-key services, designing the marketing, developing the lists(s) and sending out the direct mail pieces.

Purchasing lists that already exist is far less expensive than having lists developed. However, you should be careful about the expense involved and use caution, depending upon lists. Many lists are compiled from subscribers to publications. Frequently, however, it is less expensive to place an advertisement in the publication than it is to purchase the list and send out direct mail pieces. Although the purchase of a list and the sending of a direct mail piece often will get the attention of the potential client rapidly, the cost can be much greater. Remember, it normally takes three exposures to an advertisement before notice is taken of the advertisement. Sometimes tour companies advertise six to nine times for the same price it would cost to purchase a list and send out direct mail pieces to the same target audience.

Lists are also developed from sources other than magazine subscriptions. In purchasing lists, the marketing executive should ask where the names came from and how recent the names are. Some lists are of poor quality.

Lists are usually sold on a per name basis. Frequently, there is a minimum that can be purchased. Usually the more expensive the list, the better the quality. Some tour operators have been successful by purchasing expensive lists and sending out expensive direct mail pieces. However, you should always be aware of costs. In planning programs which depend on lists, you should experiment by undertaking sample mailings with partial lists and finding what the return on investment will be. In some cases, the cost will be inexpensive for the marketing project (list plus direct mail), but the purchase of tours resulting from the list/direct mail marketing project will be so little that the cost will exceed the income.

In other cases, the cost of list purchase and direct mail will be high, but the number of expensive tours purchased will also be high. It is still necessary to measure the return on investment. Although tours can go out full, the return may still be poor because the cost of the list and the direct mail pieces are so high or because the names purchased and the number of mailing pieces which must be sent out for each booking that results is so considerable. Through experimentation many companies have found combinations that give them consistently good returns on investment.

Many tour companies also work closely with targeted clubs, organizations, and associations. By developing direct mail pieces sent to the membership of a club, company, or association and by having the sponsorship of the executives of the organization, sometimes reflected in a letter from a chief executive in keeping with the direct mail piece, the return on investment is usually better. However, the tour company usually pays a price for this highly selective and highly qualified mailing list. Tour companies often return to the sponsoring club, company, or association between five and 15 percent of the cost of the tour in exchange for the name list, a letter from a Chief Executive, and sponsorship of the tour.

Other Media Marketing

Other media marketing may involve magazine advertising, newspaper advertising, radio, and television. Magazine advertising has been especially effective. Two types of magazine advertising strategies tend to work better than others. One type is the selection of a publication that goes to a very narrow audience, but an audience which has a substantial amount of disposable income and time.

One tour company works with large associations of retired persons and obtains contracts from them which include the right to exclusive advertising in their monthly magazines. The exclusive advertising is not always sole advertising in that the magazine may accept ads from two or three tour operators, but usually the number of these advertisements is limited so that the type of tour products handled by each company do not overlap. Because membership is so large and the retirement income for the average retiree is so substantial, the tour company can work strictly on the basis of numbers.

One such tour company explains its marketing philosophy by saying that historically it has found that a tour will fill if magazine advertising can attract inquiries from one tenth of one percent of an organization from which the subscription list is between one and one-half million and two million. Using this ratio, they approach appropriate organizations and apply their formula. Advertisements which have worked in the past are slightly altered to meet the needs of the specific group of retirees. This company advertises only a single tour product, but that tour is normally an expensive international tour with substantial profits built in. The tour operator points out that the same tour could be purchased by buyers at a lower cost if the tour participants purchased it from another marketing source. The tour operator must cover the expensive cost of the magazine advertisement and pass that cost on to tour members. However, because the retirees wish to travel together, they are willing to pay a premium. This tour operator's tours always fill with only a single advertisement in a single publication issue.

The other type of magazine advertisement which has been especially effective for tour companies is one in a publication oriented to the type of activity around which the tour is centered. This has been especially effective for adventure tour operators. For example, a tour operator which offers bicycle tours of Switzerland advertises in specialized cycling magazines. A tour operator which offers scuba diving trips advertises in diving magazines. As with all other forms of marketing, tour operators need to experiment to determine which type of ad works best. They also need to experiment with publications to find out which specialized publication is most effective. However, by combining advertisement experimentation and specialized publication experimentation, many tour operators have found a successful route to substantial profits.

Radio and newspaper advertising usually work best only when appealing to a large general audience for a tour that is tied in with a personality who is associated either with the radio or the newspaper or with a local figure who is well known in the community. For example, classical music tours hosted by the disk jockey from a city's largest classical music radio station can often be successful when advertised on that radio station simply because of the listening audience's loyalty to the disk jockey. Tours to football bowl games advertised in the sports section of the team's home town newspaper or a local radio station can be successful when hosted by the sports editor or a radio sports personality. But without such figurehead tie-ins, general circulation newspaper and radio advertising is often not effective.

Television advertising, because of its expense and because of its inability to narrowly target selective audiences, is seldom used. However, when a tour is advertised on television, using a well-known local figure (especially when the tour is advertised during a program featuring that figure), the tour can sometimes be successful. For example, when a local television culinary program chef hosts a culinary tour, advertising during the chef's television program will often appeal to his listening audience. This same approach is sometimes even more successful when it comes to advertising on one of the lesser-known, but local television channels. Although the viewing audience may be smaller, those who are viewing the local channel will often be devoted to the activity around which the show is centered. Usually they will be more closely tied to the show's host. In addition, the advertising cost will be much smaller. These factors can result in a better return on investment.

The Individual Tour Marketing Budget

The *individual tour marketing budget* must be substantial enough to result in filling the tour, but it must also be small enough to not add so substantial a cost to the tour that it becomes unaffordable for potential clients. Many tour operators will budget between five and 20 percent of the total cost of the tour for marketing. After the tour is totally costed out, including profits, the marketing percentage is added to determine the overall marketing budget. This provides a parameter or framework within which the marketing costs must be kept.

The next step in the development of the budget is to identify the marketing strategies which, based upon history and the knowledge of the marketing director, should be most effective in filling the tour. These strategies are costed out. Usually more than one strategy will be used. Frequently, these will be a combination of direct mail, selected media, and telemarketing. However, they will vary from tour to tour, depending upon the nature of the tour itself. The cost of each marketing strategy is identified and a projected number of clients is also estimated, usually estimating a range of clients which can be expected to sign up as a result of the specific marketing strategy used.

For example, the marketing director might determine that between 20 and 25 tour participants can be expected to sign up as a result of the direct mail campaign. A projected return on invesment will be calculated for each marketing strategy considered and normally all considered marketing strategies, their costs, and their projected effectiveness in terms of numbers of clients who can be expected to sign up for the tour are listed in a hierarchical manner based upon cost, return on investment, or on numbers of projected clients resulting from the strategy.

By ranking marketing strategies on a single piece of paper, the marketing executive can make specific recommendations for one or more marketing strategies to be adopted in conjunction with the tour being planned. If it does not appear that effective marketing strategies can be designed within the constraints of the projected and budgeted costs, the marketing executive usually goes back to the senior executives and the planning department and either obtains a sufficient budget to be effective (usually changing the total cost of the tour) or the tour will be eliminated in favor of more potentially profitable tours.

The Individual Tour Marketing Schedule

Having identified a marketing budget and marketing strategies for the tour, the marketing executive next plans a *schedule* for the implementation of the strategies. The timing must occur in an order that will produce the results needed at the required time. In other words, since refundable and nonrefundable deposits are required by vendors in order to run the tour, a sufficient number of people should have signed up for the tour early enough to make certain that nonrefundable deposits are a good risk when they are paid. In some cases, it is impossible to obtain a sufficient number of payments when nonrefundable deposits are due. Nevertheless, tour operators make a strong effort to protect themselves by at least having deposits in before vendor payment deadlines.

As with multi-tour marketing, the marketing schedule for individual tours must consider the availability of personnel to carry out marketing strategies. If the staff is very small and the schedule calls for the implementation of a large number of marketing strategies for the many different tours being offered and these strategies involve the use of personnel, you must remember that no person can be in two places at the same time and the effectiveness of the marketing strategies may suffer if two or more are scheduled for the same time.

Developing Marketing Plan Components

After identifying a marketing budget, selecting marketing strategies, and scheduling marketing strategies, the tour company marketing executive can turn attention to each component of the individual tour marketing plan. These components may include the development of a media plan, an advertising plan, a public relations plan, a direct mail plan, a telemarketing plan, and the development and distribution of a brochure. These marketing plan components are usually worked on simultaneously, but usually the planning for each component must be completed at an early stage and included in the marketing schedule. Although the planning need not be total prior to finalizing the marketing schedule, it does need to be in close to final format.

The Individual Tour Media Plan

The individual tour media plan starts with an identification of each media which will be used. Each agreed upon marketing strategy is reviewed and if either a part or all of that marketing strategy includes the use of media, then it is broken out into the media plan. The written media plan starts with a one or two paragraph description of the media components of the marketing plan. It identifies which strategies include the use of media. Next, descriptive paragraphs are included for each media used usually in order of volume of usage.

Next, each media will be addressed individually with a recommendation of the specific publication, radio station, newspaper, or television show to be used as the media backdrop for the advertisement. Reasons for this selection will be identified. A rough draft of the actual advertisement (print media) or script (radio or television) will often be included together with a justification for the rough draft and what return on investment can be expected.

The media plan will have its own schedule for both media product development and for print or airing times. This schedule will need to mesh with other marketing plan schedules.

The Individual Tour Advertising Plan

The individual tour advertising plan is sometimes included with the media plan or it is a separate plan. Whereas the media plan will concentrate on identifying the reasons for the media selected (the particular magazine, newspaper, radio station, or television station selected, and the specific section of the newspaper, radio program, or television program to which the advertising will be tied), the advertising plan concentrates on and emphasizes the advertising message itself. Scripts or advertisement mock ups are usually included. A budget is included. Run dates are suggested. With many plans, justification for the selection of the particular advertisement and projections of the return on investment are included.

The Individual Tour Public Relations Plan

There is a strong public relations component with some tours. However, in many cases, no public relations activity is included in the marketing plan for that individual tour.

Often one of the easiest public relations tie-ins is to obtain an article about the tour in the same publication where the advertisement is placed. Some newspapers and magazines have a policy that they will not automatically include *gratis* articles about tours just because advertisements are placed with the publication. Other publications, however, will write a substantial amount about the tour in editorial copy at no additional cost for those who advertise in their publications. The same can be considered with both radio and television. In some cases, stations have a policy that they will not endorse advertisers during talk shows or other presentations. In other cases, especially when a personality with the station or newspaper will act as a guide on the tour, substantial editorial comment can be expected. This editorial support is normally provided on a *gratis* basis.

Other public relations activities may include such things as press releases, public service announcements (PSAs), speaking engagements, state or national tourist industry literature inclusions, and so forth. These cost either nothing for the tour operator or the cost may be only the cost of time and paper stock. In other words, there is no budgeted cost.

The public relations plan will list all public relations efforts the company plans to make in promoting the individual tour. However, frequent public relations opportunities occur and the company should plan to take advantage of these even if they are not included in the prepared plan.

The Individual Tour Direct Mail Plan

The *direct mail plan* is made up of three parts. These include:

1. the mail piece(s) the item(s) that will be mailed;
2. the direct mail budget; and
3. the direct mail schedule.

The direct mail pieces need to be thought through carefully. Keep in mind that the average buyer needs at least three exposures before noticing a product or service. Therefore, many marketing executives send out multiple direct mail pieces. This can be more expensive, however, multiple mailings have been proven to better draw the attention of the potential client. The average consumer in the United States receives a substantial amount of direct mail pieces. Many of these are never read. Therefore, the marketing executive needs to consider how to get the attention of the recipient of the direct mail piece right away and lead that recipient from an initial glance at the direct mail piece into reading the piece. Postcards are one of the most efficient and effective direct mail pieces.

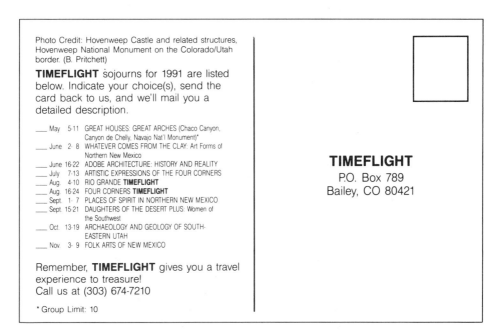

Photo Credit: Hovenweep Castle and related structures, Hovenweep National Monument on the Colorado/Utah border. (B. Pritchett)

TIMEFLIGHT sojourns for 1991 are listed below. Indicate your choice(s), send the card back to us, and we'll mail you a detailed description.

___ May   5-11   GREAT HOUSES: GREAT ARCHES (Chaco Canyon, Canyon de Chelly, Navajo Nat'l Monument)*
___ June   2- 8   WHATEVER COMES FROM THE CLAY: Art Forms of Northern New Mexico
___ June 16-22   ADOBE ARCHITECTURE: HISTORY AND REALITY
___ July   7-13   ARTISTIC EXPRESSIONS OF THE FOUR CORNERS
___ Aug.   4-10   RIO GRANDE **TIMEFLIGHT**
___ Aug. 16-24   FOUR CORNERS **TIMEFLIGHT**
___ Sept.   1- 7   PLACES OF SPIRIT IN NORTHERN NEW MEXICO
___ Sept. 15-21   DAUGHTERS OF THE DESERT PLUS: Women of the Southwest
___ Oct. 13-19   ARCHAEOLOGY AND GEOLOGY OF SOUTH-EASTERN UTAH
___ Nov.   3- 9   FOLK ARTS OF NEW MEXICO

Remember, **TIMEFLIGHT** gives you a travel experience to treasure!
Call us at (303) 674-7210

* Group Limit: 10

TIMEFLIGHT
P.O. Box 789
Bailey, CO 80421

FIGURE 4-1 SAMPLE TIMEFLIGHT TOURS DIRECT MAIL POSTCARD. Full-color postcards present an excellent opportunity to generate an interest in a tour. This one has been provided by TIMEFLIGHT of Bailey, Colorado.

The photo leads the recipient to read the short message. This is especially true if the picture on the front is appealing, intriguing, or unique. Glance at the postcard TIMEFLIGHT Tours uses in Figure 4-1. If you were the recipient, wouldn't you turn it over and read the message?

Direct mail pieces normally are lightweight in order to save postage. Usually they do not exceed one page, folded three or four times. Flyers are often used in direct mail as well (see Figure 4-2). These can be printed on both front and back. Brochures are often included in the direct mail program. You should avoid, however, mailing numerous pages of small type. This type of material is less likely to be read.

Mailing costs frequently are a concern in budgeting direct mail since the cost of postage has gone up substantially in recent years. Many tour operators qualify for reduced cost "bulk" mail. However, this mail is the type that is most frequently thrown away. To increase readability, some tour operators use first class mail. Bulk mail, while it is less expensive, carries with it two other disadvantages: Delivery time can be many days after the date when the bulk mail is delivered to the post office. Also, it must be packaged, bound, and delivered to usually only one or two designated post offices in a city. Much personnel time can be involved in preparing bulk mail. You should balance the budget benefits of bulk mail against the disadvantages before making a decision as to which type to use.

The direct mail budget should consider not only costs, but time as well. Although the timing of the direct mail is considered in the direct mail schedule,

THE DU PONT COUNTRY CLUB
PRESENTS

**4 SEASONS TOURS
AND TRAVEL**

CALIFORNIA
AND
OREGON

**SEPTEMBER 23-OCTOBER 3, 1991
11 DAYS/10 NIGHTS**

$1,645 per person

Deposit $100

Final payment due August 10,1991

SAMPLE THE FINE WINES OF CALIFORNIA AND OREGON. EXPERIENCE A JET BOAT RIDE ON THE ROUGE RIVER! ATTEND A PERFORMANCE AT THE WORLD-RENOWNED OREGON SHAKESPEARE FESTIVAL! MARVEL AT THE PACIFIC OCEAN POUNDING THE COAST OF OREGON! RELAX FOR A FULL DAY AT OREGON'S SUNRIVER RESORT. JOURNEY WITH US ON THIS EXCITING TOUR INTO SOME OF THE NORTHWEST'S MOST BEAUTIFUL SCENERY.

Sept. 23, Day 1 - DU PONT COUNTRY CLUB/SAN FRANCISCO
Morning departure from the Club to Philadelphia airport to board your flight to San Francisco. Transfer to your hotel at Fisherman's Wharf. Remainder of afternoon free to explore on your own. A gala get-acquainted dinner this evening.
HOLIDAY INN   MEALS IN FLIGHT, D

Sept. 24, Day 2 - SAN FRANCISCO
A morning sightseeing tour of the city including the restored Victorian homes, the Palace of Fine Arts and the Golden Gate Bridge. Lunch in Tiberon with remainder of day free.
HOLIDAY INN   L

Sept. 25 - Day 3 - NAPA AND SONOMA VALLEYS
Cross the Golden Gate Bridge into these peaceful, beautiful valleys of the wine country where you'll board the elegant Napa Valley Wine train for a gourmet lunch and sightseeing. This afternoon free time in Sonoma to explore its colorful Plaza, Mission and smart shops. Check-in at our nearby hotel.
SONOMA VALLEY INN   L

Sept. 26, Day 4 - WINE TASTING/REDWOOD/EUREKA
Today begin a magnificent journey through northern California and Oregon. Before lunch, stop for wine tasting at a California winery. Next visit Humboldt State Park, heart of the giant California Redwoods. Spend tonight in Eureka, CA.
EUREKA INN   L & D

Sept. 27 - Day 5 - ROUGE RIVER/SHAKESPEARE
Drive into Oregon for lunch and a thrilling jet boat ride on the wild and scenic Rouge River. Then you're on your way to Ashland, famous for its Oregon Shakespeare Festival Theatre. Before tonight's performance, you can explore the wealth of shops and artisan crafts.
ASHLAND HILLS INN   L & D

Sept. 28 - Day 6 - CRATER LAKE NATIONAL PARK
Travel today to America's deepest and bluest lake formed nearly 60 centuries ago. Your drive along the rim of the lake gives you breathtaking vistas. Your journey in the afternoon takes you into the heart of high desert country bordered by the towering Cascade mountains. Two nights at Sunriver Lodge and Resort.
SUNRIVER LODGE AND RESORT   L & D

Sept. 29, Day 7 - SUNRIVER RESORT
A full day at leisure for relation and recreation. Golf is available on two championship courses, plus tennis and miles of walking trails. For those who prefer touring, you'll sightsee the high lake region along the Cascade Lakes highway.
SUNRIVER LODGE AND RESORT   B

FIGURE 4-2. 4 Seasons Tours and Travel direct mail piece. (Reproduced with permission from 4 Seasons Tours and Travel, Wilmington, Delaware.)

Sept. 30, Day 8 - CASCADE MOUNTAINS/EUGENE/SALISHAN LODGE
A beautifully scenic day as you cross the Cascade Mountains over the McKenzie
Highway to Eugene for lunch and sightseeing. Continue to the Oregon coast and
your resort hotel overlooking the Pacific.
INN AT SPANISH HEAD   L & D

Oct. 1 - Day 9 - OREGON COAST/PORTLAND
Drive north along the rugged coast, past picturesque light houses to Cannon
Beach, a delightful town where you can have an independent lunch browsing in the
many shops. Continue towards Portland, stopping enroute for wine tasting of
Oregon's fine wines. Arrive in Portland, your home for two nights.
PORTLAND HILTON   B

Oct. 2 - Day 10 - PORTLAND/COLUMBIA RIVER/STERNWHEELER CRUISE
Tour Portland and then drive along the mighty Columbia River with stops at
Multnomah Falls and Bonneville Dam to watch salmon make their way upstream on the
dam's ladders. This evening board the Columbia Gorge Sternwheeler for dinner and
a cruise on the Wilamette River.
PORTLAND HILTON   D

Oct. 3 - Day 11 - PORTLAND/PHILADELPHIA/WILMINGTON
Say farewell to the west as you board your flight to Philadelphia where your
motorcoach will be waiting to transfer you to the Club.
                              MEALS IN FLIGHT

TOUR INCLUSIONS:

Roundtrip transportation from the Club to Philadelphia airport.

Accommodations for 10 nights in deluxe and first-class hotels based on two
persons sharing.

Meals include 2 breakfasts, 6 lunches and 6 dinners.

Sightseeing as per itinerary.

Taxes and gratuities for included meals, hotels, maids and sightseeing guides.

Baggage handling.

Services of a tour director from 4 Seasons Tours and Travel.

Conditions: Tour is based on a minimum of 30 passengers. In the event of insufficient
participation, tour price will be adjusted accordingly, or alternately, tour will be
cancelled and all money refunded. Tour price is subject to any surcharge the airline may
impose.
A deposit of $100 is due with each reservation. Final payment is due 8 weeks
prior to departure.

Cancellations are subject to penalties less than 8 weeks prior to departure as
required by airline, hotels, sightseeing and for non-refundable theater tickets.

Responsibility: 4 Seasons Tours and Travel acts only as agent for passengers in arranging
transportation, accommodations and services included in this tour. Neither 4 Seasons Tours
nor the Sponsor, is liable for loss, damage, injury or expense on account of delay,
failure or accident of any conveyance or service from any cause whatsoever, whether or not
due to or caused by negligence of any company or person. Air carriers are not liable for
loss, damage or injury while passengers are not aboard their aircraft.

TO RESERVE: COMPLETE THE FORM BELOW AND RETURN WITH YOUR DEPOSIT OF $100 TO:

4 SEASONS TOURS AND TRAVEL   For more information call us at 594-1030
1010 N. Union St., Suite 6   Kent & Sussex counties call 1-800-273-3232
Wilmington, DE 19805   Out of state call 1-800-458-1030

- -
DU PONT COUNTRY CLUB
CALIFORNIA AND OREGON   Guest must pay an additional $35

Enclosed is my deposit of $_____ for each of the following reservations on the
California and Oregon Tour departing September 23, 1991.

Mr/Mrs/Miss_____Membership # _____

Address_____Zip_____Phone_____

Mr/Mrs/Miss_____Membership #_____

Address_____Zip_____Phone_____

FIGURE 4-2 (continued)

the personnel time involved will have a direct relationship on the cost of the direct mail program and it may have a direct effect on other work in the tour company. If people will be brought from other tasks to take on the direct mail projects, it is necessary to coordinate their work so that other aspects of the tour and the company do not suffer.

The direct mail schedule is an annual schedule which identifies the departure date of the tour and works back from that date in order to develop sufficient direct mail so that enrollment will occur at the time that the tour operator requires it. Many direct mail pieces are sent too early (before the client is ready to make a "buying" decision) or too late (not giving potential buyers enough time to plan their schedules). Marketing executives need to balance the schedule so that enrollment comes early enough to fill the tour, but the direct mail piece is not sent out too early to arrive before clients are ready to buy.

The Individual Tour Telemarketing Plan

Increasingly tour companies are finding that tour marketing works for them. This is especially true for tours of a special nature. These are tours which appeal to a select audience. Frequently, they are referred to as *special interest tours*. Because it is usually fairly easy to obtain mailing lists of those who have special interests and because people with special interests often have both the time and the money to travel, telemarketing to those on high-quality lists can often result in strong enrollments for a tour. For example, a tour company which specializes in providing buying tours for jewelers obtains lists of jewelers and mails brochures to each. A telemarketing follow-up call encourages the jeweler to take the tour. A bicycle tour operator obtains lists of potential clients from bicycle shops throughout the U.S. Mailings regarding the tour are sent to all on the lists. Follow-up telephone calls encourage enrollment.

Telemarketing programs are most effective if you use trained telemarketers who work on a full-time basis for the tour company and who are paid on an incentive basis. Experienced telemarketers, working with good lists, are normally able to close on several sales per eight-hour work period. However, top quality telemarketers are highly compensated since only a small percentage of those who undertake telemarketing are able to effectively sell tours consistently. Telemarketers' productivity levels vary widely. Therefore, when you find a successful telemarketer, it is essential that you compensate that person well. Effective telemarketing compensation plans include a flat hourly compensation rate, a bonus for each sale commitment received, and a higher bonus for exceeding a realistic quota level each work day or week.

Utilizing "800" numbers is usually cost effective when telemarketing to potential clients throughout the country. Working with credit card companies and allowing credit card charges for tours is vital to the effectiveness of telemarketing. It is also essential that a follow-up written confirmation (mailed within 24 hours) be sent to those purchasing tours as a result of the telemarketing effort.

The Brochure and Its Development

For most tour companies, the brochure is the major printed sales piece. Its major purpose is to present an overview of and to sell the tour. However, it also presents conditions for refunds or cancellations. The brochure is literally a legal document. It needs to be specific in terms of what is and is not offered on the tour, what is and is not included, and list any exclusions. Any limitations should be spelled out. Brochure drafts should be reviewed by legal counsel before they are sent to the printer for typesetting.

Shells

A *brochure shell* is a multi-color brochure with photos, but with no printing other than perhaps the printed name of the shell's sponsor (see Figure 4-3). Shells are provided by state and national tourist bureaus, airlines, and some resorts. They are usually provided on either a *gratis* basis or at a very nominal cost. Sponsoring organizations (state and national tourist bureaus, airlines, and resorts) take advantage of printing price breaks because of the considerable number of shells produced at the same time. Some sponsoring organizations will offer a variety of shells, while others (usually resorts) may have only one shell. (If that sponsoring organization's shell is to be used, there will be no choice as to the type, the number of panels, or the photos that appear.)

FIGURE 4-3 SAMPLE BROCHURE SHELL.

Courtesy of United Airlines.

Shells provide an economical way for tour companies to produce a brochure in full four-color. Color gets attention! It sells considerably better than black and white. However, four-color printing is very expensive. By using inexpensive shells, an excellent sales piece can be provided at an inexpensive cost. The printer sets the tour operator's print copy around the photos (usually above and below). When the printer runs the shells through his printing press, the type will appear on top of the white or blank spaces of the shell producing a good-looking brochure.

Shells come in many types and sizes. The most common is an 8-½″ × 11″ sheet folded twice. This looks much like a letter folded. Each folded section becomes a "panel" on which tour information is printed vertically. A four-fold shell is produced using the same approach as the three-fold shell by folding a sheet of 8-½″ × 14″ paper once more so as to create four panels. Other shells are in unusual sizes and may have as few as one or as many as six or seven folds. These are less popular, often more expensive to mail, and sometimes will not fit into a travel agency's brochure folder rack.

While most shells are produced on a white matt or a glossy finish, a few shells are produced on a color stock. In some cases color ink provides an additional "different" image. Many colored ink on colored stock combinations can be very effective. But be very careful when selecting ink colors for colored paper stock. Some color combinations do not work well together. Some work well when the print is bold, but will not work when it comes to reading small type. Using silver ink on burgundy paper stock is an example of this. It works well when the print is large, but it is almost unreadable when the print is small.

The Brochure Cover

The brochure cover includes some mandatory items and others which are customary. Mandatory items include a title, a date, and, for air tours, an *inclusive tour* (IT) number.

Many air carriers provide an additional commission on the airline ticket issued for a tour client if that ticket is issued in conjunction with an international tour which meets the requirements of being what the airlines refer to as being an inclusive tour. Inclusive tours have assigned numbers which may be obtained by tour operators from a block of numbers allocated to air carriers. The tour operator requests its own number block from the airline or airlines which provide air transportation in conjunction with the air tour. The additional commission is small, but it can make a substantial difference in profits for the travel agency selling the international air tour.

To qualify the air transportation ticket issued in conjunction with a tour for the additional commission, the tour must be categorized as an inclusive tour. In order to obtain this designation, the tour operator must provide a minimum of two ground arrangements and the air transportation must be on an air carrier which is a member of the inclusive tour program. One of several additional requirements includes publishing the IT number on the front of the brochure and submitting two copies of the brochure to the air carrier which provides the IT number.

Perhaps of greatest importance, however, is having a title on the cover. The title should be one that sells. It should stand out, be recognized, and ideally, it should be remembered by readers. The title should describe the tour in between one and four words and, ideally, it will bring about feelings of nostalgia, excitement, or desire to travel to the destination simply by the use of its name. The title should be bold enough that it can be read on the brochure from some distance while the brochure is sitting in a brochure rack. Brochure racks may cover as much as the bottom one-half of the brochure. Therefore, the title should appear in the upper one-third to one-half of the brochure itself.

Brochures should be dated showing the year in which they are effective. Many travel agencies get concerned about selling out-of-date tours. By having the year of effectiveness published on the front cover in small print, agency staffers will know whether or not the brochure is still in effect.

Many select brochure shells which have a photo on the front cover. Although a photo is not required, the additional appeal a photo on the front cover gives to a brochure is sufficient reason to include it. Therefore, most tour brochures include a four-color photo. In working with pre-printed shells, however, the tour operator will have no choice.

Inside the Brochure

The interior of the brochure and the back page of the brochure should include several sections. These include tour features and highlights, a tour member itinerary, information on deposits and costs, and information on conditions, refunds, and protection clauses (if appropriate).

The tour features and highlights section often appears on the second panel or inside flap. This is often the section that best sells the tour. It highlights those tour features that are considered to be of greatest importance to potential tour members. It is not an itinerary; it is simply a listing of outstanding tour features. This section may include references to both the number and type of included meals. It usually stresses the most important tour sights. It may emphasize special features regarding hotels or other lodging facilities used. If the tour manager is a person of some fame, this can be pointed out in the features section. In other words, the features may be anything that is deemed to be of considerable value or importance to the potential tour member.

The itinerary is not a detailed itinerary due to lack of space. Often, it is broken down into morning, afternoon, and evening segments for each day of the tour. If it is a short tour, this can prove to be a very effective itinerary development process. Other itineraries provide only a skeleton of the highlights of the tour. These are listed on a day-by-day basis. The itinerary on the brochure seldom includes the optional activities for which an additional cost is levied.

Deposits, payment deadlines, and all aspects regarding costs, including the total amount of cost, should be detailed on the inside of the brochure. Many do not like to highlight costs since brochures are generally designed to encourage one to make a purchasing decision prior to considering costs. Nevertheless, the amount of the deposits, a schedule for payment, and the amount of full payment for the tour should be spelled out somewhere on the brochure.

The small print on a tour brochure consists of identifying conditions of carriage or of participation, policies on refunds, and any protection clauses. Review other brochures to get an idea what small print they include prior to developing the small print for your brochure.

The Brochure Self-Mail Flap

Many brochures are more effective when they include a *self-mail flap* to be used by the reader to sign up for the tour. If interested in taking the tour, the reader need only complete the information on the self-mail flap and mail it in. This is a panel which is often perforated. It is like a postcard addressed to the tour operator, usually having a prepaid postage permit imprinted in the upper right-hand corner of the address side.

With the permit, the person mailing the self-mail flap does not need to pay the postage. It will be billed to the tour operator by the post office. On the reverse side there are blanks for the name, address, and contact phone number of the client. The client pays the deposit (or full payment by entering his credit card number, expiration date, and the spelling of his name as it appears on his credit card. If more than one tour has been promoted on the brochure, space to check the block identifying the desired tour is included. These self-mail flaps on brochures that are sent or distributed to potential clients can result in a substantial number of additional enrollees on tours. However, they are not needed on the brochures which are distributed through travel agencies. Agency staffers call the tour operators' toll-free (800) numbers to book tours for their clients.

Other Brochure Considerations

The weight of the brochure is important. It should weigh little enough so that whether it is mailed by itself as a self-mailer or with a cover letter, it will require only one stamp. Quality printing is also necessary. The ink should be quick-dry. Paper stock should be absorbent rather than have a slick finish (which smears easily). Machine folding gives the brochure a professional touch.

Marketing with the Brochure

Brochures can be used in many ways for marketing. Often, they are response items sent to those who telephone with requests for tour information. They are sent in bulk to travel agents for their use in selling to their clients. Brochures are especially beneficial when making presentations to groups. A copy can be placed on the chair of each person in the audience or copies can be given to audience members as they enter or exit the room. Brochures can be carried with salespersons in their jacket pockets or purses so that they can be given out at an appropriate time.

Tour brochures, therefore, are a handy marketing tool, providing the tour company with a way of getting key information about the tour to current and potential clients at a very low cost.

Summary

Unlike other segments of the travel industry, successful approaches to marketing tours vary considerably with the tour company, the type of tour conducted, and destinations served by the tour. A tour company needs to understand both its product and its market before developing a marketing plan.

The more successful tour companies develop *annual marketing plans* which become increasingly sophisticated from year to year. These plans include marketing strategies, a marketing schedule, and a marketing budget. Optional plan elements include a direct mail plan, a telemarketing plan, and a sales plan.

The *marketing budget* is normally based on a percentage of projected next-year expenses, the percentage being similar to that which was used in the previous year. Marketing strategies are selected based on their proven ability to provide a substantial return on investment. The marketing schedule considers staff time limitations and the times when reservations or new bookings are preferred and needed.

When a *media plan* is developed, it considers all media that will be used. Normally, it also includes a media run schedule.

An *advertising plan* combines the media plan with the advertising budget. It also includes the PR company selection criteria, media placement recommendations, and tie-in or cooperative advertising suggestions. When an annual public relations plan is adopted, it consists of public relations strategies and a PR schedule.

Sales plans identify the type of sales structure to be adopted. These vary from the employment of a large sales force to working with multi-line sales representatives. It identifies client bases and sets out production goals.

The *direct mail plan* identifies direct mail pieces to be used. Lists that will be purchased or compiled, staff considerations relating to producing and mailing the direct mail pieces, and the integration of the direct mail plan with other marketing plans are also important considerations.

Telemarketing plans identify ways to integrate telemarketing with other marketing plans and programs. Production guidelines are determined, compensation plans are set out, and telemarketing goals are identified.

Direct mail, telemarketing, and sales need to be integrated to bring about synergistic results. Clients need a minimum of three exposures before they notice and potentially consider to buy. All three of these plans can be adopted to expose clients to a series of effective marketing messages.

The marketing of inbound tours may be to either tour companies based inside or outside the United States. Marketing may also be directed to clubs, associations, and other organizations which are planning trips to the local destination area. Both off-the-shelf local tours and tailor-designed local tours may be offered. Additional services may include meet-and-assist, transfers, and local sightseeing trips. Tours provided for international visitors may be offered to them directly or, more traditionally, will be provided on contract to tour companies headquartered in other countries. Inbound tour company marketing frequently centers around inquiry list purchases, request for proposal solicitations, and international conference representation.

Marketing plans can be developed in two ways: Either the company can develop an annual marketing plan which will be the company's blueprint for marketing throughout the coming year or marketing plans can be created for each individual tour or type of tour.

When developing an individual tour marketing plan, it is first important to identify whether or not the tour will be marketed to the general public or to a specific target audience. Pre-formed groups are usually easier to sell. Targeting to the general public is much more difficult. Tour companies use a wide variety of approaches or strategies to achieve this.

The development of an *individual tour marketing budget* is similar to the process utilized in developing an annual marketing budget. With a budget and with marketing strategies identified, the marketing schedule is established. As with the annual marketing plan, individual tour marketing plans may include a tour media plan, a tour advertising plan, a tour public relations plan, a tour direct mail plan, and a tour telemarketing plan. However, the foundation marketing element for most tours is the tour brochure.

Tour brochures consist of several sections. The brochure cover shows the title, a date, and for international air tours, an IT number. The inside flap identifies tour features and highlights. Other items included on the brochure include information about deposits, payment deadlines, a brief itinerary, and information on refunds and other policies. Many brochures also contain a self-mail flap on which potential clients may fill in tour registration information in order to sign up for the tour. Brochures need to be lightweight and machine folded. They may be used in many ways for marketing.

DISCUSSION QUESTIONS

These questions may be discussed by two or more students outside of class as a fun way of reviewing this chapter or they may be discussed by everyone during class for a more wide-ranging discussion.

1. There are three major components of a marketing plan. Two of these are the strategies and the schedule. What is the third component?

2. What is considered to be perhaps the most difficult part of developing an annual marketing plan?

3. What is a tie or co-op advertisement and how can this be beneficial to both the tour company and its client travel agencies?

4. What are the most common sales force arrangements found in the tour industry?

5. How might direct mail, telemarketing, and sales be merged and interrelated to bring about a synergistic effect in marketing tours?

6. How does the marketing of inbound tours differ from the marketing of outbound tours?

7. Why might a tour company develop an individual tour marketing plan?

8. How does the reunion as a sales strategy work?

9. What factors are considered important in purchasing lists?

10. What is a "shell" and where might tour operators obtain shells?

ROLE PLAY EXERCISES

1. Two students may participate in this role play either out of class as a fun way to review the chapter or as an in-class exercise. One plays the role of a tour student and the other plays the role of a tour company executive. Please read the script and then pick up the conversation in your own words.

   TOUR STUDENT: I don't understand how you can get the media to use public service announcements which you develop to promote your company or your tours. Isn't that what you have to pay for as paid advertising?

   TOUR COMPANY EXECUTIVE: It's a fine line. Public service announcements are supposed to be just that. They are announcements of information that can be of public service benefit. For example, when we prepare an announcement on tips for securing one's home when leaving on vacation, the PSA will usually be run by radio stations and often in newspapers.

   TOUR STUDENT: How does this help you?

   TOUR COMPANY EXECUTIVE: Some PSAs help us very little. It is customary for radio stations and newspapers to give us credit for providing the information and therefore we get our name in front of the public at no cost. However, with some PSAs we can have a logical tie-in with one or more of our tours and get some exposure for the tour. For example, in conjunction with some of our ecological tours we prepare public service announcements that . . .

   CONTINUE ON YOUR OWN

2. Two students may participate in this role play either out of class as a fun way to review the chapter or as an in-class exercise. One plays the role of a tour student and the other plays the role of a tour company executive. Please read the script and then pick up the conversation in your own words.

TOUR STUDENT: This marketing thing seems more complicated than I think it ought to be. Why do you need such things as telemarketing, direct mail, a PR plan, an advertising plan, and a media plan? Isn't that overkill? Why don't you just put together a tour, tell people about it, and run it? That's what one of my high school teachers did for a trip to Washington, D.C. She just sent letters home to our parents with the students in her class and didn't have any trouble getting enough students to go. Can't you do the same kind of thing?

TOUR COMPANY EXECUTIVE: People who run one or two tours with a locked in target group seldom need to do very much marketing. In many cases, they do not treat the tour field as a business, but put together the tour so that they can have an interesting trip for themselves or so that they may have another small amount of add-on income. Tour companies run tours all the time. They have to if they are going to pay their expenses and their staff and still make a profit. This means building in reasonably good profits and it also means developing marketing that the company can consistently count on to fill the tours.

TOUR STUDENT: But do you really need all of those plans and programs?

TOUR COMPANY EXECUTIVE: Some tour companies do and others do not. It depends upon . . .

CONTINUE ON YOUR OWN

3. Two students may participate in this role play either out of class as a fun way to review the chapter or as an in-class exercise. One plays the role of a tour student marketing intern and the other plays the role of a tour company marketing executive. Please read the script and then pick up the conversation in your own words.

TOUR STUDENT MARKETING INTERN: I appreciate your letting me work with you on developing the marketing for this new rafting tour off the coast of Finland. You asked me to review the list information from three list companies and make some recommendations. I've talked with the list companies on the phone and gotten some of their literature. It seems like comparing apples with oranges.

TOUR COMPANY MARKETING EXECUTIVE: Sometimes it is difficult to make a decision because the list companies give us information in so many different formats that making a comparison is almost impossible. What have you decided to recommend?

TOUR STUDENT MARKETING INTERN: I'm not sure. One company has some very good prices. They boil down to only 9¢ a name. When I called them they said they get their names from outdoor magazine subscribers. Another company I checked with charges a lot more. Their cost is 63¢ per name. The list is smaller though and they say they get their names only from rafting companies in the United States which provide the names and addresses of those who have gone on their rafting trips in the past. On the basis of cost per name, I've got to recommend the first company, but

TOUR COMPANY MARKETING EXECUTIVE (INTERRUPTING): Will they really be the most beneficial source? Our mailings cost over 60¢ per mail piece and that is not including the cost of postage. Considering this factor, why would you recommend the 9¢ a name company over the one that is more expensive?

TOUR STUDENT MARKETING INTERN: The less expensive company offers the advantage of . . .

CONTINUE ON YOUR OWN

GROUP DISCUSSION SITUATION: WHITTLER TOUR MARKETING

Fork whittler, Mimi Morney, has always wanted to go to the Scandinavian Whittlers' Museum in Ankara, Turkey. She has worked with the local Tours-Are-Us franchise for several years putting together local totem pole whittling day tours. These have had mixed success. In the beginning, several of the tours had to be cancelled because there were not enough individuals in the community who signed up for the tours. However, when the manager of the franchise allowed Mimi to increase the cost of the tour by $12 per person and allocated $10 from that $12 for marketing and when Mimi started giving on-bus fork whittling demonstrations enroute to the totem poles, she was able to generate enough public knowledge of and interest in the tours that she began to fill them on a regular basis.

Mimi recently approached the President of the Tours-Are-Us franchise and convinced her that a tour to Ankara, Turkey should be developed and marketed to local whittlers. She also suggested that it be marketed in Scandinavia since it would feature the Scandinavian Whittlers' Museum. The tour has been approved and is scheduled to leave 14 months from now. Mimi has been directed to concentrate her marketing efforts on selling the tour to members of the Greater Los Angeles Whittler's Association, an organization in which she has been a member for the last 43 years.

The seven day, six night all-inclusive tour has been priced at $4,918 per person. The company has allocated a budget of $298.22 per person for marketing expenses and requires a minimum of 20 persons to breakeven. With less than this, the tour will be cancelled. The tour bus to be used is a 42 seat bus complete with a full Western bathroom. It has been agreed that no more than 38 of the seats will be sold, but that Mimi may sell up to 38 seats and may take a five person waitlist. Mimi will be paid an agreed-upon contractor's fee for designing, selling, and conducting the tour. She will be paid no bonus for the first 25 people who sign up for the tour. However, Mimi will receive a bonus of $110 per person for each additional person after that. Therefore, she is interested in filling the tour to capacity.

You and your associates are considered marketing experts in the tour industry. Mimi has turned to you for advice in the past and is asking your assistance in developing a marketing plan that will help her to make sure the tour is filled to capacity. You are expected to review the information provided and make recommendations to Mimi so that she may develop a tour marketing plan complete with marketing strategies, a marketing schedule, and a marketing budget. Prepare a paper presenting your recommendations. Identify how and why you reached the conclusions and are making the recommendations that you present. Make sure your entire paper is no longer than three pages in length. Also make sure that the paper is double spaced and typed. This is a formal paper prepared for your instructor. Describe your marketing recommendations. Be prepared to also present your recommendations verbally in class if your instructor suggests that you do so.

EXERCISE

Break into groups of no more than three students working together. Yours will probably be the same group that has been working together in the development of a one-day tour since the beginning of the course.

Develop a "mock up" or draft of a brochure for your one-day tour. If you wish to obtain a shell from the state tourist board or the chamber of commerce in the destination area to which your tour will be going, feel free to do so. Since this is a one-day bus tour, it will be inappropriate to use an airline shell and since there will be no overnight arrangements, it would also be inappropriate to use a hotel's shell or the shell of a resort.

Alternatively, you may wish to use an 8-½" × 11" sheet that can be folded into three panels and printed on both sides. Once this has been developed, it can be reproduced in a light color (beige, for example) and on a heavy paper stock before folding. This makes a nice brochure.

Be sure to include all of the sections on your brochure that were discussed in this chapter. You might wish to look at a number of tour company brochures before preparing the mock up of yours. Review the wording used by tour companies and identify what type of wording you desire. You should not copy from a brochure that is published, but you may use the basic concepts that are similar in relationship to such important areas as tour deposits, refunds, and cancellation policies.

CHAPTER 5

Established Tour Operator's Initial Tour Development Process

OBJECTIVES

Upon completion of this chapter, the student will be able to:

1. Identify the major sources of ideas for new tours.
2. Prepare detailed tour manager and bus driver tour itineraries.
3. Develop an initial draft tour budget.
4. Describe the points that should be considered before making each of the go/no go decisions when considering developing and offering a new tour.

Pre-Tour Planning and Preparation

For the established tour operator, the decision to develop and offer a new tour is a multi-step process involving several "go/no go" decision points. It normally starts with rough initial research or an educated recommendation. That research or recommendation concept of a new tour is given a rapid review before a first go/no go decision is made. If the first go/no go decision is positive, initial research that is greater in depth will be undertaken. State and national tourist boards and potential venders are contacted and usually there is follow-up research.

At this stage, a second go/no go decision is made. If the decision is still a positive one, normally a research familiarization trip is undertaken and an initial client itinerary is developed. Vender contacts are made and venders are usually questioned in depth.

A number of key questions are posed and ultimately a third go/no go decision is made. This final go/no go decision is usually made on the basis of a wide variety of factors based on the tour's profit projection.

The Germ of a Tour Idea

The idea for a new tour normally comes from either a person within the tour company recommending a tour concept which, because of political, economic, or other new developments, appears to be "ripe." Alternatively, and more often with an established tour operator, a new tour idea develops out of a review of questionnaires completed by previous tour members. Tour planners review post-tour evaluation forms which ask about future tour preferences. When a tour planner sees that a large number of past tour participants are interested in taking a tour to a specific destination, frequently that destination becomes the nucleus of a new tour concept. Other new tour concept sources are tourist bureau executives and travel agents, both of whom may make recommendations to the tour company.

The First Go/No Go Decision

The first go/no go decision is normally made by several executives reviewing the potential tour. It is determined on the basis of three factors. The first is whether or not a sufficient number of persons would take the tour to justify the cost of developing and running the tour. Because initial research can be expensive, tour companies normally expect to run a minimum of 10 tours to recuperate research costs, assigning approximately one tenth of the research costs to each of those first 10 tours. Therefore, if at least enough interested tour participants for 10 tours cannot be expected, there is a strong probability that the tour concept will not be developed.

A second factor considered is cost. A review of expected costs can rapidly be done and while the cost projections will not be totally accurate, it can be expected that they will be very close (plus or minus between 10 to 15 percent of the final tour cost). Based upon this analysis, projections as to whether or not the tour could be expected to make money (a profit) for the tour company can be made.

The third initial consideration is the ability to operate the tour. While a tour concept may have considerable merit and be both popular with potential clients and profitable for the tour company, the tour may not be practical to operate because of political or other reasons. In some cases, obtaining documentation for a sufficient number of tourists to enter the destination country may not be possible. Perhaps the hotels in the country are too few or of an inferior quality for the tour project being planned. And there are many other reasons why a tour might not be practical.

Based upon these and any other factors, a decision is made to either proceed with planning for the tour or a decision is made not to go forward. This is the first go/no go decision.

Initial Research

Initial in-depth research is undertaken in several ways. In addition to reviewing the evaluation forms of past clients, many tour companies will also send out questionnaires to a large number of previous tour participants. These questionnaires will ask as many as 50 questions regarding client preferences relating to the considered tour. The company will research tours of a similar nature currently offered by competitors. Many will study published tour guides written for travelers going to the destination. They will consider the suggested itineraries, the destination hotel and restaurant recommendations, sightseeing suggestions, and guide book notes.

The Role of State and National Tourist Boards

State and national tourist boards play a crucial role in the development of new tours. They are in business to sell their area as a destination. Because tour operators represent an opportunity to bring a large number of visitors to their area, state and national tourist board executives are usually anxious to assist in the development of new tours to their area. Most board executives provide whatever information is sought during the research stage when a tour planner is developing the new tour concept. They will frequently provide the names of other tour operators who have used vendors in their area. In this way, they assist the tour planner in the selection of quality vendors. Some state and national tourist board executives will also work with air carriers, local hotels, and local sightseeing destination points in putting together tailored, free familiarization trips designed specifically for the tour planner. In a telephone or a letter contact with a tourist board official, the tour planner advises what type of vendor he wishes to see during the trip or, in many cases, identifies specific vendors by name. The tourist board official will then contact all appropriate companies and individuals and set up a schedule of meetings so that the tour planner can maximize the benefits received from his time in the destination area.

The Second Go/No Go Decision Point

The additional research conducted and the discussions with tourist board members lead many tour planners to a second formal go/no go decision. This is often a decision made at a meeting specifically called to consider whether or not the new tour being considered has a sufficiently good potential for success to commit the personnel time and expense involved in planning the tour.

Much more information is available now and the projections of potential cost, income, and profits from the new tour can be more accurate at this stage than they were at the time the first go/no go decision was made. The tour company officials know that from this point in the planning process considerably more money will be spent in developing the tour. Therefore, this go/no go decision is considered by many to be the most important and the most crucial of the three go/no go decisions. Usually the decision to go forward with the planning is a decision the tour company will stick with even though there is usually a third formal go/no go decision meeting later.

Since that last go/no go decision meeting is often a reconfirmation of the second go/no go decision (unless some change or unforeseen element is discovered during the balance of the tour planning) it is at this second formal go/no go decision point that most tour companies make the "real" decision as to the tour's offering.

The Research Familiarization Trip

The *research familiarization trip* is conducted differently by different tour companies. There are two basic schools of thought. One is that the planner should go through as many parts of the projected tour as possible without identifying himself to potential vendors so that he can see how the "average tourist" is treated by the vendor.

When the tour planner undertakes a familiarization trip with the goal in mind of discovering how the tour member will be treated by vendors, the planner usually makes reservations independently from the company. In other words, the reservations are called in on a personal basis in order to reserve rooms in hotels, seats on planes, and perhaps even transfer arrangements. Sightseeing activities are either booked on sight or arranged through a travel agency, obtaining vouchers prior to departure on the trip.

As the tour planner proceeds from one vendor to the next, simulating the projected tour as close as possible to the way in which it will be conducted on a group basis, he/she makes copious notes and is often able to separate vendors into categories ranging from extremely good to extremely bad. This approach towards starting the familiarization trip as a tourist who is not distinguished from any other tourist has the major advantage of giving the tour planner the opportunity to evaluate vendors and their services from the standpoint of a person from the general public who is not being catered to because he will be bringing in a large number of tour guests.

It has the major disadvantage of being both time consuming (the amount of time spent by the tour planner on the familiarization trip is usually at least twice the amount of time for the actual tour) and expensive. A large number of tour companies feel, however, that this additional expense, in terms of both time and money, is worthwhile because of the benefit of being able to see what the tour would be like and how the vendors will perform in a situation where the vendor is not providing special services and special attention to a recognized tour planner.

The second approach used to undertake the research familiarization trip and the approach most often used by tour companies is to contact all potential vendors in advance, make arrangements to meet or be met by these vendors, and move from one stage of the tour to the next by having vendors escort the tour manager as the tour manager makes notes. When the familiarization tour is conducted in this manner, a tourist board executive will put together the ingredients and will make the initial contacts.

The tour planner is usually given a great deal of attention and service. Frequently, he receives, on a *gratis* basis, much more than the average tour member would receive. Airlines sometimes fly the tour planner in first class, transfer services provide limousine transfers, hotels put tour planners in suites, and sightseeing companies usually select their best local guide to personally escort the tour planner. This special attention provides the planner with an ability to be able to get the answers to questions as he moves from one part of the tour to the next while providing him/her with a comfortable familiarization trip. However, it has the disadvantage of giving the planner a skewed viewpoint toward all aspects of the tour.

An increasing number of tour companies are undertaking familiarization trips by combining both the first and second types of trip. In other words, the tour planner undertakes all possible aspects of the tour first as an unidentified individual traveler. Right before or shortly after the third go/no go decision, the tour planner returns, meets with vendor representatives, and repeats each part of the tour as an identified tour planner receiving the special attention normally accorded the position. Using this combination approach, the tour planner has a much more realistic view at the end of both familiarization tours than he could be expected to have if he only went out meeting vendor representatives and progressing from one part of the tour to the next while enjoying luxury accommodations and facilities.

The Initial Client Itinerary

To undertake the research familiarization trip, the tour planner must have already drawn up a basic rough draft of the projected itinerary. However, one of the purposes of the familiarization trip is to prepare an initial client itinerary that will be used to plan the first client test trip. The research familiarization trip can identify itinerary problems that you may not have thought of in advance.

For example, you may find that transportation transfers may actually take either a shorter or a longer amount of time than previously thought by reviewing the literature. Some sightseeing points may be found to be closed during the hours that would best fit into the projected itinerary. Hotels and other vendor services (transfer buses, restaurants, etc.) may turn out to be of much poorer quality than the tour planner had thought. In each case, during the familiarization trip the tour planner will usually attempt to find an acceptable alternative.

If an acceptable alternative is not available, or if there are time constraints which cannot be met, ingredients of the client itinerary may be changed. After returning from the familiarization trip, the tour planner takes all points into consideration and develops what will be an initial client itinerary on which to base the test tour(s).

Vendor Contracts

Chapters 9 and 10 discuss vendors and vendor contracts in detail. However, in the initial tour development process, vendor contract development is essential. Although some tour companies will initiate a tour with letters of agreement from vendors, it is suggested that full and tight contracts be drawn up between vendors and the tour company even at this early stage. These may not be the final contracts, since the tour company may not wish to commit itself to a large number of repeat dates for vendor usage until the tour company has an opportunity to determine how well the tour will sell as well as to determine a history which may identify the degree of ongoing popularity of the tour.

However, even for an initial one, two, or three time tour run, solid contracts are needed. They may not include the price breaks the tour company would like to have because of the inability of the tour company to make long-term or substantial commitments in advance at this stage in the tour's development, but in spite of the fact that the price breaks may be less, a tight contract is still needed. Before developing the contracts, it is recommended that the tour planner review the points made in Chapters 9 and 10 regarding vendor contracts.

Dry Runs

At this stage in a tour's development some companies will run one or two dry runs or "test" tours to the destination limiting the marketing conducted in conjunction with these test tours to only one or two small regional areas. They will then evaluate the test tours through written evaluations completed by both the tour manager, the tour participants, and often by in depth oral interviews with both the tour manager and tour participants. These tests and interviews are designed to identify weak points in the tour before marketing it on a national or widespread regional basis.

Key Questions

After undertaking the research familiarization trip, developing a client itinerary to be used on test trips, preparing and getting agreement to vendor contracts, and running the test dry run trips, the tour planner should ask three key questions before making the third and final go/no go decision, although tour planners often ask many more questions than this at this stage.

The first key question is, "How much client demand is there?" Projections from the questionnaire results provided in the surveys to previous clients can often be projected with a reasonable degree of accuracy over a short period of time. However, the ultimate answer to this question can only be an educated guess. By studying current and projected political, social, and economic situations, both at home and in the destination area, and by reviewing the questionnaire responses, experienced tour planners can usually project with a high degree of accuracy an acceptable range for most tours. The problem is more often the difficulty of separating the emotional desire to run a tour from the practical results which may sometimes suggest that the real demand is not there to support and justify it. The tour planner needs to be realistic and look at the facts, eliminating emotional preferences as much as possible.

A second key question is, "How practical is the tour?" With some tour destinations, the potential for problems is simply so high that tour planners should reject running tours to these destinations simply because the probability is that, on a continuing basis, problems which will have a major affect on the tour will likely arise time after time. In areas that are highly underdeveloped or which have a history of major political change, tour planners should seriously consider the potential for problems and weigh this potential against projected profits.

When the projected profit level is low for tours for which no problem is expected to occur, the tour company may expect to make some money from the tour over a period of time. However, when the projected profit is low on a tour that is going into an area where the probability is that there is a high likelihood of problems, the tour company should strongly consider not running such tours since the likelihood of ultimately not making any profit is much higher and the likelihood of losing money on the tours is considerably greater.

Ultimately, the most important question for most tour companies and tour planners is, "How potentially profitable is the tour?" Obviously, if the tour is a low-risk tour and the projection for client demand is high, then a tour that shows consistently high potential profitability should be considered much more rapidly and seriously than a tour where potential profit is low, risks are high, and client demand is not strong.

Potentially, low-profit tours should always be questioned, especially if there are alternative tours which are potentially very profitable. This is sometimes difficult for tour planners and tour executives to face since, in many cases, the profitable tours are far less romantic and far less exciting than those which are not as profitable.

A few years ago, in a discussion with a major adventure tour operator, the owner pointed out that short domestic adventure tour trips were consistently the most profitable products in the inventory of tours offered by his company. However, he stressed that they were boring after awhile not only to those who were planning the trips, but also to reservationists, tour executives, and virtually all those who worked in the company. He stressed that tours to far off points throughout the world were far more exciting to work with and, therefore, even though some of these were unprofitable or marginally profitable, the tour company had, in his opinion, wrongfully emphasized these tours, deemphasizing the highly profitable, short, domestic adventure tours. Because of this emphasis, far less profit had been made by the company and stockholders became upset. He pointed out that he was in the process of changing the orientation, but regretted having paid attention to his emotions instead of the practical bottom line relating to potential profitability.

The Third Go/No Go Decision

The third go/no go decision is usually the last one. If all factors undertaken since the second go/no go decision are positive, then normally the third go/no go decision is also a positive decision and the tour moves forward into operation.

This is usually the case. However, on occasion, one or more factors are discovered, usually during the research familiarization trip(s) or one of the test trips. These factors may be serious enough to recommend against proceeding with the tour. Therefore, it is important that the tour planner go through the process of holding a formal meeting in order to make a final go/no go decision at this stage.

Once the decision has been made to go forward, normally the tour company incorporates the tour into its inventory of tours and conservatively runs a few tours during the first scheduled year of operation. These will be reviewed before making a decision to expand the number of tour offerings in future years.

Summary

For the established tour operator, the decision to offer a new tour involves three go/no go decision points. The first go/no go decision is made after an initial recommendation based upon a review of a small amount of initial research.

The second go/no go decision is made after contacting state and national tourist boards and potential vendors following intensive follow-up research. Usually, at least an initial familiarization trip will be made prior to the second go/no go decision.

The third and final go/no go decision is made after reviewing itinerary details, vendor contract possibilities, and productivity/profit figures. Detailed client itineraries and detailed vendor contracts are prepared. There may be another familiarization trip taken. When the final go/no go decision is made, the tour company has a good idea how well the tour will run, whether or not they will be able to make a profit, and will be able to project fairly accurate productivity levels and profit figures.

DISCUSSION QUESTIONS

These questions may be discussed by two or more students outside of class as a fun way of reviewing this chapter or they may be discussed by everyone during class for a more wide-ranging discussion.

1. Why is the decision to develop and offer a new tour considered by many to be a multi-step process?

2. From what sources might the idea for a new tour come?

3. What are the three major factors that form the basis for determining the first go/no go decision?

4. What are some of the reasons why a tour company might not have the "ability" to operate a proposed tour?

5. In what way might state and national tourist boards assist in the development of a new tour?

6. Why do many consider the second go/no go decision to be the most important and the most crucial of the three go/no go decisions?

7. What are the two types of familiarization trips that researchers might go on in checking out vendors and key aspects relating to the potential tour?

8. At what point in time does the tour planner develop what will be an initial client itinerary on which to base the first tours?

9. Why might the tour company run one or two dry runs or "test" tours, limiting the marketing conducted to only one or two small regional areas, before offering a full schedule of tours in all marketing areas?

10. What "key questions" should the tour planner ask before making the third go/no go decision?

ROLE PLAY EXERCISES

1. Two students may participate in this role play either out of class as a fun way to review the chapter or as an in-class exercise. One plays the role of a tour student and the other plays the role of a tour company planner. Please read the script and then pick up the conversation in your own words.

   TOUR STUDENT: I don't understand this go/no go nonsense. Why do you need to go through such a formal process?

   TOUR COMPANY PLANNER: We have found from experience that this is the most efficient way to screen tour possibilities and come up with new tours that are profitable and that our clients like.

   TOUR STUDENT: But you have been in the industry for many years. You must know the signs that indicate that a possible tour will go over well and the signs that indicate that it won't. Why don't you just decide based on what you see and hear in the industry that you are either going to offer a new tour or you aren't?

TOUR COMPANY PLANNER: It would be nice if it worked that way. However, it is essential to . . .

CONTINUE ON YOUR OWN

2. Two students may participate in this role play either out of class as a fun way to review the chapter or as an in-class exercise. One plays the role of a tour student and the other plays the role of a tour company planner. Please read the script and then pick up the conversation in your own words.

    TOUR STUDENT: I understand you get a lot of help from state tourist bureaus when you are developing a new tour.

    TOUR COMPANY PLANNER: That's right. Most of them give us a great deal of assistance.

    TOUR STUDENT: When I want to take a vacation, I call the state tourist bureau of the state where I'm going. They send me an envelope stuffed full of information on places I should see, hotels I might want to stay in, even restaurants. But, it is so much that I feel overwhelmed. Don't you feel when you get that material that it is a case of overkill?

    TOUR COMPANY PLANNER: State tourist bureaus work differently with those of us who plan tours than they do with people who write in saying they want to visit the state. For those of us in the tour planning field, state tourist bureaus . . .

CONTINUE ON YOUR OWN

3. Two students may participate in this role play either out of class as a fun way to review the chapter or as an in-class exercise. One plays the role of a tour student and the other plays the role of a tour company planner. Please read the script and then pick up the conversation in your own words.

    TOUR STUDENT: I understand that sometimes you go on a familiarization trip and don't tell anyone that you are working with a tour company. Is that right?

    TOUR COMPANY PLANNER: That's correct. It is important for us to understand how we would be treated as just a member of the general public.

    TOUR STUDENT: Then, why work in the industry? Isn't the whole idea of having a job in travel getting the opportunity to go on trips for very little money and going first class?

    TOUR COMPANY PLANNER: Sure, a number of us work in the travel industry so that we can travel and we certainly enjoy the first class treatment. However, on these familiarization trips, we . . .

CONTINUE ON YOUR OWN

GROUP DISCUSSION SITUATION: NITTLES MIDNIGHT SWAMP TOUR

Nitty Nittles has been a tour guide for Creepy Crawly Tours of Miami, Florida for the past 18 years. She is an excellent guide and continuously gets good evaluation comments from those who have gone on her tours. Long ago, Nitty became the guide with the longest years of seniority and it seems like she just continues to pile up the years of experience as she continues to provide excellent guide service for Creepy Crawly Tours.

The tour company specializes in offering exotic, erotic, and austere evening and night adventure tours. For many years, Nitty has been attempting to get the tour planner to offer a midnight swamp tour which she would like to guide. However, time after time when the subject was brought up the tour planner indicated that the idea would have to be bounced off of senior executives and would have to go through a fairly strict process of being considered. It seemed that the tour planner had an exact process which was applied to every new tour idea and if the tour concept did not meet specified criteria at each stage in the process, the tour idea was "dead in the water."

Nitty pushed hard. Two years ago the tour planner gave in and investigated offering the tour. She told Nitty that investigation proved the tour would be unsafe. "There simply are not enough safeguards to make certain that our clients can make it back alive and in good health," commented the tour planner. That was the end of Nitty's idea.

Three weeks ago, the tour planner died quite suddenly. Some whispered that Nitty had something to do with the unexplained rapid death and it was obvious that Nitty was not sorry. She had always wanted to be a tour planner. Nitty stressed to the Creepy Crawly manager and owners that her vast experience as a guide prepared her extremely well for tour planning. They agreed and told Nitty they would give her a chance.

Of course, Nitty's first tour to be considered was her midnight swamp tour. She has been working on the development of the tour and is very pleased with the results. As she predicted, preliminary responses from previous tour members indicated that there was a high interest in the tour. Many signed up for it as soon as it was announced. Vendors have been lined up and are all very cooperative. Most are vendors Nitty has worked with over the years as a tour guide, so she is on a first name basis with them.

One of the boat tour vendors, however, yesterday suggested to Nitty that she might want to consider the safety factors. He pointed out that if she took one of his boats out at midnight and returned it at four in the morning (the midnight swamp tour schedule), Creepy Crawly Tours would have to sign a waiver of responsibility since the boat company would not take any responsibility for the safety and well being of those using their boats that late at night in the swamp. Nitty suggested that the boat owner was being overly cautious, but she said she would take responsibility. Nitty rapidly scribbled her name to the waiver.

Instead of offering a scaled down version of the tour, Nitty announced 45 departures of the tour over the next two and a half months and included this in the brochures sent to all past clients, travel agents, and sightseeing companies that sell Creepy Crawly Tours' one-day or shorter tours locally. The first tour is scheduled to go out tonight. The tour concept is extremely popular. There are at least 30 people on the waiting list for tonight's inaugural.

Management, however, seems to be having second thoughts. The President of the company has asked Nitty to stop by his office about 10 P.M. this evening to discuss some concerns he has about the safety of tour participants on the tour. He pointed out on the phone that he was sure Nitty had taken all these factors into consideration and was not overly concerned. He just wanted to check with her regarding the precautions that she has made.

Nitty now has some concern about the meeting with the President since she has not taken any of the warnings seriously. Nitty has been running tours in Miami for many years and she is convinced that there is no need for concern. Her problem, however, is how to convince the President during the meeting. Nitty has gotten a group of her associates in the guiding field together to discuss tonight's meeting and the tour.

You and your associates constitute this group of Nitty's co-workers. You are expected to review the above information and advise and counsel Nitty as to what she should say and how she should handle the meeting with the President. Be prepared to present your suggestions in a paper that will be no longer than three pages in length. Also make sure the paper is double spaced and typed. Be prepared to also present your suggestions verbally in class if your instructor suggest that you do so.

EXERCISES

1. Break into groups of no more than three students working together. Yours will probably be the same group that has been working together in the development of a one day tour since the beginning of the course.

Go back to the initial one-day tour itinerary developed as the exercise in Chapter 3 and from that draft itinerary, develop specialized itineraries for clients, the tour manager, and each of the key vendors (i.e., the bus driver, each sightseeing point used, and the restaurant if a restaurant meal is scheduled). The tour manager's itinerary should be broken down into 15-minute segments with suggestions to the tour manager for each on-bus segment and other time periods when there will be intensive tour manager/tour client contact. The bus driver itinerary should include descriptions of where the bus should be parked, times of arrival, drop off and pick up points, and times of departure.

2. Break into groups of no more than three students working together. Yours will probably be the same group that has been working together in the development of a one day tour since the beginning of the course.

Review the budget recommendations and the exercises in Chapter 2. Go back to the initial one-day tour itinerary developed as the exercise in Chapter 3. From that draft itinerary and from any revisions made in the first exercise in Chapter 5, develop an initial draft budget based upon projected costs and projected income. Keep in mind that you need to include all costs, including a portion of the research cost, all marketing costs, all personnel costs (including the guide—even if you or your group will perform the role of guide), and a miscellaneous expenses cost. In addition, a profit should be projected. Make your budget realistic (i.e., one that is within reason for marketing your tour at the cost per person that is projected as the tour sales cost).

DRAFT ITINERARY PREPARATION FORM

ITINERARY FOR: **Client Itinerary** _____

DAY ONE - EARLY MORNING

0600 _____

0630 _____

0700 _____

0730 _____

0800 _____

0830 _____

0900 _____

DRAFT ITINERARY PREPARATION FORM

ITINERARY FOR: _____

DAY ONE - LATE MORNING & EARLY AFTERNOON

0930 _____

1000 _____

1030 _____

1100 _____

1130 _____

1200 _____

1230 _____

DRAFT ITINERARY PREPARATION FORM

ITINERARY FOR: _____

DAY ONE - MID AFTERNOON

1300 _____

1330 _____

1400 _____

1430 _____

1500 _____

1530 _____

1600 _____

DRAFT ITINERARY PREPARATION FORM

ITINERARY FOR: _____

DAY ONE - LATE AFTERNOON - EARLY EVENING

1630 _____

1700 _____

1730 _____

1800 _____

1830 _____

1900 _____

1930 _____

DRAFT ITINERARY PREPARATION FORM

ITINERARY FOR: _____

DAY ONE - LATE NIGHT

2000 _____

2030 _____

2100 _____

2130 _____

2200 _____

2230 _____

2300 _____

DRAFT ITINERARY PREPARATION FORM

ITINERARY FOR: **Tour Manager Itinerary**

DAY ONE - EARLY MORNING

0600 _____

0630 _____

0700 _____

0730 _____

0800 _____

0830 _____

0900 _____

DRAFT ITINERARY PREPARATION FORM

ITINERARY FOR: _____

DAY ONE - LATE MORNING & EARLY AFTERNOON

0930 _____

1000 _____

1030 _____

1100 _____

1130 _____

1200 _____

1230 _____

DRAFT ITINERARY PREPARATION FORM

ITINERARY FOR: _____

DAY ONE - MID AFTERNOON

1300 _____

1330 _____

1400 _____

1430 _____

1500 _____

1530 _____

1600 _____

DRAFT ITINERARY PREPARATION FORM

ITINERARY FOR: _____

DAY ONE - LATE AFTERNOON - EARLY EVENING

1630 _____

1700 _____

1730 _____

1800 _____

1830 _____

1900 _____

1930 _____

DRAFT ITINERARY PREPARATION FORM

ITINERARY FOR: _____

DAY ONE - LATE NIGHT

2000 _____

2030 _____

2100 _____

2130 _____

2200 _____

2230 _____

2300 _____

DRAFT ITINERARY PREPARATION FORM

ITINERARY FOR: **Vendor Itinerary**

DAY ONE - EARLY MORNING

0600 _____

0630 _____

0700 _____

0730 _____

0800 _____

0830 _____

0900 _____

DRAFT ITINERARY PREPARATION FORM

ITINERARY FOR: _____

DAY ONE - LATE MORNING & EARLY AFTERNOON

0930 _____

1000 _____

1030 _____

1100 _____

1130 _____

1200 _____

1230 _____

DRAFT ITINERARY PREPARATION FORM

ITINERARY FOR: _____

DAY ONE - MID AFTERNOON

1300 _____

1330 _____

1400 _____

1430 _____

1500 _____

1530 _____

1600 _____

DRAFT ITINERARY PREPARATION FORM

ITINERARY FOR: _____

DAY ONE - LATE AFTERNOON - EARLY EVENING

1630 _____

1700 _____

1730 _____

1800 _____

1830 _____

1900 _____

1930 _____

DRAFT ITINERARY PREPARATION FORM

ITINERARY FOR: _____

DAY ONE - LATE NIGHT

2000 _____

2030 _____

2100 _____

2130 _____

2200 _____

2230 _____

2300 _____

DRAFT ITINERARY PREPARATION FORM

ITINERARY FOR: **Driver Itinerary**

DAY ONE - EARLY MORNING

0600 _____

0630 _____

0700 _____

0730 _____

0800 _____

0830 _____

0900 _____

DRAFT ITINERARY PREPARATION FORM

ITINERARY FOR: _____

DAY ONE - LATE MORNING & EARLY AFTERNOON

0930 _____

1000 _____

1030 _____

1100 _____

1130 _____

1200 _____

1230 _____

DRAFT ITINERARY PREPARATION FORM

ITINERARY FOR: _____

DAY ONE - MID AFTERNOON

1300 _____

1330 _____

1400 _____

1430 _____

1500 _____

1530 _____

1600 _____

DRAFT ITINERARY PREPARATION FORM

ITINERARY FOR: _____

DAY ONE - LATE AFTERNOON - EARLY EVENING

1630 _____

1700 _____

1730 _____

1800 _____

1830 _____

1900 _____

1930 _____

DRAFT ITINERARY PREPARATION FORM

ITINERARY FOR: _____

DAY ONE - LATE NIGHT

2000 _____

2030 _____

2100 _____

2130 _____

2200 _____

2230 _____

2300 _____

DRAFT ITINERARY PREPARATION FORM

ITINERARY FOR: **Sightseeing Itinerary**

DAY ONE - EARLY MORNING

0600 _____

0630 _____

0700 _____

0730 _____

0800 _____

0830 _____

0900 _____

DRAFT ITINERARY PREPARATION FORM

ITINERARY FOR: _____

DAY ONE - LATE MORNING & EARLY AFTERNOON

0930 _____

1000 _____

1030 _____

1100 _____

1130 _____

1200 _____

1230 _____

DRAFT ITINERARY PREPARATION FORM

ITINERARY FOR: _____

DAY ONE - MID AFTERNOON

1300 _____

1330 _____

1400 _____

1430 _____

1500 _____

1530 _____

1600 _____

DRAFT ITINERARY PREPARATION FORM

ITINERARY FOR: _____

DAY ONE - LATE AFTERNOON - EARLY EVENING

1630 _____

1700 _____

1730 _____

1800 _____

1830 _____

1900 _____

1930 _____

DRAFT ITINERARY PREPARATION FORM

ITINERARY FOR: _____

DAY ONE - LATE NIGHT

2000 _____

2030 _____

2100 _____

2130 _____

2200 _____

2230 _____

2300 _____

DRAFT ITINERARY PREPARATION FORM

ITINERARY FOR: **Restaurant Itinerary**

DAY ONE - EARLY MORNING

0600 _____

0630 _____

0700 _____

0730 _____

0800 _____

0830 _____

0900 _____

DRAFT ITINERARY PREPARATION FORM

ITINERARY FOR: _____

DAY ONE - LATE MORNING & EARLY AFTERNOON

0930 _____

1000 _____

1030 _____

1100 _____

1130 _____

1200 _____

1230 _____

DRAFT ITINERARY PREPARATION FORM

ITINERARY FOR: _____

DAY ONE - MID AFTERNOON

1300 _____

1330 _____

1400 _____

1430 _____

1500 _____

1530 _____

1600 _____

DRAFT ITINERARY PREPARATION FORM

ITINERARY FOR: _____

DAY ONE - LATE AFTERNOON - EARLY EVENING

1630 _____

1700 _____

1730 _____

1800 _____

1830 _____

1900 _____

1930 _____

DRAFT ITINERARY PREPARATION FORM

ITINERARY FOR: _____

DAY ONE - LATE NIGHT

2000 _____

2030 _____

2100 _____

2130 _____

2200 _____

2230 _____

2300 _____

CHAPTER 6
Itinerary Development

OBJECTIVES

Upon completion of this chapter, the student will be able to:

1. Identify the five itineraries and describe the relative importance of each.
2. Develop and refine one-day tour itineraries for tour members, the tour manager, the bus driver, vendors, and step-on guides.
3. Prepare a list of one-day tour step-on guides and hosts/hostesses, identifying the background and qualifications of each and recognizing whether or not the guide/host/hostess will work from a scripted or a nonscripted presentation.
4. Explain similarities between preparing the ingredients called for in a recipe designed to create a culinary experience and preparing the ingredients necessary to design an outstanding one-day tour experience.

The Five Itineraries and Their Individual Importance

An itinerary is an itinerary. Many people think in terms of "the" itinerary. However, most tour operators prepare multiple itineraries for the same tour. These are designed to meet the individual needs of the tour member, the tour manager, the bus driver, vendors, and step-on guides. There can be as many as five or more itineraries depending upon which person(s) the tour operator decides need(s) a special itinerary for his or her purposes. There are normally separate and distinctive itineraries for the client (see Figure 6–1), the tour manager, and the bus driver. While some tour companies provide a generic "vendor" itinerary and some prepare individual itineraries for each step-on guide used, many give vendors and step-on guides copies of either the client itinerary or appropriate segments of the tour manager's itinerary.

Each of the other itineraries is based upon an individualized expansion from the client itinerary. The tour manager's itinerary will probably be the most

FIGURE 6–1 SAMPLE CLIENT ITINERARY

Santa Fe Bus Tour Itinerary

Friday, September 29

7:30 A.M.	Depart Denver from The Swartz House
9:30 A.M.	Breakfast in Pueblo at the Crested Moon Indian Resort Main Dining Room
10:30 A.M.	Great Hall Mansion—Guided Tour
11:45 A.M.	Depart Pueblo
3:30 P.M.–4:00 P.M.	Arrive Las Vegas, New Mexico
Upon Arrival	Check in at Hotel Las Taaxicis
5:00 P.M.	Dinner at Hotel Las Taaxcis
6:30 P.M.	Dessert & Artist Presentation in the Observatory
7:45 P.M.	Depart for Hotel Las Taaxcis

Saturday, September 30

8:00 A.M.–9:00 A.M.	Breakfast at Hotel Las Taaxcis
9:15 A.M.	Depart Las Vegas, New Mexico
10:30 A.M.	Arrive Santa Fe
10:30 A.M.–12:30 noon	Free time in Santa Fe at the Plaza Area
12:30 noon–3:00 P.M.	Spanish Iron Works & Sulpture Garden
3:30 P.M.	Check in at the Peabody House
6:30 P.M.	Wine and Cheese Gathering—Peabody House Garden Area
7:30 P.M.	Dinner on your own

Sunday, October 01

7:30 A.M.	Breakfast Buffet at the Peabody House
8:15 A.M.	Depart Santa Fe to Mid Century to visit and tour the New Spanish Gallery
1:30 P.M.	Picnic in the New Mexican Grand Rose Garden
2:30 P.M.	Depart for Santa Fe
3:00 P.M.–6:00 P.M.	Free time to relax, shop, and explore
6:45 P.M.	Reception in Peabody House Garden before dinner
7:15 P.M.	Depart for La Placeda

FIGURE 6–1 (*continued*)

7:30 P.M.	Dinner at La Placeda
9:00 P.M.	Depart for the Peabody House

Monday, October 02

8:00 A.M.	Breakfast Buffet at the Peabody House
9:30 A.M.	Depart the Peabody House for Museums
10:00 A.M.–10:50 A.M.	Guided Tour—The Anthropology Museum
11:00 A.M.–12:00 noon	Guided Tour—Hispanic Art Museum
12:00 noon–12:30 P.M.	Free time to explore other local museums or rest
12:30 P.M.	Depart for the Peabody House
12:45 P.M.–2:00 P.M.	Light Lunch at the Peabody House with three invited local artists
2:00 P.M.–6:30 P.M.	Free time to explore, relax, and enjoy Santa Fe's Plaza and/or Canyon road
6:45 P.M.–8:30 P.M.	Group Picture at the Peabody House and Dinner at La Hacienda
9:00 P.M.	Dessert at the Peabody House

Tuesday, October 03

7:30 A.M.	Breakfast Buffet at the Peabody House
8:30 A.M.	Depart Santa Fe for Taos with optional stops along the Rio Grande Valley— including Indian Pueblos
10:30 A.M.–1:00 P.M.	On your own to explore Taos
1:00 P.M.	Depart Taos for Denver
6:00 P.M.–7:00 P.M.	Arrive at The Swartz House in Denver

Reproduced with permission from SW Tours, Littleton, CO.

expansive, including numerous special notes, recommendations and suggestions for the tour manager. The bus driver's itinerary will include such things as parking instructions, timing information, and so forth.

Vendor itineraries will have specific information relating to that part of the itinerary with which the vendor deals. The same normally is true for individual step-on guide's itineraries when a special itinerary relates to only that portion of the tour handled by that guide. If the tour picks up a step-on guide at each location, at several locations, or at specific sites, the step-on guide will receive a copy of the client itinerary to get a feel for the entire tour and also a tailored specific itinerary detailing that part of the itinerary for which the step-on guide will have responsibility.

The Client Itinerary—The Starting Point

In developing an itinerary, the tour planner starts with a client itinerary. This is normally built around transportation and accommodation considerations. Clients prefer 10:00 A.M. departures for air trips whether the flight is taken at the start of a tour or is one between cities scheduled enroute during the tour (see Figure 6–2). This means that if clients are meeting at a destination airport to start their air tour, they will normally meet at approximately 8:30 A.M. or 9:00 A.M. If the trip is in conjunction with a domestic air tour, clients will arrive at their destination in time to pick up luggage at the airport and make transfers so as to allow check-in at the first destination city hotel at or before 6 P.M. This has a number of advantages, including normal availability of a selection of rooms at that time. The hotel can usually fulfill its obligation to provide rooms of the type reserved by the tour operator to clients even if the hotel is overbooked. The probability is that other hotel guests will be arriving after 6:00 P.M. Early hotel arrival also allows guests to unpack at a leisurely rate and to have dinner at the hotel or at a nearby restaurant without being pressured to unpack rapidly.

If the air tour is one involving international flights, the departure from hometown America may well be after 10:00 A.M. because some flights going into Europe, the Middle East, and Africa leave after 6:00 P.M. from New York City or other East Coast cities. This means that your client will be flying all night. If the destination is Europe, clients will arrive in the destination city early the next

FIGURE 6–2 SAMPLE ARRIVAL/DEPARTURE TIME CHART

Time	Activity
7:00 A.M.–9:00 A.M.	Arrive at airport hotel for "Day Room" flight layovers
8:30 A.M.–9:00 A.M.	Meet at airport for air tour start
10:00 A.M.	First day and subsequent day flights
	Ideal daily sightseeing bus departure time for elderly and wealthy tour groups
	Ideal time to schedule the initiation of bus or air transfers between cities and countries
2:00 P.M.–4:00 P.M.	Start of "free time" when a formal evening function is scheduled
6:00 P.M. (or earlier)	Arrive at new hotel (arrival time for first night at a hotel)

day. For very early morning arrivals in London, obtaining hotel accommodations can be a problem since it is probable that hotel rooms will not be available when the group arrives.

The tour planner may elect to book *day rooms*. These are usually available after 7:00 A.M. but, in many cases, they are only found at selected airport hotels. Since many of your clients will have been awake all or most of the previous night on the flight, tour members will be tired and will not normally be interested in taking a sightseeing trip. Nevertheless, the best thing they can do is to undertake some activity and go without sleep a little longer so that they push their systems to become accustomed to the European timetable.

Most tour operators provide clients with free time after the initial hotel check-in. If the hotel check-in is not until after 12:00 noon, often an overview city sightseeing tour is scheduled on a bus with recliner seats as tour members transfer from the airport to the downtown hotel. This allows them to nap on the bus if they choose to do so. For most clients, however, obtaining early check-in and getting to their rooms as soon as possible is usually preferred. Most tour planners will schedule free time so that tour members can get a nap. The earliest scheduled activity will be in the late afternoon with perhaps a brief sightseeing activity or a welcome cocktail party. This is normally the only thing scheduled for the day of arrival.

For most tours going to the Middle East and Africa, a transfer somewhere in Europe will be needed and destination arrival will be in the afternoon or evening of the second day. In this case, tour members will have been awake for a very long time unless they are among the relatively few who can sleep well on airplanes. Housing should be obtained immediately upon arrival. Tour participants will need to have the balance of the day free so that they may relax and catch up on their sleep.

For tours destined to the Far East, the same type of problem occurs. Travelers going to Australia, New Zealand, and the Far East are on the airplane for such a long period of time that it is essential they get into a hotel as soon as possible and get an opportunity to relax and sleep. Tour members should be encouraged to adapt their systems to the countries being visited as rapidly as possible so that they sleep during the night in the destination countries rather than making partial adjustments to a U.S. time schedule. When a trip begins with a flight to a far-away international destination, tour activity scheduling should start the morning after arrival with either no or very little planned activity on the day of arrival.

Tours going to Latin America will generally find that tour members have little difficulty in adjusting their body clocks since seldom will the time differences be of any major difference. Often flights for these destinations will leave the United States during the morning hours and will arrive in Central or South America in the late afternoon or evening. This means that clients can be transferred to their hotels and get a good night's sleep on a schedule that is quite similar to what they would experience in their hometown in the United States. Often, short tour activities can start the first evening.

Schedule Planning

In planning the schedule, tour planners should first block out all flights on a day schedule sheet. Next, accommodation arrangements are scheduled. Sightseeing activities are then added, followed by scheduled meals, free time, and other activities.

One- and Two-Day Local Tour Scheduling

In preparing itinerary schedules, many will be considering a one-day or a two-day local tour prior to planning longer distance or international air tours. Since the one- or two-day tour is normally a bus tour, the scheduling sequence is somewhat different than with air tours. However, transportation is usually still a major focus because the time that it takes to drive between points often is the determining factor as to what can be scheduled when. Meals, however, are also a major factor in scheduling one- and two-day bus tours. However, you should start planning these short bus tours with the single major activity in mind. Work backward and forward from that activity to schedule other parts of the tour. Therefore, the central focus of the tour or the "tour event" becomes the most important scheduling factor.

After placing the central focus tour event onto the initial draft schedule, the tour operator next identifies tour events of secondary importance and determines the transportation time needed between each event. Then these are entered into the first draft tour schedule. Usually no more than three tour events per tour day are scheduled. Of course, transporation time from the point of departure in the hometown city to the first event and the transportation time back to the hometown city drop off point from the last event may well determine that fewer than three events can be scheduled. Much depends upon the nature of the group, but it is seldom that more than three "events" can be or should be scheduled on a one-day tour.

The "events" are usually sightseeing activities. For adventure tours, they are usually adventure activities such as ballooning, rafting, snow skiing, and other similar popular sports. When the "tour event" is an activity, it is frequently the only event scheduled on a one-day tour, as participation in the activity is why tour members undertake such a tour. Even here, however, sometimes an afternoon meal or a nearby museum, picturesque vista, or other activity which would be of interest to tour members, taking relatively little time, might be and often is included in the tour.

The itinerary planning for one- and two-day bus tours, therefore, starts with the "tour event" and moves to inclusion of secondary tour activities. Bus transportation is scheduled, usually in conjunction with the planning of the tour event and secondary tour activities. Meals, registration, and departure at the beginning of the tour and completion activities are planned as the final ingredients to the one-day tour schedule.

The two-day, weekend bus tour itinerary is planned in much the same way. However, the addition of overnight accommodations, evening meal, and often one or more evening activities is planned along with the pre-departure, return, and meal planning, constituting the last part of the itinerary plan.

The client itinerary for a one- or two-day tour is usually a short enough itinerary that it can be included on the tour brochure or as a separate sheet of paper given to the client at the beginning of the trip. It highlights the basics of what the client needs and wants to know relating to the activities and the order in which these activities are scheduled. It provides key information such as check-in time, departure time from the point of origin, the departure location for the bus tour or the departure airport terminal for the air tour, and the time and location for completion of the tour. It does not include much detail, since most one- and two-day bus tour clients are not overly concerned with detail throughout their itineraries.

Multi-Day Scheduling

Multi-day tour itineraries are designed similarly to one- and two-day bus tour itineraries. At most, there will be morning, afternoon, and evening segments. Often, at least one of these three time block segments will be left open as "free" time. When traveling between hotels by bus, a 10:00 A.M. departure and a before 6:00 P.M. arrival should be planned. Limited sightseeing enroute is appropriate as long as it does not result in arriving at the destination hotel much after 6:00 P.M.

The Tour Manager's Itinerary

The tour manager's itinerary is the most comprehensive of all of the itineraries prepared. By working with this itinerary, the tour manager should be prepared to manage all aspects of the tour from the beginning to the end. Many tour manager's itineraries will run several pages in length. Because they are so lengthy, a large number of tour companies prepare tour manager's itineraries on a day-to-day basis with no more than one day's activities appearing on any single page. Some even break each day down to a separate page each for morning, afternoon, and evening. In this way, the tour manager does not need to take all of the itinerary with her in carry-on luggage throughout the day, but can leave non-pertinent parts of the itinerary back at the hotel, in her under-the-bus luggage, or in her flight-checked luggage.

The Importance of 15-Minute Time Blocks

Experienced tour companies do not break itinerary line items on an arbitrary quarter hour basis, but rather list activities based on the duration of each activity and it's time sequenced scheduling. However, many who are new to itinerary development will find initial planning easier if they have the itinerary identify each activity that will be undertaken on a 15-minute by 15-minute time block basis. The first draft of the tour manager's itinerary, broken into 15-minute segments, will allocate as much as one-third of a page for each time block. Once the draft tour manager's itinerary has been completed, revised, and prepared in a form that begins to resemble the final format, each of the pages can be grouped together and retyped with activities scheduled one after the other. Ideally, even though the 15-minute time breaks may be kept, each six- to eight-hour time block can be prepared in such a way that it will fit on a single sheet of paper.

Tour Manager Itinerary Notes

Notes that are suggestions or recommendations to the tour manager can and should appear on the itinerary in the appropriate sections based upon when the tour manager will need to know the information. Some tour companies list itinerary activities sequentially on the left-hand side of the page and leave the right-hand side of the page open for notes to be added by either the tour planner or the tour manager before the tour starts and by the tour manager after the tour starts. Itinerary notes will include such items as the names of contact people in each location being visited, special seating arrangements in theaters or other performance auditoriums, tip suggestions, and so forth.

The Bus Driver Itinerary

When special versions of the itinerary are provided for bus drivers, the reason is to give them an opportunity to understand the information they need to do a good job. The itinerary should include notations of drop-off points, turnaround points, pick-up points, areas that are difficult to maneuver, hazardous driving areas, special routes because of weak bridge (posted and unposted bridge weight limitations), and so forth.

In some cases, the driver will have an opportunity to park the tour bus in a central location close to the sightseeing point or sightseeing activities, but when this is the case, frequently there is a special bus parking area. This should be identified on maps which are referred to with notes on the itinerary. If the driver is expected to drop off tour participants, take the bus to a location some distance away, and return at a designated time to pick up passengers, these times should be noted, the location where the bus can be parked should be indicated, and the pick up point should be identified on the itinerary.

Bus driver itineraries will sometimes call for driving at a slower pace between designated points that are especially scenic so that tour participants can enjoy the scenery and perhaps take photos from the bus. Bathroom waste dumping locations need to be identified and waste dumping should be scheduled to avoid smelly bus bathrooms. Other special notes may be appended to the itinerary for the bus driver as well.

Individual City/Country Step-on Guide Itineraries

One- and two-day bus tours seldom use step-on guides. Usually, but not always, the tour escort conducts the entire tour alone. However, multi-day air tours and some multi-day bus tours often draw heavily on the expertise of step-on guides. These are local experts who know the sights, the history, and the scenery that is being visited usually better than anyone from outside the area. Tour operators often contract with inbound travel firms or destination management companies for step-on guides. Alternatively they contract directly with step-on guides so that these experts will accompany the tour on those portions of the tour for which they are experts. These are usually four-hour to eight-hour segments in the community or area in which the step-on guide lives.

When step-on guides are used, tour companies frequently provide these guides with detailed itineraries relating to the segment of the tour for which the step-on guide will be providing guide service. They also usually provide the guide with a copy of either the overall client itinerary or, less often, a copy of the tour manager's itinerary. The step-on guide can better prepare the presentation when the itinerary is provided in advance. The guide will have an excellent idea how long to make presentations because the time durations spent in each destination area will be clearly identified.

Other Vendor Itineraries

Many vendors will neither need nor want a copy of the itinerary. However, some will find specific parts of the itinerary helpful. Sightseeing hosts or hostesses (sometimes called docents) who escort the tour group through their facility will often find it beneficial to know where their destination comes on the tour's full day's schedule. For example, if the group is being escorted through an art museum by a museum hostess/guide who is an expert in the art housed at the museum, the hostess/guide may find it beneficial to know where the tour has been earlier in the day and where it will go later. She will be able to better understand the time constraints necessary so that they can be adhered to. Frequently, when these local site hosts and hostesses receive a copy of the itinerary, they can make suggestions regarding what the tour member(s) might want to consider doing during free time later and they often can suggest special purchases in the area where the tour members will be housed or where they will be visiting next. At the very least, hosts and hostesses are in a position to understand more about the group and to tailor their comments.

Rather than being a prepackaged recording type of presentation, dialog comments on where the tour members have been and where they are going can be included in presentations. Often these are people who are steeped in local culture and history. Giving them a complete itinerary takes advantage of their unique knowledge.

Other Vendors Needing Itineraries

Other vendors who often appreciate receiving copies of client itineraries include lodging sales and marketing executives as well as restauranteurs. Although not all lodging sales and marketing executives will take advantage of having a copy of the client itinerary, some, especially those affiliated with resorts, often make a special effort to meet the group and to make a welcoming speech upon arrival. This presentation is usually a short one. Highlights of the hotel or the resort are identified so that tour members can enjoy the lodging facility to the fullest.

When the sales and marketing executive has a copy of the itinerary, references to points visited during the past few days or points that will be visited can be incorporated into the presentation. Also, if the tour is running late and staff is kept waiting for the tour members to arrive, with a copy of the itinerary the resort sales and marketing executive can call to the place last visited and determine whether or not the tour is on schedule. Of course, the same benefits accrue to a front desk manager or employee who is expecting a bus load of tour members to come in so that the front desk can be prepared for the arrival.

Restauranteurs sometimes also appreciate having a copy of the client itinerary so that they can be more prepared for the group when they arrive. As with the resort sales and marketing executive, some restaurant owners like to make a welcoming presentation offering a few comments about the restaurant. This is especially true when the restaurant is located in a historic area and has a history of its own or is a part of the history of the area, if it is a "theme" restaurant, or if it is a special interest restaurant.

Itinerary Mix Planning

Good itineraries can be thought of in a manner similar to good recipes for cakes, pies, or other sweets. They include ingredients, many of which can be good in and of themselves. Combined together in just the right mix, they provide an outstanding culinary or tour experience. Not only must you start with good ingredients, but often the secret to a memorable tour is the mix itself. There needs to be just the right amount of sightseeing, the right number of quality meals, the proper entertainment in the right amount, and so forth.

Quality is often related to cost. Some of the most memorable experiences of tour memebers who have taken many tours, however, are memories of events and experiences that were inexpensive. A woman who for many years has taken expensive tours remembers as her favorite meal a picnic consisting of local cheese, breads, wines, and other picnic ingredients purchased in a small French village and brought on the bus to a mountain meadow where tour members sat among the lush grasses and had a delightful picnic. For the proper time and with the right group this works.

By reviewing comment sheets from past tour participants, conducting in-depth interviews with previous tour participants and by studying recommendations received from current and past clients, the tour planner should review the wide range of potential tour ingredients and work with them to come up with an increasingly more popular and an increasingly more satisfying tour. Like any presentation to large groups, a tour can be honed and perfected over a period of time, making it increasingly better as the tour company gets more and more experience in offering the tour. Alternatively, a tour can be offered repeatedly, continuing mistakes or ingredients that make for a less than perfect mix time after time simply because it continues to sell and fill. A fine line needs to drawn between overworking a tour (making too many changes in it) and offering a tour that has been insufficiently evaluated and, therefore, has had few of multiple needed changes.

The Sightseeing Foundation

For most tours there is no question but that the foundation for the tour (often the reason for tour participants to go on the tour in the first place) is the sight-seeing. Sightseeing can be destination oriented, but it can also be found enroute. When it is destination oriented, what is seen getting to the destination is usually considered to be of no interest to tour participants. In such cases, transportation time needs to be filled with some on-bus activity. When there is sightseeing from the point of departure to the major sightseeing destination and back, usually because the scenery is so spectacular, less on-bus activity should be planned. In fact, in some cases where the scenery is especially beautiful, tour members prefer not to be taken away from their ability to see the scenery by any on-bus activities.

In most cases, the sightseeing foundation will be specific sightseeing destinations. This may be natural scenery such as drives through the national parks. It may also be cities such as Paris, Rome, London, and so forth. It may be antiquity such as Williamsburg, Virginia. Or it may be any one of a number of other types of destination sightseeing. Whatever the sightseeing foundation, tour members should be given every sightseeing advantage as compared with members of the general public.

Although it need not be emphasized (it usually should be noted) in the literature, it is beneficial for tour members to sense that they have an advantage in their sightseeing as compared to those who may have gone to the destination on their own. These advantages may include presentations by experts or perhaps lectures and discussions which may not be available to the average visitor. If there is an event to be seen, excellent seating should be reserved in advance for tour members. At the Scottish Highland Games, for example, one section in particular has the best view in the center of the field. Reservations in this section are made as much as a year in advance as this preferred seating is sold out quickly. Although buses may not be able to park close to the entrance area, tour members may find an advantage by being on a tour bus that drops them directly in front of the main entrance rather than having to walk half a mile or further from where private cars are parked.

It is the sight or sights themselves, however, that should be described on the client itinerary. They should be described accurately but in terms that elicit interest, excitement, and a strong desire to be there.

Food and Beverage Functions

Generally speaking, food and beverage functions should be varied. Much depends upon the nature of the tour group. Those participating in adventure tours who have been very active throughout the day will probably be quite hungry in the evening and an appropriate meal should be planned. On the other hand, tour members who have been on tour buses throughout the day usually have had an opportunity to snack or eat heavy breakfasts and lunches and will seldom want to have a substantial amount of food in the evening. Many of these tour members will be more interested in the presentation and the quality of the food or entertainment that may be available at the dining establishment than the quantity of the food.

Tour planners should seriously consider the number of food and beverage functions that are included on the tour. Many tour members prefer to have some food and beverage functions that are "on their own" so as to provide them with an opportunity to eat at a wider variety of restaurants as well as to reduce the cost of the tour. Tour planners also should realize how substantially a reduction in two or even one meal per day can reduce the total cost of the tour. However, some meal functions should be included on most tours since they often present opportunities for unique tour experiences. By buying meals as a group, tour members can sometimes take advantage of lesser costs or obtain preferred seating and these circumstances should always be explored when considering included meals.

The itinerary should list each included food and beverage function and special functions should always be emphasized. Whatever food and beverage functions are planned, highlights of these should be included in the itinerary. If, for some reason, little food and beverage will be served during an "included" meal, tour members should be advised. They can then plan to have a meal on their own if they are normally heavy eaters.

Entertainment

Included entertainment is not always noted on itineraries, but should be. Some tours lend themselves to excellent entertainment opportunities, while others provide relatively few entertainment options. If entertainment is included with a meal, mention should be made of it or it should not be mentioned, depending upon whether or not it is considered an important function. When a live band is playing in the evening at the restaurant where dinner is included on the tour, it is often beneficial to mention this, especially if dancing is available. Those couples who are on the tour who enjoy dancing will usually appreciate knowing that they can plan for this. On the other hand, if there is a strolling musician at the restaurant and no other musical or entertainment activity, the itinerary may or may not mention the fact that the restaurant has a strolling musician. The tour planner should use his own judgment in making this itinerary listing decision.

On-Bus Activities

On-bus activities are seldom mentioned in the itinerary unless they are unique and special. Running commentary by the tour manager is expected and a mention of this is not appropriate. With videos available on buses, however, some tour companies are now indicating in the itineraries, especially for long-distance highway travel by bus, that a first run film will be featured or that some other videotaped feature which might be considered of special importance to the client will be shown. Again, the tour planner should consider whether or not the bus activity is something which would be considered of importance to the tour member before listing the on bus activity on the client itinerary.

Included vs. Optional Itinerary Ingredients

The tour planner should consider a number of options and determine whether or not they should be "included" activities or made optional for tour members. If an activity is considered special, if a substantial number of tour members can be expected to believe that the activity would be a highlight of the tour and especially if the activity is limited in terms of the numbers of people who can either participate in it or view it, serious consideration should be given to making the activity an "included" one. However, the tour planner must always recognize that included activities add to the cost of the entire tour and some tour members may not find the included activity to be either special or important.

When the decision is made that an activity is optional, the client itinerary usually identifies the availability or the potential availability of the activity and notes that it is optional. This is especially true when your clients might otherwise believe that the activity is an "included" feature of the tour. For example, an evening nightclub sightseeing tour in a major city might be of interest to a number of tour participants, but not to all. Therefore, the itinerary might read, "Free time after dinner. For those who do not wish to retire early, an optional nightclub tour will be available." By noting this on the itinerary, tour members can plan accordingly and will know that there will be an additional cost if they plan to participate in the optional nightclub sightseeing tour.

The Importance of Free Time

Many who are new to developing tours may not appreciate the importance of free time. Generally, the longer the tour in terms of the numbers of days, the older the average age of tour members, and the more expensive the tour, the greater the need to have free time allocated to passengers.

For example, on a one-day domestic bus tour, participants will often want to see and do as much as possible and will expect relatively little free time. However, on a four-week deluxe grand tour of Europe, it can be expected that most of the tour participants have been to most of the destinations before and will have a few favorite places in mind to revisit in the main cities. They will probably be well-read, having reviewed a number of guides. In many cases, they will want to visit a number of the top stores and boutiques, having prepared a specific shopping list in advance. For all of these purposes, tour members will want and expect to have a substantial amount of free time.

It is also generally recognized that those who are the wealthiest are usually older tour members. But with age comes a more rapid tiring. Although older people seldom sleep as much as younger people, they tire more rapidly. Therefore, shorter segments of high-intensive activity should be planned. Some older clients will be accustomed to taking short naps in the afternoon, but often will stay up quite late at night. Others, however, will not nap and will get to bed early. While many older clients are early risers, a large number do not wish to start a tour right away in the morning. They may wish to undertake touring activities at a slower pace.

As with air trips, many tour members have found that a 10:00 A.M. departure from the hotel for daily sightseeing is usually a good time when working with clients on luxury tours or with clients who are older. This gives clients plenty of time to take a morning stroll if they wish to do so or to have a leisurely breakfast before departure from the hotel. This is especially important if the tour is leaving one hotel and going on to another city and another hotel, necessitating packing and hotel check out for each tour member before leaving on the tour bus in the morning.

Many tour operators will schedule planned sightseeing or other activity for a two- or three-hour morning session and a two- or three-hour afternoon session. Approximately every two days, either a full morning or a full afternoon will be left for free time. Evening events are planned for a little more than two/thirds of the evenings on tour when it is a long tour, but some will reduce this down to fewer than half of the evenings. Often, when an evening function is planned, the afternoon is provided as free time. This is especially true if the evening event is formal, such as attending a play, an opera, or a formal party. Many in the tour group will want to spend time getting ready for the evening event and will not want to rush back from a sightseeing trip having only 45 minutes or an hour to prepare.

As noted, one-day and other short tours, especially for adventure activity-oriented and younger tour members can often be filled much more completely with planned activity. However, if the central theme of the tour is a theme park or an event where there will be many booths (the Strawberry Festival, a visit to a rural gambling town, Disneyworld, etc.), tour members will usually want to be let off the bus and given the entire time at the destination free to do their own thing.

The only exception to this is when there is some special event associated with the theme program such as a parade. For such an event, the tour operator should obtain good seats in advance and make these available to the clients. Seating tickets can usually be given to tour members in advance so that if they decide to see the parade or other event, they may do so. However, if they decide to shop, visit booths, or simply stroll around the area instead of attending the parade, they will have that option.

Scripted vs. Nonscripted Presentations

As with enroute on-bus presentations, presentations by local sightseeing guides and hosts or hostesses at destination antique buildings, museums, and other interesting destination sights can either be scripted or nonscripted. Usually hosts and hostesses who make presentations which are nonscripted do a better job and their talks are better received.

A step-on guide commenting about spectacular caves in her area pointed out that she felt the scripted presentations of hosts and hostesses taking tour groups through the caves ruined the cave visits to such a degree that she now advises clients prior to entering the caves to lag at the back of the tour taking in the sights in the caves themselves and ignoring the "banter" of the cave hosts/hostesses. The jokes, she said, are feeble. The history is inaccurate and incomplete, and the modulation of the presentation is nonexistent. When hosts and hostesses take groups of tour members through the cave every 45 minutes for eight hour shifts, day after day, year after year, it is not surprising that their presentations become lifeless and are usually in monotone.

On the other hand, tours can be very interesting with guides who work without scripted presentations, especially if they are knowledgeable and excited about their subject. Sometimes, tour planners are given no choice of local hosts, hostesses, docents, and guides. They are assigned by the sightseeing vendor on a first come, first served basis. Wherever there is a choice, however, nonscripted presentations are usually preferred, especially when presented by knowledgeable individuals.

The Sightseeing and Itinerary Budgets

Sightseeing, being the focus for most tours, should have primary budget consideration. In preparing the budget, you should start with sightseeing costs and then work in other costs. Sightseeing event admission tickets should be included whenever a tour goes to an area where all or most tour members will be together.

Tour members seldom appreciate arriving at a sightseeing destination, getting off of the tour bus, and standing in line to pay for a ticket which could otherwise have been purchased in advance by the tour company at a less expensive group rate. Although this may save on the overall cost of the tour, it is usually a false savings because tour members expect to have the sightseeing included. While they may not express dissatisfaction during the tour (they usually do, however), it is unlikely that they will sign up for future tours when they encounter even one situation such as this.

When there is a choice of seating for events, most companies obtain the best possible seats for their tour members. This is not always possible to do in advance. For example, at many casino shows, seating is provided on a first come first served basis. However, those who provide large tips are usually given the best seats. Tour companies should know these cost factors and budget for the cost of the tips required to get good seats.

Itinerary preparation budgets, for most tour companies, constitute small budget items. Most will store itineraries on computers and reproduce them on a standard form. A particularly nice format is a booklet created on sheets of paper cut to a small enough size, sandwiched between sturdy plastic covers and bound with spiral binding (see Figure 6–3.). This booklet can be small enough to fit in a man's shirt pocket or a woman's purse. This allows the tour member to flip to

FIGURE 6–3 SAMPLE ITINERARY BOOKLET

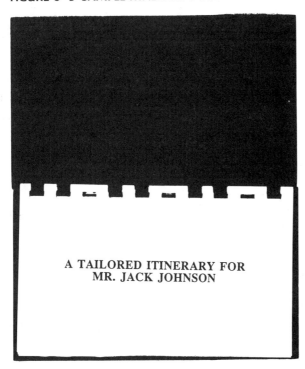

A TAILORED ITINERARY FOR
MR. JACK JOHNSON

the appropriate page for the section of the itinerary being covered that day or portion of the day, but the plastic covers provide a sufficient protection to the itinerary that it does not get ripped or torn enroute. The itinerary booklet, therefore, usually survives the trip and is an interesting conversation piece when discussing the trip with friends, relatives, and associates after the trip is over.

These itinerary booklets, however, do cost more than standard print sheet itineraries. The companies that use them usually consider them to be a good investment in that they provide an excellent return on investment. The cost is seldom more than $3 or $4 per booklet when prepared on a regular basis for all tours offered by the company.

Summary

There are five versions, and sometimes more, of the basic itinerary developed for a tour. All other versions are based upon the client itinerary. In addition to that, there are usually itinerary versions for the tour manager, the bus driver, vendors, and step-on guides. Sometimes vendors and step-on guides will use some type of "generic" itinerary which may be the same as or a portion of the client itinerary. In addition, occasionally itineraries other than these five will be prepared.

The client itinerary is the starting point. This should be client-based. In other words, it should be centered around the client and should always consider what the client might like most to do. For example, after flights on which the client will be traveling all night, usually little activity should be scheduled so that the client may relax and have a substantial amount of free time to start getting accustomed to the country of arrival and to start overcoming jet lag.

One- or two-day local tours are usually bus tours. Bus transportation time, therefore, is usually an important consideration. However, they usually have a central feature or focus as well as tour events of secondary importance. Even the transportation is based on being able to participate in or see the central focus purpose of the trip. Two-day (weekend) trips include overnight accommodations. Therefore, evening activities will often be planned as well. Multi-day tour itineraries are normally broken into three time frames—morning, afternoon, and evening.

The tour manager's itinerary is far more detailed than the client itinerary. Some break out tour manager activities into 15-minute time segments, identifying everything of importance that is scheduled to happen each 15-minutes of the trip. This usually works better for short one-day trips than for multi-day international trips. Many tour manager itineraries will leave considerable space for the tour manager to write in notes as the tour is conducted.

The bus driver itinerary will give specific instructions to the bus driver for such things as parking, locations to meet clients, and so forth. It usually is accompanied with a packet which will include maps, vendor contact information, and so forth.

Individual city and country step-on guides are given either a detailed itinerary for their portion of the tour (plus a copy of the client itinerary for the whole tour) or they receive only a client itinerary copy. By having the full itinerary, they can include comments and recommendations regarding portions of the tour outside their areas.

The same is true for the hosts, hostess, docents, and guides working for vendors. Although these vendors usually appreciate receiving specialized itineraries dealing with their particular portion of the tour, they can often provide more information for tour members if they have a copy of the entire itinerary. Both lodging and restaurant vendors sometimes appreciate having copies of itineraries as well.

In preparing the itinerary mix, it is important to include variety. Sightseeing, meals, entertainment, and free time are just a few of the daily ingredients a tour itinerary should include. To assist in developing the best possible combination of ingredients, it is helpful to review the comment sheets from past tour participants. Focus on the foundation of the tour (i.e., sightseeing).

Variety is usually the key word most appreciated when it comes to food and beverage functions. On inexpensive tours for people with strict budgets, the quantity of the food is often a concern. However, on expensive tours, especially for those with the elderly, quantity is frequently less important than the quality and the presentation.

Entertainment may or may not be listed on the itinerary, but it is usually better to make a reference to it when it is included in the price of the tour. On-bus activities should be varied and one should always keep in mind that free time on the bus is appreciated, especially when there are a large number of announcements and considerable running commentary by the tour manager, as well.

The longer international tours will need to include more optional itinerary items than the shorter one- or two-day domestic bus tours. The itinerary should clearly identify these as optional activities for which an additional cost will be levied.

You should keep in mind that many of the more expensive lengthy tours, especially those that go to only one or two countries, may include tour participants who have been to the destination before or who have special interests in visiting specific points in the countries. In addition, many of the participants on these tours are elderly, sometimes tiring rapidly. Therefore, there should be no pressure on tour members to participate in scheduled tour activities. There should also be a reasonable amount of free time built into these itineraries. Every couple of days, either a full evening or a full afternoon should be scheduled as free time and whenever there is a formal evening function, free time should be allocated prior to that function so that tour participants can change clothes and get ready.

Itineraries should include a mention of presentations, but wherever possible, these should be nonscripted presentations. Knowledgeable and interesting guides—especially those who are so involved in their destinations that they do not need scripts, should be sought.

Primary budget consideration for the tour should be given to sightseeing. Wherever possible, admission tickets should be included in the price of the tour and the best seats possible should be reserved. Client itineraries should be packaged in both a convenient and a good-looking format. The cost of bound booklets seldom exceeds more than $3 or $4 per booklet. The itinerary itself can then become a memorable and often an important souvenir.

DISCUSSION QUESTIONS

These questions may be discussed by two or more students outside of class as a fun way of reviewing this chapter or they may be discussed by everyone during class for a more wide-ranging discussion.

1. Why are there several itineraries and what unique purposes do each serve?
2. Which itinerary is "the starting point" and why is it this one that is the starting point?
3. How might the tour planner handle a tour when arrival in the European destination city is very early in the morning and tour members have been on the plane, flying all night?
4. What relationship is found between the central focus tour event, tour events of secondary importance, and other aspects of the tour when planning the initial draft schedule of the itinerary?
5. What points are important to consider when developing a tour manager's itinerary and why might some leave considerable space on the tour manager's itinerary?
6. In addition to the itinerary, what supplemental documents might be provided to the bus driver to assist him/her in following the itinerary?
7. Why might step-on guides, hostess/guides, hotel front desk employees, and restaurant owners all find having a copy of the itinerary beneficial?
8. How might the planning of an itinerary be compared to following a good recipe for a culinary experience?
9. Why is free time important and which types of tours should include more free time than others?
10. In preparing a tour budget, why should you start with sightseeing costs and why might you spend as much as $2 or $3 for each tour member itinerary?

ROLE PLAY EXERCISES

1. Two students may participate in this role play either out of class as a fun way to review the chapter or as an in-class exercise. One plays the role of a travel

the features on this one are far more luxurious and far better in terms of quality standards.

TRAVEL STUDENT: In studying the features, I can see that. But won't most of the potential tour members look at all this free time and the smaller number of features and decide instead to take a less expensive trip with a lot more activities and less free time? Are they really sophisticated enough in their travel buying that they understand the quality differences?

TOUR PLANNER: Some are sophisticated enough to understand this, but most are not. However, the people who spend money on luxury tours want free time. Free time is important to them because . . .

CONTINUE ON YOUR OWN

GROUP DISCUSSION SITUATION: MERPLE'S BLOW TO THE BLEETING BLELTS TOUR

"This is the third relative to die and leave me money this year," thought Merple Maximillions. "When Uncle Nerfie's estate is settled, it should bring me up to a net value of a little over $2 million. I think I'll splurge and take that tour of South America I've been wanting to take," thought Merple.

That was last week. Merple, 86 years old now, has traveled extensively around the world. She outlived and out-traveled four husbands. Merple has been an avid traveler since her first marriage when she was 13 and it seemed to Merple that each husband tried to keep up with her, but eventually gave up on traveling as much as she did.

Merple has a very understanding travel agent. They get along well and the travel agent seems to sense what kinds of things Merple wants to see and do on her trips. For many years, the agent planned FITs for Merple, but since she had her fourth leg break, right above the ankle this last time, Merple has opted to go on tours instead of on her own. Rarely, but often enough to concern Merple, her leg just simply gives out on her. She wants to make sure she is with a group of other people when this happens and not off some place on her own.

Last week, when Merple decided to use Uncle Nerfie's money for the Latin America trip, she called her travel agent and she has been dscussing potential tours ever since. None of them seems to have exactly what Merple wants save one, Bleeting Blelts' Below America tour. It is at the right time and it includes all the destinations Merple wants to go to.

However, the hotel in Rio is not at the Copacabana Beach and Merple really looked forward to spending some time on the beach as well as having a hotel room with a full beach view. "The Copacabana Beach in Rio has the most 'interesting' men of any beach in the world," Merple confided to her agent. "You can't see men in bikinis that small anywhere else in the world," she whispered confidentially. Merple was really hoping that the tour would have at least three days in Rio and that the hotel would give her the kinds of views she had the last time she was in Rio. "Can't we just get them to let me take a taxi over to one of the hotels on the beach, extend my stay in Rio for a couple of days, and pick up the tour after it has left Montevideo and gets into Buenos Aires," she asked.

Merple's travel agent is torn between wanting to get Merple what she wants and being concerned about her oft lame leg. She is also concerned about whether or not she should confide with the tour company reservationist to explain the situation. If she does, the tour company will probably not take Merple in the first place because her leg is so bad. "Even if they do take her," thinks the agent, "they certainly won't want to take responsibility for her being on her own at a beach with nobody around to take care of her if her leg gives way. Surely the tour company will be thinking 'suit', 'suit', 'suit'. If I don't tell them the truth, however, and they agree and then something happens to Merple, I might very well be the person who is sued."

"On the other hand," thinks the agent, "Merple isn't the kind of person to sue and she already has more money than she needs. Why not give her the kind of trip that she really wants by simply ignoring the potential problems and asking the tour company to go ahead and make the arrangements. If they think she is in perfect health, they will probably work out the beach hotel and the longer stay in Rio," thinks the agent. "Besides, the commission will be great."

The agent has confided with several other agents who specialize in luxury tours. You and your associates constitute this group of "other agents." You are expected to consider the above information and advise and counsel the agent as to what she should say to the tour company and how she should handle the matter with Merple. Be prepared to present your suggestions in a paper that will be no longer than three pages in length. Also make sure the paper is double spaced and typed. Be prepared to present your suggestions verbally in class if your instructor suggests that you do so.

EXERCISES

1. Break into groups of no more than three students working together. Yours will probably be the same group that has been working together in the development of a one-day tour since the beginning of the course.

Go back to the draft one-day tour itineraries developed as Exercise 1 in Chapter 5. From those draft itineraries, develop more complete versions based upon the material presented in this chapter. Identify which of the vendors will need specialized itineraries and prepare an itinerary to fit the needs of each of those vendors. Make certain that the tour manager itinerary has sufficient space for the tour manager to make notes and that each detail of the trip is included. Review the tour member itinerary, making certain that it fits the needs of and the interests of the tour member. Go back and change the itinerary to fit tour member needs, if necessary. Several changes may be based upon information learned in this chapter.

CLIENT'S ITINERARY

DRAFT ITINERARY PREPARATION FORM

ITINERARY FOR: _____

DAY ONE - EARLY MORNING

0600 _____

0630 _____

0700 _____

0730 _____

0800 _____

0830 _____

0900 _____

DRAFT ITINERARY PREPARATION FORM

ITINERARY FOR: _____

DAY ONE - LATE MORNING & EARLY AFTERNOON

0930 _____

1000 _____

1030 _____

1100 _____

1130 _____

1200 _____

1230 _____

DRAFT ITINERARY PREPARATION FORM

ITINERARY FOR: _____

DAY ONE - MID AFTERNOON

1300 _____

1330 _____

1400 _____

1430 _____

1500 _____

1530 _____

1600 _____

DRAFT ITINERARY PREPARATION FORM

ITINERARY FOR: _____

DAY ONE - LATE AFTERNOON - EARLY EVENING

1630 _____

1700 _____

1730 _____

1800 _____

1830 _____

1900 _____

1930 _____

DRAFT ITINERARY PREPARATION FORM

ITINERARY FOR: _____

DAY ONE - LATE NIGHT

2000 _____

2030 _____

2100 _____

2130 _____

2200 _____

2230 _____

2300 _____

TOUR MANAGER'S ITINERARY

DRAFT ITINERARY PREPARATION FORM

ITINERARY FOR: _____

DAY ONE - EARLY MORNING

0600 _____

0630 _____

0700 _____

0730 _____

0800 _____

0830 _____

0900 _____

DRAFT ITINERARY PREPARATION FORM

ITINERARY FOR: _____

DAY ONE - LATE MORNING & EARLY AFTERNOON

0930 _____

1000 _____

1030 _____

1100 _____

1130 _____

1200 _____

1230 _____

DRAFT ITINERARY PREPARATION FORM

ITINERARY FOR: _____

DAY ONE - MID AFTERNOON

1300 _____

1330 _____

1400 _____

1430 _____

1500 _____

1530 _____

1600 _____

DRAFT ITINERARY PREPARATION FORM

ITINERARY FOR: _____

DAY ONE - LATE AFTERNOON - EARLY EVENING

1630 _____

1700 _____

1730 _____

1800 _____

1830 _____

1900 _____

1930 _____

DRAFT ITINERARY PREPARATION FORM

ITINERARY FOR: _____

DAY ONE - LATE NIGHT

2000 _____

2030 _____

2100 _____

2130 _____

2200 _____

2230 _____

2300 _____

BUS DRIVER'S ITINERARY

DRAFT ITINERARY PREPARATION FORM

ITINERARY FOR: _____

DAY ONE - EARLY MORNING

0600 _____
_____
0630 _____
_____
0700 _____
_____

0730 _____
_____
0800 _____
_____
0830 _____
_____
0900 _____
_____
_____

DRAFT ITINERARY PREPARATION FORM

ITINERARY FOR: _____

DAY ONE - LATE MORNING & EARLY AFTERNOON

0930 _____
1000 _____
1030 _____
1100 _____
1130 _____
1200 _____
1230 _____

DRAFT ITINERARY PREPARATION FORM

ITINERARY FOR: _____

DAY ONE - MID AFTERNOON

1300 _____
1330 _____
1400 _____
1430 _____
1500 _____
1530 _____
1600 _____

DRAFT ITINERARY PREPARATION FORM

ITINERARY FOR: _____

DAY ONE - LATE AFTERNOON - EARLY EVENING

1630 _____
1700 _____
1730 _____
1800 _____
1830 _____
1900 _____
1930 _____

DRAFT ITINERARY PREPARATION FORM

ITINERARY FOR: _____

DAY ONE - LATE NIGHT

2000 _____
2030 _____
2100 _____
2130 _____
2200 _____
2230 _____
2300 _____

SIGHTSEEING POINT #1 ITINERARY

DRAFT ITINERARY PREPARATION FORM

ITINERARY FOR: _____

DAY ONE - EARLY MORNING

0600 _____
_____
0630 _____
_____
0700 _____
_____

0730 _____
_____
0800 _____
_____
0830 _____
_____
0900 _____
_____

DRAFT ITINERARY PREPARATION FORM

ITINERARY FOR: _____

DAY ONE - LATE MORNING & EARLY AFTERNOON

0930 _____
_____
1000 _____
_____
1030 _____
_____
1100 _____
_____
1130 _____
_____
1200 _____
_____
1230 _____
_____

DRAFT ITINERARY PREPARATION FORM

ITINERARY FOR: _____

DAY ONE - MID AFTERNOON

1300 _____
_____
1330 _____
_____
1400 _____
_____
1430 _____
_____
1500 _____
_____
1530 _____
_____
1600 _____
_____

DRAFT ITINERARY PREPARATION FORM

ITINERARY FOR: _____

DAY ONE - LATE AFTERNOON - EARLY EVENING

1630 _____
_____
1700 _____
_____
1730 _____
_____
1800 _____
_____
1830 _____
_____
1900 _____
_____
1930 _____
_____

DRAFT ITINERARY PREPARATION FORM

ITINERARY FOR: _____

DAY ONE - LATE NIGHT

2000 _____
_____
2030 _____
_____
2100 _____
_____
2130 _____
_____
2200 _____
_____
2230 _____
_____
2300 _____
_____

SIGHTSEEING POINT #2 ITINERARY

DRAFT ITINERARY PREPARATION FORM

ITINERARY FOR: _____

DAY ONE - EARLY MORNING

0600 _____
0630 _____
0700 _____

0730 _____
0800 _____
0830 _____
0900 _____

DRAFT ITINERARY PREPARATION FORM

ITINERARY FOR: _____

DAY ONE - LATE MORNING & EARLY AFTERNOON

0930 _____
1000 _____
1030 _____
1100 _____
1130 _____
1200 _____
1230 _____

DRAFT ITINERARY PREPARATION FORM

ITINERARY FOR: _____

DAY ONE - MID AFTERNOON

1300 _____
1330 _____
1400 _____
1430 _____
1500 _____
1530 _____
1600 _____

DRAFT ITINERARY PREPARATION FORM

ITINERARY FOR: _____

DAY ONE - LATE AFTERNOON - EARLY EVENING

1630 _____
1700 _____
1730 _____
1800 _____
1830 _____
1900 _____
1930 _____

DRAFT ITINERARY PREPARATION FORM

ITINERARY FOR: _____

DAY ONE - LATE NIGHT

2000 _____
2030 _____
2100 _____
2130 _____
2200 _____
2230 _____
2300 _____

student and the other plays the role of a tour planner. Please read the script and then pick up the conversation in your own words.

TRAVEL STUDENT: Why fool with all of these various itineraries? I don't understand why you don't just do one complete itinerary and then photocopy that for everybody to use.

TOUR PLANNER: It would certainly be simpler if we could. However, multiple versions of the itinerary are needed because . . .

CONTINUE ON YOUR OWN

2. Two students may participate in this role play either out of class as a fun way to review the chapter or as an in-class exercise. One plays the role of a travel student and the other plays the role of a tour planner. Please read the script and then pick up the conversation in your own words.

TRAVEL STUDENT: I don't understand. On the one hand you emphasize that the bus is important on one-day tours and that one should concentrate the itinerary on the distances the bus is capable of traveling to and from in a day. On the other hand, you say that the central focus of sightseeing is important.

TOUR PLANNER: Both are important. The central focus around which the tour is built is definitely the place to start for multi-day trips. It is also often the most important point around which to build a one-day tour. However, practically speaking the bus is also important, especially for a one-day trip.

TRAVEL STUDENT: I'm still confused. It sounds like you are saying both are equally important. You have to start somewhere, don't you?

TOUR PLANNER: Yes, and the place to start is . . .

CONTINUE ON YOUR OWN

3. Two students may participate in this role play either out of class as a fun way to review the chapter or as an in-class exercise. One plays the role of a travel student and the other plays the role of a tour planner. Please read the script and then pick up the conversation in your own words.

TRAVEL STUDENT: This 18-day tour of Asia you are putting together looks like a lot of fun. At $7,200 per person, I guess it ought to be.

TOUR PLANNER: You might be surprised how much some people are willing to pay for tours that they consider enjoyable. As you know, we have some tours where the breakdown of price per day is substantially more than on this one.

TRAVEL STUDENT: There is one thing I don't understand. On this tour you have a substantial amount of free time. On many of the less expensive tours there is very little free time. It looks like these people are paying a lot of money and are getting a whole lot less on their tour.

TOUR PLANNER: I understand why it appears that way. Actually, when you look at what is included on this tour compared to the less expensive tours,

SIGHTSEEING POINT #3 ITINERARY

DRAFT ITINERARY PREPARATION FORM

ITINERARY FOR: _____

DAY ONE - EARLY MORNING

0600 _____

0630 _____

0700 _____

0730 _____

0800 _____

0830 _____

0900 _____

DRAFT ITINERARY PREPARATION FORM

ITINERARY FOR: _____

DAY ONE - LATE MORNING & EARLY AFTERNOON

0930 _____

1000 _____

1030 _____

1100 _____

1130 _____

1200 _____

1230 _____

DRAFT ITINERARY PREPARATION FORM

ITINERARY FOR: _____

DAY ONE - MID AFTERNOON

1300 _____

1330 _____

1400 _____

1430 _____

1500 _____

1530 _____

1600 _____

DRAFT ITINERARY PREPARATION FORM

ITINERARY FOR: _____

DAY ONE - LATE AFTERNOON - EARLY EVENING

1630 _____

1700 _____

1730 _____

1800 _____

1830 _____

1900 _____

1930 _____

DRAFT ITINERARY PREPARATION FORM

ITINERARY FOR: _____

DAY ONE - LATE NIGHT

2000 _____

2030 _____

2100 _____

2130 _____

2200 _____

2230 _____

2300 _____

RESTAURANT ITINERARY

DRAFT ITINERARY PREPARATION FORM

ITINERARY FOR: _____

DAY ONE - EARLY MORNING

0600 _____

0630 _____

0700 _____

0730 _____

0800 _____

0830 _____

0900 _____

DRAFT ITINERARY PREPARATION FORM

ITINERARY FOR: _____

DAY ONE - LATE MORNING & EARLY AFTERNOON

0930 _____

1000 _____

1030 _____

1100 _____

1130 _____

1200 _____

1230 _____

DRAFT ITINERARY PREPARATION FORM

ITINERARY FOR: _____

DAY ONE - MID AFTERNOON

1300 _____

1330 _____

1400 _____

1430 _____

1500 _____

1530 _____

1600 _____

DRAFT ITINERARY PREPARATION FORM

ITINERARY FOR: _____

DAY ONE - LATE AFTERNOON - EARLY EVENING

1630 _____

1700 _____

1730 _____

1800 _____

1830 _____

1900 _____

1930 _____

DRAFT ITINERARY PREPARATION FORM

ITINERARY FOR: _____

DAY ONE - LATE NIGHT

2000 _____

2030 _____

2100 _____

2130 _____

2200 _____

2230 _____

2300 _____

2. Break into groups of no more than three students working together. Yours will probably be the same group that has been working together in the development of a one-day tour since the beginning of the course.

Guide List

Determine who the local step-on guides and hosts/hostesses will be. Review Figure 6–4, a sample tour guide list. Prepare a guide list with the title "Guide List for (Name of your tour)" at the top. This list should have the name and title of each guide/host/hostess, contact information for each person and should note

FIGURE 6–4 SAMPLE TOUR GUIDE LIST

Jack Brakman	$15 per hour	4 Hour minimum

Jack is a retired business executive and is available at almost all times and on almost all days. He leaves town in October and February each year, however. Jack is physically active, always wears a suit and tie, and handles himself in a very professional manner. He is especially good on military history and the history of downtown Denver. He has read at least twelve books on the history of Denver and is excellent at bringing out the interesting tidbits—many of them humorous during his tours. Jack does not work with a script, but prides himself on his knowledge (often block by block) of downtown Denver. Jack is also excellent on Colorado Springs tours, one of the most knowledgeable of all guides regarding the Air Force Academy and the Olympic Training Facility. Jack's voice carries well without a mike for groups of up to twenty, but he needs a mike for larger groups. In addition to his specialties, Jack has experience with and can handle the following destinations: Pike's Peak Cog Rail, Manitou Springs, Cave of the Winds, Rocky Mt. National Park, The Broadmoor, Georgetown, Silverthorne, Red Rocks, the Denver Foothills, and Estes Park. Contact: 555–4433 (If not available, Jack's wife, Eleanor, keeps his schedule and can confirm an assignment—otherwise, leave a phone message).

Roxanne Axel	$18 per hour	2 Hour minimum

Roxanne is a retired school teacher who has done step-on guide work and over the road work for nearly twenty years. She is very active in the Professional Guides Association of America—especially the Rocky Mountain Chapter. Roxanne authors a guide column in the local guide association newsletter titled, "Roxanne's Rubricks." She is considered THE authority on Colorado—especially Front Range Colorado guide facts. Roxanne prides herself on being professional, dressing well, and always arriving at least thirty minutes prior to the contracted arrival time. Roxanne knows most of the tour bus drivers in Colorado and her rapport with them is exceptional. Her presentations are clipped, factual, and straightforward with some, but not a lot of humor. Roxanne is an expert on the Molly Brown House, the Ninth Street Historic Park (including Golda Meir's house), culinary Colorado, and Colorado's Wild West image (Buffalo Bill's Grave, the Cowboy Museum, etc.). Roxanne's vast experience gives her an edge over most other guides for all Colorado tours, except hard adventure tours, which she does not do. Roxanne is available throughout the year and guide work is her only occupation. Contact: 210–3489 (leave a message—she will probably be gone—leading a tour).

the experience and background for each person. Finally, a note should be made as to whether or not the guide/host/hostess will be working from a script or will be making a nonscripted presentation.

3. Break into groups of no more than three students working together. Yours will probably be the same group that has been working together in the development of a one-day tour since the beginning of the course.

Optional and Free Time Activity List

Identify optional activities available to tour participants. Most of these will be available during allocated "free time." However, some may be available during scheduled activity times. For example, if you are planning a shopping tour during part of your one-day trip, you may also offer tour participants one or more other optional activities during the time of the shopping tour in case some of the members wish to do something other than shop.

These activities should be identified clearly as being "optional" during a scheduled activity or during free time. Optional activities should also be clearly identified as being free (at no expense) or additional expense activities. If there is an additional cost, each cost should be clearly identified in terms of the amount of the cost and the person or persons who will be paid. If payment must be rendered in some way or form other than that which is customary, advise accordingly. For example, some sightseeing companies only accept cash payment and others will only accept credit card payment. Some of the credit card acceptance vendors will only accept specific credit cards. These limitations should be noted.

CHAPTER 7

Pre-Tour Management and Processing Considerations

OBJECTIVES

Upon completion of this chapter, the student will be able to:

1. List the documents which might be required from clients taking multi-day international tours.
2. Prepare a visa checklist for a multi-day international tour.
3. Explain the documentation required by countries with strict currency controls and the reasons why tourists and tour companies should make certain that documentation control forms are maintained and recorded accurately.
4. Describe major points to be considered by tour members and tour managers regarding luggage.

Pre-Tour Document Considerations

A wide variety of tasks for both the client and the tour manager need to be completed by the tour company prior to the start of the trip. This chapter identifies major pre-tour tasks and breaks them down into:

1. document considerations;
2. monetary considerations;
3. luggage considerations;
4. special event handling considerations; and
5. pre-tour client handling.

The chapter will also address the tour manager's personal pre-tour preparation.

For international tours, the tour company needs to consider the documentation required from clients and for the tour company itself. Keep in mind that many governments will not let a traveler clear customs if all documentation is not in order. Required client documents may include from none to all of the following:

- currently valid passports;
- currently valid tourist visas;
- health cards with all required immunizations (shots) documented;
- completed entry cards;
- completed currency control forms; and
- in some cases, a paid-for airline ticket for travel out of the country.

Frequently, if the traveler does not have all required documents or if the documents are not in order and up-to-date, the destination country will require the airline to take the traveler back out of the country at no cost to the country refusing admission. Because this can be a substantial expense to any air carrier, most airlines now check all documentation of departing passengers, before allowing travelers to board their flight. Tour companies, of course, need to do everything possible to ensure that clients and the tour manager meet or exceed minimum documentation requirements. One way to make sure this is accomplished is to use a *control card* (see Figure 7-1). A *tour member card* is kept in the file of each member so as to remind the file reader to check if all documents are there. A *group tour control card*, kept in the business file for the tour, reminds the reader of the documents (as well as pending actions) required for the tour and for the tour manager.

In many cases, it is easy for American tourists to travel to Western Europe, Canada, and parts of the Caribbean because many of these destinations do not require Americans to have visas, passports, health cards, currency control forms, or return airline tickets. Some require entry cards, but typically they can be completed on the plane or right before entry into the country if necessary.

Most other countries do require at least a currently valid passport and currently valid visa. Many also require health cards. The U.S. government usually will require a currently valid health card for travelers returning from countries where diseases are known to be prevalent. Currency control forms are also required in a few countries. Several of these countries are strict in terms of the documentation requirement concerning all currency brought into that country. The amount of currency brought into the country must balance with currency and receipts brought out of the country.

Relatively few countries require travelers to have departure airline tickets proving that they can depart from that country at the time of entrance. Tour members seldom have a problem with this since their tickets are round trip. However, since some tour companies sell ground-only packages, it is beneficial to check with clients to make certain that they have their tickets before they start the tour if the tour is sold on a ground-only basis.

FIGURE 7-1 GROUP TOUR CONTROL CARD
(TO BE MAINTAINED IN BUSINESS FILE)

TOUR _____		DATES _____
ACTION REQUIRED	REQUIRED BY (DATE)	STATUS OR DISPOSITION

THIS CARD IS TO BE KEPT IN THE FRONT OF THE FILE AT ALL TIMES. IT IS TO BE USED AS A CONTINUING MEMORANDUM RECORD OF ACTIONS REQUIRED AND TAKEN. KEEP IN NEAT AND READABLE FORM.

Reproduced with permission from 4 Seasons Tours and Travel, Wilmington, DE.

Client and Tour Manager Passports

Tour companies are not allowed to apply for passports for their clients or for their tour managers. These must be applied for by the individuals themselves. They may route these applications through an approved passport processing visa service rather than through the passport office of a local post office, if they so desire. The tour company can obtain blank passport application forms and mail these to clients with directions regarding how the client can obtain a passport. Many tour companies do this. The tour company can also require tour members and the tour manager to send their passport numbers and expiration date for their passports to the tour company and may (some do) refuse to issue tour documents until and unless these numbers are received. Some tour companies request photocopies of the face page of client passports so that they may record all pertinent passport data, keeping this information on file until the client returns from the trip. Therefore, if the passport is lost enroute, this information will assist in obtaining a replacement passport as rapidly as possible from the closest U.S. embassy.

Client and Tour Manager Visas

Visas are issued by the consulates of the countries being visited. Tour companies are not allowed to issue visas and most tour companies will not process visa requests on behalf of clients. However, most tour companies provide clients with a listing of the visas that are needed. Some countries require visas while other countries do not. Therefore visas may not be needed for all countries being visited. On some tours, especially those to parts of Western Europe, no visa will be required if the tour member is a U.S. citizen.

When visas are needed, and especially when they are needed for several countries, tour companies normally recommend that clients obtain visas through a local visa service. Although these services do charge clients a processing/service fee to obtain visas for them, visa services are skilled at identifying which visas are needed and obtaining them in the correct order so that none will expire prior to the date the client will be departing from the issuing country. This is especially important for travelers undertaking lengthy tours which go to many countries, especially in the Far East, the Middle East, Africa, and Latin America. As with passport front pages, many tour companies require clients to send photocopies of the visa pages from their passports to the tour company prior to issuing tour documents so that the tour company can be certain that all needed visas have been obtained. In addition, as with passports, having a photocopy of the visa may be beneficial in obtaining a replacement visa if the passport is lost and a new one must be issued prior to the use of the visa.

Since visas are normally issued in the language of the country being visited, most travelers are unable to determine whether or not an accurate visa has been issued. If a mistake was made on the date of entry, the duration of validity, or a required exit date, and if this data appears in a language with which the traveler is totally unfamiliar, there is no way for the traveler to know that an error was made. Many tour companies, however, will employ a native or a person who knows the language of the destination country to review visa copies to make certain that the data is correct. In this way, if mistakes are made, they can often be caught and corrected prior to the tour departure.

Client and Tour Manager Health Cards

Yellow, World Health Organization health cards are required by many countries as documentation booklets for registering immunizations required of travelers entering their country. These may be obtained either at no cost or at a very small cost through doctors, clinics, and some hospitals in the United States. They may also be ordered directly from the World Health Organization. Many tour companies maintain an inventory of these blank booklets and mail one to each client when the tour is going to destinations requiring immunizations.

Tour companies need to be especially careful about flights booked for their clients returning to the United States. Even when a traveler may have been to only a few countries exempted from United States requirements for immunizations for American citizens returning from the country, if the traveler is returning on a flight which originated or stopped in a country where diseases are known to infect members of the population, the U.S. government normally will not allow returning citizens or others to enter the country without having up-to-date immunizations protecting them from such disease(s).

Therefore, if travelers are returning to the United States from England, for example, and the return flight originates in countries in Asia, the Middle East, or Africa where there is a substantial amount of disease, then the U.S. citizen traveler will be expected to have protective immunizations prior to reentering. Most tour companies, therefore, will book flights which originate in the country of destination for those returning back to the United States or will purposely avoid using flights originating in or stopping in a country where there is a disease.

The U.S. government and the World Health Organization list immunization requirements for each country of the world. All major computer reservation systems incorporate these lists in their programs so that travel agents may access up-to-date information on immunization requirements. However, for legal reasons it is wise to refer travelers to their own medical practitioners (doctors) to obtain a listing of doctor recommended immunizations. Some tour companies protect themselves by sending clients a list with a cover letter indicating that the list is compiled as a combination of WHO (World Health Organization) and U.S. government documented requirements for pertinent countries (those on the itinerary). The letter urges travelers to see their own doctor to determine any additional recommended immunizations and to obtain the shots. Tour company officials, not being doctors, should neither recommend immunizations

FIGURE 7-2 ACCIDENT REPORT FORM

4 SEASONS TOURS AND TRAVEL

1010 North Union Street #6
Wilmington, DE U.S.A. 19805
(302) 594-1030 Telex: 281241

ACCIDENT REPORT FORM

NAME OF PASSENGER(S) _____

ADDRESS _____

PHONE _____

ACCIDENT OCCURRED AT _____

_____

_____

TIME _____

MEDICAL ASSISTANCE _____

   1. Describe treatment, if any _____

_____

_____

   2. Any medication prescribed _____

SIGNATURE OF PERSON GIVING TREATMENT _____

ESCORT SIGNATURE _____ DATE _____

PASSENGER SIGNATURE _____
& RELEASE

Reproduced with permission from 4 Seasons Tours and Travel, Wilmington, DE.

nor administer medications. They should draw upon experts both before the tour and (in accidents or medical emergencies) during the tour (see Figure 7-2).

All countries, including the United States, require that the WHO Yellow Health Booklet be completed by the doctor administering the shots indicating the date of immunization and the signature of the doctor who administered the immunization for each shot or immunization administered. It is important for both the client and the tour company to review the WHO shot record to make certain that both the date of administration of the shot and the signature of the doctor appear. Some countries have been known to refuse to admit travelers when the date of the shot or the signature of the doctor have not been recorded.

As with visas and passports, some tour companies require travelers to send them a photocopy of their health cards showing the signatures and dates of immunization. These photocopies are reviewed to make certain that all necessary shots have been obtained and will still be in effect throughout the duration of the tour. The photocopies are then retained until the end of the tour in case the shot record is lost.

Client and Tour Manager Entry Cards

Most countries requiring entry cards have a standard card which is provided free to tour operators. Many tour operators maintain an inventory of entry cards for each tour destination country. These can be sent to tour members for completion and returned to the tour company, but because many are very short (requiring only the name, address, and phone number of the client), some tour companies either will send them to clients, but not require that they be completed and returned, or give them to the tour manager to distribute on the airplane enroute. They are collected by the tour manager prior to entering the country. If they are mailed to the client without a requirement that the client return them, a note accompanying the blank card suggests to the client that they retain the completed card and keep it with their passport so that it may be filled out and presented at the time of entrance at the destination country. Usually, the tour manager is given an additional supply of blank cards in case the client loses or forgets to bring the one that was provided in the mail.

Some countries will provide airlines with a supply of blank entry cards, requiring inflight services personnel to distribute these shortly before arrival at the destination airport. When this is the case, the tour company does not need to be concerned with having a supply of cards or with receiving cards back for review prior to departure on the trip. However, even when this is the case, it is usually wise for the tour manager to bring extra blank cards in case a client loses the card after it has been completed.

Client and Tour Manager Currency Control Forms

Few countries require currency control as it relates to tourists, but those that do have currency controls do not follow a single standard. Currency control requirements can vary substantially from country to country. Generally speaking, however, when tourist currency control is maintained, the client is required to document all currency brought into the country and to record this currency on a currency control form. As the client exchanges money and makes purchases in the country, receipts for the currency exchange and receipts for the items purchased must be retained by the traveler. When the traveler departs from the country, either the same currency control form or a separate currency control document will be completed indicating the amount of money brought into the country, the exchanges made, the purchases made, and the amount of money brought out. All must balance.

It is essential in working with currency control that travelers be advised and understand completely the rules, regulations, and processes involved. If the tour company does not thoroughly explain these, it is easy for a tour member not to understand, and to either throw away or loose one or more of the necessary documents. It is especially important, under these circumstances, to warn travelers against exchanging money at locations other than government authorized locations (usually government banks) in spite of the fact that the black market currency exchange rate may be substantially better. Normally, nonbank currency exchanges are considered illegal. The traveler can face either stiff fines or imprisonment as a penalty for their use.

When tours are run to countries which maintain currency control, normally the tour company will send an explanation letter together with a copy of the currency control form to clients prior to departure. They will usually require the tour manager to explain currency control in detail prior to entering the country and to remind clients during their stay in the country that they must maintain all required documents and not to exchange money at a location other than an authorized bank.

Currency control forms should not be completed by clients prior to departure. Instead, they should be completed immediately before entering the country. Usually, these are completed on the flight enroute or on the tour bus immediately before crossing the border into the country. They can only be accurately completed after the last purchase is made by the client before entering a country having currency control requirements.

Client and Tour Manager Airline Tickets

Only a few countries require travelers to have departure airline tickets before they allow the traveler to enter the country. For all-inclusive tours in which both land and air are purchased from tour companies by the tour client, documenting the departure ticket is not a problem. Normally, the tour planner prepares this documentation, listing departure airline tickets for each client prior to the start of the tour so that the customs officer receives a central list showing the ticket numbers for each client in the party. This listing is made up well in advance in multiple copies by the tour company, since all airline tickets are issued for and processed through the tour company.

However, for tours which are marketed on a ground-only basis, the tour company will normally require proof of round trip air ticket purchase from the client prior to accepting the client on the tour. This is a listing of the routings and ticket numbers. The form is completed by the client and returned to the tour company. To ensure accuracy, some tour companies ask for a photocopy of the entire airline ticket. The tour company prepares a master list from the completed forms.

Other Client and Tour Manager Documents

Some tour companies, on occasion, will require other documents from clients and the tour manager. Forms identifying client preferences such as smoking and non-smoking, meal restrictions, and so forth are usually requested but are seldom required.

Pre-Tour Monetary Considerations

Pre-tour monetary considerations include concerns about fund transfers, vendor payments, and the cash and documents carried with the tour manager enroute. In addition, some companies prepare written guidelines for clients, making recommendations regarding how they might wish to prepare for their financial needs while traveling.

Fund Transfers

With the value of the U.S. dollar vis á vis other currencies changing on a rapid basis, tour companies find themselves in the position of advertising tour costs in U.S. dollars and collecting dollar payments for tours while making payments to vendors for tour services in the vendor's currency. In recent years, this has made it very difficult for many tour companies to make a profit. When faced with this problem, the tour operator has few choices. One is to go ahead and run the tour at the price announced, either breaking even or, in some cases, losing money because of the transfer valuation differences.

A second alternative is to increase the price to tour members after announcing and publishing a lower price. This makes the tour operator look bad and it often results in a loss of tour members who decide not to take the tour at the higher price. A third alternative, opted for by many, is to price the tour based upon projected exchange rates, allowing substantial leeway in case of a large exchange rate differential between the time of the pricing of the tour and the payment to tour vendors. This, however, can result in the tour operator pricing himself out of the market by not being competitive with other tour companies offering the same or essentially the same tour.

One of the best options for tour operators, however, is to market the tour a long time before departure, collecting substantial up-front deposits at about the same time that vendor deposits are required. When tour client deposits and tour vendor payments come in and are made shortly after pricing and publicizing the tour, the tour operator will usually find far less currency fluctuations than might occur if there are six to eight months between the pricing and the payments. Also, if required deposits are substantial, sufficient funds may be transferred to the destination country and held in a bank, earning interest in the currency of the country until the monies are needed to pay tour vendors. This, of course, also reduces the risk undertaken in dealing with currency fluctuations.

One effective fund transfer technique is to identify seasonal patterns relating to exchange rates and to transfer funds into accounts in the countries where vendors need to be paid at the time of year that historically is best in terms of exchange rate. These seasonal fluctuations in exchange rate highs and lows are not found in every destination country. However, by studying exchange rates in all tour destination countries, many tour companies have found that patterns often exist and that they can save money by making their fund transfers at the time that is most favorable. Even when historical study does not reveal a pattern, tour companies still save exchange processing fees if they lump financial exchanges into no more than two or three per year per country since a processing fee is levied each time an exchange is made.

Vendor Payments

Vendor payments are normally made on a pre-determined basis with the payment dates entered into the vendor contracts. Payments may include:

1. one or more pre-payments of all or of a portion of the ultimate amount owed;
2. on the spot payment at the time of check-in of the group or at the time of check-out of the group;
3. post-tour billing to a credit card number which has been provided in advance;
4. post-tour billing by the vendor itemizing the services and products provided and with normally a thirty or a sixty day payment period; and
5. another less conventional agreed-upon arrangement.

Variations of each of the standard payment arrangements are found. Vendors and tour operators negotiate payment details to determine a mutually agreed upon arrangement and then write this into their contract. The payment arrangement which is most favorable to a tour operator, of course, is one where the tour operator is billed after the tour receives the products or services provided by the vendor. The tour operator then has between 30 and 60 days to make payment. This, of course, is the least favorable arrangement for the vendor. Therefore, this arrangement is seldom obtained by the tour company, but if the tour company agrees to other terms favorable to the vendor (such as service price) or if the vendor is anxious to obtain the business, these arrangements sometimes can be worked out.

Pre-Payment Arrangements

With many vendors a pre-payment deposit will be required either at the time the reservation for services is made or at the time the contract is issued. Some bus companies, for example, have a standard requirement that a nonrefundable deposit must be paid at the time a firm reservation for the bus is made. They will not put the bus on their reservation schedule until a deposit is received. The same arrangement sometimes occurs with hotels in blocking group space and with sightseeing vendors in reserving spectator seats or in providing tour group access to a sightseeing point of interest (for example, an antique building). With most vendors, however, the requirement for an up-front deposit, and especially for a nonrefundable deposit is totally negotiable depending upon the demand or expected demand for the product or the service.

For example, a small Boston tour operator periodically sells a European tour which takes place during the off season. Because hotel rooms are almost empty, the planner is able to negotiate good terms for the dates when the hotel rooms are booked. Although the terms he requires are considerably more liberal than the hotel is accustomed to providing, the options available during the height of off season are so considerable that he can dictate his own terms. There simply are no other tours coming through at the time nor are there other clients. Therefore, the hotels (and many of the other vendors) have no choice but to accept his terms if they wish to have the hotel rooms occupied during the time that his tour group is in their city.

On the other hand, tour operators planning tours which go into the same city during the height of the season have little or no negotiating ability. Hotel marketers know they will fill the rooms. Therefore, they need not negotiate favorable terms for the tour operator.

On-The-Spot Payment

On-the-spot payment arrangements are made with some vendors more often than with others. It is a rare arrangement to make, but such an arrangement occurs with some transportation companies and sightseeing firms. For example, in taking short train trips, a reservation can be made on the phone. However, since payment will be made on the basis of the actual number of people who go on the short train sightseeing trip, and since some members of the tour group may elect to go shopping or to engage in some other activity, frequently the vendor will accept a check or cash payment at the time the tickets are actually picked up and for the actual number of persons on the trip.

In a similar manner, it is customary to pay for restaurant meals based upon the food and drinks actually consumed. This, of course, is a payment that is made on the spot after the meal is over. Hotel vendors will vary in terms of on-the-spot payment, but relatively few will require payment at the time of check out. Many hotels work with tour companies by billing the company for the actual number of rooms used (unless they are short of the guaranteed amount) with payment not expected until one week or longer after the rendering of their bills.

Credit and Post-Tour Billing

Credit card payment acceptance is common with many vendors. Although some companies which are new to the tour industry will find that they must pay vendor bills on the spot or in advance, experienced tour companies often are given an option to pay against a bill received after the tour has left the city. This post-tour billing arrangement is customary in the industry, but only for experienced tour companies.

Other Vendor Payment Arrangements

Although the pre-payment, on-the-spot payment, credit card payment, and post-tour billing arrangements are the standard arrangements used in the industry, any combination of these is not unusual. Other types of arrangements are also sometimes found in dealing with vendors.

Tour Manager Traveling with Cash and Documents

One of the concerns that many tour companies have is the need for tour managers to travel with substantial amounts of cash and with valuable documents. Tour managers normally carry large briefcases resembling those carried by pilots. These are separated into compartments for each particular type of item so that it is easy for the tour manager to find the document or material needed at the required time. These briefcases are bulky and heavy. Frequently, tour managers find themselves in a position, however, of needing to leave them in the sightseeing bus or in the hotel, especially at times when there will be a substantial amount of activity throughout the day. The amount of activity can cause the briefcase to be a hindrance.

Arrangements for the handling of cash and documents vary, but most tour companies plan for tour managers to have access to a local bank account every two or three days so that they need not carry all monies needed on the tour. In almost all cases, hotel safety deposit boxes are used to secure cash and documents at night or during multi-day stays in hotels. Most tour managers will have a smaller briefcase which fits into the larger one in which the cash and documents needed for the day can be placed while the balance is kept in the hotel safe. This arrangement normally works well and minimizes the amount of risk taken by the tour manager in carrying cash and documents.

Pre-Tour Luggage Considerations

For single-day tours with no overnight stay involved, it is wise to advise clients that they should not plan to bring anything other than a small bag for a jacket or raincoat, if necessary, and any small items they may wish to have with them while on the bus. Travelers should be discouraged from bringing suitcases or large bags with them on one-day tours since these tend to take up room on the bus and are seldom needed.

For multi-day tours, it is most beneficial to prepare and mail a list of recommended items to bring. Most air carriers severely limit the amount of free luggage that can be taken with a client especially that which may be brought on board the plane in the cabin with the traveler. The limit imposed when traveling internationally tends to be much more readily enforced than the usually more generous limits allowed within the United States. Clients should be reminded, especially on lengthy international tours, that they will want to bring souvenirs back home and that they should leave space in their luggage for such items.

In most cases, it is wise to recommend that clients bring multi-purpose clothing (that which does not need to be dry cleaned) or wash and wear articles. A suggestion many will appreciate is to bring a portable clothes line. This cord has suction cups at both ends and can be placed in a bathtub. Wash and wear items left after one's morning shower will usually be dry upon returning to the room after a day of sightseeing.

If the tour is a budget or medium-priced tour and if the tour is a fast-moving one with only one or two days at most in any hotel, clients should be advised that getting dry cleaning completed during a stay may be very difficult and will usually be expensive. In addition, finding soap with which to clean wash and wear clothing is frequently difficult. Some tour companies recommend that a small amount of soap flakes be packed for hand washing wash and wear items.

For multi-day bus tours, it is usually wise to recommend a suitcase which will be kept in the storage/luggage compartment below or at the back of the bus when traveling between cities. A small carry-on bag may be kept with them at their seat or in an overhead rack above their seats for any items that clients may need enroute. More than this is usually inappropriate and should be discouraged.

Pre-Tour Special Event Handling Considerations

When there are special events included on the tour, often there are also special types of handling or arrangements that must be worked out in advance so that the clients may maximize their enjoyment and participation in the event. If the event is one where they will be seeing a parade or a performance, especially when it is outside, arrangements need to be made, if it is at all possible for seating in an area that will provide the best possible view. Normally, this means reserved, ideally including roped off sections. If possible, entrance to the event prior to general audience entrance is desired. A decision will need to be made as to whether or not individual tickets will be given to each member of the tour or if all tour members will be required to enter together. In either case, this should be thought out in advance and preparations made for either tickets for distribution or a gathering point and time so that everybody is together when entering.

In some cases, special transportation arrangements may need to be made or other types of special handling will need to be arranged. Whatever the arrangements, the tour planner should think through the entire process and, if at all possible, consider what might go wrong and plan to be able to overcome any obstacles.

Pre-Tour Client Handling

Before departing on a tour, clients expect to hear from the tour company. Normally, the first contact comes at the time when reservations are made. Sometimes reservations are made by the client. Other times reservations are made by the travel agency. Either way, the client expects to have a confirmation of the reservation and a receipt for payment (see Figure 7-3).

Follow ups to the reservation should be made on a regular basis. Most clients prefer to be contacted on a frequent basis. Often small tour companies obtain a substantial number of repeat clients partly because of the way the client is treated on the tour, but also because of the way in which the client is treated before and after the tour by staff at the tour company headquarters. Clients like to feel that the tour company cares about their individual needs and concerns. Most clients will not call the tour company every day asking questions, but would like to have the opportunity to call from time to time when questions may arise. They would also like to receive periodic briefings from the company. Many welcome the receipt of forms to be completed. Clients feel that after obtaining their passports, visas, and the like, and sending copies to the tour company, a letter advising that all documentation has been completed and all documents are in order is appropriate. This type of letter makes the tour member feel comfortable. It is a closing to this part of the pre-tour preparation for the client.

Tour clients also like to hear from the tour manager prior to the tour. They want to get to know the tour manager to some degree prior to the start of the tour. This often can occur when tour managers check in early. For many tour companies, this is a part of the tour manager's personal pre-tour preparation, but there are other parts of their preparation as well.

The Tour Manager's Personal Pre-Tour Preparation

Most tour managers prepare well for their tours. Of course, they all must pack the clothing they will wear, making certain that all needed items are included. They take nothing extra. It would add to the weight or the bulkiness. They also must make sure that personal hygiene materials and equipment are included.

```
                    4 SEASONS TOURS AND TRAVEL

                 1010 N. UNION STREET, STE. #6

                    WILMINGTON, DE  19805


        We have received your deposit in the amount

    of $_____  for your reservation (s) on the


    _____


    departing _____.

    Party Reserved: _____


    If you should have any questions, please feel free
    to call us at (302)594-1030.


            THANK YOU FOR YOUR RESERVATION!
```

```
4 Seasons Tours and Travel
1010 N. Union Street, Ste. #6
Wilmington, DE  19805




                _____


                _____


                _____
```

FIGURE 7-3 RESERVATION RECEIPT

Reproduced with permission from 4 Seasons Tours and Travel, Wilmington, DE.

Most professional tour managers will make an effort to arrive at the tour company headquarters offices one or two days prior to the departure of the tour so that they may either attend a formal briefing or they may brief themselves prior to the tour's departure. This briefing includes a review of client documents. Some tour companies encourage tour managers to pick up the phone and call clients using an 800 toll-free number. They conduct brief discussions with each tour member that they can reach by phone. This increases company costs, but it prepares both the tour manager and the tour members in a way that usually starts the tour member/tour manager relationship very comfortably.

The ultimate responsibility for assisting clients from point to point throughout the tour lies with the tour manager. Therefore, it is in the tour manager's best interest to make certain that all documentation is in order. If there is something that is missing or needs correction, the tour manager should make an effort to obtain the missing item or correct the problem as rapidly as possible.

Tour managers frequently review vendor arrangements in advance. Sometimes they will start their confirmation calls during their headquarters visit one or two days prior to starting the trip. In many cases, they will contact every vendor, making certain that they have the names of the contact people who will be working at or on-site at the time that they arrive. Wherever possible, they will speak with those individuals personally to make sure they know the names of the people to ask for and that those individuals know their name.

Some companies have tour managers attend a formal briefing reviewing all financial documentation, all itinerary items, and the tour manager itinerary. These reviews are conducted by the director of the documentation section, the tour planner, usually a financial executive, and sometimes other tour company employees.

Summary

Pre-tour management and processing includes making certain that all documents are in order, addressing and taking care of monetary concerns, advising clients and assisting tour guides with luggage and baggage handling considerations, preparing for special events, and handling the special pre-tour needs of both clients and tour managers. Documents may include all, some, or none of the following:

- passports;
- visas;
- health cards;
- entry cards;
- currency control forms and
- airline tickets.

Pre-tour monetary considerations include concerns regarding fund transfers and vendor payments. The cash carried by tour managers during the tour is another area of concern.

Clients will need to be advised regarding the luggage they will be allowed to take with them during the trip as a whole. Carry-on bags usually may be brought on day trips.

For special events, it is necessary to make certain that all arrangements have been completed in advance. Appropriate seating should be reserved wherever possible.

Pre-tour client needs are handled by tour companies in different ways. Most have some type of forms that need to be completed. Many will call the client after the reservation has been taken to obtain further information or to determine any special needs or concerns of the client. Some tour companies require their guides/managers to telephone tour members one or more days prior to the tour. Some ask the tour manager to arrive at the tour company headquarters one or two days in advance to review paperwork, obtain a pre-tour briefing, and to review client files. It is at this time that they sometimes also call clients long-distance to get to know them prior to the start of the trip.

DISCUSSION QUESTIONS

These questions may be discussed by two or more students outside of class as a fun way of reviewing this chapter or they may be discussed by everyone during class for a more wide-ranging discussion.

1. What documents might be required of tour members when entering and exiting countries visited during their tour?

2. Why might it be easier for American tourists to travel to Western Europe, Canada, and parts of the Caribbean?

3. What are the advantages to clients in working with a visa service to obtain visas rather than communicating directly with the consulates of the countries involved?

4. In countries having strict currency controls, why might a tourist be better off by exchanging money at locations where the exchange rate may well be substantially less beneficial to the tourist than at other places where currency might be exchanged?

5. What is one of the best ways a tour operator might counter the potential problem of a decrease in exchange rate (and the value of the U.S. dollar) between the time the tour is announced and the time when payments for tour services are due?

6. Why is the Boston tour operator discussed in this chapter able to offer inexpensive Winter tours of Europe almost every year?

7. For what kinds of services/products might tour companies be required to make on-the-spot payments?

8. What precautions might tour managers take to insure the safe keeping of money they are required to have in order to make payments enroute during a tour?

9. How do some tour managers handle the problem of the need to travel lightly on short sightseeing trips or one-day tours in spite of the fact that they must bring a substantial amount of luggage with them on an international multi-day tour?

10. What pre-tour preparations do many tour companies recommend and expect from their tour managers?

ROLE PLAY EXERCISES

1. Two students may participate in this role play either out of class as a fun way to review the chapter or as an in-class exercise. One plays the role of a tour member/client and the other plays the role of the tour manager in charge of the tour. Please read the script and then pick up the conversation in your own words.

   TOUR CLIENT: I brought an extra suitcase that is completely empty. Aunt Bea asked me to stop at Harrods and pick up a full set of her Spode china in their bargain basement. Will I have any problem bringing this with me on the rest of the tour and getting it through customs when I return back to America?

   TOUR MANAGER: We will only be in downtown London one day on the tour and that is the very first day in Europe. If you bring your suitcase with you and explain to store personnel as soon as you enter, it should be possible for them to pack the china in the suitcase quite well. However, no matter how well they pack it, you should be concerned about potential breakage enroute.

   TOUR CLIENT: I bought a hardback suitcase that is quite large. If they pack it well, won't that eliminate breakage?

   TOUR MANAGER: Probably not. You may very well have to open your suitcase several times enroute for customs inspection and even if they do perform an outstandingly good job of packing, the way suitcases are treated at airports there is a good chance some or possibly all of the china will break.

   TOUR CLIENT: I promised Aunt Bea a full set of china. How do you recommend that I handle the matter?

   TOUR MANAGER: You have several options. Perhaps the best option is to . . .

   CONTINUE ON YOUR OWN

2. Two students may participate in this role play either out of class as a fun way to review the chapter or as an in-class exercise. One plays the role of a tour client and the other plays the role of the tour manager in charge of the tour. Please read the script and then pick up the conversation in your own words.

TOUR CLIENT: These people here in Ugaristan don't know what they are doing. When we entered the country this morning I conveniently forgot to declare about $450 U.S. Nobody searched me or stopped me at the airport. I'm going to exchange it on the black market and buy precious stones to take back home. I'll simply put them in my pocket when leaving the country. I should make enough profit to more than cover my costs for the entire trip.

TOUR MANAGER: What you have already done is dangerous. I would recommend that you . . .

CONTINUE ON YOUR OWN

3. Two students may participate in this role play either out of class as a fun way to review the chapter or as an in-class exercise. One plays the role of a tour client and the other plays the role of the tour manager in charge of the tour. The tour manager is on the phone talking with the client and the time is one or two days before departure of the tour. Please read the script and then pick up the conversation in your own words.

TOUR MANAGER: I'm calling to introduce myself and to find out a little bit about you. We will be on tour together for the next couple of weeks and I want to make sure that it will be an enjoyable experience. Our records indicate that we have received copies of all your documentation except the copy of your immunization records.

TOUR CLIENT: It went out this morning. We just got the German Anti-Cobra-Venom Protection shot at 10 A.M. I wanted to make sure that it was recorded on the shot record before sending a copy to you, but we sent it overnight express mail. You should have it tomorrow.

TOUR MANAGER: That shot was optional for the Ugaristan tour and not recommended for the tour of Scandinavia. In fact, the cold weather we can expect to encounter in Scandinavia may cause a negative reaction to the shot.

TOUR CLIENT: I want to protect myself and my spouse against any possbile danger. When I saw the shot as optional on the Ugaristan trip I thought we ought to get that protection along with every other shot. In all, we probably had the doctor immunize us for about 42 different things. Are you a doctor? What right do you have to tell me that I should or should not get optional shots?

TOUR MANAGER: No. I'm not a doctor. But . . .

CONTINUE ON YOUR OWN

GROUP DISCUSSION SITUATION: SISSY STORMTROOPER'S UNDOCUMENTED CHOLERA IMMUNIZATION

Sissy Stormtrooper considers herself an unabashed coward. When it comes to shots, she is totally fearful. For years, Sissy has wanted to go to Calcutta during the Monsoon season to experience the excitement and the danger of the Monsoon. She has finally found a tour that has four days of free time in New Delhi and her travel agent assured her that she can fly down to Calcutta and spend the entire four days there. "It will be during the height of the Monsoon season," commented her travel agent, Nutty Mumbles. "Therefore, no tour operator will run a tour into Calcutta. It is just too dangerous. But if you choose to go there on your own, they will know nothing about it," mused Nutty.

Sissy purchased the India Highlights tour and Nutty Mumbles issued separate tickets for her to go into Calcutta. All arrangements were finalized a week ago. Finally, Sissy can relax as the plane takes off from JFK airport for India. "Next stop, New Delihi," thinks Sissy.

Someone approaches Sissy's seat. "I'm Takilla Turist, your tour manager for this trip," the six-foot, two Amazon-like woman intimates. "How are you doing?"

"I don't feel too well," whispers Sissy. "I think it may be a reaction to the cholera immunization. I kept postponing having it, but finally I went to a small clinic near JFK just before the flight," confides Sissy.

"No wonder you're feeling down, honey," suggests the Amazon woman. "You waited a long time for the immunization, didn't you?"

"Yes, I'm just a coward about shots. And they were in such a rush at the clinic. It certainly didn't help. Actually, I got there after they had closed the doors. I had to bang on the front door. I told them it was an emergency—that my flight left in two hours. The doctor had left, but a nurse gave me the immunization. The only thing was, the nurse entered the record of the immunization in my shot record, but the doctor wasn't there to sign it."

"It's unsigned!" the shocked tour manager exclaimed. "How did you get on the plane?"

"Well, since the doctor wasn't there and it would be illegal for the nurse to forge the doctor's signature, she wrote in the signature block where the doctor would normally sign the words 'Not Available'" Sissy whispered. "The nurse told me this had happened before. Since nobody actually reads the signatures of doctors, scribbling the words 'Not Available' in an almost unintelligible scroll, no one ever understands. They think it is the doctor's signature," reassured Sissy. "I'm sure there won't be any problem. I am feeling really bad, though. I just want to sleep to get rid of this fever, if you don't mind."

"I understand, honey," consoles Takilla. "I'm going to review all tour members' documents shortly. Let me take yours now and then you can just rest. I'll wake you up when we get to India," comforts Takilla.

Takilla is concerned. She takes Sissy's shot record and returns to her seat. Takilla reviews the record. She is shocked at how much the nurse's handwriting stands out. The statement, 'Not Available' is icy clear in its bright blue ink. Not only is it a bolder color than the ink in which all other signatures have been recorded, but it is in larger script as well. Knowing the health officials in New Delhi, Takilla has a strong concern about the ability of Sissy to get through immigration clearance. "Even if she makes it into New Delhi, when she returns to

New York City will U.S. health authorities let her back into America?" Takilla mentally muses.

Consider the situation. Decide among yourselves what you would do and how you would handle the situation if you were Takilla. Discuss the matter among yourselves. Be prepared to present your suggestions in a paper that will be no longer than three pages in length. Also make sure the paper is double spaced and typed. Be prepared to also present your suggestions verbally in class if your instructor suggests that you do so.

EXERCISE

1. Break into groups of no more than three students working together. Yours will probably be the same group that has been working together in the development of a one-day tour since the beginning of the course.

Review the itinerary below for the company's ASIA HIGHLIGHTS TOUR. Draw up a client document list identifying the documents each client will need to have in order to take this trip. Prepare a draft letter to clients advising them how they might obtain documents, the documents needed, and the way in which you (the tour company) will need to receive proof of documentation prior to the trip. Do not forget in your letter to advise when documents are needed. This trip leaves on January 05, next year and returns on January 31 next year.

ITINERARY

05 JAN FLY FROM LOS ANGELES TO BANGKOK	13 JAN BANGKOK	24 JAN TOKYO
06 JAN ARRIVE BANGKOK	14 JAN BANGKOK - KUALA LUMPUR	25 JAN TOKYO - HAKONE
07 JAN BANGKOK - PHITSANULOK - SUKOTHAI	15 JAN KUALA LUMPUR	26 JAN HAKONE - NAGOYA - TOBA
08 JAN SUKOTHAI - LAMPANG	16 JAN KUALA LUMPUR - SINGAPORE	27 JAN TOBA - ISE - KYOTO
09 JAN LAMPANG CHIANG RAI	17 JAN SINGAPORE - DENPASAR	28 JAN KYOTO - HIROSHIMA
10 JAN CHIANG RAI - CHIANG MAI	18 JAN DENPASAR	29 JAN HIROSHIMA - INLAND SEA-OSAKA
11 JAN CHIANG MAI	19 JAN DENPASAR	30 JAN OSAKA-TOKYO
12 JAN CHIANG MAI - BANGKOK	20 JAN DENPASAR - HONG KONG	31 JAN TOKYO - LOS ANGELES
	21 JAN HONG KONG	
	22 JAN HONG KONG - MACAU	
	23 JAN MACAU - HONG KONG - TOKYO	

CHAPTER 8
Tour Manuals

OBJECTIVES

Upon completion of this chapter, the student will be able to:

1. Explain what a tour manual is and why it is needed.

2. Write a draft tour manual for a one-day tour.

3. List the eight sections of a tour manual.

4. Explain what a tour report is and what information is needed to complete it.

What is a Tour Manual?

Tour manuals are policy and procedure manuals for guides, tour directors, and tour managers. They provide an understanding of how the tour company wants the tour to be conducted, providing guidelines for the ways in which tour guides, tour directors, and tour managers should handle situations which may come up. A tour manual is basically a reference book. It is seldom read cover to cover, although some tour companies require their guiding employees to read it completely when they are first hired and to sign a document indicating that they have read, understood it, and will follow its procedures. After that, it is normally treated as a reference to turn to when there is a concern or problem.

Why Have a Tour Manual?

Tour manuals provide a way for the tour company to develop tour standards. Since it is impossible for the guide or tour manager's supervisor to be with the tour while it is enroute, the tour manual provides an answer to questions which will allow for some uniformity of handling. It helps to establish a standard and a reputation for the tour company while giving guides and tour managers an answer to policy questions on location. In many cases, this means that a problem can be resolved right away rather than waiting until directions can be received from headquarters. Therefore, the manual can expedite the handling of difficult or uncomfortable matters.

How Many and What Kind of Manuals Should Be Used?

In developing manuals, tour companies usually find that a *policy and procedure manual* for each department or a single policy and procedures manual for all departments at the headquarters office is beneficial. However, the tour manual is designed for use by tour company guiding employees while they are out on tour. Therefore, the tour manual is normally a separate publication from the policy and procedures manual(s) designed for use at headquarters. The tour company, therefore, will usually have either two manuals (the tour manual and an internal policy and procedures manual) or more manuals depending upon how they decide to develop policy and procedures guidelines.

Tour Manual Ingredients

The contents of the tour manual will vary from company to company, but most have similar sections. Bill Teasdale, President of Premier Tours of Colorado, undertook a study of National Tour Association member tour manuals by requesting copies of manuals from 42 arbitrarily selected tour companies. Based upon the results of that study and two National Tour Association certification papers (*Operational Procedures for the Group Tour Manager* by Patricia Barnett, CTP with Barnett Tour and Travel, Inc. and *Tour Director Staff Development and Operator's Analysis* by Paul Weldin, CTP of Pressley Tours Inc.) the following content guidelines have been developed.

Most tour manuals have at least eight sections, though some are longer and some are shorter. These sections are broken down into the following categories, although they do not always appear in this order or with these titles:

1. General day-to-day responsibilities;
2. Specific tour policies and responsibilities;
3. Enroute;
4. Post-tour procedures and responsibilities;
5. Vendor relationships;
6. Guide/tour member relationships;
7. Emergency handling; and
8. Other.

Appendix number one contains tour manual sample pages. It incorporates suggestions from the Barnett and Weldin papers, from tour manual samples, and from correspondence received during the tour manual study.

General Day-to-Day Responsibilities

The general day-to-day responsibilities section of the tour manual normally includes, but is not limited to, sections relating to the image of the guide, general responsibilities, general rules, and daily routines. The image section emphasizes the appearance of the tour manager. Many guidelines are general, but others are very specific in their expectations. For example, some manual regulations are so specific that they require the tour manager to take a bath or a shower each day. Some have specific physical requirements, suggesting that guiding employees must keep in good physical condition. Some include size and weight measurement requirements which may not be exceeded. Some are even more specific. For example, several give a maximum and a minimum weight allowance in proportion to the height of the tour manager.

Many tour companies have uniforms and a number of tour manuals will describe requirements regarding how the tour manager should look when wearing that uniform. Some are specific. For example, one states that uniforms should always be pressed and that uniform jackets should be worn at all times except those which the manual describes. Many do not allow the wearing of caps, hats, or sunglasses. The wearing of company provided name tags is usually required when the guide/tour manager is on duty.

The general responsibilities and general rules section(s) vary considerably, but most tour manuals contain them. These usually relate to overall responsibility/rules. For example, many indicate that the tour guide/manager will be held accountable and responsible for the tour on a 24-hour basis from the time that the tour departs to the time that it returns. A number of manuals are very specific about fraternization with tour members and several stress the importance of treating tour members equally. One manual even requires guides to keep a listing of the compliments given to each tour member throughout the tour so that compliments are equally dispersed and all tour members are complimented on something. Many have rules relating to apparent attitude such as being gracious, smiling, and so forth.

The daily routines part of the general day-to-day responsibilities section of the tour manual is usually an overview list identifying what is expected of the guide/manager from the time the person wakes up (several manuals recommend a wake-up time) to the time when the guide/manager goes to bed. These are normally listed in a numerical sequence taking the guide/manager through the day in terms of each activity or procedure that tour companies expect to be completed each day. Confirmation calls and required daily paperwork completion are included in almost all tour manuals, but most manuals include between nine and 40 other daily routine specifications.

Specific Tour Policies and Responsibilities

Many break tour policies and responsibilities into three sections relating to the timing of the tour. The first section is the pre-tour. Some will break the pre-tour into that which is done one or two days before the tour operates and that which is done the first morning of the tour immediately prior to departure by air or bus.

The second section is enroute. It relates to the policies and procedures expected to be followed during the tour.

The third and last part of the specific tour policies and procedures relates to the post-tour. This is the follow-up that occurs when the tour bus returns or when the tour members disembark from the returning air flight.

The first part of the tour preparation section for tour managers covers the policies and procedures which relate to reporting for the tour. This will be either to the headquarters office or to the point of tour departure. For lengthy international tours, it is customary for tour managers to report to the headquarters office for a pre-tour briefing. For short one- or two-day bus tours, however, tour guides frequently report to the point of departure and operate as step-on guides. This first section relating to reporting usually covers policies regarding compensation, tickets, housing, and so forth for the tour leader who reports to headquarters one or two days prior to the departure of the tour.

The next part of this section relates to pre-tour study and coordination of the itinerary, the time schedule, maps, and routings. Many require the guide to review the tour manager detail book. This explains all aspects of the tour. It is normally studied one or two days before the tour. If the tour manager has a question or a concern regarding some aspect of the handling of the tour enroute, this is the time to ask that question.

Many expect tour leaders to review client information. They want the tour guide to get to know pertinent details regarding tour members even before meeting them. Some expect and require tour guides to call tour members and speak with them on the phone one or two days before departure, making sure that all is in order for their trip. In this way, a rapport is developed between the tour leader and the tour members even before the tour departs. Most expect the tour leader to start making an effort to match individuals with names. Tour member medical cards are also usually reviewed so that tour leaders can make sure those needing special attention will receive it. This is especially important for tour members who may have difficulty in walking and will perhaps need room assignments close to elevators.

If the tour is a bus tour, it is at this time that all tour supplies are reviewed to make sure everything that will go on the bus is ready, packed, and available. During this pre-tour orientation period, financial considerations are reviewed and the tour leader will obtain the money and other financial documents needed to take on the tour. Often there is a briefing required with the company's chief financial officer. The procedures for all of this are set out in the tour manual.

For bus tours, a standard routine is normally identified in the beginning section of the manual. This routine normally starts with a client check-in process. Although the client check-in varies from tour company to tour company, most specify exactly how the client check in should be conducted.

Along with the client check in, or immediately following it, baggage check-in and control will be discussed. As with client check-in, the baggage check-in process and procedure are usually specified in detail in the tour manual. This normally includes tagging each piece of baggage with a color-coded baggage tag and completing a baggage control form which lists each bag, sometimes with a description.

While some tour companies specify in the tour manual that the tour leader should go to the car barn to inspect the bus in the morning prior to going to the client check-in point, most do not require it. They usually specify that a complete inspection of the motorcoach will take place at the time the coach arrives at the point of departure. Many tour manuals have a checklist which must be completed and turned in with post-tour paperwork. This checklist will normally have minimum standards which must be met before acceptance of the motorcoach.

Prior to disembarking, most tour manuals specify a detailed supply loading procedure. This often identifies exactly where on the bus each supply item will be stored and, in many cases, it will include an order of loading which the tour company expects to have followed.

Passenger loading policies and procedures are set out in this section of the tour manual as well. Many, but not all tour companies will specify seating arrangements and seating procedures. Some state that they allow open seating.

Enroute Policies

Enroute policies and procedures detailed in the tour manual start with those functions and activities which occur on the first day of the tour. They detail a variety of routines that must be followed. They also discuss on-bus activities. The first day start-up will often have sections for:

1. the welcoming of the tour members;
2. the introductions of tour members and the tour leader;
3. the on-bus equipment explanation;
4. an explanation of rules and policies;
5. the discussion of how emergencies will be handled;
6. seat rotation;
7. the procedure for passing out and explaining tour member packets;
8. disembarkation procedures; and
9. the way in which passenger counts are to be taken.

Most tour manuals dedicate part of this section to a discussion of on-bus activities. Some tour companies limit certain types of on-bus activities. Most tour manuals specifically state that they do not allow off-color or ethnic jokes and they usually specify that alcoholic beverages may not be consumed or brought onto the tour bus. Many recognize the wide variation in tour member group types as well as the many differences in skills and attributes brought to the job by tour leaders. Therefore, many tour manuals allow a wide range of activities that may be engaged in on the tour bus, but most provide some parameters within which tour leaders are expected to work.

Enroute routines frequently specified in the tour manual discuss those routines which the tour company expects to be followed on a daily basis in relationship to working with vendors, hotel check-in and check-out routines, restaurant routines, sightseeing point routines, and other routines.

Post-tour Procedures and Responsibilities

Many break down the post-tour procedures and responsibilities section of the tour manual into three distinct parts. The first part relates to the closing activities and interfaces with tour members as the tour bus arrives back at the final drop off point. The second section covers the completion of the post-tour report. The third and final section is a verbal debriefing which occurs with some tour companies, but not with others.

Tour companies often rely heavily on repeat clients and direct much of their marketing to current and repeat clients. When this is the case, much of the required final activities involved in closing out a tour as the tour bus nears the drop-off point or as the flight is ready to disembark to return to the point of origin relates to activities designed to encourage tour participants to take a future tour with the company. Because this is so important, many tour companies have detailed tour completion procedures and requirements in their tour manuals. Often, this process starts with thank yous extended by the tour leader to tour members. Some companies require the tour leader to not only compliment the tour members as a whole for being such a good group, but also to identify strengths in each and every individual tour member and to thank tour members individually for their contributions.

Tour members are usually asked to complete a written tour evaluation form which is designed to assist the tour planner in making changes to the tour. The form also asks what future tours the tour member might want to take. This information is used in marketing other tours to the tour member. The timing, processing, and collecting of evaluation questionnaires are detailed in the tour manual. The evaluation is usually a short form. Therefore, it is sometimes accompanied by a requirement to have an oral discussion with tour members regarding the strengths and weaknesses of the completed tour. Increasingly, however, tour companies are eliminating this verbal evaluation process since if one or more negatives occurred, it can get tour members thinking about the negatives and not the positives, thereby reducing sign-ups for future tours.

Perhaps most crucial to the tour company is future tour promotion. Frequently, tour manuals stress that tour leaders will hand out brochures or schedules for future tours. Tour manuals often urge tour leaders to become familiar enough with other and future tours so that they can answer any questions about future tours. Many tour companies ask tour leaders to submit the names of tour members who they believe are interested in one or more future tours so that the marketing department may contact them.

The *tour report* is a paperwork detail required by almost all tour companies. A copy of the blank report is usually included in the tour manual. Many tour manuals include detailed completion instructions. Some even provide samples so that tour leaders will understand how to complete the report. Most reports contain both narrative and fill-in-the-blank sections. The manual guides tour leaders in completing the tour report by leading them step-by-step through its completion.

A crucial section of the report is a financial balancing where the tour leader must identify the amount of money used from the beginning of the tour, detailing the expenditures, and identifying the balance on hand at the conclusion of the tour. This balance on hand, of course, is returned to the tour company accountant or bookkeeper. Again, the tour manual specifies exactly how this accounting process is completed.

Another section often found in post-tour written reports relates to vendor evaluations. The tour manual usually includes *vendor evaluation forms* and samples of how the form has been completed by others. Some manuals include a policy which stresses that tour leaders will not be able to obtain their compensation for running the tour until the tour report is completed and turned in, complete with financial balancing and vendor evaluations.

The *verbal debriefing* of the tour leader is a requirement of only a few tour companies. When this is a requirement, the tour manual will indicate the policy requiring verbal debriefing and will normally explain what is expected from the tour leader during the debriefing session. This varies from company to company, but it normally includes finding out from the tour leader which tour members are good prospects for future tours and identifying the strengths and weaknesses of vendors which have provided services or products.

Other Tour Manual Sections

Other tour manual sections include sections relating to vendor relationships, guide/tour member relationships, and the handling of specific emergencies. Each of these sections will detail the policies and procedures of the tour company. Although most of these sections in the tour manuals are brief and to the point, some can be lengthy and specific. Emergency handling sections of the tour manual are normally broken down into types of emergencies, detailing exactly what the tour company expects the tour leader to do in each emergency situation.

Administrative Section

Most tour manuals will have a section relating to administrative policies and procedures dealing with tour leaders. These sections are titled in a variety of ways, but because they deal with administrative matters, they are usually entitled *administration*. Although the administrative sections can be lengthy and can cover a wide variety of administrative concerns, many are short and deal with only a few administrative matters. Almost all have a section relating to compensation. Many detail how compensation is calculated as well as when compensation can be expected. Most specify the paperwork that must be completed before compensation will be rendered.

Tour assignments is another section often found in the administrative part of the tour manual. This can be a sensitive area because many employees working for tour companies on a regular or full-time basis are concerned with the way in which they are assigned to tours. Most tour executives feel that if the tour assignment process and procedure is specified in the tour manual, any major problems relating to tour assignments can be reduced or eliminated.

Tour Manual Development

Tour manuals are developed in a variety of ways. Unfortunately, guidelines do not exist in the industry. Perhaps, it is for this reason that tour manuals vary so considerably in terms of their structure and their content. However, all tour companies find as they start offering tours that guidelines, rules, policies, and procedures are needed for tour guides and tour managers. Many start the development of the tour manual by simply putting down in writing those things which they tell tour leaders in pre-tour briefing sessions.

Frequently, debriefing sessions with guides and tour leaders identify problems. When these problems repeat themselves, tour companies establish policies and procedures designed to solve them. These are then incorporated into the tour manual. Sometimes they work and sometimes they don't. Again, briefing sessions will show when they need to be changed or altered.

By working with a tour manual and by continually developing and refining it, tour companies can have a guideline and a set of policies and procedures for tour leaders to follow which can be beneficial to both the company and the tour leader.

Summary

A tour manual is a reference book. It is a set of policies and procedures designed to aid the tour guide in understanding what the company wishes to have done and the way in which procedures should be implemented as the tour progresses from beginning to end. There are many types of manuals and tour company policy and procedures manuals are not limited to tour manuals for guides.

However, the tour manual is unique in that it provides directions for guides while they are on tour and unable to reach the headquarters office for policy and procedures decisions.

Tour manuals range from being very short to quite lengthy, however, most include sections relating to carrying out day-to-day responsibilities, guidelines for working with vendors and tour members, emergency handling instructions, and a wide range of other directives. Many manuals break these down into broad categories based upon when they are needed. For example, some manuals will break the guidelines into pre-tour activities, enroute activities, and post-tour activities. Other sections deal with administrative matters and with marketing concerns.

DISCUSSION QUESTIONS

These questions may be discussed by two or more students outside of class as a fun way of reviewing this chapter or they may be discussed by everyone during class for a more wide-ranging discussion.

1. What is a tour manual?
2. Why should a tour manual be developed and provided to guides?
3. Into what eight categories are tour manuals often divided?
4. What type of guidelines might tour manuals provide relating to the image of a tour guide?
5. What pre-tour policies and procedures guidelines might be included in a tour manual?
6. What policy and procedure guidelines relating to on-bus activities might be included in tour manuals?
7. What post-tour procedure and responsibility guidelines might be detailed in a tour manual?
8. What marketing and promotion activities required of tour guides might be specified in a tour manual?
9. Where might a tour guide find an example of a tour report and what types of information might a guide expect to be required to provide in completing a tour report?
10. Why do some tour manuals include a section relating to tour assignments and tour scheduling?

ROLE PLAY EXERCISES

1. Two students may participate in this role play either out of class as a fun way to review the chapter or as an in-class exercise. One plays the role of a new (to working with this company) tour guide and the other plays the role of an ex-

perienced tour guide (one with many years of experience working with this company). Please read the script and then pick up the conversation in your own words.

NEW GUIDE: I have read the tour manual and I'm surprised at how detailed it is compared with the manual used by the company I worked for before.

EXPERIENCED GUIDE: Most of us find it very helpful. How does it differ from the one used by the tour company you used to work for?

NEW GUIDE: There are a number of differences and there are several sections that weren't even in the manual developed by my previous employer. For example, this section on tour assignments seems much more detailed than necessary. We had nothing regarding tour assignments in the manual I worked with before.

EXPERIENCED GUIDE: I think most of us are happy we have the tour assignment section in the manual. Everybody understands exactly how tours are assigned and there is no arguing about them.

NEW GUIDE: That's hard to believe. We used to fight constantly over getting assigned to the better tours. What is it about a manual that stops all the arguing?

EXPERIENCED GUIDE: It's really pretty simple. The manual points out clearly that tours are assigned on the basis of . . .

CONTINUE ON YOUR OWN

2. Two students may participate in this role play either out of class as a fun way to review the chapter or as an in-class exercise. One plays the role of a new (to working with this company) tour guide and the other plays the role of an experienced tour guide (one with many years of experience working with this company). Please read the script and then pick up the conversation in your own words.

NEW GUIDE: This is the only company I have ever worked for that requires me to fill out an end-of-tour report before I can get paid for the tour.

EXPERIENCED GUIDE: The company has found that that is the only way they will get end-of-tour reports completed and handed in right after the tour is over.

NEW GUIDE: It sure works. But I don't understand why they need all of this information.

EXPERIENCED GUIDE: It sometimes does seem like a lot of information. Let me explain each of these categories on the report and why the information is necessary. Let's start with . . .

CONTINUE ON YOUR OWN

3. Two students may participate in this role play either out of class as a fun way to review the chapter or as an in-class exercise. One plays the role of a new (to

working with this company) tour guide and the other plays the role of an experienced tour guide (one with many years of experience working with this company). Please read the script and then pick up the conversation in your own words.

NEW GUIDE: I don't know if I'm going to be able to live up to these uniform, dress code, and image requirements. When I worked for the other tour company I just got up, threw on some clothes—I usually wore jeans—and took the tour out. Why is this company so fussy about the way we look?

EXPERIENCED GUIDE: It's really very simple. If you were paying a lot of money to go on a tour, wouldn't you expect the guide to project a professional image?

NEW GUIDE: Yes, and I admit the image of our guides is a lot better than the way some of the guides looked who worked for the company I worked for before. But, all of this seems like it is going overboard.

EXPERIENCED GUIDE: Let me take each of these requirements and explain why the company has them. Let's start with . . .

CONTINUE ON YOUR OWN

GROUP DISCUSSION SITUATION: PLITHY PLOD'S FIRED UP EVALUATIONS

Plithy Plod has almost memorized the tour manual. She has read it so many times that she can quote sections of it by heart. She felt this was her security blanket when she conducted her first tour on her own. However, Plithy is upset with herself because in spite of the fact that she knows that she should have obtained evaluations before tour members left the tour, she did not do so.

In many ways, Plithy's first tour was successful. It was just a three-day tour, but everything seemed to flow like clockwork. The tour members were a cohesive group. They got along well with one another and Plithy was able to work well with them. Plithy is a plodder and a detail-oriented person. She made absolutely certain that each rule, regulation, and procedure set out in the tour manual was followed.

Some of the tour members felt Plithy went overboard with her continual counts of tour members as they got off the bus, as they entered sightseeing points, as they moved from one place to another, and as they returned to the bus. However, they were good natured about it.

Just as Plithy was going through the end-of-tour procedures a few miles before the bus returned to the tour company's parking lot and shortly before the evaluations were to be started, one of the tour members at the back of the bus smelled a strong stench and screamed, "Fire!"

Almost before anyone could react, flames were seen coming from the back of the bus. The driver immediately pulled the bus over to the side of the road and stopped. But before he could get out of the bus, Plithy had grabbed the fire extinguisher, dashed out the front door, and was spraying everything in sight.

The driver calmed Plithy down as the visible flames evaporated. By this time, several cars had stopped and the siren of a police car could be heard. It was not long before the police were on the scene. While they talked with Plithy and the tour members about the situation, the bus driver radioed to the car barn for a back-up bus and in less than 10 minutes the new bus had arrived.

With the fire out and the police reports completed, Plithy helped the tour members move to the new bus (their own bus could not be restarted). All luggage and equipment was moved and the tour members got underway again for the final few miles back to the tour company's parking lot.

It seemed that in that few miles driven back to the parking lot everybody was talking and asking questions. Plithy was the heroine of the tour and members were congratulating her for her fast action. Several said they would write to the tour company stressing how Plithy's fast action had probably saved their lives. Plithy was aglow in all of the attention. When the bus pulled in to the parking lot Plithy remembered to thank the tour members and to ask them to come again on another tour. Several said it was the most exciting tour they had ever been on and that they would sign up for another one right away.

Once the tour members had all departed, Plithy started gathering her materials together and conducting a bus inspection to make sure no one had left anything on board. Suddenly, Plithy came to a shocked realization. She remembered that she had failed to obtain completed evaluations from the tour members. They had all left the parking lot now and it was obviously too late. Plithy sobbed in her despair that she had failed to complete one of the most important tasks detailed in the tour manual. "And I know that section of the manual by he⁻ʳᵗ," cried Plithy to the bored bus driver. "How could I have let them all go without getting evaluations completed?"

Plithy's mood had swung from jubilation to despair. But she remembered the other guides from the company were throwing her a "first tour party" at her apartment. They would be there to start the celebration as soon as she had completed the paperwork, released the bus, and returned home. Upon entering the apartment, Plithy recounted the events of the day to all of you, the other guides who are at her party ready to celebrate.

Consider the situation. Decide among yourselves what Plithy should do and how you will advise Plithy. Discuss the matter among yourselves. Be prepared to present your suggestions in a paper that will be no longer than three pages in length. Also make sure the paper is double spaced and typed. Be prepared to also present your suggestions verbally in class if your instructor suggests that you do so.

EXERCISE

1. Break into groups of no more than three students working together. Yours will probably be the same group that has been working together in the development of a one-day tour since the beginning of the course.

Study the tour manual sample pages in the appendix and review the discussion of tour manuals provided in this chapter. Next, go back to the brochure and other materials developed relating to the one-day tour your group has been working on since the beginning of the course. Prepare a rough draft tour manual to be used by the guide for the one-day tour your group is planning. Make sure that it includes all pertinent sections, policies, and procedures that you would expect to have followed.

CHAPTER 9

Tour Buses and Bus Drivers

OBJECTIVES

Upon completion of this chapter, the student will be able to:

1. Prepare a bus driver packet for a one-day tour.
2. List nine major factors to consider when selecting a tour bus.
3. Prepare a bus management plan for a one-day tour.
4. Explain how much and when bus drivers should be tipped.

Introduction

As with so many other aspects of a tour, having top quality tour buses and drivers can make all the difference in the world to the success of a tour. Usually, this means working with tour bus companies which are known for their excellence.

Perhaps one of the best ways to understand the importance of tour buses and tour bus drivers is to talk with clients who have returned from tours and who remember as highlights the poor quality of the tour bus or the driver. One experienced worldwide tour member tells of an exciting tour he took in North Africa and one of the first points made in his discussion of the tour relates to the poor quality of the tour bus. He recounts that the brochures emphasized the large windows giving a panoramic view, the fully air-conditioned modern motor-coach comfort, and the clean, fully equipped restroom on board providing, "top of the line comfort." He points out that while the windows were large, they were also so dirty is was difficult to see the sights. While the restroom existed, the aromas that came from it were so bad that no one would use it. The restroom door did not fully close and it banged back and forth constantly throughout the duration of the trip. While there was a hole in the ceiling where the air conditioner obviously should have gone, it was obvious to all tour members aboard that if an air conditioner had ever been housed in that space, that event occurred many eons ago. Of importance is the fact that this client who had experienced many tours stressed the poor bus quality as one of the first points discussed when remembering and recounting the events relating to his North African tour.

Generally speaking, if a tour member is provided with an outstandingly good tour bus and driver, the memory of this quality blends with the memory of other good aspects of the tour. It does not stand out. However, if the bus or the driver is particularly bad, that memory stands out sharply as a negative point.

Tour bus companies which are known for their excellence, adhere to rigid maintenance standards for their buses. These standards not only apply to the mechanical aspects of the buses, but they also apply to the cleanliness and the interior upkeep. Many bus companies will not release a bus for a tour before it is totally cleaned both inside and outside. A thorough check system is completed after every tour and even the smallest of maintenance needs is addressed in a timely manner.

Stringent rules are often maintained regarding what can and what cannot be taken aboard the bus. A number of companies will not allow cold coolers, mechanical equipment which might rip upholstry, or heavy objects which might place stress on or damage seats or overhead compartments. Some buses are equipped with seats and other furnishings which can be easily removed or replaced when they need to be repaired or when damage is so severe that a new replacement is the only viable option. Others, however, are not. Excellent bus companies usually employ drivers who take pride in both themselves and their buses and who make certain that the bus is kept in a constant state of top quality.

Usually, companies must pay more for drivers who are outstanding. The quality of drivers is frequently seen first in their image. The professional driver will dress impeccably and will make certain that his uniform is both clean and neat. He not only knows all aspects regarding his bus and how to drive it, but he knows how to perform all major mechanical repairs. Although many repairs cannot be made on the side of the road, he is fully briefed in how to fix those mechanical breakdowns which can be repaired rapidly when there is a roadside problem.

The experienced bus driver will have covered the route he is driving several times and he will know not only the best ways to travel from point to point, but he/she will often know the history and background of the sites and the area traveled on the sightseeing trip. In many cases, the driver will be an experienced guide as well as a driver, so he/she can be relied upon to fill in for the guide when and if necessary.

Factors to Consider in Selecting a Bus Company

Some of the more important factors to consider in selecting a bus company include the experience of the company, pricing arrangements, the bus company's reputation, the quality of both the product (the bus) and the service, the bus company's cooperation, the availability of buses when needed, and bus company rules.

Once a tour company has worked with bus companies, the history of the tour company's experience usually becomes a primary consideration in making a decision as to the use of the bus company for future trips. If the historical experience is good, the bus company which provided the good experience is usually considered first or among the first of the companies which are contacted when a bus booking is needed in the future. The reverse is true for those companies which have provided a less-than-desirable experience. In considering their experience with bus companies, tour planners usually consider all aspects of the experience. This includes the two major categories of both service and product. Service boils down to booking activities, on-bus driver services (if the driver is working for the bus company), and follow-up contacts (billing, payment, and so forth). The product is the bus itself.

Service starts when contacting the sales and marketing department or the reservations department of the bus company. The service and performance of these two departments is critical in that they can make the difference between a comfortable trip which comes in on budget and an uncomfortable trip which may be charged at a considerably higher figure. Bus company sales and marketing executives are charged with meeting and beating the competition in terms of the buses provided, the services rendered, and the pricing. It is beneficial for the tour arranger to negotiate pricing with sales executives and to review alternative ways of being able to reduce prices without significantly reducing quality. Sometimes pricing is based on mileage. Sometimes it is based on time, and in some cases, the costs are based on a combination of both mileage and time. There may be cost supplements for specially equipped buses. Options should be reviewed with the sales executive to make certain that the best possible pricing is being offered.

If the booking is made through the reservations department, frequently all aspects will be handled by phone. Here, too, it is usually wise to negotiate, if possible. Because bus company reservations departments frequently have less incentive to satisfy clients, the tour planner's experience with the reservations department tends to be less satisfactory than when making arrangements with sales and marketing executives.

Working through the bus dispatcher in obtaining an available bus at the time the tour planner needs it to pick up clients can sometimes be a problem. This is a major experience factor considered by tour planners when selecting a bus company. If the dispatcher is cooperative and works to correct any errors in pickup point arrangements or time arrangements, this cooperation is usually considered when planning future bus rentals. The reverse is also true.

Experience with the bus product is also important. Tour planners expect to get the type of bus that has been agreed upon. When they get a bus which is superior to that which was agreed upon, they tend to remember it in a favorable manner. However, when an inferior bus is obtained, this experience is also remembered. It is a strong incentive not to book with that company again.

Follow-up is important as well. If there are mechanical difficulties or other problems with the bus, the rapid repair of the mechanical problems or the replacement with a new bus will give the tour planner a much better feeling toward using the bus company again. In addition, if there are no billing problems, this too will encourage the tour planner to use the bus company again. However, if repairs are not made promptly, if a replacement bus is not provided rapidly, and/or if billing problems occur, this experience is considered to be negative and will dictate reluctance by the tour planner as to future use of the bus company.

Pricing is a very important factor to consider in selecting a bus company. Although most bus companies attempt to stay competitive in terms of pricing, it is rare for the tour planner to obtain exactly the same price for a bus tour from each bus company contacted. The reason for this is that companies have different prices for their buses and the ways in which prices are calculated vary from bus company to bus company. If price is based on mileage, much depends upon how the mileage is calculated. Although the mileage will be similar, the routes used to take base mileage calculations may vary from company to company. Tour planners should be especially careful about add-on pricing. There can be taxes and supplements that are added to base quotes. These need to be determined in advance so that comparison pricing will indicate exactly the same type of quote between each requested company.

The reputation of the bus company is important. Sometimes tour planners need to arrange for a bus departure from a location in which they have little or no experience in selecting bus companies. Frequently, other tour planners in the area are contacted. Often a bus company with a poor reputation will not be selected even when their pricing may be considerably less expensive.

Reputation can go beyond just good or bad. It can be, and often is, dependent upon the particular aspects being evaluated. A tour bus company can have an excellent overall reputation, but have a poor reputation when it comes to dealing with dispatchers, reservations, or the buses maintained in its fleet. Of course, it can also have a bad reputation overall and a good reputation for particular services or products. Whatever the breakdown of its reputation, bus companies need to be aware of the fact that tour arrangers are concerned about their overall reputation. It is rare for a tour operator to work with a bus company that has developed a bad reputation.

An important factor to consider when selecting a bus company is the quality of the company itself. This quality is normally emphasized most when considering the company's product (i.e., tour buses). Quality is certainly easy to measure when looking at a piece of equipment. However, the quality of the bus company is more than just its buses. The perceived quality relates to all aspects of the company. This definitely includes the structure of the company, the quality of the employees (especially those who interface with tour planners), and the quality of each aspect of the company that will have a direct or, in many cases, an indirect bearing on the tour.

Cooperation is very important. Frequently, an attitude of cooperation permeates the entire bus company operation. This makes the company a very desirable firm with which to work. It is not unusual for a tour arranger to contract with the bus company whose prices are higher (sometimes substantially higher) when the quality of the product and the cooperation extended by those working for the company are clearly superior to the quality and the cooperation found with less expensive companies. Many feel that the additional cost is worth it.

Tour bus availability is still another factor to be considered. No matter how good the company is, if the company does not have a bus available on the dates when the bus is needed, then another bus company will need to be found. Although some bus companies will maintain very large fleets of buses so that they can handle any booking that comes through, many companies are much smaller and are unable to guarantee the availability of the bus during last minute peak reservation periods.

Bus company rules constitute still another important factor to consider. The rules that frequently are considered to be most onerous by tour arrangers are those rules relating to the bus and the operation of the bus. Other rules which may result in a tour arranger not working with a bus company relate to financial arrangements. In some cases, substantial amounts of nonrefundable deposits are required. In other cases, full payment is required a long time in advance. These types of rules can create substantial hardships for a tour operator. Therefore, many tour operators seek out bus companies with more flexible pricing and payment rules.

Although tour managers may appreciate some of the rules set by tour companies regarding what can be brought aboard their buses and how clients can act on board the buses, many tour managers find these rules to present unworkable situations for them. In one case, the bus company did not allow anyone to occupy the first four seats. In another case, a bus company did not allow any smoking aboard its bus. In still another case, a tour bus company refused to let more than one passenger at a time get up from his/her seat and move in the aisles of the bus. Regulations of this type are considered prohibitively restrictive by many tour planners. Therefore, it is important for the planner to know all rules that apply on the tour bus and to consider selecting a bus company with rules that minimize hardships.

Factors to Consider in Selecting a Tour Bus

Tour buses come in many sizes, styles, and types. What is "appropriate and best" for one group is not necessarily appropriate and best for another. There are basic points that need to be checked out for any group with some groups requiring special features. Those factors which need to be considered for any tour group include:

1. the size of the bus;
2. the seats on the bus;
3. amenities on board the bus;
4. bus microphones;

5. bathrooms aboard the bus;

6. windows;

7. heating and air conditioning;

8. the mechanical condition of the bus; and perhaps most important

9. the cost of the bus.

Many consider the most important factor in selecting a tour bus, other than cost, to be the size of the bus. Tour buses used to come in 39 and 43 seat sizes only. It was rare to find any other size. However, in the last 10 years, in both the United States and Europe, tour buses have been manufactured which are both considerably smaller than 39 and considerably larger than 43 seats. Today, there are tour buses that are literally the size of two buses, having a multitude of special features. There are double-decker tour buses and even a hotel tour bus with facilities that convert into sleeping compartments.

The relationship between the size of the bus (number of seats) and the cost is a critical relationship. Bus leases are priced on the basis of the size of the bus, the number of miles or kilometers traveled, and the amount of time the bus is in use. Once the bus has been negotiated for, deposits made, and contract agreements signed, the tour operator is locked into the cost of the bus. This cost will remain the same whether one seat is occupied or all seats are occupied. In other words, the cost of the bus is a fixed cost. It does not change depending upon the number of people taking the tour.

Therefore, one of the most important factors to consider, if the tour operator is to expect a profit, is the number of passengers (i.e., paying members on the tour). If there will be 36 or 37 passengers, a 39 seat tour bus will be appropriate. However, if there will be 40 or 41 passengers, a 39 seat bus will be too small so a 43 seat bus will be needed.

Since many bus companies now have buses that are substantially smaller or larger than 39 seats, it becomes very important for the tour operator to determine in advance the exact number of tour participants. The closer the tour operator is able to come in projecting the number of tour participants and matching that number to the number of seats on the bus, the greater the likelihood that the tour operator will be able to make a profit. Obviously, if a tour operates with 10 people and a 39 seat bus has been contracted, the tour operator will pay considerably more than necessary for the bus. The cost difference between the cost of a small bus (appropriate for a ten person tour) and the 39 seat bus will come directly out of profits or it will create a loss.

The type of bus frequently determines the type of seating. One can go from the extreme of leasing a school bus, still in its bright orange paint and with child quality seating, to the luxury of an over-the-road cruiser with deep, plush, seats which recline to a comfortable sleeping angle. In many localities it is also possible to obtain buses with relatively few seats per square foot, even wider and more comfortable seats (similar to those in a first-class cabin of an air carrier), and seats that swivel.

Certainly, the luxury type of seating is preferred by customers, but the per seat cost can be triple or quadruple what the cost is for a less-comfortable bus. In most cases, tour members will be adequately comfortable on a tour bus with standard tour bus seating (two padded seats on each side of the aisle with a recline of 10 to 12 percent). However, by pricing a variety of buses and negotiating with bus companies, a shrewd operator is sometimes able to obtain even more comfortable seating at a price for the bus that is equal to standard tour bus seating pricing. Therefore, it behooves the tour operator to shop and check out the equipment owned and operated by bus companies.

A wide range of amenities are being offered by tour bus companies. Many of these can make an important difference in the comfort level of the tour member. Two of the more innovative amenities are the sound system and the videotape playback system.

Stereo sound systems have been installed in a large number of tour buses. This amenity can be seen as both a comfort and a discomfort by tour members. Some bus companies and, by default, some tour operators allow bus drivers to play radio music chosen by the bus driver over the sound system. It is not at all unusual for the choice of music to be different than the choice of many of the tour members. Although music that a tour member may not care for, when played at a very low volume, may not be especially disturbing, frequently the music is played at a sound level that interrupts passenger conversation. This is disturbing. Most tour operators agree that if a stereo sound system is used, audio tapes selected by the tour operator should be the only ones that are allowed to be played. These should be played at a very low volume and at times when the sound will not disturb passenger conversation, guide presentations, or the rest and relaxation of tour passengers. Many agree that elevator-type orchestra music is best.

Many newer tour buses are equipped with videotape playback units. Screens are set into the bus raised over the seats at intervals of about every eight to ten rows. In some tour buses, the screens are found only on the right side of the tour bus and in a few tour buses only two screens are located on the bus. When the screens are too few in number or when they are so large that they take up so much room one cannot be seated underneath a screen, then the videotape playback system may present a problem rather than a benefit. However, after some initial experimentation, tour buses are generally manufactured today with videotape playback units that are spaced in such a way that they do not interfere with passenger comfort and there are enough of them on both sides of the bus that they can be seen comfortably by passengers sitting in all tour bus seats.

Of course, the key to desirability with videotape units on board tour buses is the same as it is when considering audiotapes. This key relates to the quality of the presentation. If the videotape is a presentation on a site or a destination that will be visited shortly, it can be expected that most tour members will be interested. This is especially true if there is good narration, a good flow of information and photography, and the entire videotape presentation is relatively short.

However, some tour operators have allowed videotapes to be played which are of little or no interest to tour members. When this occurs, frequently not only is the sound disturbing, but the picture is disturbing as well. Some have allowed cartoons. In other cases, films that depict scenes which are considered in poor taste by many of the tour members have been played. Therefore, as with sound systems, the tour operator needs to control the videotape system and screen material to make sure that it is not only appropriate, but that it is of considerable interest to the vast majority of tour members.

Food and beverage dispensing facilities constitute another amenity available on an increasing number of tour buses. Some buses have installed complete bar service for passengers, whereas others have facilities to provide four-course hot meals and/or snacks served by the on-bus equivalent of airline stewardesses.

Microphones on tour buses are considered by most in the industry to be standard equipment. However, there are still some tour buses that do not come equipped with them. Therefore, you should always check the availability of the microphone and include having a working microphone on the bus in the tour bus contract. When checking out a bus at the time of bus pick-up prior to departure on a tour, the tour manager should always check the microphone to make sure that it is working.

Additional microphone points that need to be checked include the quality and loudness of the sound and the length of the microphone cord. Many tour bus microphones are designed only for the bus driver to be able to speak. Therefore, the cord length is only sufficient for speaking from the driver's seat. However, tour managers usually stand at the front of the bus between the aisles of the seats. They need a microphone that will extend that distance. Many tour bus companies include in their inventories microphone cord extensions or microphones with long cords which can simply be plugged into the bus audio system. However, these are normally not provided unless they are requested. Therefore, always ask in advance and, if necessary, order microphones with sufficiently long cord lengths.

Another tour bus feature that has come to be expected is bathrooms. There are still some tour buses that do not have them but this is becoming increasingly rare. Since the average age of tour members is getting older with the aging of America, the necessity to have bathrooms on buses is becoming more important. There is a strong correlation between age and bladder retention control. A general guideline to use is that if tour members are to be on the bus for 30 minutes or longer, a bathroom should be on board.

Many older buses have bathroom doors that will not stay fully closed. When picking up the bus, the tour manager should make certain that bathroom doors close and lock from the inside and that they can be closed and stay closed from the outside.

The cleanliness of the bathroom is also important. A quick check of bathroom facilities prior to departure from the bus barn will insure that necessary ingredients such as paper towels, toilet tissue, and soap are in the bathroom in sufficient quantity. It is wise for the tour manager to also turn on the water at the sink to make sure that there is a steady flow of water and to confirm good drainage out from the bottom of the sink. The manager should flush the toilet to determine that it is not stopped up. Finally, all bathroom facilities should be checked for cleanliness.

Tour bus windows are another point of consideration. Wrap-around windows which go clear to the middle part of the ceiling are most desirable. Some of these are tinted to reduce glare from the sun during sunrise and sunset. Most tour bus windows which are of the wrap-around type do not open since these tour buses have climate-controlled heating and air conditioning.

Many tour buses, however, are still equipped with windows that can be opened and closed. This creates a concern when some tour members can get excessively cold if a window is left open near them and when air conditioning can be allowed to escape during the hotter months of the year. If the bus is equipped with individually controlled windows, the tour manager should check to make sure that all windows are in proper operating condition before accepting the bus. Rules for the opening and closing of windows should be established so that those in aisle seats will not be unnecessarily uncomfortable because of the thoughtlessness of those sitting next to windows.

In areas of temperature extreme, heating and air conditioning can be very important. Many tour buses operate with heating and air conditioning units which do not function properly (or at least sufficiently to heat or to cool the entire bus adequately). Heating and air conditioning should be checked out by the tour manager prior to the departure of the tour bus and before accepting it for the tour. Because the problems with heating and air conditioning are so prevalent, some tour managers have included paragraphs in the bus rental contracts which levy penalties against the bus company if heating and air conditioning do not operate adequately during the tour. If tour managers check at the bus barn and accept only buses with well working heating and air-conditioning systems, the probability is strong that the systems will continue working well throughout the tour.

Each bus option has a cost and there is a relative cost increase as options escalate in number and quality. Some bus options, however, will be very inexpensive or may be provided at no cost. Heating, air conditioning, and built-in microphones normally fall into this category. However, for microphones with extended cords there may be a very small additional cost. Buses with wrap-around windows sometimes are provided at a standard cost, but in other cases a supplement may be levied for them. Some tour bus companies also charge extra for buses with bathrooms aboard and it is standard for tour bus companies to levy an additional fee for buses with full bar service or for special facilities for food and beverages. For other amenities, the tour bus company may or may not request an additional fee.

Tour Bus Negotiation

The key to keeping tour bus charges within budget is negotiation. From the standpoint of the tour operator, everything is negotiable. Tour bus executives, however, price buses on the basis of time, mileage, or time and mileage. Add-on charges are levied for extras. The rate for a standard tour bus, therefore, might be $1 or $2 less per hour than the rate for a bus with full bar service.

Keep in mind that bus companies must abide by the law. Local state, and federal laws limit their ability to negotiate such areas as route and driving time. Local laws may prohibit crossing certain bridges because the bus is too heavy. State and city laws may prohibit the use of specified streets or highways by tour buses. Federal law prohibits drivers from driving more than 10 hours a day (if more than 16 passengers are carried or if the loaded bus weighs more than 26,000 pounds). Routings and itineraries must be planned with these legal points in mind. Do not expect the bus company to even consider waiving compliance with local, state, and federal laws.

In negotiating, it is wise to determine the basis on which the particular bus company quotes its charges. In other words, you should first determine whether or not the charges are per hour, per mile, or some combination of both. It is also wise to obtain a determination early in the negotiation phase as to how much the tour bus company needs your business.

This is not always easy, but supply and demand comes into effect when negotiating tour bus charges. If the supply of tour buses available in a community at the time the tour operator needs to have a bus is considerable and the demand for buses is low, the tour operator will probably have a good negotiating position. Of course, the opposite is also true. If the tour operator needs a bus during peak season, or during a period of time when all buses in the community can easily be leased, the negotiating position of the tour operator is worse.

Some tour bus companies will have a standard schedule of rates and the company will not allow its sales representatives to negotiate prices at all. Although some tour bus companies will calculate the amount of time used to the minute, this is rare. Usually a time-based charge will be calculated from the hour the bus departs from the bus barn to the hour when it returns to the barn.

In some cases, however, bus companies will make time calculations based upon the time the bus departs from the tour departure point until the time the bus returns to that point. Obviously, the latter arrangement is usually preferred. However, you should be careful with the former arrangement since it is not at all unusual for tour bus drivers to stop for breakfast after picking up their buses in the morning and before arriving at the tour departure point.

Although some bus companies will be somewhat flexible in calculating late charges for buses that return after the time designated in the contract, most bus companies will levy a substantial penalty when buses return after the contracted time. This is especially true if the bus company provides a driver with the bus and the driver will have to be paid overtime as a result of the bus returning late. Although it is not common, drivers have been known to purposely delay their return in order to build up overtime. When this occurs, tour managers should point out the need to stay on schedule to the bus driver, provide a lower tip or no tip if the driver appears to delay returning on purpose, and report the concern to the bus company.

When tour bus charges are based on mileage, the mileage will be calculated by the bus company based on its charts and maps. A rough mileage will be included in the contract. Sometimes this is an exact use-mile figure, but frequently it is a range that may extend over a period of five to 20 miles as the estimated or the calculated use-mileage.

When the contract calls for a mileage charge, it is standard to estimate the cost based upon the estimated or calculated use-miles and an additional charge for any mileage beyond that which is estimated or calculated. The tour operator should go over the route to be driven on the tour since it is not unusual for the bus company to calculate estimated use-miles based upon the shortest distance and not based on the most picturesque or scenic route unless that route is specified by the tour operator. It is wise to provide the bus company representative with a copy of the exact route drawn on maps so that the company can calculate the estimated use-miles. As with time calculations, a few bus drivers attempt to take routes other than those designated so that they may increase the penalty costs. This is rare, but the tour manager should be on guard to make certain that the routes agreed upon are followed.

As noted earlier, the cost of tour bus leases can increase when special features are included on the bus. Although tour bus companies usually have a menu of rates based upon features, these rates are usually very much negotiable. It is wise for the tour operator to prepare a listing of options needed and to bring this to the rate negotiation meeting. This list should be prepared in a hierarchical manner so that the features appearing at the top of the list will be those of greatest concern and desire and those appearing at the bottom will be those of least importance.

Typically, the negotiator will attempt to obtain one or more free features for each paid feature. Although the features should be discussed in a hierarchical order, when it is not possible to obtain a feature on a *gratis* basis, the tour operator should move to one or more features that can be negotiated to be provided on a *gratis* basis and ask that these be included free since the paid-for feature will require a higher overall charge. Although some of the features on the list may well be features that are not particularly important to the tour manager, wherever possible during the negotiation meeting, all factors on the list should be discussed.

After negotiating price and other arrangements, it is typical to wait for a contract to be developed by the bus company and then review it based upon the tour operator's notes taken during or made right after the negotiation meeting. Bus company negotiators can make errors in their notes or forget what was agreed to between the time of the negotiation meeting and the time the contract is drawn up. Therefore, it is always wise for the tour operator to prepare and mail a review letter to the bus company negotiator immediately after the negotiation meeting, preferably the same day. This letter should be a detailed review of the agreed upon arrangement.

Although some tour companies will employ their own bus drivers who meet the specifications of the tour bus company, more frequently drivers are provided by the tour bus company and the cost for the bus lease includes payment to the bus driver. Some drivers are definitely better than others. As the tour operator works with a bus company and gains experience with that company, the tour operator normally compiles a listing of drivers who are used and identifies the better ones.

It is not unusual to specify a driver (a back-up should also be listed) when entering into contracts for the bus. Usually, the contract specifies that the company will provide the driver named, but most add the two words, "if available." Most bus companies will make every effort to provide the services of the driver specified. However, that driver may be particularly popular and may have been already requested for a tour on the date(s) needed. In addition, there could be any number of other reasons why the specified driver might not be available on the date(s) desired. It is because of these factors that it is wise for the tour operator to indicate a second preference and to be willing to sign the contract when the bus company requires the, "if available," phrase to be included.

When the tour operator is dealing with a new bus company (a company with which the tour operator has no previous experience) and there is no history on which to base driver selection, many tour operators will call other local tour companies and ask for their recommendations regarding drivers. Frequently, the operator will ask the bus company for references (i.e., the names of companies and organizations that have leased buses from them in the past). When calling these references to evaluate the bus company, the tour operator also asks for the names of preferred drivers. Using this combination of approaches, the tour operator is able to compile a listing of preferred drivers so that even the first tour will be handled by a better driver.

In selecting a driver when there is no historical basis, (for example, when using a newly formed tour bus company), the tour operator should compile a listing of criteria to be met by the driver. For example, the tour operator may specify that the driver should be experienced on the route (i.e., a driver who has driven that particular route a minimum of four or five times in the recent past). Another criteria may well be that the driver be an experienced tour bus driver. Sometimes a minimum of three years of driving experience is required, but others use a five-year minimum. Frequently, the tour operator will request a driver who is also a guide. This provides a back-up for the tour manager. Some specify physical criteria that needs to be met. On occasion, for example, tour buses have flat tires. It takes a driver with some degree of strength to be able to change a tire. Therefore, tour operators may specify that the driver needs to be at least strong enough to change a tire. Sometimes, there is also a height requirement specified by the tour company. However, physical requirements for drivers are rare.

Bus drivers driving while under the influence of alcohol constitute a serious concern. Many bus companies require abstention from alcohol (usually for a specified number of hours before the start of a tour and total abstention during a tour) as a requirement for the drivers they employ. However, the tour manager should be especially watchful for signs of drinking. A change in bus drivers should be made, even at the last minute, and even at the risk of delaying departure of the tour, if it appears that the driver has been drinking and is even slightly under the influence of alcohol. Of course, the same applies for a driver who has taken any type of non-prescribed drugs.

The Driver Request Process

The driver request acceptance process may vary somewhat from bus company to bus company. A few bus companies are sophisticated enough that they have client profiles in their computer systems and it is possible to simply indicate verbally to the sales representative the names of preferred drivers and the order of preference. The bus company will keep this request on file. Each time a bus order is placed by the tour firm, the bus company will access the client profile, identify driver preferences, and assign available drivers to the tour company based upon the tour company's indicated preferences and the availability of preferred drivers. Any time a change in driver preference occurs or one wishes to change the preference hierarchy, a call to the bus company's sales representative is all that is needed. The change will be made in their computer.

Most bus companies, however, are not this sophisticated. Some will not accept or honor bus driver requests from clients at all, but most will make an effort to accommodate client requests. While a verbal request will frequently be all that is needed, it is usually wise to make the verbal request each time a bus order is placed. Back up the verbal request with a written letter when each bus order is placed. In addition, or alternatively, the names of preferred drivers can be added to a paragraph in the bus contract each time the contract is prepared or to the letter requesting a bus each time a bus order request letter is mailed.

It is always wise to check with the bus company between 48 and 72 hours prior to the departure date to find out which driver has been assigned. If a list of preferred drivers has been provided and none on the list are assigned, it is perfectly acceptable to ask the bus company if they will make a change to one of the drivers on the preference list. Sometimes it is impossible for the bus company to accommodate a client's driver request even when the list includes three or four names, but this is rare.

The Importance of the Bus Driver Itinerary

The bus driver itinerary was discussed in detail in an earlier chapter along with all other needed itineraries. While some tour companies do not prepare separate itineraries for bus drivers and they simply provide the bus driver with the same itinerary used by the tour manager or the same itinerary as that which is given to tour clients, those tour companies which do prepare a bus driver itinerary find that the drivers appreciate having an itinerary which is designed to meet their special needs. In addition, preparing a bus driver itinerary can force the tour company to recognize special driver needs and address those needs in advance. This reduces the possibility of bus access problems and parking problems once the tour is underway. Even when the tour has been run a number of times, sometimes a last minute substitute driver must be accepted and used. The substitute may not know the route and special itinerary points unique to the tour group. Without a bus driver itinerary to work from, the driver may ask questions from the tour manager or ask for routing assistance. If a bus driver itinerary is provided, these questions will be fewer. Therefore, it is important to have a bus driver itinerary and to review it from time to time with drivers when the same trip is run repeatedly. Many times, a driver can make beneficial change suggestions in the itinerary for future offerings of the trip.

Driver Routing Maps and Driver Parking Maps

As a part of the bus driver packet of materials one usually includes driver routing maps and driver parking maps. Several maps should be included. One should be a clear routing map showing the highways to be taken from the point of origin to the final destination and back. Ideally, this entire route will be shown (and highlighted) on one map. Additional maps should be provided for each city or town where one will get off of the major highway. The city/town map also should show the route from the point of leaving the highway to the furthest destination point in that city or town and back to the highway. Again, this route should be highlighted. The same type of routing map will apply to any lengthy site over which the driver will be expected to traverse (such as state parks).

Detailed parking maps should also be provided. Some sightseeing vendors provide tour operators with routing maps with bus parking points identified on the map. These can be obtained simply by asking for them either in writing or by phone. Many facilities, however, do not have pre-prepared parking maps. When this is the case, the tour operator needs to keep bus parking in mind when undertaking familiarization trips and developing the tour itinerary. When talking with vendors you should always ask where the best bus parking is located and one should look at access routes to that parking as well as routes exiting the bus parking locations (with one-way streets they are not always the same).

Most chambers of commerce will have city maps and the tour operator can put together a driver itinerary with parking points marked on the chamber of commerce maps. The American Automobile Association and state or national tourist offices are other sources for excellent map companies which are often able to provide exactly what the tour operator needs in a uniform size and with streets identified boldly enough that drivers can glance at the maps and easily follow them while driving.

The tour planner should keep in mind that if tour bus parking is not available at or near the sightseeing, meal stop, or other point convenient for tour members to get off of the bus and to return to the bus, it may be necessary for the bus to stop as close to the sightseeing point or restaurant as possible, unload tour members, and for the driver to then take the bus to a parking point some distance away, returning to pick up tour passengers at a designated later time. Although this arrangement should be a last resort, when it is necessary it should be thought through thoroughly in advance. Even under this type of circumstance, one must find the closest point where tour buses are allowed to park. Sometimes bus parking must be reserved and a bus parking permit or fee must be paid in advance. This should be checked prior to the start of the tour and drivers should be briefed well in advance of arrival.

In some terrains, or on very narrow streets, it may be impossible for larger tour buses to maneuver. The difference in maneuverability between a 39 seat bus and a 43 seat bus may seem to be small, but there are routes where the larger bus simply cannot go. Under such circumstances, you should ask the locals what is possible, check with bus companies which may have provided buses to drive in the area in the past, or as a last resort, actually have an empty bus drive the route prior to the tour to make certain that the bus can make it. If a smaller bus must be used, you'll need to know that prior to finalizing the tour planning. If no bus can drive over the route because of the difficulty of the terrain, you'll need to know that as well.

Special buses may be fun and exciting for a tour group, but sometimes they present special problems as well. A tour company had some surprises when they arranged for a double-decker sightseeing bus similar to British city buses for a client tour group wishing to go to a city center sightseeing destination that had been served by the company many times in the past without difficulty. What they had not thought about in advance, however, was the mature trees growing in the neighborhood. After knocking down two limbs and scratching the bus considerably during the course of the first tour conducted with the double-decker bus, the tour company eliminated use of that type of bus for future visits to that sightseeing point. It was an expensive way to find out that the bus could not clear the trees.

The Bus Driver Packet

Although some tour operators do not specifically have a packet of material prepared in advance for bus drivers, a number of tour operators and tour managers feel strongly that the advanced preparation of the packet of materials will help to reduce the possibility of misunderstandings and assist in ensuring a comfortable, smooth flow to the tour itself. The bus driver packet may include many items and it varies from being a very small file folder of pertinent documents to including as many as 10 to 15 items which may be contained in a file folder or a file folder plus other container.

The following are some of the documents and other items which might be included in the bus driver packet. Listed in order of importance, they include:

1. a copy of the driver contract;
2. a driver briefing sheet;

3. appropriate vouchers;

4. the bus driver itinerary;

5. routing and parking maps;

6. vendor contact lists appropriate for the driver;

7. a copy of the bus contract;

8. the daily briefing sheet;

9. the driver's name tag;

10. a copy of the tour brochure;

11. copies of the client itinerary and of the tour manager itinerary;

12. a copy of the tour member name list;

13. a copy of the rooming list;

14. any give-aways which might be provided for tour members; and

15. sightseeing brochures.

Driver Contract

While most tour bus companies insist that tour operators employ drivers working for their (the bus) company, there are some bus companies which only lease buses without drivers while others allow or provide an option for the leasing of buses without drivers.

When a bus is leased without a driver, then it is the responsibility of the tour operator to contract with a driver separately. Under such circumstances, a copy of the *driver contract* is usually included as a part of the bus driver packet. Normally, this is the first item to be reviewed with the driver when going through the details of the material in the bus driver packet. Some companies prefer to not include a copy of the driver contract with the bus driver packet, but to include it only in the material retained by the tour manager during the course of the tour so that the tour manager will have it available if a point in the contract needs to be reviewed. Most companies, however, believe that both the driver and the tour manager should have a copy of the contract and that the major points of the contract (and all other driver packet items) should be reviewed the first morning of the tour and prior to the tour's departure.

Driver Briefing Sheet

Separate from a driver contract, some tour operators include a *driver briefing sheet* in the bus driver packet. This is especially necessary when there is no separate contract for the bus driver and contract details relating to the bus driver are included in the overall bus lease contract. The driver briefing sheet spells out what is included during the tour for the bus driver and what is not included. If the driver will be provided with meals which are paid for by the tour manager along with those meals paid for by the tour manager for the entire tour group, this is pointed out. If vouchers for meals are included, this is also pointed out on the briefing sheet. If the driver is expected to stay with the bus at sightseeing points, this preference is noted. However, if the driver is to be provided with the option of going along with the tour members at sightseeing places, this option is also noted on the briefing sheet.

The driver briefing sheet will also spell out details relating to bus pick up at the bus barn, cleaning of the bus which is expected both before and during the course of the tour, food and beverage loading arrangements (if appropriate), and tour member pick up arrangements at the initial point of departure.

The briefing sheet should also identify the exact termination point for the tour, any special arrangements for unloading passengers at that time, and other bus unloading procedures which may include food and beverage unloading, final bus cleaning, details regarding when and how the driver will be tipped, and details regarding the process of returning the bus to the bus barn. Some tour companies will provide daily driver briefing sheets if the tour is one which will extend over several days. However, most companies will include driver information on a daily basis on the daily briefing sheet for the tour as a whole rather than having a separate daily driver briefing sheet.

Vouchers

The bus driver packet may or may not include vouchers. When vouchers are included, they may be for meals, for admission to sightseeing places, or for any number of other purposes. Usually they will be the same vouchers which are provided for tour members. However, in some cases, free vouchers are provided by restaurants and sightseeing vendors for both tour managers and tour bus drivers. When this is the case, they are sometimes stamped, "Gratis—For Bus Driver Only" (or similar wording) or they may be color-coded. The vouchers should be reviewed with the bus driver rather than just given to the driver so that the driver understands clearly which vouchers are being received and for what purposes.

The Bus Driver Itinerary

One of the most important documents to review in detail with the bus driver is the bus driver itinerary. This is broken down into specific time blocks identifying exactly when the bus driver should be at each location so that the bus driver will be certain to arrive and depart from each point on time and not delay the smooth flow of the tour by being late. Many companies consider it essential to review the bus driver itinerary in detail with the driver prior to leaving the bus barn.

Routing and Parking Maps

Detailed maps with the routing clearly marked should be provided to the driver and the route should be discussed in detail with the driver. In addition, parking maps should be provided and gone over with the driver. Special notes should be made if the driver feels that there might be a problem with any aspect of the route or the parking that has been planned.

The Vendor Contact List

Although the driver will not need contact information for all vendors on the tour, the driver should be provided with the names of the contacts for vendors where some type of interface may be needed. For example, if the driver will be parking in a restaurant parking lot, having the name of the restaurant manager might be beneficial in case the driver needs to contact someone at the restaurant during the time tour members are eating their meal. This might occur if there is a parking problem, such as another patron parking in such a way that the bus is blocked from exiting from the restaurant parking lot. Provide the driver with the name of contact people at hotels and sightseeing points as well.

Bus Contract Copy

Just as with the driver contract, some tour operators do not choose to provide a copy of the bus contract for the driver, but make certain that the tour manager has a copy of the contract in case it becomes necessary to refer to it. Others provide copies for both the driver and the tour manager.

When the bus contract is included in the driver packet, it is wise to go through the pertinent points with the driver. It is especially important to review contract mileage and time constraints so that the bus driver understands the importance of not exceeding the specified mileage and time maximums. Although sometimes exceeding these contract numbers is necessary, most tour operators require tour managers to specify that the driver must obtain permission from the tour manager before exceeding the terms/limitations specified in the contract. Of course, any other limitations or specifications contained in the contract should be reviewed with the driver as well.

Daily Briefing Sheet

If the tour is one which runs for several days, it is customary for the tour manager to prepare a *daily briefing sheet* for all who will work any aspect of the tour. On the daily briefing sheet will normally be points of importance to the driver. Therefore, the driver should receive a copy of the daily briefing sheet. This briefing sheet may contain notes regarding necessary itinerary changes, different locations for drop-off and/or pick-up of clients, and other points that result from special situations which were not known about and not considered prior to departure on the tour. Pertinent aspects of the daily briefing sheet should be reviewed when the briefing sheet is turned over to the driver and preferably before the first departure of the day.

Other Materials

Other items included in the bus driver packet include name tags and tour brochures. Although bus companies usually provide standard name tags for their drivers, not all do so. Many tour operators prepare name tags for all tour members and will include a prepared name tag for the bus driver as well. It is usually expected that the driver will wear the tour name tag. Tour brochures also are included if they are included in tour member packets. Tour companies normally provide tour brochures for each tour run by the company. Normally, a copy of the tour brochure is included in each tour participant's packet of materials. A copy should also be included in the bus driver packet.

While the bus driver itinerary is the itinerary of greatest importance to the bus driver, some tour operators also include copies of the client itinerary and the tour manager itinerary in the bus driver packet. The bus driver can compare the driver itinerary with the tour member itinerary and will have an understanding of where the tour manager can be expected to be at any particular point in time in case the tour manager needs to be contacted at some time other than while on the bus (for example, in the evening while at the hotel).

Tour member name lists and rooming lists are also sometimes provided to the driver so that the driver will get to know the names of each person and put a name with a face.

Sometimes tour operators provide give-aways to tour members. These may be T-shirts that have a photo or a design pertinent to a destination point. Alternatively, it might be a distinctive bandana, a button containing the tour group logo, or some other fairly inexpensive give-away. In many cases, the same give-away is included in the bus driver packet so that the bus driver will fit in with the rest of the group. If all tour members are wearing their T-shirts, bandanas, or buttons, the driver may also wish to wear his/hers.

Other brochures are also included if they are included in tour member packets. These will usually be the brochures produced by sightseeing and hotel vendors. Some tour companies include other items in the bus driver packet as well. These vary depending upon the nature of the tour and the degree to which the tour company wishes to brief or prepare the driver in advance.

Interacting with the Bus Driver

Tour bus companies vary in their policies regarding interaction with the tour bus driver. Some discourage interaction during the time that the driver is driving, especially when the route is a particularly precarious route or the weather conditions are bad. Under such circumstances the tour manager is expected to understand the danger or potential danger and should make certain that the driver is left free to concentrate on driving.

Under other circumstances, however, drivers may be encouraged to interact with tour members and contribute to the tour. Many drivers are very knowledgeable regarding the areas where they drive and they can supplement the tour manager's ability to brief tour members on the sites and other aspects of the areas being traversed. You must be careful to limit some tour drivers to make certain that they do not contradict the tour manager or take over the role of tour management. However, an experienced tour manager will know how to handle this and will maintain control at all times.

The bus driver and the tour manager should interact regularly so that all points where there may be a potential problem are reviewed and worked out in advance. Briefings between the tour manager and the bus driver should always occur prior to the first departure of the day and every effort should be made to make certain that briefings and discussions with the driver are conducted at a time and a place away from tour members. Some companies set up specific arrangements for a daily briefing session each morning of the tour and a daily debriefing session each evening. These are often held in the tour manager's hotel room.

The Local Driver/Guide

In Europe, it is not at all unusual for a tour which covers five or six countries to use a combination of a full-time guide who accompanies the tour from the beginning to the end, and a local guide, who is a specialist in a particular city, area, or country who stays with the tour only during the time in that region. In the United States, this is less common. However, in America it is becoming popular for tour companies to work with local *guide/drivers*. This is especially true with short sightseeing trips arranged for clubs, organizations, and associations which may have a meeting of some type in a city and arrange for a half-day or a full-day sightseeing trip in conjunction with the meeting. Frequently, the person contracted to handle the tour will be a driver/guide. The club or organization may have its own person, often a member, who drives the bus from city to city, but instead of arranging for a local step-on guide, a driver/guide will be contracted. Often the driver/guide will be an independent contractor, but equally often it will be a person who works for a bus company and who drives/guides on contract. In other cases, the driver/guide will work for the bus company on contract to tour companies handling inbound tour groups from other countries or pre or post convention trips for associations.

This arrangement is exactly the same as it is when a tour operator contracts with a bus company for a driver only except that the driver/guide cost will usually be greater than it will if contracting for just a driver. However, of course, the tour company saves money because it does not have to employ a guide in addition to a driver.

Although driver/guides frequently provide excellent quality tours, he/she is expected to do double-duty. It is difficult to find driver/guides who are able to perform both functions with a high level of expertise. Although the technical knowledge of a driver/guide may well be, and often is, equal to that of the step-on guide or the usually more experienced full-time guide, it is not possible for the driver/guide while on the tour bus to have the type of interaction with tour members that a step-on guide or a tour manager is able to have. The driver/guide must keep his eyes on the road and, therefore, he is unable to establish the same rapport with tour members as the guide who works with the microphone going up and down the aisle of the bus delivering a running commentary and pointing out sights that are passed enroute.

Driver Tipping

Tipping bus drivers is handled in several ways. The more professional tour companies almost unanimously take the approach that driver tips are included in the cost of the tour. They stress that the driver should be tipped only by the tour guide/manager. Normally, 10 to 15 percent of the bus lease cost is included in the overall tour budget for driver tips. The tip is presented when there is a change in drivers or when the tour is over. Traditionally, the tip is a cash amount. The money is placed in a small sealed envelope. This is handed to the driver normally right before the bus leaves for the bus barn at the conclusion of the trip.

It is customary for the tour manager to thank the driver, and hand the tip to the driver in a manner that is personal, quiet, and non-public. Most tour companies strongly discourage making a public display of giving the tip to the driver. Since the time of tipping normally is just before the bus leaves, most find that the best arrangement is for the tour manager to conduct a final check to make certain that all tour member items have been removed from the bus and, as the tour manager is disembarking from this last check, the driver is thanked and the tip is offered.

Tips are designed to provide a financial way of thanking the driver for excellent service. The term "tip" is an acronym meaning "to insure promptness." However, we have come to expect not just promptness, but also quality of service and excellence of service. Most tour companies ask the tour manager to evaluate the quality, excellence, and promptness of service and to tip accordingly. If the driver has performed in an outstandingly good manner, then it is expected that the tour manager will provide a full tip. However, if there are shortcomings on the part of the driver, then less than the full tip is given. If the driver has performed badly and especially if the driver has created problems during the trip, most tour companies expect that the driver will be given no tip whatsoever.

Because it is expected that the amount of the tip will vary depending upon the service provided, tour companies make certain that tour managers receive the full amount of the tip for the driver. This is in small bills and the envelope is not sealed. Therefore, if the service is less than what one should expect to receive, the tour manager is able to remove some of the bills from the tip prior to sealing the envelope and giving the sealed envelope to the driver. Of course, when this occurs, the tour manager is expected to return the balance of the money (that which was deducted from the tip) back to the tour company.

Tour companies rapidly develop reputations. A company which provides customary tips on a regular basis for excellent service rapidly earns a good reputation. Often, drivers compete to excel in their work for such tour companies. On the other hand, tour companies which uniformly provide poor tips or no tips also earn a reputation among bus drivers. Many bus drivers consider themselves professionals and strive to provide a professionally good job even for those tour companies which have earned themselves a poor reputation for tipping. However, it is generally agreed in the industry that those tour companies which tip well tend to obtain a more consistent level of excellent service than those which do not.

Summary

The importance of selecting a good tour bus company is frequently realized only by the negative aspects of client memories of bad tour buses. Quality bus companies make certain that they maintain well-equipped buses which are kept clean and thoroughly maintained. Excellent bus companies also hire experienced drivers who take pride in both themselves and their buses. These drivers meet and exceed stringent dress codes. They have the mechanical ability to repair many small problems enroute and their knowledge of the history and background of the sites covered is sufficiently extensive that they can be relied upon to fill in for the guide, if necessary.

When a tour planner selects a bus company for a tour, usually the first criteria to be considered is the tour company's historical experience in using the bus company. When past experience is good, the tour company seldom looks further. However, when past experience has been negative, the tour company will usually not go back to the bus company under any circumstance. Other factors that are considered include pricing arrangements, the bus company's reputation in the community, the quality of the bus, the service provided by the bus company, the cooperation of the bus company, the availability of buses when needed, and bus company rules.

Once a bus company has been selected, the tour planner will consider the specific bus to be rented. The needs of tour groups can vary considerably from one tour to another. The bus selected should be appropriate for the tour. Factors which need to be considered include:

1. the size of the bus;
2. the seats on the bus;

3. amenities on board the bus;

4. bus microphones;

5. bathrooms aboard the bus;

6. windows;

7. heating and air conditioning;

8. the mechanical condition of the bus; and

9. the cost of the bus.

After selecting the tour bus company you want to work with and your preference in tour buses, the next step is to negotiate a contract for the bus. Usually, the first point of negotiation relates to the cost of the bus. Although time and mileage are the standard factors used in calculating bus costs, negotiating for a better price frequently depends upon the supply of tour buses in the community at the time the bus is needed for the tour and the demand for those buses at the same time.

Frequently, it is easier to negotiate for a tour bus that is newer and/or fitted out with a larger range of amenities and to obtain such a bus at little or no additional cost than it is to obtain a reduction in the basic fee determined through the bus company applied time and mileage calculations. Often, the better quality bus can be obtained simply by asking for it. Other points that frequently can be negotiated include reducing or eliminating the charges on "additional miles" or "additional time usage" when you exceed the estimated mileage or time use. Although few companies will waive the additional charges altogether under any circumstance, frequently a buffer amount of miles and time will be thrown in on a gratis basis by the bus company, if one pushes for this in the negotiation. One should always go into the negotiation with a hierarchical listing of the features one wants in the bus and you should always review the completed contract to make sure that all points negotiated and agreed to have been included in the contract.

Many will not consider the negotiations complete until agreement has been made on the bus driver to be used. Most bus companies will allow a tour company to provide a list of preferred drivers, but many companies will not guarantee the use of any of the drivers on the tour company's preferred list. Many will make an effort to honor the request, but because of scheduling difficulties, most tour bus executives hesitate to guarantee that a specific driver will be provided. However, tour planners should consider keeping a list of preferred drivers and pushing hard to get agreement to use one of the drivers on the list.

Factors to consider in the selection of a driver include the previous history of using the driver, the driver's driving experience, the driver's familiarity with the route to be covered, and having a driver who has sufficient strength to be able to change a tire. While a verbal request for a specific driver is frequently all that is needed, it is always better to include the driver request in the contract or in a separate letter to the bus company.

In addition to negotiating for a top quality bus and requesting an excellent driver, the tour company should provide the bus driver with the tools to do an excellent job. These tools include a bus driver itinerary, driver routing maps, driver parking maps, and a bus driver packet. The packet may vary in its contents, but it usually includes not only an itinerary and both routing and parking maps, but also the following:

1. the driver contract;
2. a driver briefing sheet;
3. appropriate vouchers;
4. vendor contact lists appropriate for the driver;
5. a copy of the bus contract;
6. the daily briefing sheet;
7. the driver's name tag;
8. a copy of the tour brochure;
9. copies of the client and the tour manager itineraries;
10. a copy of the tour member name list;
11. sightseeing brochures; and
12. any give-aways which might be provided for tour members.

Enroute, unless the bus driver is expected to be both a guide and a driver, it is wise to minimize interaction with the driver. The bus driver should be given the freedom and opportunity to concentrate totally on the job of driving the bus. Briefings and discussions with the bus driver should take place before the daily departure of the tour bus and/or at sightseeing or rest stops.

If, however, a driver has been asked to perform the dual roles of both guide and driver, a part of the job of the driver will be to point out sightseeing points enroute. Although this means that the driver will be performing double duty, many drivers are fully capable of doing so. Some drivers get enthusiastic. It is wise to caution them against turning around and looking at the tour members while discussing sights. The driver should keep his eyes on the road even when he is enthusiastic in describing the sights along the way, thereby curbing a natural tendency to have face-to-face direct interaction with tour members.

The tour company should plan driver tips. Normally 10 to 15 percent of the bus lease cost is the maximum amount of tip provided. This is prepared in small bills and an appropriate envelope for the tip is included together with the money for the tip in the package of materials given to the tour manager prior to departure on the tour. The tour manager should evaluate the quality of service and should not provide the full tip if service was not excellent. Reputations for tipping are established rapidly and can make a difference in the quality of service provided by tour bus drivers. Therefore, tour planners and guides should take bus driver tipping seriously, but should nevertheless avoid overtipping.

DISCUSSION QUESTIONS

These questions may be discussed by two or more students outside of class as a fun way of reviewing this chapter or they may be discussed by everyone during class for a more wide-ranging discussion.

1. What are some of the negative types of memories a tour member might have if the tour company makes a poor choice in the selection of a bus company, a tour bus, or a tour bus driver?
2. What type of "image" do tour bus companies look for in the selection of drivers?
3. What factors do tour companies consider in selecting a bus company?
4. What are examples of "add-on pricing"?
5. What factors do tour companies consider in selecting a tour bus?
6. For what reasons is the size of the bus considered to be the most important factor in bus selection, other than cost?
7. Who should select the audio tapes played on tour buses and what type of music is recommended?
8. What is the general guideline used to determine whether or not a bus with a bathroom on board should be leased?
9. Why should bus contracts be reviewed by tour company executives before they are signed?
10. Why is having a bus driver itinerary considered to be important?

ROLE PLAY EXERCISES

1. Two students may participate in this role play either out of class as a fun way to review the chapter or as an in-class exercise. One plays the role of the tour planner working for the tour operator and the other plays the role of the bus company sales representative working for the tour bus company vendor. Please read the script and then pick up the conversation in your own words.

   TOUR PLANNER: I understand you have a wide range of buses in your fleet. Our tour group consists of tenth year university fraternity alumni and their wives. It is an active group and they will be going into some mountainous terrain. Some of the area will be steep graded roads, so we need a rugged bus that will hold between 30 and 40 passengers. The tour members will be staying at a chalet pretty far up the mountain.

BUS SALES REPRESENTATIVE: Most of our buses are equipped for mountainous terrain, but a few of the larger, better-equipped buses we allow only on paved highways. Will you need something with rear or under-the-bus cargo storage or will they just be bringing overnight bags?

TOUR PLANNER: It's just one overnight and two full days of touring. Probably the overhead racks on board the bus will be enough since most will be bringing only carry-on-bags. They do want to show a videotape and they have asked for an open bar on the bus. Can you accommodate that? And what kind of costs are we looking at?

BUS SALES REPRESENTATIVE: It will be hard. We will have to bring in a bus. I calculate that total mileage will be 632 miles and at a rate of . . .

CONTINUE ON YOUR OWN

2. Two students may participate in this role play either out of class as a fun way to review the chapter or as an in-class exercise. One plays the role of a new tour planner and the other plays the role of an experienced tour planner. Please read the script and then pick up the conversation in your own words.

NEW TOUR PLANNER: This is the first time I've ever had to make a tour bus booking. What do I do?

EXPERIENCED TOUR PLANNER: The first thing you need to do is to check out the bus companies that you will potentially use. Once you have made a decision on a company, then you will need to negotiate with them.

NEW TOUR PLANNER: Those seem to be the general guidelines, but how do I find tour bus companies to contact in the first place? And what criteria do I use in selecting a bus company?

EXPERIENCED TOUR PLANNER: Those questions will take a few minutes to answer, but I will do my best. Let's start with how to find bus companies from which to make a selection. One of the best ways to begin is to . . .

CONTINUE ON YOUR OWN

3. Two students may participate in this role play either out of class as a fun way to review the chapter or as an in-class exercise. One plays the role of a new tour planner and the other plays the role of an experienced tour planner. Please read the script and then pick up the conversation in your own words.

EXPERIENCED TOUR PLANNER: Did you find a bus company that will work for you—and are you pleased with your selection?

NEW TOUR PLANNER: Yes, I appreciate your advise. I found a company I'm very pleased with—thus far. I'm just beginning to negotiate with them. I'm still hesitant. Not about the company. I'm sure they are good. But about my negotiating ability. I'm not sure what to ask for, what to say, how far I should push. And after agreements have been reached, I'm not too sure about the contracting process or what I should do to follow up. Can you give me some advice on these matters?

EXPERIENCED TOUR OPERATOR: Sure. Take it step by step. Let's go over each step. First . . .

CONTINUE ON YOUR OWN

GROUP DISCUSSION SITUATION: CROAKING CRIPPLES' TIPS FOR SCREEMING MIMI

Harried Hanna is the youngest and newest tour manager working for Croaking Cripples Tours. She is nearing the end of her first senior citizen group tour for Croaking Cripples Tours. It was a one-day tour into the Everglades of Florida. It featured a full afternoon of snake hunting in the marshes. The company provided individual snake containers so that each senior citizen could bring two or three snakes back to the senior citizen home to train as their personal pets.

The bus driver, Screaming Mimi, seemed nice enough at the beginning of the tour, although she showed up 15 minutes late because she said the waitress at the place where she stopped for breakfast was trying to fix an overhead fan and didn't get her coffee to her on time. Nevertheless, Screaming Mimi assisted in helping some of the normally wheelchair-bound seniors up the steep steps of the bus during the loading process. However, Screaming Mimi monopolized the microphone during the drive to the Everglades, telling tour members her own version of how the Everglades were settled by Mexican royalty escaping after their revenge against Montezuma. Her story became more colorful as she sipped from some type of bottle contained in a paper bag.

Problems with Mimi, however, started when she could not find the Everglades. An hour after scheduled arrival at the Everglades and after having spent 45 minutes driving from one Miami-area shopping center to another, she eventually found a road leading to the Everglades and although the seniors had to skip lunch, they were able to have enough time to collect most of the snakes they wished to train as pets. Screaming Mimi then objected to the seniors placing their snake boxes on empty seats as she said that the wet boxes would leak water into the fabric of the seats and besides, she noted, the escaping snakes would probably be more comfortable slithering in the bus floor carpeting rather than on the fabric of the seats. After considerable arguing. Screaming Mimi finally agreed to let the seniors place their snake boxes on the empty tour bus seats.

Harried Hanna has noted that Croaking Cripples Tours has provided her with a tip envelope and $43 for a tip. However, she feels that Screaming Mimi was not the the best quality tour bus driver and is considering reducing the total amount of tip to be given to Screaming Mimi.

In your group session consider how you would handle the tip for Screaming Mimi and how much you would tip her. In your group session, select one person to chair the group. All will have an equal vote on decisions. In the group session you are expected to reach agreement on the tipping arrangements and prepare a written paper on your suggestions for tipping to be presented to the entire class by the chair of your group.

EXERCISE

Break into groups of no more than three students working together. Yours will probably be the same group that has been working together in the development of a one-day tour since the beginning of the course.

Prepare a bus management plan and a bus driver packet for your one-day tour. The packet should include detailed routing maps with the routing clearly marked on them. Bus parking location maps should also be provided unless bus parking locations are clearly identified on the routing maps. A driver contract should be included, if it is not a part of the bus contract. Both a bus contract and an analysis of the bus contract should be included. Prepare a bus driver itinerary which will include notes on parking and on either staying with the bus while tour members are on tour or providing for bus security during the time tour members are off of the bus.

As a part of the bus management plan, prepare a driver selection criteria sheet. Also prepare a plan for a bus barn pick-up of the bus, cleaning of the bus, food and beverage loading (if appropriate), and tour member bus termination point arrangements. These arrangements should include all return activities. These should include food and beverage unloading, plans for ecologically sound trash removal, bus cleaning, a driver tip plan, and bus return to the bus barn.

CHAPTER 10
Tour Vendors

OBJECTIVES

Upon completion of this chapter, the student will be able to:

1. Identify the kinds of vendors with which tour operators are most likely to work.
2. Draft rough sightseeing and food service vendor contracts.
3. Explain the types of problems which one might encounter when working with small- , medium- , and large-sized sightseeing vendors.
4. Compare the advantages and the disadvantages of booking air travel arrangements through travel agency vendors rather than directly with air carrier vendors.

While tour operators work with many kinds of vendors, the major vendors with which they contract are:

1. hotels and resorts;
2. transportation vendors (air carrier or bus); and
3. sightseeing vendors.

Because work with bus companies is so considerable, the last chapter was devoted to that industry alone. This chapter will concern itself with the other major vendors that the tour company deals with to a lesser degree.

Hotel and Other Lodging Vendors

In working with hotel and other lodging vendors, the tour operator must strike a balance in obtaining quality accommodations at a price that is affordable for the target market being solicited for participation in the tour. One of the initial concerns is to identify what is considered "quality" lodging for tour participants.

Americans want private baths and most Americans, even many who are married, while they may not be hesitant about sharing a room, will almost always be hesitant about sharing a bed. Tours are normally sold on a two person per room basis on what is usually referred to in the industry as a *double*. Those wishing to have a single room are usually charged a single room supplement.

Therefore, the first step is to find lodging that meets the basic requirements of two beds in a room with a private bath.

It should go without saying that the hotel needs to be near scheduled sightseeing points. An experienced tour guide reports being shocked to find that a little-known museum was on her tour group's itinerary with an arrival time at 10 A.M. When she asked the driver how many blocks the museum was from the hotel, she was upset to learn it was nearly 500 miles—an impossible drive no matter what time in the morning they left the hotel. This suggests that the tour planner did not take a familiarization trip prior to developing the itinerary.

Additional qualifications will be required based upon the type of tour involved and its target audience. For example, some senior citizen groups will request rooms that do not require uphill walking or stair climbing.

After identifying all essential lodging factors and listing those that would be desirable, a checklist can be designed. Lodging properties that meet these requirements can often be located through several sources. Hotel guides are sometimes beneficial. The *Official Hotel and Resort Guide* lists a number of hotels and resorts which work with tour companies. Many of these have a large number of rooms, all of which are priced the same and many of which have identical floor plans, furnishings, and views. This is especially beneficial for tour groups since most tour members are sensitive to one or more of the tour members having a bigger room, a more desirable floor plan, or a better view. The *Star Guide to Elegant Properties* is beneficial when tours are using more expensive hotels or resorts. Other guides can also be beneficial.

State and national tourist bureaus also can be helpful in finding appropriate lodging. By providing bureau staff members with a checklist of requirements, they can often make specific recommendations, indicating the pros and cons of each property.

Once one or more properties have been identified as beneficial, travel to the destination area to see the properties should be considered. Usually state or national tourist bureaus can assist in designing a familiarization trip which will allow for a visit to each of the several properties under consideration.

Negotiations with properties should be initiated on an appointment basis, meeting with the top marketing executive in each property if at all possible. It is suggested that the negotiated arrangements agreed upon through discussions with property executives be detailed immediately after each meeting. Confirm agreements through the required completion of your own hotel information confirmation form. (See Figure 10-1 for an example of a hotel information confirmation form.) Discuss potential renovations or other disturbances that might affect tour members during their stay and confirm with selected properties that no negative changes, construction, or other known potential disturbances are

trentway tours ltd.

680 THE QUEENSWAY, P.O. BOX 772, PETERBOROUGH, ONTARIO K9J 7A2 (705) 748-6411 TELEX 06-962880

YOUR PROMPT ATTENTION TO SUPPLY THE CORRECT INFORMATION ON THIS FORM WILL SPEED THE DELIVERY OF OUR BOOKING CONFIRMATIONS FOR THE DATES YOU ARE HOLDING FOR OUR GROUPS.

PLEASE MAKE CORRECTIONS IN THIS AREA

TELEPHONE NO. ____________ TELEX NO. ____________

RATES	FROM DAY	FROM MO.	FROM YEAR	TO DAY	TO MO.	TO YEAR	SINGLE	TWIN	TRIPLE	QUAD.	QUINT.

RATES NET: YES ☐ NO ☐ or COMMISSIONABLE @ ____________

BAGGAGE HANDLING (Round Trip) $ ____________

DEPOSIT PER TOUR: YES ☐ NO ☐ if yes, AMOUNT $ ________ BY ________ (DAY MO. YR.)

OR

DEPOSIT HELD IN ESCROW UNTIL FINAL TOUR YES ☐ NO ☐ if yes, AMOUNT $ ________ BY ________ (DAY MO. YR.)

NUMBER OF COMPLIMENTARY ROOMS PER BUS: ____________

PLACE AND PERSON/DEPT. TO WHICH OUR ROOMING LISTS AND LAST MINUTE CHANGES SHOULD BE FORWARDED

PLEASE MAKE CORRECTIONS IN THIS AREA

TELEPHONE NO. ____________ TELEX NO. ____________

TRENTWAY TOURS LTD.
PETERBOROUGH, ONTARIO

CONTACT :
TITLE :

Member of: ntba NATIONAL TOUR BROKERS ASSOCIATION; ONTARIO TRAVEL INDUSTRY CONFERENCE; ONTARIO MOTOR COACH ASSOCIATION; ACTA ALLIANCE OF CANADIAN TRAVEL ASSOCIATIONS; AMERICAN SOCIETY OF TRAVEL AGENTS

PLEASE RETURN THE COMPLETED FORM AND RETAIN ONE COPY FOR YOUR FILES
YOUR PROMPT ATTENTION IS REQUESTED

FIGURE 10-1 SAMPLE HOTEL INFORMATION CONFIRMATION FORM

Reproduced with permission from Trentway Tours, Peterborough, Ontario, Canada.

planned for the time when the tour group will be at the hotel or resort (see Figure 10-2).

Prior to departure from the home city, a prioritization of lodging properties should be prepared. Normally, properties are ranked from first choice through third choice. Often a second visit to the first choice property is undertaken to go

trentway tours ltd.

FAX (705) 748-2452

680 THE QUEENSWAY, P.O. BOX 1987, PETERBOROUGH, ONTARIO K9J 7X7 • (705) 748-6411 TELEX 06-962880

MEMO TO: ALL SUPPLIERS

RE: ACCOMMODATION AND TRAVEL INDUSTRY ACT

When we were negotiating our contract with you, we stressed the importance of your advising us of the existence of any construction or renovation at or near your facility that might affect our passengers adversely. Our failure to convey to our clients such information can give rise to serious ramifications under Ontario's Travel Industry Act.

A further section of that Act obliges us to ensure that the accommodation is, upon our passengers' arrival, in the same condition as was represented to him at the time of sale. We take this opportunity to ask categorically if there has been, or will be during the course of the visit of the passengers named on the accompanying rooming list, any change in the conditions, facilities, buildings or amenities to be provided since the date the rooms were contracted. Your prompt reply by fax, SAM, telex or telegram is requested.

Sincerely yours,
TRENTWAY-WAGAR INC.,

James J. Devlin,
President.
JJD/dn

Member of:

FIGURE 10-2 ACCOMODATION AND TRAVEL AGENCY ACT FORM

Reproduced with permission from Trentway Tours, Peterborough, Ontario, Canada.

over any points where there may be concerns. During this second visit, or shortly after returning back to the tour headquarters office, a *letter of agreement* should be drawn up indicating the tour company's understanding of the booking terms. This letter of agreement is sent to the property, which may accept by signing a copy and returning it or the property may not agree to one or more of the terms and will correspond accordingly.

Sometimes several changes need to be made in the letter of agreement before it is finally acceptable to both parties. Obtaining a letter signed by both parties is the goal. A contractual agreement is usually prepared based upon this letter of agreement.

Many lodging properties will want to use their own contracts, some requiring sole use of their contracts. When use of a lodging property contract is required, the tour company should attempt to have onerous clauses struck and initialled or write in additional clauses favorable to themselves.

Price as a Hotel Selection Factor

In addition to locating accommodations that meet quality standards, it is important that the tour planner also find accommodations that are within the price range identified as ideal for the tour. This is more of a challenge during the "in season" than when hotels are empty in the off season. However, with enough shopping, it is usually possible to find a hotel that will be within the price range and which also will meet the quality standards needed. Use a hotel cost sheet (see Figure 10-3 for an example) to project the total cost for each property and the price per person per night for each property.

The Hotel Marketing/Sales Department and Its Ability to Commit

Initial prices can often be negotiated downward. It is important, therefore, to identify a person in the marketing/sales department who is in a position to commit the hotel. You should negotiate with that person. However, there are times when a hotel marketing executive may not be in a position to commit. This is sometimes a difficult matter to determine up front.

In some cases, especially when a hotel is in the process of being sold or if a hotel is owned by one person or a small group of people, the owners may not back a commitment made by the marketing department. By staying in touch with the marketing executive with whom the contract is signed, you should be able to find out when the marketing executive has overextended his ability to negotiate.

Wherever possible, it is better to find this out early. One of the best ways to do this is to require the hotel marketing/sales executive with whom the negotiation is undertaken to sign a binding contract with a penalty clause included if the hotel fails to provide the services and facilities agreed to in the contract. Some hotels are reticent about signing such contracts, but this is one of the few ways

```
                        HOTEL COST SHEET


HOTEL NAME:    _____


ADDRESS:        _____


TELEPHONE:      _____


KEY CONTACT:_____


HOTEL DATES:_____


ROOM REQUEST:_____


    SINGLE                                      DOUBLE


_____              RATE              _____

X _____         NUMBER OF ROOMS        _____

_____            SUB-TOTAL           _____


X  _____          NUMBER OF NIGHTS        _____


_____            SUB-TOTAL           _____


+_____     SF LODGERS/CITY TAX(.09875)  _____


_____            SUB-TOTAL           _____


+ _____    COMMISSION 15% PLUS TAX     _____
                      (OPTIONAL)
                    TAX (1.05875)

_____             TOTAL              _____


DIV _____        NUMBER OF PERSONS        _____


_____          COST PER PERSON       _____


_____        BAGGAGE PER PERSON      _____


_____             TOTAL              _____
_____    PRICE PER PERSON PER NIGHT  _____
```

FIGURE 10–3 SAMPLE HOTEL COST SHEET

Reproduced with permission from Rojo Tours, Santa Fe, NM.

that a hotel can be encouraged to stick to its commitments. If the hotel market-ing/sales executive is hesitant to sign either a contract or a letter of agreement, ask if the contract must be signed by the general manager or one or more own-ers. If so, ask that person(s) to sign the contract.

Working with Air Carrier Vendors

Tour companies have the option of working through a travel agency to get the airline group space needed (sharing commissions with the travel agency) or ap-proaching the airline directly. If the tour company has a history of running a large number of air tours, the tour company will usually be in a position to ne-gotiate a better price and better terms than the company could obtain if it went through a travel agency.

However, if the tour company is new or if it normally runs bus tours, the tour company will often obtain a better price by working through a travel agency. Airlines generally provide price reductions only to their better clients. Travel agencies buy considerably more airline seats from them than do tour op-erators, especially small tour operators. It is for that reason that many tour com-panies are better off to negotiate price and ticketing arrangements through a large travel agency which handles a substantial number of bookings. Often it is because of the very large number of seats blocked for its clients that an agency is able to obtain far better per seat pricing for tour members than a tour com-pany could receive. When this is the case, not only will the tour member usually obtain a better seat (preferred seating), but the tour company is able to pay a lower price for the air carrier seats it occupies.

After a tour company has worked through a travel agency on several air tours and has purchased a substantial number of air carrier seats, the tour com-pany is in a position to meet with air carrier marketing executives and negotiate future tour group fares and ticketing. The time needed to evolve to this position varies. Some tour companies run few multi-day, long-distance tours while others run this type of tour quite often.

Airline Group Desk vs. Airline Sales Rep vs. Other Contact

If the tour company decides to go directly to the air carriers in order to nego-tiate for air fares for tour members and/or free or reduced rate air tickets for tour leaders, the tour planner will be referred to the *airline group desk*. However, most air carrier group desks are not given a large amount of negotiation flexi-bility. They are provided with set rules laid out in writing. Any organization wishing to obtain low "group" rates must abide by all rules in order to qualify for those rates.

However, air carriers are like all other industry vendors. They have low-booked flights and high-booked flights. Airline executives are usually far more concerned about booking additional seats on low-booked flights than on those flights which will fill up anyway even without group bookings. Therefore, when the tour operator can help an air carrier in filling traditionally low-booked flights, the tour executive should consider negotiating with a different airline contact than the airline's "group" desk reservationist.

The sales representative for the airline is a good person to contact and, in some cases, the sales representative will be able to obtain lower (occasionally even unpublished) fares. However, like group desk reservationists, most sales representatives are locked into working with only a limited range of negotiating ability before they must have it cleared with higher level executives. Therefore, many find that if they start the negotiation process with a high-level airline executive rather than a sales representative, they are more successful in either obtaining lower fares or getting low-fare requirement waivers.

If the tour planner wishes to obtain special services other than cuts in air fare (such as VIP services, special onboard services, facilities, or considerations, or assistance in post-arrival baggage handling or customs clearance) and if the tour planner wants to have these special arrangements guaranteed by the airline and contracted for in writing, it is usually better to negotiate these at as high a level as possible. Most of the time neither the local sales representative nor the group desk reservationist will be in a position to agree to any aspect of special facilities or special handling. Again, the ability to obtain these services and concessions from carriers will depend upon how badly the airline needs to have the seats filled.

Selecting an Air Carrier

While the price per person is an important factor in selecting an air carrier (sometimes it is the only factor that can be considered), other factors should be investigated and looked into when the price is the same or quite similar. These factors include:

1. native carrier preference in ground handling;
2. inflight services; and
3. inflight food and beverages.

Some countries give preferential treatment to their native carriers when processing clients through arrival customs and baggage handling. If there is a strong degree of difference in handling, use of the native carrier when flying into the capital or another large city should be given serious consideration. There are instances where arriving passengers coming in off of flights of foreign carriers (not native to the country of arrival) have had to wait until the passengers disembarking from two or three native carrier flights are processed first. While this may seem unfair, tour members caught in this political native carrier preferential arrangement can become quite disgruntled and schedules planned for immediate post-arrival arrangements can be thrown off considerably.

On-board facilities are also important. Obviously, if one plane is a Boeing 707 and the other is a Boeing 747, the seat size differences and the resulting comfort level of clients will be substantial. Therefore, the type of aircraft flown can be important. However, beyond the type of aircraft, you may also wish to consider such factors as the amount of reading material available on the flight, the number of seats in the plane's configuration (which determines to some extent the amount of leg room and the amount of tilt of chairs), and any special facilities on board (for example, a few carriers now have a stand-up bar in the economy section of their 747 aircraft).

Food and beverage should also be considered. Some carriers consistently win prizes for their outstanding food and beverage services. But the food and beverages served on other carriers can be mundane, small in portion size, and unattractive. With all other things being equal, if you can obtain an outstanding food and beverage service, passengers are happier.

You should also be aware that there are several air carriers which do not serve alcoholic beverages. For some groups (Alcoholics Anonymous members), this is okay. For other groups, for example, the International Beer Drinkers' Association, this arrangement is not okay. Many passengers are simply uncomfortable without being able to have an alcoholic beverage.

All of these factors, however, fall into the "nice-to-have" category and, in most cases, the tour planner should not pay extra for them but should attempt to gain them within the constraints of the budgeted air price. If two or more carriers offer the same price, the tour planner may want to consider these additional evaluation points.

Sightseeing Vendors

Sightseeing vendors vary considerably in type and in degree of sophistication. Vendors can be classified in several ways, but probably the easiest way is by type of site. For example, there are vendors who offer tours of antique or other special buildings. There are also multi-building vendors who offer tours of facilities which consist of several buildings. There are also theme park vendors which usually offer an opportunity to see a large number of buildings, landscapes, events of some type (usually staged), and/or performances (sometimes live and sometimes multi-media). There are sightseeing vendors which offer garden or other pure landscape vistas. And, there are event-oriented sightseeing vendors who offer the opportunity to see one or more events (sometimes on a once-a-year or other occasional basis and at other times on a continuing basis). There are also transportation-oriented sightseeing vendors.

Each of the sightseeing vendors ranges in its degree of sophistication based primarily on factors relating to the size of the sightseeing activity and the number of tourists who visit the sight. Many small sightseeing activities and facilities, especially historic ones, are managed by volunteers. In a few cases, the volunteers are given training, but often they receive no training at all. In dealing with vendor volunteers, especially those who are untrained, the tour planner needs to be especially wary. It is not at all unusual to have problems when a vendor depends upon volunteers to reach agreements and to provide services. Often agreed-upon arrangements are never written down and the person who set up the arrangement is no longer working with the sightseeing vendor when the tour group arrives. Most tour planners try to stay away from visiting this type of site because of the high potential for problems.

A higher level of sophistication, but usually one that is less professional than many tour planners would like, is often found with the small sightseeing vendor who typically provides access to an antique home, an historic building, or even, in some cases, a group of buildings. Although there may be a paid person working at these sightseeing destination points, the paid person may very well also be a caretaker who doubles as a guide and admission ticket sales person. In these facilities, the types of problems that you can run into include:

1. mixing tour group members with general public members for tours;

2. leaving the tour group in the middle of the tour to admit other people to the building or facility or for other administrative purposes resulting in delays and an unprofessional presentation; and

3. not being available at the site at the time the tour group shows up.

The caretaker/guide may be out to lunch, ill, or some problem necessitating absence may have occurred.

Larger facilities tend to do a better job. However, with this next level up there can still be problems. Problems encountered in working with the mid-sized sightseeing vendor often center around a misunderstanding of arrangements. Frequently, the person who makes arrangements with tour groups is not the person who collects tickets and handles the tour when it arrives. One must get all arrangement details written into contracts when dealing with mid-sized tour vendors. Find out who will be on duty at the time that the tour group arrives and, if possible, talk with that person directly either in person or on the phone to make sure in advance that there are no misunderstandings.

Although the potential for misunderstanding between the tour planner and the group coordinator also applies to large and more sophisticated sightseeing vendors, it occurs far less frequently. The larger sightseeing vendors tend to serve many tour groups. They usually understand what tour groups need. Because their reputation is on the line, they tend to have sophisticated, streamlined operations. They follow through efficiently and effectively. Tour planners feel most comfortable working with this type of vendor. However, it is not always with this type of vendor that tour members are happiest. Many tour members want to see the off-the-beaten-track sights and because of that, it is necessary for tour planners to weigh the advantages and disadvantages of working with each potential sightseeing vendor before arbitrarily saying no just because the vendor is small or uses volunteer help.

Another consideration, of course, is price. Some sightseeing destinations charge a considerable amount for entrance fees. The tour planner needs to determine whether or not the high admission price is acceptable in view of what tour members can be expected to receive in terms of pleasure in viewing, experiencing, or participating in some aspect of the sightseeing destination. In some cases, the felt return on investment by tour participants may well be too little. For example, a midwestern-based tour operator once included balloon trips in many of his itineraries. Although many tour members seemed to enjoy the trips, the evaluations at the end indicated that they felt the value received from the balloon trip was not in proportion to the perceived value of other trip components which were approximately the same in cost. He made the balloon trips optional and found that almost none of his tour members took them. His tour enrollments increased because the cost of the tour without the balloon trip was substantially reduced.

Non-price considerations include the ability to obtain confirmed arrangements, the past history of the tour vendor/tour operator working relationship, and the degree of hardship placed on tour members in experiencing or viewing the sightseeing point.

Other Vendors

A wide range of other vendors may be used by the tour company. Chief among these are restaurants and ground operators. Ground operators tend to be umbrella companies which provide a variety of services. They offer these services, normally in a menu format, to tour companies, incentive travel houses, and to other group travel firms. The food service vendors used should be those accustomed to serving tour groups. Usually a contract can and should be developed for working with the restaurant, cafeteria, or other food service vendor. Other vendors may include limousine services, other transportation vendors, and those who assist in lining up guest expert presenters. In each case, contact the state or national tourist bureau and other local experts for recommendations and develop a listing of criteria to use in the selection process.

Summary

Tour companies work with many types of tour vendors. The major ones are hotels and resorts, transportation vendors (air and bus), and sightseeing vendors. In working with lodging vendors, it is necessary to strike a balance between booking quality accommodations and obtaining reasonable costs. Quality levels will be determined by the budget of the tour as well as the quality expectations of tour participants. The search for accommodations meeting these and other criteria may start with a perusal of hotel and resort guides or by obtaining state and/or national tourist bureau recommendations.

Negotiation meetings are scheduled with the executives of the potential accommodation vendors. Comparisons of accommodations, price, and other factors are undertaken before a contract is signed. The ability to negotiate will be based upon the degree to which the property needs the tour business. Once this is determined, identifying the best person with whom to negotiate is the next task. This is often a marketing executive, but it may be an owner, a co-owner, or a chief executive officer.

In obtaining air reservations and ticketing, you should determine whether or not it will be beneficial to work through a travel agency or directly with the air carrier. If the tour company is new or has very few air tours, a travel agency will probably be able to obtain more negotiated benefits and cost reduction than the tour company will. If you work directly with an air carrier, however, you should start with the highest marketing executive who has the authority to negotiate. Group desk personnel and airline sales representatives often are locked into only negligible negotiating ability. If pricing from two or more carriers is either the same or close, other factors should be considered in making a final decision. Three of these factors are ground handling carrier preference, inflight services, and inflight food and beverage. These three factors, however, normally fall into the nice-to-have category and are usually considered only after making certain that the lowest fare per person is obtained.

In selecting sightseeing vendors, you should be wary of potential problems that occur when dealing with small sightseeing vendors, medium-size sightseeing vendors, and larger ones. Each has its own set of potential problems, but you should take precautions in avoiding each set of problems. Normally, having a letter of agreement or a contract, especially one that includes penalty clauses for nonperformance or for performance to a lesser standard than that agreed to in the contract is one of the best ways of assuring that the vendor's performance will be that which is expected.

Other vendors with which the tour company will frequently interface include ground operators and restaurants. Here, too, it is recommended that contracts to be agreed to by the vendor restaurants and the vendor ground operators. Again, having penalty clauses in the contracts may help. Other vendors with which one may consider working include limousine services, other transportation vendors, and guest expert presenters.

DISCUSSION QUESTIONS

These questions may be discussed by two or more students outside of class as a fun way of reviewing this chapter or they may be discussed by everyone during class for a more wide-ranging discussion.

1. What three major types of vendors do tour operators work with most?

2. Between what two factors should a tour operator strike a balance in working with hotel and lodging vendors?

3. What two basic qualifications should you consider as the first step in dealing with lodging vendors?

4. What are two of the guides which tour planners might consult in identifying potential hotels with which to contract?

5. Why should tour operators obtain the signature on the accommodation contract of the owner or the chief executive officer when contracting with accommodation vendors?

6. Why might a tour operator prefer to book airline seats for air tours through a travel agency rather than directly with an air carrier?

7. What are the pros and cons of booking air reservations through an airline group desk as compared with working with an airline sales representative to make the reservation?

8. What three factors might be considered in selecting an air carrier if the prices charged by two or more carriers are very similar or are identical?

9. What are the disadvantages of working with small-, medium-, and large-sized sightseeing vendors?

10. Why might it be beneficial to work with a contract when arranging for tour meal functions and negotiating with food service vendors?

ROLE PLAY EXERCISES

1. Two students may participate in this role play either out of class as a fun way to review the chapter or as an in-class exercise. One plays the role of a new tour planner and the other plays the role of an experienced tour planner. Please read the script and then pick up the conversation in your own words.

    NEW TOUR PLANNER: I've only worked with bus tours, thus far. It's a pleasure to have an opportunity to work on an air tour. What are the major differences in working with vendors, other than contracting with air carriers for the seats rather than with bus companies for a bus?

    EXPERIENCED TOUR PLANNER: Actually, the vendor with which we work most on air tours is a travel agency; not an air carrier.

    NEW TOUR PLANNER: That doesn't make sense to me. Can't we obtain the airline seats cheaper and get more of the creature-comfort benefits for our travelers if we negotiate with the air carrier directly than if we go through a travel agency?

    EXPERIENCED TOUR PLANNER: One might think so. However, . . .

    CONTINUE ON YOUR OWN

2. Two students may participate in this role play either out of class as a fun way to review the chapter or as an in-class exercise. One plays the role of the CFO (Chief Financial Officer for a company) and the other plays the role of the

company's tour planner. Please read the script and then pick up the conversation in your own words.

CHIEF FINANCIAL OFFICER: You asked me to alert you when we reached a level of $1 million in terms of air bookings for our tour members. As you know, we increased our air tours this year by over 30 percent. We haven't quite reached the $1 million mark yet, but we should get there within the next 20 days. Why is it important?

TOUR PLANNER: In negotiating with air carriers, as well as the travel agency we customarily use for booking air space, it seems to me that the $1 million mark is the point at which we can start doing considerably better by negotiating directly with air carriers as compared with continuing to use our travel agency. Now that I know we are so close, I will schedule a series of meetings with the air carriers. But I will need back up documentation from you showing exactly what we have booked in terms of dollar value—and this should go back for a minimum of two years. I need to show patterns.

CHIEF FINANCIAL OFFICER: I understand what you are doing and I appreciate your efforts to try and save us money. However, I have a concern about getting at least the same range of financial and nonfinancial benefits that we have been getting through the agency. Won't we lose more money by having to employ someone to work directly on the negotiations and to call in the reservation information to the airline. Surely there will be more personnel hours taken up this way. And, I expect you will spend a lot more hours with the airlines than you currently do with the agency. As you know, your time is valuable and you cost the company a lot of money.

TOUR PLANNER: I understand your concerns. Let me address each of them. First, . . .

CONTINUE ON YOUR OWN

3. Two students may participate in this role play either out of class as a fun way to review the chapter or as an in-class exercise. One plays the role of a tour planning assistant and the other plays the role of the company's tour planner. Please read the script and then pick up the conversation in your own words.

TOUR PLANNING ASSISTANT: I know our tour members on the Atlantic Horrors Tour consider the Revolutionary Murder Center both a major and an exciting tour stop. However, we have had problems with the last three tour groups that stopped there. The caretaker is getting so old that he is making mistakes. He takes tour members from one room to the next and locks the doors after him. He thinks everyone is with the group and by the time he has reached the end of the tour, he has locked some of the tour members in two or three of the different rooms. Since the lights are out and the tour members are aware that this is a place where many murders have been committed, they tend to be fearful. Remember that 98-year-old woman you were concerned about?

TOUR PLANNER: Yes, don't tell me she had a heart attack or something like that.

TOUR PLANNING ASSISTANT: Not quite that bad. You said she was too old and she moved too slowly to keep up with the group. Well, when the caretaker unlocked the door where she had been trapped for almost 15 minutes, you should have seen her run out of that place. She made a mad dash to the bus and refused to budge from her seat for the rest of the evening.

TOUR PLANNER: I'll bet your next question is going to be whether or not we can eliminate the Murder Center from the tour.

TOUR PLANNING ASSISTANT: That's right. Can't we find something to substitute it with or just eliminate it altogether.

TOUR PLANNER: I know there are problems, but . . .

CONTINUE ON YOUR OWN

GROUP DISCUSSION SITUATION: THE DETHRONED BARONESS OF HENSLEY

Brikette Hensly of the House of Hensly in Little Labrador, Tennessee has been the Resident General Manager for the House of Hensly for the last 20 years. Originally, her family owned the majestic Hensly Hotel. It was her grandfather who converted the hotel into what was then called the House of Hensly because of the multi-million dollar renovation and the addition of several acres of landscaped gardens surrounding the main building. This made it one of the more famous and one of the most expensive luxury resorts in America.

Brikette's brother, Henry, inherited the House of Hensly and lived well on the Hensly wealth for many years. He had little concern about the House of Hensly and spent most of his time traveling and gambling. Brikette, meanwhile, reigned over the House of Hensly and because of her tight reign, she was called the Baroness of Hensly. Henry, however, squandered the wealth and had to sell the House of Hensly to a banking group about seven years ago in order to pay his gambling debts. Henry died mysteriously shortly afterwards, leaving Brikette with an uncomfortable, but barely workable contractual arrangement to work with the banking group which now owns the House of Hensly.

She retained a small amount of stock, a place on the Board of Directors, an apartment wing as her personal residence, and a very good compensation. Most important to Brikette, however, she retained her reign over the House of Hensly, being appointed the top-paid executive in exchange for all the aforementioned benefits.

Almost from the beginning the House of Hensly has catered to small deluxe tours. Sven Svorgenthral, a small special interest tour operator, has used the House of Hensly for many years for his small groups of wealthy tour members. They usually fly in on private chartered aircraft on a Friday afternoon and spend three days at the House of Hensly. A luxury motorcoach is leased and the tour members take short trips to Nashville, the mountains, and to other sights each day, returning to the House of Hensly for a sumptuous dinner and a quiet evening of chamber music entertainment.

Sven reserved 20 private rooms, each with a second or third floor view of the House of Hensly gardens for his latest tour group made up of top members of the Association of Retired Diamond Thieves. He made the reservation directly with Brikette and because of their many years of experience in working together, he was able to obtain special touches such as the ice carving in the form of the famous "Green Diamond" which formed the centerpiece for the buffet feast served the evening of arrival.

When their aircraft arrived yesterday, Brikette was on the luxury motorcoach personally welcoming the retired thief tour members, having the driver of a second van pick up all luggage from the aircraft and transfer it back to the House of Hensly. Brikette had the motorcoach driver take the long way back to the House of Hensly and enroute she stopped the motorcoach several times to explain some of the more interesting sights that they were passing. Before arriving at the House of Hensly Brikette distributed room keys to each tour member and gave them a verbal tour of the property and the gardens.

The luggage had already arrived. Suitcases had been unpacked and clothing hung up in closets or placed in enormous chests of drawers when the luxury motorcoach arrived. The tour members were ushered into the drawing room where cocktails and hors d'oerves were served. Again, Brikette welcomed the guests and gave them a short tour of the first floor public rooms before they, sipping their cocktails, made their way to their individual rooms. After relaxing and changing for dinner, an eight course meal was served. That evening a quartet of accomplished musicians featuring a world-renowned harpist entertained the House of Hensly guests in the Great Drawing Room while well-trained serving staff members unobtrusively kept everyone supplied with cocktails and caviar.

The whole evening went smoothly and Sven went to bed congratulating himself on having put together yet another outstandingly good tour.

This morning, however, has been a shock. Sven woke up about 3 A.M. to the sound of loud noises downstairs. Rushing into a robe and dashing downstairs, he found movers taking file cabinets and stacks of books and papers into moving vans. Two older, executive type men were directing the activity and Brikette was screaming at everyone in sight. Sven demanded an explanation, but as soon as Brikette started a sobbing tale, going back to the old story of Henry's gambling, one of the older gentlemen interrupted. He introduced himself as a senior banker with the institution that currently owns the House of Hensly. He explained.

It seemed that Brikette's contract with the ownership group expired at midnight. The bankers had advised her several times that the contract would not be renewed and that she should make other arrangements for her own personal affairs since a new Executive Resident Manager would be placed in charge of Hensly House when Brikette's contract came to an end.

About two months ago, when Brikette first heard that her contract would not be renewed, she called every board member and ranted and raved on the phone. She even got her lawyer on the phone. But several days ago, Brikette was told by her own legal counsel that she had no recourse but to comply. Brikette ignored the situation, refused to turn over any papers, and stayed until the ugly scene which had been witnessed a short time ago by Sven.

Shortly after the Banker's explanation and after Brikette refused to depart, the county Sheriff and two of his deputies escorted Brikette out of the House of Hensly. The Banker then approached Sven and advised him that he and his tour members would have to leave the resort by 10:00 A.M., as the entire House of Hensly would be closed by noon in order to conduct a complete inventory.

Sven was both angry and disturbed. He returned to his room and finding the contract he had signed with Brikette many months ago, he went back to the banker, waving the contract in his face. The banker's only response was to call the sheriff and ask the sheriff to explain. The sheriff was polite enough, but he explained that Brikette had no legal right to sign the contract in the first place. Therefore, according to the sheriff, the contract was null and void and, commented the sheriff, "If your group is not out by 10:00 A.M., my deputies and I will bodily escort them from the premises."

Consider the situation. What should Sven do. Decide among yourselves how you would handle the situation if you were in Sven's place. Discuss the situation among yourselves. Be prepared to present your suggestions in a paper that will be no longer than three pages in length. Also make sure the paper is double spaced and typed. Be prepared to present your suggestions verbally in class if your instructor suggests that you do so.

EXERCISE

Break into groups of no more than three students working together. Yours will probably be the same group that has been working together in the development of a one-day tour since the beginning of the course.

Develop draft letters of agreement for one of the sightseeing companies and one of the food service firms you will be working with on your one-day tour. In a meeting with the vendors, go over the letters of agreement, but make sure the vendors understand that you will not actually be running the tour and that this is being undertaken as a class project only. Determine whether or not the vendors would sign the letters of agreement you have developed if you actually were running the tour and if the vendors indicate that the letters would not be signed, determine why. Negotiate factors with the vendors until the letters of agreement reach the point where you as a tour development team and the vendors are in agreement. Again, however, do not have the letters signed since the purpose of the letters is for a learning exercise only and not a real tour.

CHAPTER 11

Tip Management

OBJECTIVES

Upon completion of this chapter, the student will be able to:

1. Identify those individuals who provide services during a typical tour who should receive tips and to identify those service providers who normally do not receive tips.

2. Prepare a tip management plan for a one-day tour.

3. Explain the process used in accounting for tips after a tour is over.

4. Identify the flaws in the traditional approach to tipping and to explain how these flaws can be overcome.

Introduction

Tip management is consistently at the top of the list of concerns expressed by tour managers, tour planners, and tour executives. Budgeting for the right amount of tips, tipping at a time and in a sequence that produces the desired service, maintaining dignity for both the giver and the receiver of tips, and insuring that cheating and theft are avoided constitute problems all tour companies face and need to overcome.

Tip Budgeting

Tips, especially tips for tour guides, are often requested of tour members. Sometimes these are not included as part of the tour package. However, quality tour operators include all tips in the tour package and note this in their brochures. They fire tour guides who solicit tips, but, with few exceptions, they allow voluntary tipping.

Because tips are included, however, tour planners struggle with tip budgeting until they find the formulae that works for them. Although there are standard tip percentages that work in many industries, there are wide variations both within segments of the hospitality industry and from geographical area to geographical area throughout the world.

In budgeting, as in most other aspects of tip management, the goal is to obtain a high level of quality service for tour members. Therefore, when budgeting for tips, plan to tip enough to make certain good service is provided and it is provided consistently. Talk with any seasoned hotel or resort bellman who works a large number of tours. He will tell you that some companies overtip, other companies tip an average amount, and some tour managers tip substantially below "expected" tip levels. If he is honest, he will also tell you that his service for those who tip well and who tip on an average basis is different than the service provided to those who are poor tippers. In most cases excessive tips do not insure better service, but poor tips definitely insure inferior service. The best approach is to determine what the tip should be. Then budget and tip that amount.

But how do you find out what is the "right" amount of tip? The answer is as simple as asking. The tour planner, while on site visits, should include a question about tips at each hotel visited. Obviously, only one hotel will be used in a city, but if during site visits bell captains are asked what the going rate of tips is at each of the hotels visited or considered, an averaging can be determined and one will usually find that there is little variation in the expected tip level at each of the hotels in the type or property range considered by the tour operator. There may be a difference from city to city or from one category of hotel property to another within a city, but seldom is there a difference within the same hotel category in a city. In addition to asking vendors themselves about tips, also ask inbound operators and state or national tourist board experts. The tour companies which tip too much or too little tend to be those which adopt an across-the-board percentage for all tips or companies employing tour planners who simply make an educated guess as to what the tip should be.

Who Gets Tips

Not everyone who provides a service is tipped. However, tips should be offered to all who provide service and who customarily receive tips. Bus drivers are usually tipped. Except in major U.S. cities, step-on guides are normally not tipped unless they spend a substantial amount of time (two or more days) with the tour. Outside the U.S., it will depend upon the country, the type of tour, and the company for which the step-on guide works.

Hotel bellmen are tipped. The entire amount of the tip goes to the bell captain with the request and expectation that the bell captain divide the tip among the bellmen who served tour members. The hotel concierge and the hotel doorman normally are not tipped unless special services are rendered, but they are tipped if special services are provided. It used to be that all hotel maids were tipped and in many countries it is still customary.

In America, however, tipping hotel maids is normally not done unless one is staying in the finer hotels and resorts. Then they usually are tipped. Hotel front desk staff are normally not tipped unless they provide special services.

In restaurants, it is customary to tip the Maitre' D. In some restaurants, especially outside the U.S., the Maitre' D receives the tips for waiters, sommeliers, and other helping staff and distributes them accordingly. This should be determined when visiting the restaurant on the site trip. In most cases, however, wait staff should be tipped either individually or as a group with a group tip being left for the head waiter to distribute. Bus persons are normally not tipped. They receive a portion of the tip provided to the wait staff. This is given to them by the wait staff. Sommeliers and strolling musicians are tipped separately, if tips are deemed appropriate. Guides at historic buildings and other sites are sometimes tipped and sometimes they are not. Determine this during the site visit or by asking someone with the state or national tourist bureau. The same applies for others who may provide special services.

Tips Based on Service vs. Required/Included Tips

Tips were originally designed as compensation to reward good service. The word "tip" is actually an acronym which stands for "To Insure Promptness." Traditionally, tips are offered after the service is rendered. They serve the purpose of rewarding the person who provides service for the quality and amount of service provided. This traditional approach, however, has two flaws. One of these is a growing move on the part of many establishments, especially restaurants, to include a service charge with the fees levied which would be shown on the customer's bill. Tips become a required portion of the fee; not an optional reward.

In a few cases, this required service fee is levied, but not passed on to the persons who provide the service and these people expect a tip as well. However, even when the required service fee is passed on to the person(s) rendering the service, because it is automatic, the incentive to provide good service has been removed. Frequently, therefore, service is not good.

The second problem is that even with traditional tips, the money left to reward good service is provided after the service is rendered, not before. While it still provides a reward, it is not as much of an incentive as it would be if the person providing the service knew that a certain amount of tip would be received if the service was rendered well. In many restaurants and other establishments which provide service, there is a guessing game played by waiters and other tipped personnel. They guess which patrons will provide the best tips and give excellent service to those patrons, often providing far less service for other patrons. Talking with service providers and making clear what is expected in return for an agreed-upon level of tips is certainly one of the best ways of making certain that the expected level of service is provided.

Reputation can earn a company even better service. As a tour company uses a vendor time after time and tips well, the reputation becomes established and service providers normally will consistently provide a high level of service. They know that the tour company tips well and does so on a consistent basis. This is a reputation that a company should strive for, but the company that has not yet achieved such a reputation still needs to make sure that their clients receive good service. This may mean that a frank conversation with service providers prior to rendering the service is the only answer.

Planned Tip Distribution

Tips should be distributed at a time and in a manner that has been planned in advance. Most tour companies ask tour managers to distribute tips in local currency placed in a small plain envelope. In most cases, the tip amount is determined in advance, placed in envelopes, and kept on the person, in the purse, or in the briefcase of the tour manager. The envelopes are usually not sealed until shortly before distribution. If the service provided is that which is expected, the envelope is sealed and surreptitiously passed to the person providing service.

It is important to maintain the dignity of the person receiving the tip. Therefore, the distribution is carried out in a subtle manner. If more than one person is to receive a tip at the same time, the names of the individuals can be written on their appropriate envelopes so the tour manager can be certain each person receives the correct amount. Sometimes, the names are not known in advance. Under these circumstances, titles can be placed on the envelopes instead.

Last Minute Tip Amount Change Considerations

Tips are normally placed in envelopes at the beginning of the day before leaving the hotel. The amount of money placed into each envelope is that which is expected to be the maximum tip. When service is less than expected, it is appropriate to provide a smaller tip or, in some cases, no tip at all. When the tour manager makes the decision not to provide any tip, the envelope simply is not given to the service provider. However, when the tour manager decides that service is less than expected, but that some tip is still warranted, the tour manager may slip away from the group for a minute, remove some of the currency from the envelope, and seal the envelope with a smaller amount of local currency in it as the tip. Tip reduction for poor service is facilitated by keeping envelopes open until right before tip distribution.

Developing a Tip Plan

As the tour planner develops arrangements for a tour, the planner should consider tips throughout the planning process. Key considerations should be:

1. who should be tipped; and
2. how much should the tip be.

The second question has already been addressed, but the question of who should be tipped is one that should be answered by the tour planner as the tour unfolds and as the tour planner discovers those components of the tour which require service and which will use the services of persons who should be tipped.

By keeping notes throughout the planning process, the tour planner should be able to develop a tip plan which essentially identifies the titles of those people to receive tips each day and the amount of tips. This plan includes the cost of tips in the overall tour budget and identifies when currency should be exchanged to obtain monies for tips. By giving daily tip information to the tour manager, and providing the tour manager with a tip budget, the tour manager can plan to obtain sufficient and appropriate change each evening so that tip envelopes can be prepared each morning. Developing the tip plan is the responsibility of the tour planner; not the tour manager. Implementing the tip plan is the responsibility of the tour manager.

Accounting for Tips

Tour companies expect tour managers to account for the money provided to them for tips. Most tour managers will keep a running record of the amounts of tips and the recipients of tips throughout the tour. This record should be updated each evening so that the tour manager can balance out the amount of funds left in the tip account with the tip expenditures. By keeping a daily record and a running accounting, the tour manager should always be in balance. He should have little difficulty in providing the required end-of-trip accounting records without having to spend an inordinate amount of time on them.

It is especially important that tour managers document occasions when less than the expected tip is provided. The amount left should be recorded on the tour manager's report and the reason for leaving less than the planned tip should be noted. The difference between the planned tip amount and the actual tip should be recorded, balanced with other tour financial records, and returned to the tour company after the tour is over.

Summary

Tip management consists of planning tips in advance. This means that tips must be budgeted. The tour planner identifies who should be tipped. The planned distribution of tips is based on services(s) rendered. Wherever possible, guidelines or rules for tip distribution are provided to tour managers. Tour managers are encouraged to make last minute tip changes if they deem it necessary and appropriate. A system for accounting for tips is developed and instituted.

All of these points are included in a written tip plan spelled out in the tour manual and/or the individual tour detail sheets provided to tour guides. The tip plan is reviewed either on a regular basis or after each trip and updated to reflect changing circumstances. With a good tip plan, the dual goals of tipping the exact "correct" amount (neither too much nor too little) and obtaining service at least partially because of the incentive of getting tips will be met.

DISCUSSION QUESTIONS

These questions may be discussed by two or more students outside of class as a fun way of reviewing this chapter or they may be discussed by everyone during class for a more wide-ranging discussion.

1. What are four tipping problems all tour companies face and need to overcome?
2. What is the goal of tip budgeting and tip management?
3. Is it generally true that excessive tips insure greater service and poor tips insure inferior service?
4. How does one find out what the "right" amount of tip is?
5. Does one normally find that there is a large variation in the expected tip level in various hotels in the same type or property range in the same city?
6. Which service providers are normally tipped and which ones are normally not tipped?
7. For what is the word "tip" an acronym?
8. Why are tip envelopes normally not sealed until right before the tip is delivered to the service person/provider?
9. What does the tour planner give to the tour manager so that the tour manager can obtain sufficient and appropriate change each evening in order to prepare tip envelopes for the next day?

10. How often should the tour manager(s) running record of the amount of tips and the recipients of tips be updated?

ROLE PLAY EXERCISE

1. Two students may participate in this role play either out of class as a fun way to review the chapter or as an in-class exercise. One plays the role of the tour company's comptroller and the other plays the role of the same tour company's tour planner. Please read the script and then pick up the conversation in your own words.

   TOUR COMPANY COMPTROLLER: I don't understand why the tips for this new tour, the Niagara Falls Barrel Tour, are so high. Our tips normally don't average more than one-and-a-half to two percent of total tour costs, and those are on the international deluxe tours. This Niagara Falls Barrel Tour simply includes a short bus trip with very few amenities. I understand why the insurance costs are so much greater than normal, but I sure don't understand why the tips are so substantial.

   TOUR PLANNER: It's a unique tour. There are special tips needed for services not normally needed on a tour. For example, the Falls Barrel Placer has to wade out in the water and . . .

   TOUR COMPANY COMPTROLLER (INTERRUPTING): Don't editorialize. Just give me a list of who gets what tips and why.

   TOUR PLANNER: Okay; let's start with the Falls barrel placer. She gets tipped . . .

   CONTINUE ON YOUR OWN

2. Two students may participate in this role play either out of class as a fun way to review the chapter or as an in-class exercise. One plays the role of the Duchess of Quaks, a step-on guide. The other plays the role of an Inbound Tour Company's Dispatcher. Please read the script and then pick up the conversation in your own words.

   THE DUCHESS OF QUAKS: Of course I'm the best step-on guide to conduct tours of Quakery Castle. I'm the only guide residing in at least twenty-five kilometers of the castle. What are they going to pay me to do the tour?

   INBOUND TOUR COMPANY DISPATCHER: They are paying twenty pounds for the day, including tips. It's one of those American companies and they don't understand that guides of Royal lineage expect to receive substantial tips.

   DUCHESS OF QUAKS: Well, I never . . .

   INBOUND TOUR COMPANY DISPATCHER (INTERRUPTING): Don't worry, I'm sure we will resolve the matter.

   DUCHESS OF QUAKS: And exactly how do YOU plan to do that?

INBOUND TOUR COMPANY DISPATCHER: I'll start by . . .

CONTINUE ON YOUR OWN

3. Two students may participate in this role play either out of class as a fun way to review the chapter or as an in-class exercise. One plays the role of a tour manager and the other plays the role of a hotel's bell captain. Please read the script and then pick up the conversation in your own words.

TOUR MANAGER: Your bell staff did a great job. The bags were in most of the rooms within twenty minutes of our arrival and I received several compliments on the pleasantness and courteousness of the bellmen.

BELL CAPTAIN: Thanks, we do our best to do a good job.

TOUR MANAGER: There was one exception, unfortunately. The bellman in charge of the rooms in the West Wing on the twelfth floor didn't get there until nearly an hour after we arrived. Our tour members occupied three of those rooms. They finally came down to dinner before their bags arrived. They were upset that they were unable to change. Even worse, when they came back from dinner, they found the bags in their rooms, but he put the bags in the wrong rooms. One of the tour members called the bell station and they promised to send the same bell person up to switch the bags around and get them into the right rooms. But, after twenty minutes, when he did not show up, the tour members handled it themselves. They are elderly and should not be moving heavy bags around—even just from room to room. To the best of my knowledge, the bellman still hasn't shown up to correct the problem.

BELL CAPTAIN: I regret you had a problem. Thanks for telling me about it. I will look into it right away.

TOUR MANAGER: This puts me into the uncomfortable position of wanting to tip the rest of your bell staff well—even better than normal. I'll give you the total tip and let you distribute it, as usual. But, I don't want THAT bellman to receive anything.

BELL CAPTAIN: I appreciate your attitude. However, the custom at this property is to distribute tips evenly to all bell staff members and that's what I will have to do.

TOUR MANAGER: Under the circumstances that is simply not acceptable. Let's . . .

CONTINUE ON YOUR OWN

GROUP DISCUSSION SITUATION: HAPPY HIPPY'S CHEATING CHEETUM

"Aha!" cried Paucious Pupillar, the Comptroller for Happy Hippy Tours. "I've finally gotten proof," thought Paucious as he hurriedly shuffled his way through the massive attic corridors linking the offices of the New York

Greenwich Village Brownstone that called itself home to Happy Hippy Tours. It wasn't but a few minutes later when he dashed into the lilac-laden office of Happy Hippy's President, Eunice Eunick. Brushing aside the fading blue flowers that always seemed to strew the desk of the CEO, Paucious threw down the sheaf of papers and in a triumphant whisper gurgled, "We finally got her! Cheating Cheetum's days are now numbered."

"Don't talk in riddles," the company's Chief Executive Officer admonished. "What's Cheetum done now?" Eunice knew it had to be something serious. Ayi Cheetum, the favorite niece of the banker who owned most of the stock in Happy Hippy Tours and served as its perpetual Chairman of the Board, had ruffled the feathers of Paucious Pupillar from the first day she came into the job swishing about the office, bragging that she got the highest cumulative grades of all 9,241 tour managers who graduated that year from the Purple Posie Tour Management Institute. From the first tour Ayi Cheetum took out, Paucious Pupillar exercised his eagle eye even more carefully to scrutinize every financial detail in the end-of-tour reports she filed.

Three months ago, Paucious started suspecting Ayi of cheating by pocketing portions of tip monies. It was only a sense he had at first; nothing he could prove. After the last tour, Preeny Prune, the Tour Planner, brought up in an Executive Committee meeting that several complaints had been received about the service provided in hotels that have customarily provided extremely good service. Paucious grunted out immediately that it had to be a tour that Ayi Cheetum was leading—and indeed it was. Paucious took it on himself to get a list of the hotels and to send off letters of inquiry. Now he had the evidence he wanted.

Mad and raving, Paucious' finger jutted out pointing to the paragraphs in three letters he submitted in evidence. "Some of our best resorts," he exclaimed. "Look at this letter from the Brazzaville Towers. And here's one from the Baghdad Bungalows. The most damaging letter, though, is from our finest lodging vendor, the Uganda Ameen Resort. All of them are angry about the low tips their service people receive when Cheetum brings a tour through. Now look at the financial log," Paucious Pupillar demanded as the book that seemed bigger than he was was swung upon on the desk to a pre-marked page on which in a blood-red circle Pupillar had marked the tipping amounts Ayi Cheetum had claimed to have tipped in each of the three deluxe lodging properties. There it was—clear for all to see. Her report claimed to have provided full tips for each service person. "How can she claim to have tipped everybody the full amount budgeted and still get letters complaining about the low tipping levels, if she isn't cheating," questioned Paucious. "Fire the cheat!" screamed Paucious as he triumphantly exited Eunice's office.

"The evidence certainly does look damaging," thought Eunice. "Now what do I do," she mused.

You are minority stockholders in the company and you are also friends of Eunice to whom she has turned with particularly sensitive concerns and problems in the past. Consider the situation. Decide among yourselves what you would do and how you would handle the situation if you were Eunice. Discuss the matter among yourselves. Be prepared to present your suggestions in a paper that will be no longer than three pages in length. Also make sure the paper is double-spaced and typed. Be prepared to also present your suggestions verbally in class if your instructor suggests that you do so.

EXERCISE

Break into groups of no more than three students working together. Yours will probably be the same group that has been working together in the development of a one-day tour since the beginning of the course.

Following the recommendations made in this chapter, prepare a tip management plan for the one-day tour you have been working on since the beginning of the course. Make certain that you go over the itinerary completely and identify by title each person who would logically be tipped. Undertake the research necessary to determine an appropriate tip level. Plan a tip budget and develop the tip management plan.

CHAPTER 12
Multi-Day, Multi-Destination International Air Tours

OBJECTIVES

Upon completion of this chapter, the student will be able to:

1. Compare the differences in planning for single-day domestic bus tours and multi-day, multi-destination international air tours.

2. Develop an emergency plan covering at least two-thirds of the common emergencies for which there should be plans.

3. List 5 global and 11 specific differences between short, domestic bus tours and lengthy, multi-destination international air tours which should be considered by the tour company when planning multi-day, multi-destination international air tours.

4. Describe what happens during the first day of a typical international air tour.

Introduction

The most difficult tour to plan, market, and run effectively is an international, multi-day air tour which encompasses several destinations. The novice in developing, marketing, and running tours should build up to this type of tour slowly. Run short domestic tours in the beginning and, over time, add both in terms of the number of days of the tour and the number of international destinations. When the tour company is ready to start offering multi-destination, international air tours, the experience gained from shorter domestic tours can help to overcome some of the potential problems. Concentration can be given to the unique aspects of international air tours.

Planning Differences for International vs. Domestic Tours

Five major differences will be encountered by the tour planner when moving from planning short domestic bus tours to planning multi-day, multi-destination international air tours. These five major differences are:

1. language;
2. culture;
3. documentation;
4. communications; and
5. transportation.

If the international air tour is multi-destination, there will probably be a language difference. Many feel that this single difference is a deterrent strong enough to discourage them from planning and running a multi-destination, international air tour. If the planner is not knowledgeable of the destination languages, the planner may have some concern about the ability to develop a quality tour.

However, you will learn that the majority of people with whom one interfaces in the travel industry speak English and speak it quite well. You should always be sensitive to the fact that two or more languages are involved and misunderstandings can occur much more easily, but the fact remains that English is a standard language for communicating within the travel industry throughout the world. Be patient. And, work with greater amounts of written communication rather than relying on verbal communication. It should be possible to plan most international, multi-destination air tours without the need of fluency in a language other than English.

Cultural differences are a concern for many—sometimes justifiably. For example, what is considered to be fashionably late in some countries is considered intolerable by many U.S. tour planners.

The tour planner should recognize that it is not possible to change the destination country's culture. A high tolerance for ambiguity, patience, and an attempt to both understand and accept the destination culture are all attributes that will help the tour planner. In most countries, destination vendors, such as ground operators, are aware of the U.S. concern with timeliness. Most make an effort to ensure that their services and facilities are provided in a timely manner even if it is not the custom to do so within their country. Nevertheless, there are some cultures where time considerations are not nearly as important as in the United States. Tour planners need to consider this when planning their tours.

Other aspects of the culture also are important. For example, the hours of major meals may be quite different than in the United States. In many countries, the biggest meal of the day is eaten in the afternoon rather than in the evening.

Shops are often closed in the afternoon while people take an afternoon rest. The shops then reopen in the evening. In over half of the world, it is customary to have retail shops open in the morning (usually until 12 noon or 1:00 P.M.), closed in the afternoon, and reopen at night (usually from approximately 4:00 P.M. or 5:00 P.M. until 8:00 P.M. or 9:00 P.M.). The tour planner should remember that these and other cultural patterns make destinations interesting. Take advantage of the differences. Plan within the framework of the culture.

On short domestic bus tours, there is a minimum of documentation necessary. With international air tours, you'll encounter a large number of documents which must be completed and completed accurately. Whole tours have been held up because one or more persons on the tour did not have the right visa, passport, or even a completed entry card. Just traveling between the United States and Canada, bus tours encounter the problem of U.S. tourists crossing the border without proof of citizenship. The tour can be held up during crossings in one or both directions because of a lack of needed documentation. This problem can be multiplied when traveling by air between many different countries far from the shores of the United States. Remember, documentation applies to the tour as a whole as well as to each individual member of the tour and the tour manager.

Communication problems also can be larger with international tours, especially if one or more of the destinations are to exotic, poorly developed parts of the world. In the United States, it is common today to fax contracts, letters of agreement, and other documents. Only a short period of time from the initial talking stage to the final signing stage is needed to complete a contract, even when the tour operator and the vendor are on opposite coasts. But this communications ability is not duplicated in other parts of the world. Transferring written communications between tour companies in the United States and vendors in locations half way around the world can involve lengthy delays and considerable potential for misunderstanding. It is important that tour planners expect communications delays but attempt to reduce all important aspects of communications to writing.

For the tour planner who has been accustomed to working with bus tours, the change to air tours can hold surprises. Both forms of transportation offer advantages and disadvantages. Although air transportation is much more rapid, the time constraints within which the planner is working are far more narrow and tour members may carry far less luggage with them. From the planner's point of view, finding the appropriate individuals with the air carrier with whom to interface can be a challenge. If possible some domestic tours should be conducted by air prior to offering an international air tour. For a company to make the transition from bus to air at the same time as they are making the transition from domestic to international is not recommended.

In addition to these global differences encountered when planning multi-day, multi-destination international air tours, the tour planner also finds specific differences to consider as they relate to:

1. working with local ground operators;

2. working with local step-on guides;

3. airport meet-and-assist services;

4. airport and hotel hospitality desks;

5. the first day processes;

6. the daily routine of a multi-day international air tour;

7. the ability to meet both group and individual needs;

8. international hotel procedures;

9. emergency planning;

10. enroute communications; and

11. border crossings.

Each of these areas will be discussed in detail.

Working with Local Ground Operators

Apart from the obvious language, cultural, and distance differences between U.S. ground operators and those located in other countries, the tour planner will find that the selection options for international ground operators will be less (there are fewer of them in most international cities than one finds in major U.S. cities). However, ground operators outside the United States tend to be much more global in the services that they provide. In America, it is rare to find a single company that will provide most (preferably all) needed services. In the major cities outside the United States, it is rare to find a ground operator which does not provide a wide menu of services (usually all that are needed).

The tour planner will often find that instead of contracting with eight or nine different vendors, as often is the case in the United States, the contract will be with a single vendor in the international destination country. The vendor may subcontract some services, but often will provide a full range of services without needing to contract out any of them. Both the narrow number of choices and the wide range of services provided make the tour planner's job easier, but both factors reinforce the need for quality.

Domestically, when dealing with eight or nine vendors for services, tour members may overlook lower than expected levels of service. However, if a poor quality ground operator in an international destination does a bad job, the poor quality may carry through to all contracted services. Tour members will definitely notice. Therefore, tour planners should be careful when selecting ground operators in other countries.

Working with Local Step-on Guides

In the United States, tour companies will often contact step-on guides directly. To do so in other countries is more difficult. In the United States, the

Professional Guides Association of America assists tour planners in identifying guides in all locals who have the desired expertise. A roster of local guides is usually kept by the tour company for each destination allowing tour planners to telephone the local guide and work out arrangements on the phone. This simple process is difficult to duplicate in other countries.

Local step-on guides in other countries are usually employed by a single company rather than by several companies. Normally, the only route available to work with them is by going through a local ground operator. The services of step-on guides are normally included in the menu of services offered by the ground operator and frequently this is the only way in which the U.S.-based tour company is able to obtain local step-on guides. If recommendations have been received from other tour companies or if the tour planner has run several tours to the destination and utilized step-on guides in the past, a request for a specific guide will usually be honored by the ground operator whenever possible. However, the ground operator tends to be the go-between. Internationally, the ability to write direct contracts with local step-on guides remains minimal.

Airport Meet-and-Assist Services

Airport meet-and-assist services provided in other countries are similar to those which are offered by ground operators in the United States. However, in many countries outside the United States, the relationship between major ground operators, the air carriers, and airport authorities are different than they are in America. It is not unusual to find ground operators who will have access to secure areas of the airport and even access to the ramp. Therefore, it is often possible to have tour groups met as they disembark from the plane. Tour members can be assisted throughout the debarkation process as they move from the plane through health checks, passport and visa checks, and customs luggage searches. Throughout this process, the ground operator's meet-and-assist personnel can translate wherever necessary and can assist older passengers with their luggage, if needed. While this expansive range of meet-and-assist services is not available in all international destinations, it is available in many of them.

Airport and Hotel Hospitality Desks

Ground service operators in other countries are usually able to provide airport and hotel hospitality desks just as these are provided in the United States. Sometimes, the availability of personnel who have fluent English language ability is not as good as one might hope, but usually the hospitality desk staffers have considerable expertise as well as fluency in English. Airport desks can sometimes be set up at the point of passenger debarkation rather than after clearing customs.

The First Day on an International Air Tour

The first day on an international air tour differs from the first day on a domestic bus tour. Those going on bus tours will normally meet at a convenient site where there is plenty of parking and where the bus can pull up for a leisurely loading. Tour members embarking on an international air tour will sometimes fly in from many parts of the country, meeting at the gateway city airport.

Although, in some cases, tour operators are able to obtain an airport meeting room from the airline, more frequently the tour guide will meet tour members at the gateway city departure gate between 45 minutes and two hours prior to departure of the flight constituting the first international leg of the tour. The tour manager will often have a sign and be sitting in a designated section of the boarding gate area. The tour manager will check documents and seating, but will seldom do more than this prior to boarding the flight. Some tour companies arrange to have tour members sit in one section of the plane, but it is not unusual for tour members to sit throughout the plane.

Experienced tour managers will usually allow the flight to start before meeting with individual tour participants. Usually 15 minutes or so after the flight gets into the air, the tour manager will make the rounds of the plane, visiting briefly with each tour member. Throughout the flight, many tour managers move from one client to the next getting to know each person. This, of course, is much easier to do on jumbo-jets than on smaller aircraft. The purpose of the meetings is for the tour manager to introduce himself and to find out any concerns the tour member may have about the trip. More complete documentation checks may be undertaken, but they are usually not needed. Seldom is anything special provided for tour members during the flight.

When the first destination city is reached, the tour manager gathers tour members together and makes an effort to disembark from the plane together. Usually, the tour manager takes a count to make certain that all tour members are together. Then the tour manager guides tour members through health and document checks and into the customs clearance area.

If a meet-and-assist service is not available, the tour manager will arrange for skycaps to group all tour member luggage as it is identified and will work with tour members as baggage is taken off the baggage carousels, checked through customs, and placed on the baggage cart for transfer to the hotel of first destination. The tour manager is usually the last person in the tour group to come through customs, but unless ground operator meet-and-assist is provided, tour members will be asked to wait together either in the baggage clearance section (going out together) or immediately outside of the baggage section. After making certain that all tour members have gone through the customs baggage check process, the tour manager exits customs, takes a count, and guides the tour members to the transfer bus.

Again, the tour manager takes a count to make certain that all tour members are present as members board the bus to transfer to their hotel. After getting seated on the bus, the trip begins into the city. Sometimes at this point the tour manager will officially welcome tour participants to the tour and review pertinent points (e.g., highlights, rules and regulations, general information not provided in the company's literature, and the like). Then the tour manager or a step-on guide (working on contract with the tour company and its ground operator) will provide sightseeing information as sites are passed enroute from the airport to the hotel. As the bus approaches the hotel, the tour manager provides information regarding activities for the rest of the arrival day and explains the processes involved in disembarking from the transfer bus and hotel check-in.

Upon arrival at the hotel, it is customary for the tour manager to ask tour members to remain seated on the bus until he has had an opportunity to interface with hotel front desk personnel. He will normally conduct a group check in of all passengers, coordinate baggage transfers to client rooms, and receive all keys (ideally in envelopes with the name of each passenger on his/her envelope). Upon returning to the bus, the keys are distributed and tour members are advised when to meet for the first sightseeing trip or other scheduled function. Usually, little is scheduled on the day of arrival. Because the air trip can be tiring, relatively few tour members want to attend scheduled activities on their day of arrival. Most will relax.

The Routine on Multi-Day, International Air Tours

Contrary to popular belief, most multi-day, multi-destination international air tours are not crammed full of activities. The majority of people taking multi-day, multi-destination international air tours are repeat tour clients. They prefer to have a comfortable, fairly leisurely tour which gives them an opportunity to appreciate the sites they visit without having to rush from one place to another. Most prefer to see the sites of greatest importance and skip those sites of less importance. Some will go back on an FIT or a specialized, in-depth, one-area, or one-country tour to visit those sites which were missed on the multi-day, multi-destination tour.

The exception to this is the grand tour of Europe. It is often composed of persons who are taking their first international multi-day, multi-destination international air tour. Frequently, they want to see as many countries as possible within a short time frame. They, therefore, often want scheduled activities from very early in the morning until very late at night, seeing as much as possible, and visiting as many countries as possible. The routine on multi-day, international air tours discussed in this chapter, however, applies to the majority of multi-day, multi-destination international air tours—those that maintain a more leisurely pace.

The Daily Routine

Typically, the day starts with breakfast. This is usually scheduled between 8:00 and 9:00 A.M., most often at 8:30. The breakfast will usually be in the hotel dining room. Tour participants will be expected to have their bags packed and ready to leave before coming down for breakfast if the tour groups is scheduled to leave the hotel for a destination that will require a change in hotels. Breakfast will normally be finished by approximately 9:30 A.M. and the tour bus will be scheduled to leave the hotel at approximately 10:00 A.M.

By far the majority of tour members prefer a 10:00 A.M. departure for sightseeing. This gives them an opportunity to have a leisurely morning and a leisurely breakfast. If they are going to be changing hotels, it also gives them an opportunity to pack without having to rush. When there is a hotel change, tour members go back to their rooms after breakfast, pick up their handbags, and proceed back down to the lobby where the tour group gathers to board the bus.

While tour members were eating breakfast, the bell staff collected the packed suitcases and placed them on the tour bus. Of course, the tour manager will need to take a count of all suitcases prior to departure to make certain that all baggage was retrieved and placed aboard the bus. Most tour members carry a small bag with them for the items they need during the day. Many pack the night before and place their pajamas and toiletry items in their carry-on bag.

The tour bus starts boarding at approximately 9:45 A.M. After the tour manager boards the bus, a final count of tour members is taken and the bus departs on time. Typically, the tour bus takes tour members on sightseeing trips which include a luncheon. If it is a short tour, it may return at approximately 1:00 P.M. or 1:30 P.M. giving tour participants an opportunity to have free time or to prepare for a late afternoon tour.

The late afternoon tour will usually be very short. It may leave at around 2:30 or 3:00 P.M. and come back around 5:30 or 6:00 P.M. Frequently, however, the 10:00 A.M. tour will be the only sightseeing tour scheduled for the day. It will bring tour participants back to their hotel at around 4:00 or 5:00 P.M. When this type of sightseeing is scheduled, the evening can be either left free for tour participants to do what they wish or a dinner and evening activity program may be scheduled.

On most multi-day, multi-destination international tours between one-fourth and one-half of all evenings include planned activity. Usually this activity will consist of a group dinner at a restaurant away from the hotel and some type of cultural activity such as a play, symphony, or special event. In most cases, the scheduled activity will conclude and tour members will be back at their hotel by 10:00 or 11:00 P.M. so that they can get a reasonable night's sleep.

Normally, during the last scheduled activity of each day as the tour bus returns to the hotel, the tour manager will go over the schedule of the next day with tour participants advising them of when and where they should meet, reminding them of free time that may be scheduled, and suggesting optional activities that tour members may wish to participate in during their free time. Any special notes will be provided to them as well at this time.

Before the first shopping excursion, tour managers review the process for paying customs, legal purchase exemptions, potential fines and the purchases for which those fines might be levied, and goods which might be confiscated if purchased. Usually, at the beginning of each day, as the tour bus leaves the hotel, the tour manager will make a few opening remarks and will review the day's activities with tour participants. He may also go into a very brief description of what the next few days will hold as well so that tour participants are always provided with a reminder of what to expect. In this way, they can plan their free time.

Usually when the tour bus reaches its destination, tour members will be asked to stay on the bus until the tour manager has an opportunity to go in and pick up the event tickets, admission tickets, or make other arrangements needed for tour participants to engage in the activity that is scheduled. The tour manager takes a count of all tour participants each time the bus departs, making sure that all members have reboarded and that no one is left behind.

Tour companies usually make a conscious effort to provide variety in the daily schedule offered to tour members. Although the departure time will usually remain 10:00 A.M., the number of sightseeing trips planned during a day and the number of evening or special activities planned will vary from day to day. This gives tour members an opportunity to have more variety in their schedules and to plan individual activities at different times.

There is seldom any pressure placed on tour members to participate in scheduled sightseeing trips. Although tour members will have paid for the entire tour, some will decide that they want to skip some sightseeing trips so that they can do things on their own or so that they can simply relax at the hotel. If they have less interest in the particular point being visited, this will give them an opportunity to have more free time and more of a leisurely vacation. Experienced tour managers understand this and allow tour members to participate selectively as they wish. However, if the tour is moving to another hotel, of course the tour members will be expected to be at the bus on time and to travel with the tour group.

When traveling long distances by air, often moving from one country to another, the flight will usually be scheduled for departure at either 10:00 or 11:00 A.M. If it is a 10:00 A.M. departure, tour members may have to leave the hotel as early as 8:30. Their customarily leisure departure may have to be moved up. If it is a very short flight, the flight may be scheduled closer to noon or 1:00 P.M. This allows tour members to stick to their usual 10:00 A.M. hotel departure and still get to the city's airport in time for a leisurely group check-in. If the air trip is a short one (normally two hours or less), evening activities can be scheduled the night of arrival, but seldom will activities in the afternoon be scheduled other than an opportunity to have an overview of the new city presented during the transfer from the airport to the new hotel.

When traveling by rail, local rail customs and regulations should be discussed with tour members before embarking for the rail station. The tour manager keeps all rail transportation and seating/sleeping accommodation tickets. Passengers board as a group and, wherever possible, luggage is transported in the passenger car(s). The rail schedule is explained to tour members and "free time" is provided so that tour members can get settled and view the scenery. Rail group activities are limited, but some tour groups make an effort to dine together.

In most cities, one of the first scheduled sightseeing trips will be a city tour presenting the highlights of the city. Further distant and more inclusive sightseeing trips will be scheduled for the second, third, or later days in a city. Usually, during the airport to hotel transfer, tour members are provided with a city map so that they can get their bearings. This and the city tour give tour members an opportunity to understand the city sufficiently well that they can get out on their own and go to the places that they wish to visit by themselves, usually by taxi. Frequently, either the first or the second night that is spent in a city includes a city nightclub tour. Some groups have less interest in nightclub tours than others, but most will want some type of a tour hitting at least a few of the major night spots.

Planning to Meet Group Needs vs. Individual Needs

Each tour member has some individual interests and needs unique to himself/herself. He/she shares group needs with other tour members. The planning of a tour normally is centered around meeting group needs. Most tour companies will conduct substantial research to identify what the preferences are of potential tour members and will build the tour around the preferences of the majority. Post-trip surveys of tour participants identify group need trends. From year to year, tour planners incorporate facets into the tour to meet new and changing group needs.

Most tour planners recognize that they cannot meet some of the individual tour member needs, especially when meeting those needs will conflict with meeting the needs of the majority of tour members. Although planners will usually go to considerable lengths to meet individual tour member needs, there is a limit. At the very least, this limit is where meeting the individual need would be harmful to the group or where the meeting of individual needs on a continuous basis will become so expensive that the tour company will lose money rather than make money. Two examples show the point.

Example 1: On a short bus tour which included Las Vegas, tour participants stayed at a downtown hotel and used the tour bus for scheduled runs to and from "The Strip" casinos. The runs were scheduled every half hour on the hour and the half-hour. One tour member got on the bus at 11:15 P.M. and insisted that the driver bring her back to the hotel. She pointed out that the driver should be able to make it to the hotel and return to the strip in time to make the 11:30 P.M. scheduled pick up on time.

"Even if you are a few minutes late in picking them up, it won't matter," she said. The driver refused and the tour member became angry. She complained loudly during the 11:30 scheduled return all the way back to the hotel. The tour members who accompanied her on the 11:30 P.M. return were very pleased that the driver took the position he did. By his action, they were not forced to wait and wonder where the bus was. The tour manager explained to the woman that the driver was following instructions and that he made the right choice in meeting the group needs, as planned, rather than taking a chance, not getting back in time and making those who had planned to leave at 11:30 P.M. have to wait.

Example 2: The co-owner of a tour company which runs adventure tours throughout the world is a man who goes to considerable effort to meet the individual needs of tour participants. His partner, however, is concerned because, in meeting individual tour member needs, he tends to spend much of the budgeted profits. An example occurred in Switzerland during a bicycle tour. One evening, after dinner, when the group was in tents camping out enroute between two cities on a picturesque mountain meadow, coffee was prepared for tour members. One man indicated that he did not like the brand of coffee being used. The tour manager (he was also the tour company co-owner) got into the van used to accompany the bicycle tour, drove to the nearest city, purchased the coffee brand the tour member preferred, and drove back.

Although this met the need of the individual tour member and he was no doubt pleased to have the brand he preferred, and while no other tour members were harmed in any way, the additional expense incurred was an unbudgeted expense. This one incident would not have made a major difference in whether or not the tour made a profit. However, combining this activity with many other unplanned expenditures continually forced what could have been profitable tours to become marginally profitable or unprofitable.

A balance, therefore, needs to be struck between meeting individual needs and the profitability of the tour or inconvenience to other tour members. Sometimes, these questions can best be considered prior to the departure of the tour and discussed among tour managers and tour company supervisors.

If policy is established, it helps tour managers to make company-preferred decisions. To assist in making these decisions before the tour, rather than on the tour, an increasing number of tour companies are sending extensive questionnaires to tour members prior to the departure of the tour asking for a wide range of preferences, likes, and dislikes. Some tour companies require tour managers to telephone tour members prior to the departure of the tour and to talk with them about their expectations so that the tour members' expectations can be brought in line with what the tour will actually offer. Most tour members appreciate this thoughtful predeparture phone conversation.

International Hotel Procedures

Some international hotels operate differently than domestic hotels. Much more often, international hotels are designed to handle tours. They are guided by the booking contract and confirmation (see Figure 12-1), but sometimes the hotel will have a specific set of written procedures for tours to follow upon arrival and throughout the stay. In some cases, there is a separate entrance to the lobby for tour buses. If canopied, the canopy is higher than it might be for cars in order to allow the tour bus to fit underneath it. The doors may be larger—big enough for carts for the transfer of suitcases. And the check-in desk may be one that is geared toward handling groups.

These hotels generally assign rooms based on a *rooming list* (see Figure 12-2) sent to them several days before the tour group arrives. Nevertheless, they prefer it if the tour manager will call from the airport (if arriving by air) or from some point outside the city (if arriving by bus) so that the staff will be prepared when the tour bus arrives. The hotel staff then preassigns rooms and the bell staff is scheduled to meet the bus. As the bus pulls up, the bell staff will immediately open the luggage containers below the bus and start unloading baggage so that, ideally, the luggage will be in the room prior to the client's arrival. Some hotels have all check-in documents prepared in advance. All the tour manager needs to do is sign the check-in roster and pick up the key envelopes with the names of tour members on each envelope. The tour manager can return to the bus right away and distribute the key envelopes. This eliminates potential lobby congestion.

Hotels frequently have their dining rooms set up to handle groups as well. As the tour member enters the dining room, he will need only to identify his room number and the tour group with which he is associated to be seated in the section reserved for his group. Often waiters are assigned to tour groups (rather than table groups) and meals can be served rapidly. When this is the case, the tip is either included in the bill or the tour manager gives the head waiter a single tip for distribution.

The concierge is normally given a copy of the tour schedule. He is then prepared to advise tour members about points of interest and activities which do not conflict with scheduled sightseeing.

Most tour companies like to work with hotels that are prepared for tours. Over a period of time, a rapport is built up between a hotel and a tour company. The hotel staff understands the unique needs of each tour company and is able to meet those needs.

Planning for Emergencies

No one likes them, but tour companies need to plan for emergencies and to brief their tour members accordingly. Clients are asked to provide emergency contact information (see Figure 12-3). Company emergency plans are incorporated into the tour manual. Common emergencies for which there should be plans include:

1. the tour manager becoming ill;

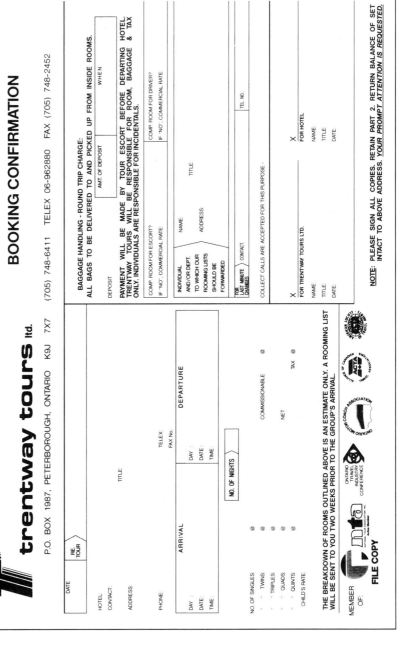

FIGURE 12-1 SAMPLE BOOKING AND CONFIRMATION SHEET

Reproduced with permission from Trentway Tours, Peterborough, Ontario, Canada.

```
         TRENTWAY TOURS              R O O M I N G   L I S T
                                                           14/08/91
    TOUR- 24004   TENNESSEE MUSIC            HOTEL - TRY02

    ARRIVING ON SUNDAY     AUG 18,1991   6:00 P.M.    GROUP 1 OF 1
    DEPARTING ON MONDAY    AUG 19,1991   8:00 A.M.
    NO. OF NIGHTS -  1

    CONTACT -  MRS BRENDA OSBORNE  OR  MRS MARCELLE ROUSE
               TEL - (705)748-6411,  TELX - 06-962880

       CAROL SKIDMORE
       ASS'T GENERAL MANAGER
       HOLIDAY INN OF TROY              TOTAL MEMBERS IN GROUP   46
       I - 75 AND OHIO RTE. 55
       TROY, OHIO                          TOTAL ROOMS   22
       45373


    BAG-CD                            BAG-CD
                  TWINS - 15          E-033 DOWNIE, MS. CAROL
    E-003 TRELEAVEN, MRS. BARB        E-033 DOWNIE, MRS. VIOLA
    E-003 TRELEAVEN, MR. DAVID
                                      E-034 GALLAGHER, MISS ANNE
    E-004 MARTIN, MR. NORMAN          E-034 GALLAGHER, MRS. LILY
    E-004 MARTIN, MRS. CLARA
                                                    TRIPLES -   3
    E-005 BOWIE, MR. LACHLAN          E-006 DENISON, MR. ALAN
    E-005 BOWIE, MRS. ISALEEN         E-006 DENISON, MRS. EVELYN
                                      E-006 DENISON, MISS JANET
    E-007 BENJAMIN, MR. HAROLD
    E-007 BENJAMIN, MRS. SHIRLEY      E-008 MILLER, MR. GEORGE
                                      E-008 MILLER, MRS. BETTY
    E-013 ROSEBUSH, MS. LYNN          E-008 MILLER, MRS. MARGE
    E-013 MACE, MS. MOLLY
                                      E-019 CHISHOLM, MRS. VERNA
    E-015 MACE, MRS. PHYLLIS          E-019 LAROUCHE, MISS GERRY
    E-015 ROSEBUSH, MRS. IVA          E-019 PHILLIPS, MRS. BERNICE

    E-022 HOBBS, MRS. JOYCE                        QUADS  -  1
    E-022 LEE, MRS. ETHEL             E-009 DONOHUE, MRS. NANCY
                                      E-009 DONOHUE, MS. KIM
    E-024 TURNBULL, MR. GLENN         E-009 HEBERT, MRS. NARDA
    E-024 TURNBULL, MRS. CAROLYN      E-009 MCELWAIN, MRS. DEBBIE

    E-025 KERR, MRS. DAPHNE
    E-025 DAVIDSON, MRS. GEORGINA                  SINGLES -  3
                                      E-027 GUINTA, MR. MICHAEL
    E-028 GALBRAITH, MR. GERALD
    E-028 GALBRAITH, MRS. MARGUERITE  E-001 DRIVER - DAVE FOX

    E-029 RINALDO, MR. ANGELO         E-002 ESCORT - SHEILA WHITE
    E-029 RINALDO, MRS. JOSEPHINE

    E-030 WILLEY, MS. KAREN
    E-030 MACDONALD, MS. LAURIE

    E-032 CHAMBO, MR. JOSEPH
    E-032 CHAMBO, MRS. SHERRON
```

FIGURE 12-2 SAMPLE ROOMING LIST

Reproduced with permission from Trentway Tours, Peterborough, Ontario, Canada.

2. illness or death of tour members;

3. delayed or canceled departure of aircraft scheduled to transport tour members;

4. bus breakdowns;

```
┌─────────────────────────────────────────────────────────────────────┐
│                          INSTRUCTIONS                                 │
│                       IN CASE OF EMERGENCY                            │
│                      FOR SINGLE PASSENGERS                            │
│                                                                       │
│                                                                       │
│     NAME: _____        │
│                                                                       │
│     ADDRESS: _____       │
│                                                                       │
│              _____       │
│                                                                       │
│              _____       │
│                                                                       │
│     TELEPHONE NO.: _____       │
│     (please include area code)                                        │
│                                                                       │
│     PERSON TO NOTIFY IN CASE OF                                       │
│     ILLNESS OR ACCIDENT: _____        │
│                                                                       │
│     TELEPHONE NO.:  Res. _____        │
│                                                                       │
│                     Bus. _____        │
│                                                                       │
│     Would you give permission to a representative of the company to collect │
│     your belongings in the event of an emergency, absolving him/her of │
│     responsibility for any loss incured?  If yes, please sign below.  │
│                                                                       │
│                              _____        │
└─────────────────────────────────────────────────────────────────────┘
```

FIGURE 12-3 EMERGENCY CONTACT INFORMATION SHEET
Reproduced with permission of Trentway Tours, Peterborough, Ontario, Canada.

5. hotel overbookings; and

6. sightseeing destination point closures.

Few companies run many tours without encountering one or more of these emergencies. With written policies and procedures in place, tour managers will be better prepared to deal with these emergencies. In addition, when an emergency occurs, most tour members are relieved to find that there is a written policy and procedure to follow. Most accept changes when they understand that an emergency situation has occurred and when they are told that the tour company has prepared in advance for such an emergency.

Communicating Enroute

Most companies find that daily contact with tour managers is important. Some require the tour manager to telephone the company at predetermined times.

These are usually times set into the tour manager's schedule in such a way that it will be convenient. Time zone changes make it difficult to time communications that will fit both the schedule of the tour manager and the tour company. Nevertheless, regularly scheduled communication is usually felt to be important. This provides the tour planner with a feel for the "continuity" of the tour and an ability to stay on top of potential problems, giving the tour manager an opportunity to discuss those potential problems.

Company and client messages and mail are usually tracked as they are forwarded (see Figure 12-4). Those of the company can be handled in two different ways. Most of the time mail and messages will be sent to the hotel where the tour manager is expected to be at the time the mail or message arrives. To be safe, some companies time the mail/message to arrive at the hotel one or two days prior to the date the tour manager is scheduled to check-in. This tends to work well, especially when using the same hotels repeatedly.

An alternative arrangement is to route mail and messages through the ground operator with which the tour company is contracting. Since the ground operator will have contact with the tour manager either immediately or shortly after the tour manager's arrival at a destination, this arrangement can work quite well. However, because some ground operators do not normally provide mail/message forwarding service, systems are sometimes not in place to be able to handle this well and mail and messages are occasionally lost. It is for this reason that the hotel arrangement is normally the preferred arrangement.

Handling client mail and enroute messages for clients is also important. Most tour companies prepare a list of addresses as well as the amount of lead time necessary for mail sent to clients. This list is sent to tour members well before they leave home (see Figure 12-5). Tour participants may duplicate the list and give one to each of the people who might wish to contact them. Usually the phone number is included together with the international country access code for each hotel.

By having the contact list, a family member or other person wishing to contact a tour member will be able to refer directly to the list and identify when mail needs to be sent or, if telephone contact is needed, in most cases they will be able to pick up the phone and call. Because a number of hotels around the world now have fax machines, written communications can be sent almost instantaneously. The fax message is placed in the client's hotel box for pick up almost as soon as it is received by the hotel.

Planning for Border Crossings

Border crossings present a unique set of circumstances for tour companies. Sometimes they need to be planned in detail. If the group is traveling by tour bus, the tour manager will normally collect all passports and completed entry cards prior to arrival at the border and will keep them together to present to border guards and custom inspectors. In some cases, the check by border guards

FIGURE 12-4 ACCOUNT COMMUNICATIONS SHEET

Date	Client Origin	Rojo Origin	Message/Action

Reproduced with permission from Rojo Tours, Santa Fe, NM.

```
TOUR #23314
13 DAYS

                              TRENTWAY TOURS LIMITED
                              ACCOMMODATION LIST
                              ATLANTIC CANADA

*****************************************************************************

DAY 1      Holiday Inn                    DAY 10     Lord Beaverbrook Hotel
           1068 Williston Road                       659 Queen Street
           South Burlington, VT                      P.O. Box 545
           05401                                      Fredericton, NB
           Phone: (802) 863-6361                     E3B 5A6
                                                     Phone: (506) 455-3371

DAY 2      Comfort Inn
           750 Hogan Road                 DAY 11     Loews Le Concorde
           Bangor, ME                     & 12       1225 Place Montcalm
           04401                                      Quebec City, PQ
           Phone: (207) 942-7899                     G1R 4W6
                                                     Phone: (418) 647-2222

DAY 3      The Delta Brunswick Inn
           39 King Street                 DAY 13     Arrive in Ontario
           Saint John, NB
           E2L 4W3
           Phone: (506) 648-1981


DAY 4      The Delta Barrington
& 5        1875 Barrington Street
           Halifax, NS
           B3J 3L6
           Phone: (902) 429-7410


DAY 6      Sydney Mariner Hotel
& 7        300 Esplanade
           P.O. Box 1054
           Sydney, NS
           B1P 6J7
           Phone: (902) 562-7500


DAY 8      Best Western MacLauchlan's
& 9        238 Grafton Street
           Charlottetown, PE
           C1A 1L5
           Phone: (902) 892-2461
```

FIGURE 12-5 SAMPLE ACCOMMODATIONS LIST

Reproduced with permission from Trentway Tours, Petersborough, Ontario, Canada.

will be quite perfunctory and the tour bus will be able to move on in just a few minutes. In other cases, a search of all luggage will be undertaken and all documents will be perused. The tour manager coordinates all interfaces with official government personnel when crossing borders by bus.

Arrival in a country by air can be handled in much the same way. All passports and entry cards are collected by the tour manager and presented together to official government personnel for clearing tour members. Some tour companies, however, prefer to have each tour member retain his own documents at the airport. As long as the tour members stay together and the tour manager stays in each processing section until the last tour member completes entry processing, the movement can go rapidly. This latter arrangement tends to be preferred by tour members. If there is a ground operator assisting, however, the former arrangement can speed up the process of getting the group through airport arrival documentation clearances in an expedited amount of time.

Summary

A multi-day, multi-destination international air tour is much more difficult to plan, run, and make a profit from than a short domestic bus tour. For that reason, many in the industry start with bus tours and, having gained experience, slowly move into developing and offering international air tours.

There are five major (global) differences in planning multi-day, multi-destination international air tours. These differences relate to language, culture, documentation, communications, and transportation. This chapter has discussed each of these differences.

In addition to these significant differences, there are also 11 specific differences that the tour planner encounters. These relate to working with local ground operators, local step-on guides, and both airport and hotel hospitality desks. They also involve differences encountered relating to the first day processes, the daily routine, international hotel procedures, border crossings, and enroute communications. Finally, they involve considering emergency planning and the ability to meet both group and individual needs. Each of these specific differences have also been discussed in detail in this chapter.

DISCUSSION QUESTIONS

These questions may be discussed by two or more students outside of class as a fun way of reviewing this chapter or they may be discussed by everyone during class for a more wide-ranging discussion.

1. What are five "global" differences encountered by the tour planner when moving from planning short, domestic bus tours to planning multi-day, multi-destination international tours?

2. What are 11 specific differences the tour planner should consider in planning multi-day, multi-destination international air tours?

3. What are the advantages and the disadvantages of the tour manager retaining all passports and other international documentation and presenting them as a group to immigration and customs authorities as the tour moves from one country to another compared to the advantages and disadvantages of individual tour members retaining their own documentation and presenting it individually at times of border crossings?

4. In much of the world retail shopping hours are different than they are in the United States. What are they and why would this make a difference to tour planners?

5. For what six types of emergencies should a tour company consider planning?

6. Is the tour planner likely to find more ground operators available from which to select in countries outside the United States or is the tour planner likely to find more in the United States?

7. Is it usually better to send company mail for the tour manager to the international hotels being used by the tour or to the international ground operators with which the company is contracting to handle the tour?

8. Is it easier to contract directly with step-on guides in conjunction with domestic bus tours or in conjunction with multi-day, multi-destination international air tours?

9. While many tour companies make an effort to meet individual tour member needs, which kind of needs should take priority over meeting individual tour member needs?

10. What is the preferred way of distributing room keys to passengers on a tour when checking in at a hotel?

ROLE PLAY EXERCISES

1. Two students may participate in this role play either out of class as a fun way to review the chapter or as an in-class exercise. One plays the role of a new international air tour planner and the other plays the role of an experienced international air tour planner who is working with the same company. Please read the script and then pick up the conversation in your own words.

NEW INTERNATIONAL AIR TOUR PLANNER: I've worked on several short domestic bus tours. It doesn't seem to me that these long tours covering North Africa and the Middle East will be much different as it relates to the planning processes. Are there really very many things I need to do differently?

EXPERIENCED INTERNATIONAL AIR TOUR PLANNER: What you actually do will be quite similar. However, the points that need to be taken into consideration will be considerably more and there will be tasks that you will encounter which you have not run across while doing short bus tours.

NEW INTERNATIONAL AIR TOUR PLANNER: It sounds like the differences might be more extensive than I had thought. What are they?

EXPERIENCED INTERNATIONAL AIR TOUR PLANNER: Let's start with the differences relating to points that need to be considered and then let's look at the different tasks. One of the first things you will need to think about is . . .

CONTINUE ON YOUR OWN

2. Two students may participate in this role play either out of class as a fun way to review the chapter or as an in-class exercise. One plays the role of a new international air tour planner and the other plays the role of an experienced international air tour planner who is working with the same company. Please read the script and then pick up the conversation in your own words.

NEW INTERNATIONAL AIR TOUR PLANNER: I'm getting ready to line up step-on guides in the cities covered on our new Latin America Extravaganza tour. I've worked with the Professional Guides Association of America to line up guides for our domestic tours. What organization do I contact for guides in Latin America?

EXPERIENCED INTERNATIONAL AIR TOUR PLANNER: I've got startling news. There is no equivalent association.

NEW INTERNATIONAL AIR TOUR PLANNER: How do I get step-on guides?

EXPERIENCED INTERNATIONAL AIR TOUR PLANNER: It is a little more difficult. Some of the approaches I take include . . .

CONTINUE ON YOUR OWN

3. Two students may participate in this role play either out of class as a fun way to review the chapter or as an in-class exercise. One plays the role of a new international air tour planner and the other plays the role of an experienced international air tour planner who is working with the same company. Please read the script and then pick up the conversation in your own words.

TOUR MEMBER: These buffet breakfasts you have scheduled every morning are great. My wife and I both like them. However, you have scheduled them to start much too late.

TOUR MANAGER: I'm glad you like the breakfasts. I regret that they are scheduled late for you. Perhaps, if you come in right at the beginning of the scheduled breakfast times, the inconvenience will be less.

TOUR MEMBER: My wife and I have always been early risers. We get up at 3:00 A.M. and always have breakfast at least by 4:30 in the morning. Just tell the hotels to have the buffet breakfasts ready then and we will make do with eating that late every day.

TOUR MANAGER: I'm afraid that won't work. There are several problems with such an arrangement. For one thing, we have the entire group scheduled to eat together and, as you know, breakfast is the time when the daily briefings are conducted.

TOUR MEMBER: Then either tell the group to change their schedule so they can eat with us or have the hotel set up a special buffet just for my wife and I and you can give us the briefing before briefing the rest of the group.

TOUR MANAGER: I would like to accommodate your individual need to have breakfast earlier, but . . .

CONTINUE ON YOUR OWN

GROUP DISCUSSION SITUATION:
SPRIGS' SURPRISE

Jennifer Sprigs woke up that morning with the very uncomfortable premonition that something was going to go wrong. Her sixth sense regarding catastrophes always seemed to be right. She kept waiting for that "something," but the morning went smoothly. "Even more smoothly than normal," she thought as she witnessed Mr. and Mrs. Grumbly enter the dining room of the Truk International Resort, smiling and actually joking with one another. "This," she thought, "has got to be a first for the tour when the Grumblys start the day in a good mood and actually liking each other."

In addition, none of the group complained when they were served the featured breakfast special, Breadfruit Breakfast Surprise, as the third and main course during this last morning repas. Jennifer started thinking, "It's the last morning of the tour. What could possible go wrong now when all we have got left is a transfer to the airport and the flight back to America?" Yet her sixth sense kept telling her that something was going to happen.

The bus was loaded. The passenger count had been taken. The baggage count checked out. There wasn't even a mistake on the hotel bill. During the brief drive to the Truk International Airport, everyone seemed to be happy, comparing notes on what they had done last night during their free time and exclaiming about the beautiful island views and the lagoon. Everyone still seemed in a jovial mood as Jennifer sneaked a glance at the passports and documents and counted just to make sure that all passports were there. They were.

"The men of Truk are handsome," Jennifer thought, as she checked in at the Airline Group Desk, "but the women are strikingly beautiful. Not only that, but everyone is pleasant." As much as she wanted to get back to America, Jennifer found herself thinking it would be nice to stay here on the island a few days by herself without the tour group, just relaxing.

And as Jennifer was mentally relaxing, daydreaming about a few hours asleep on the beach, the first catastrophe hit. The group check-in desk attendant advised that the flight would be delayed due to a mechanical problem. "It looks like it won't be more than 45 minutes," she said smiling. "And the pilot will make up the difference enroute to America." Jennifer agonizingly thought, "I've heard that one before."

Nevertheless, Jennifer advised the tour members and assured them that they would still get to Los Angeles in time to make their connecting flights back home. "There is no reason to panic," comforted Jennifer. "The pilot should be able to make up the time getting us in at the same time we have been scheduled to arrive." Several wanted to call their relatives anyway, just in case. But Jennifer assured them that they need not unjustifiably alarm their relatives back home.

The 45 minutes dragged into an hour, however, and then into an hour and a half. Tour members were restless and upset, but the gate agent was nowhere in sight and there didn't seem to be anyone around to advise just how late the flight might be.

Finally, Jennifer spotted an airline supervisor across the terminal and going up to her, insisted on being given correct information regarding the delay. "Actually," the supervisor advised, "we had hoped to get the problem resolved, but it now looks like a part will have to be flown in. Your gate agent will be making an announcement shortly that it will be tomorrow morning before we will be able to get the flight out. She will make overnight housing arrangements for you and your group at the convenient Airport Hovel Hotel."

Jennifer was aghast. This meant rescheduling all connecting flights, advising all family members who were planning to meet their relatives returning from the tour, and worst of all, it meant spending a night in the infamous Airport Hovel Hotel known throughout Micronesia for their high roach to guest ratio.

Jennifer turned to her tour manual to find out what to do during an emergency such as this. Alas, the manual had advice on seemingly every other potential problem, but nothing about canceled or delayed flights. "I'll call headquarters," she thought. Then she realized. "It's about three or four on Sunday morning at headquarters. There won't be anybody there."

"Okay," thought Jennifer to herself, "Be calm. I'll call some of my friends who are tour managers. I'll wake them up. But they will understand."

You are the friends that Jennifer has phoned. Consider the situation. Decide among yourselves what you would do and how you would handle the situation if you were Jennifer. Discuss the matter among yourselves. Be prepared to present your suggestions in a paper that will be no longer than three pages in length. Also make sure the paper is double-spaced and typed. Be prepared to also present your suggestions verbally in class if your instructor suggests that you do so.

EXERCISE

Break into groups of no more than three students working together. Yours will probably be the same group that has been working together in the development of a one-day tour since the beginning of the course.

Based upon the tour manual sample pages in the appendix and the information provided in this chapter, consider the six potential emergency areas considered to be "common emergencies for which there should be plans" and prepare an emergency manual setting out step-by-step procedures to be taken in relationship to each of the emergencies if they occur in conjunction with the one day tour that you are planning.

Note: The preparation of emergency plans for delayed or canceled departure of aircraft will be inappropriate as it relates to your tour. Therefore, ignore this emergency area in your Emergency Plan. In addition, since your trip will not include a hotel stay, ignore developing a plan preparing for hotel overbookings when the hotel refuses to accommodate passengers. The other four emergency categories should be planned for. These include:

1. the tour manager becoming ill;
2. illness or death of tour members;
3. bus breakdowns; and
4. sightseeing destination point closures.

CHAPTER 13
The Vendor Booking Process

OBJECTIVES

Upon completion of this chapter, the student will be able to:

1. Review the process of developing a vendor contract, including delivery and/or penalty clauses.

2. Prepare a written confirmation letter based upon a vendor contract.

3. Complete a daily reconfirmation call sheet form for a one-day tour.

4. Discuss the process involved in selecting sightseeing vendors.

Introduction

Vendor booking may be as easy as making a phone call or as difficult as reviewing multiple pages of multiple drafts of contracts. Most tour companies start out trusting vendors and working with telephone agreements. Fortunately, most vendors are honest, keep good records, and perform to the best of their ability either to or beyond the exact specifications agreed to on the phone. Unfortunately, there are some vendors who do not. Ultimately, tour companies run into vendors who fall into the latter category and if the tour company did not do so before, it starts working with contracts and other legal agreements. Simply because of the large potential for misunderstandings, it is always wise to document agreements.

The Importance of a Contract

Some who are new to contracting express the feeling that contracts are of benefit only if there is a legal suit and court action is imminent, but that contracts play no other role. Certainly, contracts are beneficial in the case of litigation, but that is only one, and usually thought to be a small, part of the purpose served by contracts. The primary purpose of a contract is to spell out what both parties will do and usually the compensation is spelled out as well. This can clear up both real and potential misunderstandings. Many contracts developed by lawyers, are written in legalese. They are expensive, voluminous, and difficult to understand. This sometimes results in one or both parties not reading the contract thoroughly. Wherever possible, contracts should be developed by the tour company to avoid both the cost and the jargon. Then they can be reviewed by legal counsel before being sent to vendors.

Delivery or Penalty Clauses

One of the best ways to make certain that vendors perform is to include delivery requirements and penalty clauses which require the vendor to pay the tour company if the services contracted are not provided in accordance with the contract. In standard hotel, resort, airline, and other vendor contracts prepared for the vendor by its lawyers, it is rare to find any mention of a penalty clause. If vendor contracts are adopted, a penalty clause can usually be written into the contract. Penalty funds should be reasonable in amount and ideally held by a third party in escrow. Often the practicality of getting such a penalty, however, is minimal, but one should work toward this goal. Sometimes it is only because of the penalty clauses and the concern for having to pay penalties that a vendor will make special efforts to fulfill its obligations as spelled out in the contract.

Contract Specifications and Obligations

The contract specifications and obligations will be different with each vendor. A list of requirements can be drawn up to identify what is desirable. With this set of requirements in front of the tour planner, potential vendors can be telephoned and the planner can explore what they have to offer. As they explain special features of their product compared to other products, notes should be made. Feel free to go back to potential vendors asking if they also will provide some of the features that were discussed by other vendors, but not discussed by them. Again, take notes.

After determining which vendor to use based on telephone conversations, a letter of agreement can be drawn up outlining each of the features agreed to on the phone. To make sure that all features discussed have been put in writing, the tour planner may wish to tape record the phone call (he can transcribe directly from the telephone conversation). Make sure the agreement to tape record is tape recorded so that if there is a later disagreement about this, the tape recorded agreement will provide proof of the vendor having agreed to being recorded.

Each feature should be described or discussed in the letter of agreement in a separate paragraph. Number each paragraph. Later, in any discussions, the item being discussed can be referred to by the paragraph number in the letter of agreement. Once the letter of agreement has been agreed upon, a contract can be drawn up based on it.

If the vendor pushes to use his standard contract, peruse the contract. Strike out those aspects that are not in compliance with your agreement. Write in any additional items agreed to in the letter of agreement. Initial each of these changes and require the vendor to do so on your copy of the contract.

Getting an Understanding from Vendor Sales/Marketing Executives

Keep in mind that the marketing executive and/or the sales person will want to make a sale. Sometimes this person will agree to conditions but they will not be agreed to by his superior and not agreed to in writing. Push to have the feature agreed to in writing. Indicate that a letter documenting the agreement will be required before moving forward. Alternatively, draw up the contract and submit it for signature.

Some sales and marketing executives are well thought of in their organizations and have a great deal of clout. What they agree to will be what is in the contract and what is delivered. In addition, these professional executives will often be on hand at the time of the tour's arrival making sure that quality service is provided.

An outstanding example of this is the sales manager for Grand Island Resort in Niagara, New York. When she reaches agreement with a tour company, the arrangements are detailed in the contract. But, she often goes far beyond the contract. She meets incoming tour managers, greets tour members as they get off of the bus, gets to know as many as possible by first name, makes special arrangements for tour members who may have special problems or need special services, instructs the front desk to notify her whenever a concern may arise so that she can personally take care of it, and works with all staff members to make certain that services are provided equal to or in excess of those agreed to in the contract. Tour executives like working with this type of sales and marketing professional.

Direct Vendor Representative Interfacing

In spite of the excellent way some sales and marketing executives are able to work with their companies and the entire staff, in many cases, there is less internal communication within the vendor's organization than tour planners would like. After arrangements are worked out with the sales representative, expectations are high. Upon arrival, however, the tour manager may encounter an employee, sometimes a new employee, who has none of the paperwork, has not been advised in advance, and has no access to anyone who knows about the contracted arrangements. The sales person may be out of town or otherwise unavailable. No one else knows what arrangements have been agreed to.

Because this happens so frequently, many tour planners make an effort to protect themselves, especially with vendors with which they have had previous negative experiences. They ask for the name of the person who will be on duty when the tour arrives and ask that this person be present during contract negotiations.

They communicate with this person directly, usually through confirmation calls two or three days prior to arrival. Many vendors dislike this seeming lack of trust on the part of the tour company. They interpret it as a lack of belief in their ability to communicate adequately with their staff. However, most vendors are not aware of the frequency with which tour managers encounter problems with employees who are not aware of contracted arrangements.

A second protection taken by tour planners is to provide a copy of all vendor contracts for the tour manager to bring on the tour and have available in case a vendor employee on duty is not familiar with the contracted arrangements or suggests that the arrangements are different than what the tour manager understands them to be. Having copies of the signed contracts can help to clarify points of misunderstanding.

Written Confirmations and Reconfirmations

After a contract has been developed, if there is a month or more between the time of finalizing the contract and the time when service is provided to the tour, a written review of services to be performed should be sent to the vendor with a request for confirmation. It is wise to follow this with a reconfirmation either immediately before the start of the tour or several days prior to the date when services are to be performed.

In addition, the tour manager should telephone to reconfirm 48 to 72 hours prior to the tour's arrival. Remember, reconfirm with the person who will be on duty at the time of arrival. Some companies require tour managers to keep calling in reconfirmations until they reach the employee who will be on duty. While vendors may not appreciate receiving so many reconfirmations, they help to avoid last-minute problems.

Client Data

When booking with a vendor, the vendor will need individual tour member client data. All vendors need to know the number of paid tour participants, the number of escorts or guides, and whether or not the bus driver will be accompanying the tour members. Hotels and resorts will want to know which tour members are sharing rooms and which have single rooms. Some vendors will want information on smoking or other preferences. If any tour members have any type of impairments, such as hearing or walking difficulty, this information can be valuable to vendors.

Some vendors will request information which tour members and tour companies may consider not necessary or confidential. For example, some will want to have tour member addresses and phone numbers, primarily for their use in marketing to solicit repeat clients. Most tour companies do not provide this type of information as clients may not appreciate receiving direct mail pieces after the tour. Some vendors request age, sex, or race information. Unless the tour company can see the relevance, they usually do not provide this information. However, sometimes otherwise confidential information may be needed by the vendor. Some vendors, for example, will not accept elderly persons on high-activity programs. They set age limits for rafting trips, mountain climbing, or other strenuous outdoor activities.

Needed information on clients, such as rooming lists, can be either mailed or faxed to the vendor. If necessary, however, this information can be transmitted by phone, but mail or fax avoids the potential problem of misspelling names.

Telephone Reconfirmations

The telephone reconfirmations which tour managers make while enroute consist of simply calling the vendor and speaking with the person who will be on duty when the tour arrives. The tour manager reconfirms the number of participants on the tour, the arrangements as detailed in the contract, and discusses any points of special concern.

The tour manager's daily reconfirmation call sheet lists each reconfirmation call that will need to be made that day, the name of vendor contact persons, and telephone numbers. Appropriate special notes are appended to the list. The tour manager is usually expected to make notes on the reconfirmation call list as calls are made. These indicate the name of the person with whom the tour manager conversed, the date and time of the call, and any appropriate special notes.

Working with Vendors

In planning sightseeing, tour planners are often faced with more sightseeing options than possible to reasonably schedule. This is a nice kind of problem, but it presents a selection problem. The tour planner is frequently tempted to select those sightseeing options which entail working with the vendors that will be easiest to book and that will present the smallest amount of potential difficulty. Certainly, options should not be booked where there is a real probability of problems—especially those that may result in a lack of client enjoyment. However, sightseeing options that will be of greatest interest to the majority of the tour participants are usually selected. This will depend on the target market tour members.

It is suggested that the tour planner first eliminate those sites that present insurmountable problems. Next, survey past tour participants asking them to rank the sightseeing options. The ranking process should be simple, easy, and clearly understood. Usually the best way is to rank them from a number which is the total of all sites being considered down to 1 (that site which the evaluator considers to be of greatest interest). The site of least interest to the evaluator will be the site which has been given the highest cumulative score. For example, if the listing is composed of 20 sites, the evaluator would be asked to rank the sites from 1 (most interested in visiting) to 20 (least interested in visiting). If 10 people are evaluating the sites, the site with a score of "10" will be the most popular destination and the site with a score of "200" will be the least popular. If this ranking is conducted several times with several past groups, ranking patterns can be identified and the tour planner will have a guideline with which to work in planning sightseeing trips.

Although the most important consideration in including a sightseeing point in the tour itinerary is the degree of interest expected from the target audience (i.e., the tour members), there are other factors which should be considered. One of these factors is the "fit" of the sightseeing point. When tour planners put together an itinerary, there should be a logical flow from one portion of the trip to the next. Although some sightseeing points may be of interest to participants, unless that interest level is extremely high, if the sightseeing point does not logically fit comfortably into the itinerary, it probably should be left out rather than forced into the tour.

Tours suffer when tour planners try to squeeze in every potential sightseeing point so that nothing will be missed. There are some points that should not be missed. But many can be excluded. Usually, tour members feel better about an itinerary when there is a smooth, comfortable flow to the trip. Most of the time, tour members prefer an easy pace over one that rushes them just to see everything.

Often there is little correlation between top-quality vendor efficiency, knowledge, and the ability to handle tour groups on the one hand, and interest on the part of tour members to participate in or consume the product or service offered by the vendor on the other. Sometimes, the sites tourists most want to visit, the hotels tourists would most like to stay in, and the restaurants in which tourists would most like to have meals are run by the vendors which are the most difficult to deal with. A balance must be struck to make sure that tour members are able to see the sites, stay in the hotels, and eat the meals they would like to, but to make sure that a reasonable degree of service is provided as well.

In most cases, sites, hotels, restaurants, and other vendors which treat tour members badly should be left out of the itinerary. However, the tour planner should not lose sight of the fact that it is the tour experience for the tour member that is being purchased, not the ease of operation with vendors. Therefore, tour planners may need to work with vendors and work through problems. This is not always easy, but a willingness to recognize that the vendor is trying (when making a sincere effort) and to accept small problems, goes a long way in helping to create a memorable tour and establishing long-term good relationships with tour vendors.

Summary

Many who start working with vendors, especially for short, domestic tours, believe that having a contract is not necessary. Experienced tour managers, however, feel having contracts with vendors is important no matter how short the tour. They assist in cases of litigation and they provide a vehicle for spelling out the obligations of both parties. In addition, most agree that having contract delivery requirements spelled out and penalty clauses detailed is also important.

Tour planners find that one of the best ways of working with vendors is to first meet with several potential vendors and find out what special features they offer. Planners negotiate for an agreement that is most beneficial to the tour company and develop a contract based on a letter of agreement. If the vendor requires its standard contract, write in the additional agreed-to features and remove those which are disagreeable. Initial any change and have the vendor do the same.

One obstacle may be in finding the right person with whom to negotiate. The person who verbally agrees to a contract should be a person who can commit for the company. Some sales executives can do this; others cannot. Another problem arises when a contractual agreement for services has been reached and finding that the contractual information has not been passed on to the vendor representative who will be handling the tour when it arrives. This problem can be solved by involving the representative of the vendor who will provide services in the initial conversations and contractual agreement process. In addition, confirmation calls can be made in advance. All aspects relating to the services to be provided are reviewed with the person who will be on duty at the time the tour arrives. Written confirmations can also be beneficial.

Vendors will want and need information on tour members. Some information IS necessary. Provide it! Other information is not necessary. The vendor will use it for marketing. Normally, this type of marketing information is not provided on request.

Make telephone reconfirmations with the person who will be on duty when the tour arrives. Reconfirmations should be detailed and specific. Areas of special concern should be discussed.

Many tour planners are tempted to select sightseeing vendors because they are easy to work with. However, sightseeing should be planned based on the interests of tour members. Eliminate sites that present major problems and those of least interest to tour members. Only include sites which "fit" well on the itinerary. Sightseeing companies should provide good value for cost. Ease of working with the vendor is important, but it is the tour experience that is being purchased by the client. Even if vendors are hard to work with, if they provide a unique and beneficial experience, many tour companies feel that they should make every effort to work with such vendors.

DISCUSSION QUESTIONS

These questions may be discussed by two or more students outside of class as a fun way of reviewing this chapter or they may be discussed by everyone during class for a more wide-ranging discussion.

1. Because of the large potential for what, it is always wise to document agreements between the tour company and vendors?

2. Is there usually a strong correlation between top quality vendor efficiency, knowledge, and ability to handle tour groups on the one hand and interest on the part of tour members to participate in or consume the product or service offered by the vendor on the other hand?

3. Why must tour companies and tour planners need to learn to work with vendors and work through vendor-related problems?

4. What is one of the best ways to ensure vendor performance?

5. What is the most important consideration in including a sightseeing point in the tour itinerary?

6. In finalizing a contract with a vendor, should the tour planner feel free to go back to potential vendors asking if they will provide some of the features that were discussed by other vendors, and not discussed by them?

7. How might a tour planner develop a guideline with which to work in planning sightseeing trips?

8. If you work out detailed arrangements for the handling of the tour with the sales representative of the vendor, will the tour company automatically find that the arrangements will flow smoothly, exactly as agreed upon with the sales and marketing executive?

9. What department normally prepares a daily reconfirmation call sheet for the tour manager?

10. What documentation do tour managers often bring with them and have available in case a vendor employee on duty is either not familiar with the contracted arrangements or suggests that the arrangements are different than what the tour manager understands them to be?

ROLE PLAY EXERCISES

1. Two students may participate in this role play either out of class as a fun way to review the chapter or as an in-class exercise. One plays the role of a new

tour planner and the other plays the role of an experienced tour planner. Please read the script and then pick up the conversation in your own words.

NEW TOUR PLANNER: I've always worked with vendors on just a handshake. It has worked well for me in the past, but I understand that in the tour industry contracts are usually considered the way to go.

EXPERIENCED TOUR PLANNER: Most vendors do an excellent job and it is seldom that a contract is necessary. However, with some vendors a contract is essential.

NEW TOUR PLANNER: Wouldn't it be possible for me to simply not work with those vendors who do not perform or who perform to a lesser degree than expected? Then I won't need a contract.

EXPERIENCED TOUR PLANNER: That sounds as if it might work. However, . . .

CONTINUE ON YOUR OWN

2. Two students may participate in this role play either out of class as a fun way to review the chapter or as an in-class exercise. One plays the role of a new tour operator and the other plays the role of an experienced tour operator. Please read the script and then pick up the conversation in your own words.

NEW TOUR OPERATOR: Isn't it a bit ridiculous to do a contract and then a written confirmation, and then finally telephone reconfirmations? Isn't that a case of overkill?

EXPERIENCED TOUR OPERATOR: It may seem like it, but . . .

CONTINUE ON YOUR OWN

3. Two students may participate in this role play either out of class as a fun way to review the chapter or as an in-class exercise. One plays the role of a new tour planner and the other plays the role of an experienced tour planner. Please read the script and then pick up the conversation in your own words.

NEW TOUR PLANNER: I understand your tour managers carry copies of vendor contracts with them.

EXPERIENCED TOUR PLANNER: Yes, we recently adopted that process.

NEW TOUR PLANNER: I have a real concern about releasing copies of the contracts and letting the tour managers have a copy. Surely, when they have them they will read them. Then they are aware of the exact terms of our agreement.

EXPERIENCED TOUR PLANNER: I can see why you might be concerned. If they decide to go into business in competition with you, having that knowledge might be beneficial for them. We have not had that type of problem occur. The benefits we enjoy by having tour managers retain copies of the contract, having them available while they are on tour simply boils down to . . .

CONTINUE ON YOUR OWN

GROUP DISCUSSION SITUATION:
NAG'S NIDGET NO NO

Magdelana Nag, called MagNag by friend and enemy alike, felt good and patted herself on the back last February when after two years she was finally able to get Piety Phylax, the Museum Manager for the Niggardly Nidget Museum in Niamey, Niger to agree to allow her tour group to tour the museum next month. The President of the Empty-headed Uptors of Belly Bay, New Mexico had made it very clear to Mag that they expected to have the museum visit included in their package or they would not even consider a tour of Niger and the surrounding countries. MagNag had spent years building up the reputation of Ninny Nobility Tours and knew that she needed to maintain the reputation that she could get groups into sights where no one else was able to gain access. "It's my stubbornness," she thought.

After calling Piety week after week for almost three months, Piety finally returned her call, Magdelana thought primarily just to get her to stop "bugging" her. Piety was concerned about the antiquity of the niggardly nidgets in the museum and did not want tour groups to go through. A group had not toured the museum in at least 10 years. But at the insistence of Mag, Piety finally agreed, since Mag said she would bring Empty-headed Uptors through the museum only in small groups of five at a time.

Shortly after Piety had reached agreement on the phone, a contract arrived. It had been drawn up by Magdelana Nag and it was very one-sided. Since Piety was still reluctant to allow the group to tour the museum, she held on to the contract for several weeks.

After a week had gone by without getting the contract back in the mail, Magdelana placed repeated calls to Piety. Piety knew what the reason for the call was, so she never returned the calls. But a few days later, she signed the contract and returned it to Magdelana at the Ninny Nobility Tours' headquarters.

Not a month went by before Piety got another reminder from MagNag in the form of a letter of confirmation. The letter spelled out all details of the agreement, but added a few points that Piety had not remembered agreeing upon. They were small points, though, so Piety accepted. She did nothing with the letter, since it was simply a reminder. However, Piety has noticed that every month that has gone by, she has received another copy of the confirmation letter.

This week, Magdelana Nag started telephoning in order to confirm all details by phone. Piety was out of the office, attending an international convention. But when she returned, she had 15 phone messages from Magdelana, each one asking her to return the call in order to complete reconfirmation requirements. Piety thought, "These are the requirements of Ninny Nobility Tours, not industry or destination requirements." She was angry that Magdelana continued to call and leave messages since Piety's secretary, Booksum Bloxsum, was excellent in taking messages. Booksum also confided that the last time Magdelana called, MagNag was rude, insulting Booksum and suggesting that Booksum did not give the messages to Piety. "If you had, Piety would have called me back immediately, since I am such an important client for you," insisted MagNag.

This last insult is the last straw, thought Piety. She did get on the phone and return the call to Magdelana. However, when MagNag picked up the phone, Piety let her have it with her anger. Finally, Piety screamed, "The tour is off! Don't you and your Empty-headed Belly Bay Uptors dare show your faces at our museum next week. We will lock the doors on you."

Now Magdelana doesn't know what to do. The tour has been sold out for some time and the tour members are scheduled to depart in three days. She is attending a local chapter meeting of the International Tour Planners' Association this afternoon and has already called several of you, the members, prior to the meeting. You have gathered in a private room to discuss the problem before the meeting starts. "I just did what is standard in the industry," Magdelana tells you.

Consider the situation. Decide among yourselves what you would do and how you would handle the situation if you were Magdelana Nag. Discuss the matter among yourselves. Be prepared to present your suggestions in a paper that will be no longer than three pages in length. Also make sure the paper is double-spaced and typed. Be prepared to also present your suggestions verbally in class if your instructor suggests that you do so.

EXERCISES

1. Break into groups of no more than three students working together. Yours will probably be the same group that has been working together in the development of a one-day tour since the beginning of the course.

Select one of the contracts that you developed in completing Chapter 10's Exercise 1. From that contract, prepare a confirmation letter to the vendor which will constitute a written review of the services the vendor is to provide. Before preparing the letter, make a list of all services to be rendered and/or all products to be provided to the tour by the vendor and determine how you want to present each one. You might write a paragraph about each or you might just list each one. Make sure, however, that you convey to the vendor the need to provide services/products that meet the quality standards you have specified.

2. Break into groups of no more than three students working together. Yours will probably be the same group that has been working together in the development of a one-day tour since the beginning of the course.

Prepare a reconfirmation call sheet for your one-day tour. Make sure you provide complete contact information. If possible, this will include the name of the vendor, the vendor's complete address, the vendor's phone number (including area code and any appropriate extension number), the name of the person you have been working with associated with the vendor, and the name of the person who will be on duty when the tour arrives. Briefly identify what needs to be confirmed. This information should be provided for each vendor that provides one or more services or products for the tour throughout the day of your one-day tour.

CHAPTER 14

Client Reservations

OBJECTIVES

Upon completion of this chapter, the student will be able to:

1. List the required data items a reservationist needs to obtain when making a tour reservation.

2. Complete five simulated bookings utilizing a standard reservation booking card form.

3. Identify the pros and cons of the tour operator contracting with a travel agency to take tour reservations.

4. Complete at least five simulated client confirmation forms.

Introduction

Most tour companies find that as they grow in size, their methods and approaches to handling reservations change. Small tour companies have the problem of needing to take reservations, but not having enough tours to justify having a good internal reservation system. Medium-sized companies find that they can justify an internal system, but they do not have the sophistication that many clients would like and that would give them cost advantages. Large tour companies find that they can justify high quality automated reservation systems, but that the software and sometimes the hardware needed may not be available. Therefore, there are good and bad points associated with reservations for tour companies at each size level.

In addition to considering basic reservation systems, tour companies also consider both required and optional needed reservation data. They also need to consider their clients and how clients will be making reservations. Many tour companies take travel agency reservations. These reservations come in either by phone or through a computer reservation system. All reservation calls need confirmations. The handling of both verbal and written reservation confirmations will be considered in this chapter. This chapter also reviews the dual problems of overbooking and underbooking. Ways of avoiding and/or handling both problems are discussed.

Contracting with Travel Agencies to Handle Reservations

When a tour company starts in business, it frequently starts with only a few tours to run each year. When this is the case, the company is faced with a problem concerning reservations. This problem is especially acute when the tour operation is run out of one's home, as it frequently is with a start-up operation. The company is not in a position to hire a full-time reservationist.

Therefore, either working on a contract basis with a travel agency, some other service handling reservations, or a telephone answering facility (either an answering machine or a telephone answering service) tends to be the only practical way of handling reservations. A few companies have found that a telephone answering service or an answering machine works satisfactorily. However, many consider a machine and a service to be unprofessional and some potential tour clients will not book with a company that uses an answering service or machine. Therefore, the only viable option is to work on a contracted basis.

Some use nontravel reservation booking services. These are often quite good. One drawback, however, is that the personnel of reservation services seldom have a thorough knowledge of the tour product. They are trained to ask the right questions, but if the client asks for clarification, in most cases, they are totally unprepared to answer the potential client's questions.

Travel agencies offer advantages over reservation booking services. Most agencies are relatively small. A training session with agency staff members can give agency staffers enough information to answer most questions a potential client might ask when making reservations. In addition, since travel agencies book tours on a frequent basis, agency staff members will be prepared to look out for potential problem clients. They can steer potential clients either to or away from the tour because of their counseling ability. Perhaps of greatest importance, however, are the travel agency staff members. When booking the tour, they must sound professional to the potential tour member so that there is an impression that the client is talking directly to a representative of the tour company rather than to a contracted company employee.

There are disadvantages in working with travel agencies, however. Agencies expect a 10 percent booking fee. This adds to the cost of the tour. It also takes a large percentage of the money budgeted for marketing. Another problem sometimes encountered is one of ethics. A few agencies, contracting to sell the tours of a specific tour company, will duplicate the tours identically when they find a tour that sells well. They will sell their own product rather than the product of the tour company. The potential for this problem can be reduced or eliminated through the development of a good contract with the travel agency. Nevertheless, several tour companies have found their tours duplicated closely by travel agencies with which they contracted to handle reservations. The agency was able to book a full tour for itself with few or no bookings for the tour operator.

Overcoming these obstacles is fairly easy if you recognize the potential obstacles in the beginning. By budgeting and pricing the tour adequately, the 10 percent booking commission can be built into the tour price. By using written contracts, especially those with penalty clauses, travel agencies which will steal a tour tend to be eliminated from consideration.

Developing a Manual Reservation System

When the tour company has grown large enough, an in-house reservation system will be developed. This often starts as a manual reservation system. Normally, a master listing of all who have made a reservation by tour number or tour name is kept either in a book or on a wall-chart. There will be lines numbered for each place on the tour followed by between five and 10 wait-lists. When the client or travel agency calls in a reservation, the reservationist checks the book or wall chart to determine if space is available. If it is, the name of the client is entered in the book or wall chart taking up a numbered space. A booking card is then filled out for the client giving details such as client address, phone number, the travel agency with which the client is working (if appropriate), and other data (see Figure 14-1). The booking card is then kept in a file retained for each tour. Most booking cards call for the client number on the tour to be entered in the top right-hand corner of the booking card. Booking cards are filed in numerical order corresponding with the client's assigned tour number. Usually the booking card includes blocks or lines for financial data. Deposits, additional payments, and ultimately a final payment will all be reflected on the booking card. These entries will reflect the date the check was received and the amount of money received. This manual system works well for small tour operators. For larger tour companies, however, it becomes cumbersome and is too time-consuming. Most large tour companies, therefore, develop some form of computerized reservations.

Computerized Reservations

At this point, tour company management should determine whether or not they wish to have a computerized reservation system which is an off-the-shelf system or if they wish to have one built to meet their individual needs. It is usually considered best if the company wishes to have a tailor-built system to do so at the time the company moves from a manual system to a computerized system. This is less expensive and it allows the company to start computerization with a system that meets its own needs rather than a system designed to meet the needs of a large number of tour operators.

```
┌─────────────────────────────────────────────────────────┐
│              RESERVATIONS/CONFIRMATIONS                   │
│                                                           │
│  Name: _____    Phone No. _____    │
│                                                           │
│  Contact: _____                       │
│                                                           │
│  Date: _____    Time _____     │
│                                                           │
│  No. of Passengers: _____               │
│                                                           │
│  Special Information: _____        │
│                       _____        │
│                       _____        │
│                       _____        │
│                                                           │
│  Date Confirmed: _____  Double Confirmed: _____  │
│                                                           │
│                                                           │
│              RESERVATIONS/CONFIRMATIONS                   │
│                                                           │
│  Name: _____    Phone No. _____    │
│                                                           │
│  Contact: _____                       │
│                                                           │
│  Date: _____    Time _____     │
│                                                           │
│  No. of Passengers: _____               │
│                                                           │
│  Special Information: _____        │
│                       _____        │
│                       _____        │
│                       _____        │
│                                                           │
│  Date Confirmed: _____  Double Confirmed: _____  │
│                                                           │
│                                                           │
│              RESERVATIONS/CONFIRMATIONS                   │
│                                                           │
│  Name: _____    Phone No. _____    │
│                                                           │
│  Contact: _____                       │
│                                                           │
│  Date: _____    Time _____     │
│                                                           │
│  No. of Passengers: _____               │
│                                                           │
│  Special Information: _____        │
│                       _____        │
│                       _____        │
│                       _____        │
│                                                           │
│  Date Confirmed: _____  Double Confirmed: _____  │
└─────────────────────────────────────────────────────────┘
```

FIGURE 14-1 SAMPLE BOOKING CARD

Reproduced with permission from Rojo Tours, Santa Fe, NM.

The major drawback in developing a tailored system is cost. It usually is more expensive than an off-the-shelf program. Because of cost, therefore, many companies move from a manual system to an off-the-shelf program. As they build up capital reserves, they move into the third stage (i.e., having a computer reservation system tailor-designed to meet their needs).

Although this approach means incurring a substantial amount of additional cost by purchasing the off-the-shelf system prior to developing a tailor-designed system, some companies have no choice. They cannot afford a tailor-designed reservation system at the stage in their development when they need computerization. In addition, the approach of adding an off-the-shelf system before developing a tailor-designed system gives the tour company an opportunity to take the time needed to work the bugs out of a tailored program before implementing it. They can continue with the off-the-shelf system while sophisticating the tailor-designed program.

The best references for off-the-shelf reservation systems are obtained through the national associations and the trade press. Companies marketing the systems advertise in the trade press and often will have a booth at national association meetings. You should review several systems before adopting one. Systems range considerably in cost and sophistication. The least expensive ones are designed to be used on a small office computer or on a personal computer. These systems are inexpensive, but they have severe limitations in what they can do. More expensive systems provide interfacing between computers, rapid access to individual names, and the ability to massage names or other data records for research or alternative list development purposes. Most of the inexpensive systems do not have add-on ability to make them competitive with more sophisticated systems.

Therefore, tour company executives need to determine exactly what they want from their reservation systems and develop a hierarchy of reservation system needs. Once this has been determined, an investigation into the systems that are available on the market will allow the managers to compare needs, systems, and cost. This approach provides an opportunity to purchase a system that should meet immediate needs as well as short-term future ones. If the budget is available, longer-term needs may also be met by an off-the-shelf program. You should avoid, however, buying inexpensive systems to meet immediate needs. Finding yourself trapped in a cycle of purchasing a new automated reservation system every two or three years as your budget for reservations and the need for reservation system sophistications become greater is indeed frustrating. This is a trap that is easy to fall into, and it can be very expensive over a period of time.

Required and Optional Reservation Data

Booking cards and sophisticated computer reservation systems allow tour companies to gather a substantial amount of data on each person making a reservation (see Figure 14-2). The limitation on client data normally is not prescribed

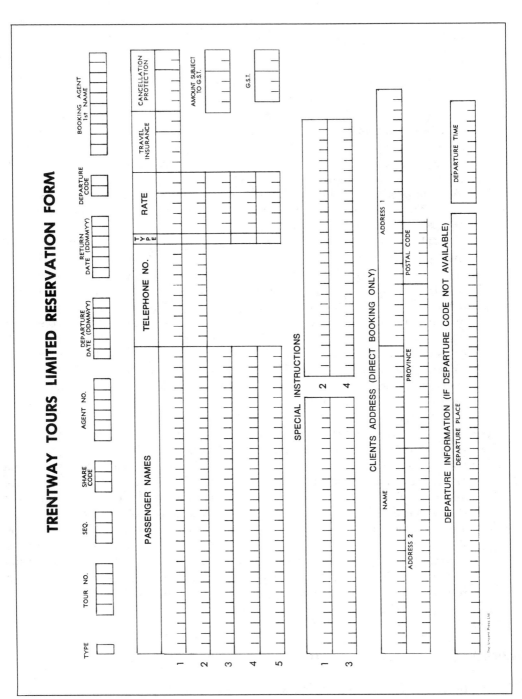

FIGURE 14-2 SAMPLE RESERVATION FORM

Reproduced with permission from Trentway Tours, Peterborough, Ontario, Canada.

by computer reservation equipment or pre-assigned blocks on a reservation card. It is limited by the amount of time the client or the client's travel agency wishes to spend in making the reservation and the client's confidentiality regarding tastes and preferences.

The most essential information is the name of the client spelled correctly. In addition, the client's address and both business and home phone numbers are usually obtained. The tour the client is booking and the starting date of the tour or the tour number need to be recorded. If the client is booking the tour through a travel agency, the name of the agency, the address and the phone number of the agency, and preferably the name of the booking agent working for the agency should all be recorded. This is the essential information. All systems should record this data.

In addition to the essential, required reservation data, optional data is often sought. For example, most companies want to know if there are limitations on the part of the client, especially physical limitations. These limitations could be as insignificant as a slight hearing difficulty or as major as being confined to a wheelchair. Some clients do not like to talk about their limitations and do not make them known even if they are asked. Some fear that they will not be accepted for the tour if they make the tour company aware of limitations. Others are simply embarrassed about having limitations. Nevertheless, if the tour company can obtain this information, the knowledge assists both the company and the tour manager. Some adventure tour companies require a filing of up-to-date physical examination records before accepting members on tours.

In addition to limitation information, most tour companies like to find out information such as age, sex, whether or not the client will be sharing a room with one or more other people on the tour, special interests, and the financial status of clients. Some of this information will often be given to the tour company without hesitation. For example, you can usually tell sex by voice or name. If the booking comes through a travel agency, the agent can be asked the sex of the traveler. Most travelers volunteer it if they wish to share a room with one or more other tour members. They know this is a cost consideration.

However, many clients are hesitant to provide other, nice-to-have data. For example, few clients are willing to provide financial income information.

Most booking cards are designed to request required data first, beneficial information which probably will be provided right away by tour members next, and nice-to-know information which may not be provided by tour members last. In asking for reservation data information, the reservationist needs to be sensitive to concerns on the part of the tour member and on the part of the agency through which the tour may be booked. Except for required and essential information, seldom are tour members pressured to provide optional information. Sometimes all optional information is gathered only through questionnaires on which it is very clearly noted that responses are optional.

Travel Agency Phone Reservations

Although bookings made by travel agencies for their clients may be transmitted to tour companies through computer reservation system interfaces, most travel agency-booked tour reservations are still made on the phone.

After consultation with the client, a tour is selected. The agent then telephones the tour company reservations office to determine whether or not space is available. Frequently, this reservation call is made while the client is at the desk of the agent. If the tour is full, the agent and client must make a second choice.

The agent's first concern when making a reservation is whether or not there is space available. Reservationists need to be aware that this will usually be the first question. If there is space, the agent may turn to the client, confirm space availability, and get a confirmation to complete the reservation. The more sophisticated agents will already have obtained this permission, however, and will continue making the reservation. They will provide the essential, required information without even being asked. The reservationist needs to take down the data, read it back to confirm accuracy, and ask any required or essential reservation information that has not been covered by the agent.

Reservationists must transact business rapidly. Reservation productivity quotas should be met and it should be remembered that agents are busy individuals. A businesslike approach on the phone is important. This should not, however, restrain the reservationist from being cordial. In spite of reservation quotas, try to be patient if the agent needs to confirm or check data with the client during the reservation phone call.

Travel Agency CRT Bookings

As agency computer reservation systems become more sophisticated, an increasing number of tour companies are listing their tours in the systems. This has several advantages. Agents have productivity goals just as tour reservationists do. An agent who is skilled in operating her computer reservation system can complete a computer booking in less than one-third the time that it takes to make a phone reservation. Therefore, many agents prefer to make reservations through their computers.

Computer reservation systems also provide more detailed information about a tour than a tour brochure provides. Some of the more sophisticated systems can even show destination photos on the CRT screen. These can be viewed by both the agent and the client in the travel agency.

The drawback to making computer reservation system bookings available as a reservation option for agents is the cost. All agency computer reservation systems have their prime affiliation with non-tour vendors. The cost of listing tours is expensive and there are booking charges as well. The combination of costs may be so high that tours have to be priced higher than the prices of competitors. Tour companies, therefore, need to be careful before listing their tours in computer reservation systems.

Agency and Client Written Confirmations

After reservations are made, clients expect to receive a written confirmation. If the reservation is made through a travel agency, the written confirmation normally goes to the agency. There is no direct interface with the client when the booking comes through a travel agency. The agent is expected to transmit the confirmation to the client.

The timing of confirmations is important. Both the client and agent often get excited about the trip when the reservation is made. To keep up that excitement and to reduce the potential of or a fear of a lost reservation, it is important to confirm reservations rapidly. Many tour companies have a policy that written confirmations will be mailed from the tour company within 24 hours (or by the end of the next business day) of the time the reservation is taken.

Written confirmations are typed or computer-generated. They verify that the client will be taking the tour. The client name is spelled out as the reservationist took it and the name of the tour is also spelled out. The departure date of the tour is noted. Any additional essential information is also confirmed. Most confirmations conclude with a paragraph or a statement suggesting that the client or the agency contact the tour company right away if any portion of the confirmation information is incorrect.

Overbookings and Underbookings

Both tour overbookings and underbookings can create problems. Overbookings are situations in which reservationists have taken bookings for many more tour participants than the maximum number scheduled for the tour. Successful tour companies find that, like with airline seats, there are clients who cancel at the last minute. Therefore, overbooking a tour gives the tour company the ability to fill those places canceled by tour members who decide at the last minute that they will not take the tour. Companies often reduce the potential problem of overbooking by levying substantial penalties on tour members who cancel at the last minute. Some companies project a profit position requiring less than a full tour.

When all but 10 seats on the tour bus are sold, the tour goes into a wait-list position. Anyone booking for a wait-listed position is advised that they may not be able to go on the tour. As cancellations are received, wait-listed persons are advised that they can be confirmed. Their wait-listed positions are absorbed by others moving up on the list. This may open up additional wait-list positions so that reservations can be taken for more people. Each wait-listed person is told that they are wait-listed and the reservationist often tells the wait-listed persons how good their chances are of being able to make the tour. This is a professional way of avoiding overbookings. However, it can result in lower profits for the tour company.

Tour companies which have marketed tours that must fill to capacity in order to breakeven or tours for which the per person profit is marginal, often find themselves needing to accept all persons who sign up for a tour and "squeezing them in somehow." This is not recommended. When tours are overbooked, clients can be upset. Many states and countries have rules against allowing tour members to stand on a tour bus. Therefore, if more tour members are sold than can be accommodated on the bus, the company is in a position of either having to get a larger tour bus or of having to cancel a person who believes himself to be accepted for a tour. This can create substantial problems for a tour company. Some companies have been sued by tour members who have been turned down for a tour because of overbooking. Tour planners should take every step possible to avoid overbookings and to project their profits sufficiently well that the need to fill tours to capacity will be reduced.

Underbookings may cause an even greater problem. If the tour has so few people that the company will lose money if it runs the tour, the tour company is then faced with the problem of either turning down tour members who have signed up or running the tour at a loss. Some companies, especially large ones, will go ahead and run a tour, even at a loss, rather than risk the reputation of having to cancel. Many companies, however, are not in the financial position where they can run tours at a loss. They are then forced to cancel the tour. This can create a bad reputation.

It is always wise to advise tour members that a tour will be run only if there is sufficient enrollment. However, even though this disclaimer may appear on the brochure and reservationists may make this statement verbally, the hard feelings that tour members may have toward the company may well persist for a long period of time after the cancellation. When cancellations are necessary, therefore, some type of compensation for the tour passengers should be considered. One of the favorite ways of doing this is to offer a reduction in price if the canceled tour member takes any other tour offered by the company within a specified period of time—usually a year. This may mean that the tour company will not make a profit from that tour member on the tour selected, but it will go a long way toward reducing the hard feelings the tour member may have and it may turn an angry client into a repeat customer.

When a tour is canceled because of underbookings, the commissions of travel agencies should be protected. When a travel agent sells a tour, the agency expects to receive at least a 10 percent commission. In the mind of an agency owner, just because the tour company did not have enough people sold does not justify taking away the 10 percent commission earned when the tour was sold. Therefore, if tours are cancelled, most agency executives believe that their commissions should be protected and paid anyway.

Summary

Tour companies have several options regarding the way in which they handle reservations. The selection from the options varies in direct relationship to the size and history of the tour company. New and small tour companies tend to work with answering services or answering machines. Usually considered a better option is to contract with a travel agency or a reservation booking service to take reservations. When this is done, a ten percent fee is standard. However, agencies can provide a professional level of service. If an agency is used, a contract should be obtained with penalty clauses in case they attempt to duplicate the tour.

In house manual systems constitute the next step up in reservations. Tour companies that are larger and that have a more substantial history frequently opt to work with computerized reservation systems, purchasing off-the-shelf programs. This provides substantially better quality reservations, greater data flexibility and faster data input. The largest tour companies have computer reservation systems tailor-designed to meet their needs. Although these are expensive, they can provide the company with a maximum degree of capability.

Tour companies find that the data needed from tour members and the travel agencies booking tour clients can be divided into two categories: that data which is essential and that which is nice to have. Essential information includes the name of the client, client contact information, the tour and the date of the tour, and the name and contact information of the travel agency and of the booking agent. Optional data varies from company to company. This is often data that can be beneficial to the tour manager and it may include information helpful in marketing to the client in the future.

Reservations can come into the tour company by phone from the agency or the client or through the agency's computer reservation system. However, the listing and booking fees involved make listing a tour company's tours on computer reservation systems expensive.

Once a reservation has been taken and confirmed verbally by the tour company, both the travel agent and the client will expect to receive written confirmations. Confirm all aspects of the tour and send the confirmation to the travel agency—within 24 hours of receipt of the booking, if possible.

Two of the major reservation problems are overbookings and underbookings. It is usually better to price tours sufficiently well that overbookings are not necessary. However, the higher the per person price of the tour, the less likely the tour will fill. Clients tend to be cost conscious in booking most tours.

Underbookings which result in canceled tours tend to make clients angry. Include a printed message on tour brochures indicating that tours must fill or they will be cancelled. This advice should also be given verbally to clients when they book. If a tour is cancelled, provide some compensation to the client. Offering a reduced rate for a future tour helps to reduce the natural antagonism a client feels when advised that the tour has been cancelled.

DISCUSSION QUESTIONS

These questions may be discussed by two or more students outside of class as a fun way of reviewing this chapter or they may be discussed by everyone during class for a more wide-ranging discussion.

1. What are several options open to small tour companies in handling their reservations?

2. What options are open for medium-sized travel agencies in taking reservations?

3. How do the larger and most experienced tour companies handle the reservations function?

4. Is it important to protect the commissions of travel agencies when a tour is cancelled because of underbookings?

5. What are two disadvantages in having travel agencies take reservations for tour companies when the tour company is too small or too young to have its own reservation staff?

6. How might a tour company turn a potentially angry client into a potential repeat customer when a tour is cancelled because it was underbooked?

7. How many wait-list lines normally appear on a booking card?

8. What is an overbooking situation?

9. What is the major drawback in developing a tailored computerized reservation system?

10. What confirmation time policy is identified in this chapter as one which many tour companies follow regarding the speed with which written confirmations will be mailed from the tour company to the travel agency or to the client who booked directly?

ROLE PLAY EXERCISES

1. Two students may participate in this role play either out of class as a fun way to review the chapter or as an in-class exercise. One plays the role of a new tour reservationist and the other plays the role of an experienced tour reservationist. Please read the script and then pick up the conversation in your own words.

NEW TOUR RESERVATIONIST: I don't understand why we need to prepare a written confirmation at all. After all, we have confirmed everything on the phone with the travel agent when taking the reservation.

EXPERIENCED TOUR RESERVATIONIST: Yes, it is all confirmed on the phone. However, . . .

CONTINUE ON YOUR OWN

2. Two students may participate in this role play either out of class as a fun way to review the chapter or as an in-class exercise. One plays the role of a tour company owner and the other plays the role of a tour industry consultant. Please read the script and then pick up the conversation in your own words.

TOUR COMPANY OWNER: We have built our business quite substantially over the last two years. Our working relationship with the travel agency that is handling reservations for us is a very good one and the arrangement seems to work quite well.

TOUR INDUSTRY CONSULTANT: I'm glad that things seem to be working out well for you. How can I help?

TOUR COMPANY OWNER: I'm concerned about the cost of working through the travel agency with which we contract in taking reservations and I also would like to get better control over the reservations function. I'm considering eliminating the contract and handling the reservations function in house. What are the pros and cons of our doing it here in our offices compared with continuing the arrangement we have of farming out the reservations function to a travel agency?

TOUR INDUSTRY CONSULTANT: There are both advantages and disadvantages. Let's start with the advantages. Probably the most important advantage to taking reservations in house is that . . .

CONTINUE ON YOUR OWN

3. Two students may participate in this role play either out of class as a fun way to review the chapter or as an in-class exercise. One plays the role of a new tour company owner and the other plays the role of a tour industry consultant. Please read the script and then pick up the conversation in your own words.

TOUR COMPANY OWNER: We are doing very well in selling most of our tours and we made a good profit last year. But we seem to have a nagging problem with a very few tours that need to be cancelled from time to time because of low bookings. There doesn't seem to be a pattern to it. It is only about one out of 22 tours, so it is not going to put us into bankruptcy. The concern I have is the loss of clients when we have to tell them that the tour has to be cancelled because of light bookings. We are losing more clients than I am comfortable with when this type of situation occurs. I am also concerned about our reputation. When we cancel, those who signed up for the tour talk with other people and the mistaken impression might get around that we are a failing company. I don't want to discourage potential or current clients from booking with us due to a false impression coming from underbooking cancellations.

TOUR INDUSTRY CONSULTANT: I understand your concerns, but there are ways of reducing the negative effect of a tour cancellation on clients who have signed up and have to be advised that the tour has been cancelled. Sometimes you can even turn a potentially unhappy situation such as this into a positive one.

TOUR COMPANY OWNER: Tell me how.

TOUR INDUSTRY CONSULTANT: The next time you have to cancel a tour because of light bookings, you might consider . . .

CONTINUE ON YOUR OWN

GROUP DISCUSSION SITUATION: THE SMYTH SMITH CANDY CASE

"Never again!" screamed Candy Apfel, the senior leisure agent at Cooky's Kooky Travel. "I can't understand why your reservation people can't get a simple name correct on the reservation, especially when I spelled it twice for your reservationist."

Merple Meekly, co-owner and manager of Brazen Buffalo Tours, was concerned. Although everyone at Brazen Buffalo knew that Candy Apfel was a perfectionist, Cooky's Kooky Travel had consistently booked clients with Brazen Buffalo Tours and over the last several years it has grown to be one of the top ten agencies in number of bookings for the tour company.

Candy continued, "I told her distinctly Bessie Smyth's name was spelled with a 'Y'. I said, 'make sure you spell the documents with a 'Y'. It is S M 'Y' T H." Now all the documents have come in spelled wrong—and the tour leaves tomorrow. The Smyths are always angry when documents are issued incorrectly. It's too late to change the documents and I will have to hear them explode this afternoon when they look at the documents and realize that still another time the spelling of their last name on documents has been messed up."

"I understand your problem, Candy. What can I do to make things right for you?" questioned Merple.

"I don't see how you can solve the problem at this point," responded Candy. "I'm going to recommend to Cooky Kooky that we never do business with your company again. We just can't risk losing clients because your reservationists can't take down names correctly. I suggest you either train your people or fire them and get somebody in who can do the job right." With that Candy slammed the receiver down on the phone, abruptly ending the conversation.

You and your associates constitute the management staff at Brazen Buffalo Tours. Consider the situation. Decide among yourselves what your company will do and how you will handle the situation. Discuss the matter among yourselves. Be prepared to present your solutions in a paper that will be no longer than three pages in length. Also make sure the paper is double-spaced and typed. Be prepared to also present your solutions verbally in class if your instructor suggests that you do so.

EXERCISES

1. Break into groups of no more than three students working together. Yours will probably be the same group that has been working together in the development of a one-day tour since the beginning of the course.

Practice taking reservations for your one day tour by taking mock reservations from three of your fellow students who are enrolled in this course. Use the three blank reservation forms which are included in this chapter on the pages following this exercise. Type or neatly print the reservation date and be sure to include your name on all three reservation sheets before banding them together.

If you would prefer to practice a variation modeled after taking reservations from travel agencies, try a role play with one fellow student playing the role of a travel agent making the booking and another fellow student playing the role of the client. You and the student who is playing the role of the travel agent will speak with one another role playing a telephone conversation in which the travel agent gives you the booking information as you request it. This information will be based upon the data received from the student who is playing the role of the client.

2. Break into groups of no more than three students working together. Yours will probably be the same group that has been working together in the development of a one-day tour since the beginning of the course.

Practice preparing typed tour confirmations for the reservations taken for your one day tour from three of your fellow students. Prepare typed letters of confirmation for each of the three reservations. Be sure your name is on each of the confirmation letters.

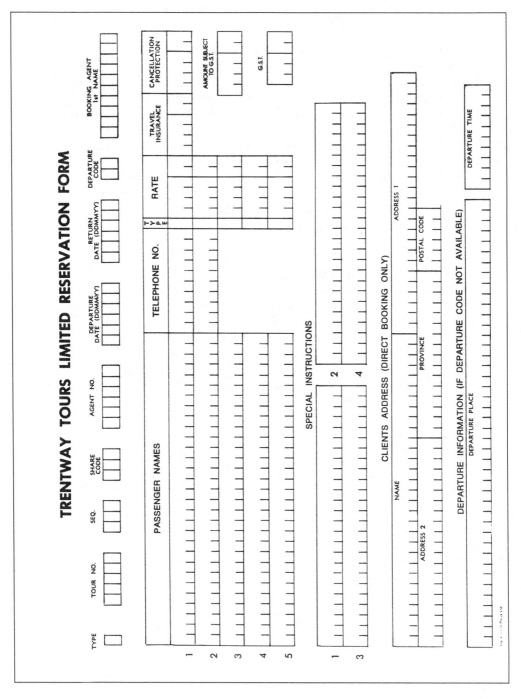

Practice Reservation No. 1

Reproduced with permission from Trentway Tours, Peterborough, Ontario, Canada.

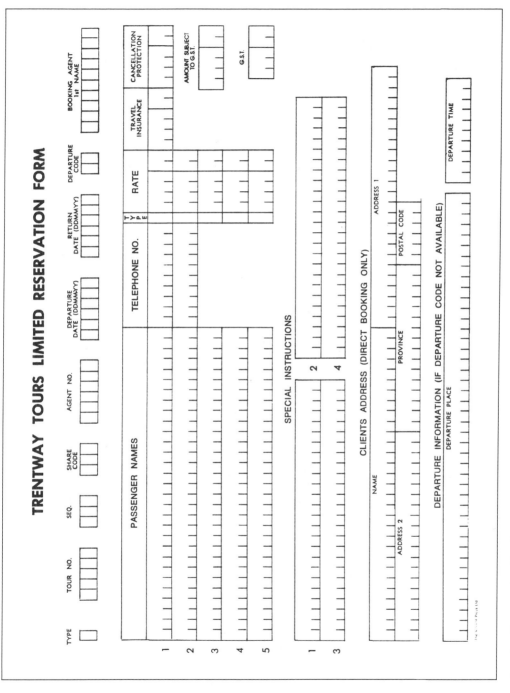

Practice Reservation No. 2

Reproduced with permission from Trentway Tours, Peterborough, Ontario, Canada.

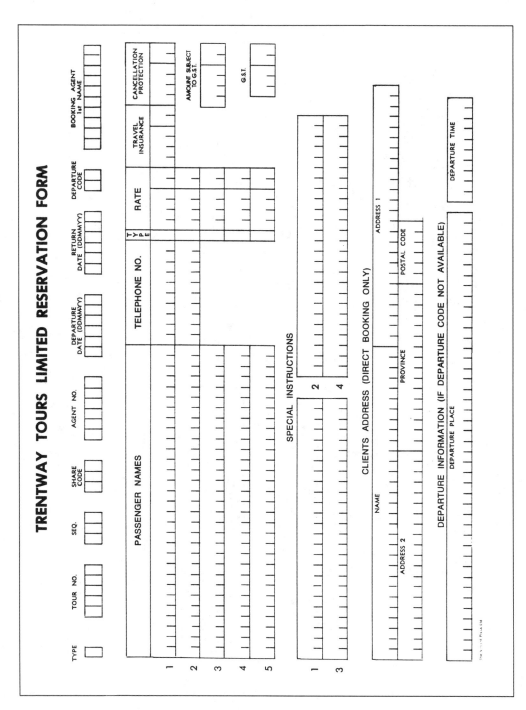

Practice Reservation No. 3

Reproduced with permission of Trentway Tours, Peterborough, Ontario, Canada.

CHAPTER 15

Post-Tour Management

OBJECTIVES

Upon completion of this chapter the student will be able to:

1. Prepare an end-of-tour client evaluation form for a one-day tour.
2. List all of the standard and some of the optional end-of-tour reports prepared after tours have been completed.
3. Explain how tour planners identify those aspects of post-tour reports which should be considered important and those which should not be considered important.
4. List the steps taken in calculating a monthly cost per reservation.

Introduction

Those new to the tour industry sometimes think that when the tour is over it is forgotten and all attention should be focused on upcoming tours. Certainly, the priorities are given to future tours, but experienced tour executives are aware that post-tour tasks still need to be completed. One of these is the post-tour report which is filled out by the tour manager. Most tour companies require tour managers to file a report at the end of each tour. Some require post-tour vendor reports as well. Many companies ask tour members to complete tour evaluations. A report on these evaluations is prepared (normally by headquarters office staff members). The tour manager and the tour planner/organizer usually complete financial and accounting reports.

The post-tour reports will be studied by the tour planner and then used in making changes to the tour. Some changes will not take effect until the next season. All future tours normally will incorporate the changes listed. Other changes, however, may need to be made right away. For example, if a hotel has changed owners and it is providing far less than what is either expected or contracted, it may be necessary to make a change starting with the next departing tour.

The end of the tour establishes a beginning point for the tour marketing and sales division. Tour member names will be added to the client list and post-marketing activities will start almost as soon as they return home. The goal is to get these people to take another tour with the company.

Tour Manager Post-Tour Trip Reports

An increasing number of companies require tour managers to file post-trip reports after the tour is over. These vary in nature and scope. The simplest are basic accounting reports. However, many tour companies want to obtain tour manager perceptions regarding what tour members liked most about the trip and what they disliked. Detailed vendor reports are often requested. Some tour companies ask for an evaluation of tour members (see Figure 15-1). This helps to identify the demographics of the people taking the company's tours.

Some post-tour reports require little more than having the tour manager check appropriate blocks or enter a few words in appropriate spaces. These may also include free-flow information. Other, more difficult-to-complete reports ask open-ended questions designed to solicit opinions on a wide variety of aspects regarding the tour. Still others are a combination of these types of questionnaires and reports.

Whatever form the report takes, most tour companies expect the post-tour report to be filed rapidly. Some companies will not compensate the tour manager until the post-tour report has been completed and turned in. Some have a debriefing after each tour. This consists of the tour manager filing a post-tour report and then reviewing it verbally with his boss and/or a panel of company executives. These individuals ask the tour manager questions about the tour, normally based upon points made in the report. A transcription of the debriefing accompanies the report. Those evaluating and considering tour changes then have this additional information on which to base change recommendations.

The Tour Manager's Post-Tour Vendor Report

Most experienced tour companies require tour managers to file a report on each of the vendors used. In many cases, this report will be a part of the post-trip report. However, in some cases, it constitutes a separate report in and of itself.

Vendor evaluation reports can be computer-generated with the name of the vendor, the name of the tour, and the number of the tour preprinted on the computer form. The questions on the form differ depending upon the type of vendor. For example, hotel vendor questions are different than the questions asked about restaurant vendors. Some vendor reports consist primarily of check-

```
                    MANAGER'S TOUR EVALUATION

     TOUR_____DATES_____

     1 2 3 4 5    MOTORCOACH(describe)_____
     1 2 3 4 5    DRIVER(name)_____
                  HOTELS(insert name, location, date)
     1 2 3 4 5       A._____
     1 2 3 4 5       B._____
     1 2 3 4 5       C._____
     1 2 3 4 5       D._____
     1 2 3 4 5       E._____
     1 2 3 4 5       F._____

                  RESTAURANTS(insert name, location, date, meal)
     1 2 3 4 5       A._____
     1 2 3 4 5       B._____
     1 2 3 4 5       C._____
     1 2 3 4 5       D._____
     1 2 3 4 5       E._____
     1 2 3 4 5       F._____

                  ATTRACTIONS(name, location, type, date)
     1 2 3 4 5       A._____
     1 2 3 4 5       B._____
     1 2 3 4 5       C._____
     1 2 3 4 5       D._____
     1 2 3 4 5       E._____
     1 2 3 4 5       F._____

                  ENTERTAINMENT FEATURES(name, location, program, type, date) .
     1 2 3 4 5       A._____
     1 2 3 4 5       B._____
     1 2 3 4 5       C._____
     1 2 3 4 5       D._____
```

FIGURE 15-1 SAMPLE MANAGER'S TOUR EVALUATION SHEET

Reproduced with permission from 4 Seasons Tours and Travel, Wilmington, DE.

```
1 2 3 4 5     ITINERARY

              TOUR OPERATORS ESCORT(s) (name, tour segment)
1 2 3 4 5     A._____
1 2 3 4 5     B._____
1 2 3 4 5     C._____


              SIGHTSEEING GUIDES(name, place, tour, date)
1 2 3 4 5     A._____
1 2 3 4 5     B._____
1 2 3 4 5     C._____
1 2 3 4 5     D._____


              AIRLINES
1 2 3 4 5     A._____
1 2 3 4 5     B._____


PASSENGERS:  No._____  TYPE OF GROUP_____

FIRST-TIMERS(No.)_____REPEAT PASSENGERS(No.)_____

GROUP MORALE?_____PROMPT?_____PATIENT?_____

MUTUAL COURTESY?_____INTEREST IN COMMENTARIES?_____

LIKED SEAT ROTATION?_____ENJOYED ENROUTE GAMES?_____

ENJOYED THE TOUR?_____TIPPPED DRIVER?_____

EXCEPTIONAL PASSENGERS(Cooperative, Congenial, Entertaining, Motivating,
      or Uncooperative, Complaining, Loners, Tardy, Contentious, Alcoholic
      Disabled)

_____
_____
_____
_____
_____
_____
_____
_____
_____
```

FIGURE 15-1 (cont'd)

offs and short responses to questions. Others are very open-ended and allow the tour manage to editorialize.

Some companies have a pre-determined processing approach for various types of vendor reports. Others treat the processing of all vendor reports the same. When there is a difference, it is usually because the company wishes to rapidly identify potential or real problems. Usually under these circumstances, the company mandates that if there were vendor problems which were serious enough to consider making a change, the tour manager should expedite the filing of the report so that it can be brought to the attention of the tour planner right away.

Tour Member's Tour Evaluation Report

Tour member evaluations serve two purposes. They remind tour members of how enjoyable the trip was and, in this subtle way, they encourage tour members to sign up for future tours. The more obvious purpose, however, is to determine the feelings of tour members regarding the tour and its ingredients.

Tour members often evaluate on the basis of emotion. Evaluation reviewers are sometimes surprised to find that it is often the less expensive features of a tour that stand out in the minds of tour members. A good tour evaluation form will ask both general and specific questions (see Figure 15-2).

Usually, if the general questions are asked first and the specific questions asked last, the evaluation will be higher. The reverse is also true. Most tour members will evaluate most tours in a similar manner. Averaging evaluation scores will be in the middle to upper level. For most tours, however, there will be skews created by one or two tour members (sometimes more) who give a very low rating or an almost perfect rating on almost all areas. These should be viewed as skews and should not be given undue importance.

What is considered important is a pattern of consistently low evaluations for sites, vendors, or any other facet of the tour. With this pattern, the tour planner often makes immediate changes, especially if the scores are low across the board.

Normally, each evaluation response is statistically analyzed to calculate a mean average in determining an overall tour member opinion. Some will attempt to eliminate the potential problems with skews by also calculating a median and a mode. The results are compared with the results from the last tour. Similar average statistics may be calculated on all offerings of the same tour run to date that year. Other statistical analyses may be calculated as well.

Post-Tour Accounting and Account Balancing

One of the most important end-of-tour reports is a financial accounting for all expenditures and income. This report consists of several sections or mini-reports.

SEAL HERE

TRENTWAY TOURS LIMITED

Trentway Tours requests your assistance! Please take a few moments to complete this questionnaire. It will assist us in correcting any problems and also with planning our future tours.

We would appreciate it if you would supply us with your name and address, however should you wish to remain anonymous your comments will still be beneficial to us.

The completed questionnaire may be sealed and given to your Tour Representative for delivery or mailed directly to our head office.

Tour No. _____   Destination _____   Return Date _____

PASSENGER COMMENTS   (Please circle one answer)

RESERVATIONS:
How did you make your reservation?
Through a Travel Agent   Yes   No
Our Office   Yes   No

If Trentway Tours Office, were our reservationists
helpful?   Yes   No
courteous?   Yes   No

If Travel Agent, were you satisfied with the communication between your agent and our office?   Yes   No

ACCOMMODATIONS:
Were the hotels/motels utilized to your satisfaction?   Yes   No

Please indicate if a specific hotel/motel was lacking in areas of cleanliness, facilities, location.

_____
_____

ATTRACTIONS:
Were the included attractions worthwhile?   Yes   No
If No, please indicate which attractions:

_____
_____

Were you allowed: sufficient time?   Yes   No
too much time?   Yes   No
not enough time?   Yes   No

Are there other attractions in the area you would like to have seen?   Yes   No

If Yes, Please name _____

GUIDE SERVICES:
Were step-on-guides informative?   Yes   No
If No, please indicate which guide(s)

_____
_____

MEALS: (if any)
Were the included meals to your satisfaction?
Menu   Yes   No
Time   Yes   No
Location   Yes   No
If No, please state problems:

_____
_____
_____

ESCORT:
Was your escort   – well informed?   Yes   No
– courteous?   Yes   No

DRIVER:
Was your driver   – capable?   Yes   No
– courteous?   Yes   No

Did he offer assistance boarding and leaving the coach?   Yes   No

BUS:
Was the coach clean at the start of the tour?   Yes   No
Was the coach clean throughout the tour?   Yes   No
Was the washroom properly equipped and serviced?   Yes   No
Was a step provided?   Yes   No

ADDITIONAL COMMENTS PLEASE:

_____
_____
_____
_____

Name: _____
(Optional)
Address: _____

Thank-you for assisting us in this manner. I trust Trentway will be able to serve you again in the near future.   TT 03

FIGURE 15-2 SAMPLE TOUR EVALUATION FORM
Reproduced with permission from Trentway Tours, Peterborough, Ontario, Canada.

The tour manager submits a report which balances all on-tour monies. This report starts by identifying the amount of the company money provided to the tour manager at the beginning of the trip. It identifies each expense by type. It balances and totals all expenses. Finally, a line is provided to identify the amount of money returned back to the tour company at the end of the trip. The total amount on the expenses line plus the total amount of reimbursement back to the company should equal the amount of money received at the beginning of the trip. Receipts should be attached to the report. Expenses such as tips, however, will not include receipts, since this and some other expenses are items for which receipts are normally not requested or provided.

The tour manager's expense report is attached to and becomes a part of the tour's financial accounting report. The tour financial accounting report identifies all income received for the tour and all expenditures made on behalf of the tour. This report is often prepared by the tour company's operations manager, but it is sometimes the responsibility of the company's in-house bookkeeper or accountant.

Some expenditures are difficult to allocate. For example, a reservationist may take calls for a large number of trips one after another throughout the day. Allocating the reservationist's expenses to a particular tour can, therefore, be difficult. The simplest way of doing this is to identify a monthly cost per reservation. The total monthly cost of the reservations function (personnel, equipment, and so forth) is divided by the number of actual reservations taken during the month. An even more accurate figure is achieved by doing the same thing on an annual basis. In other words, all reservation function costs for the year are totalled and divided by the number of reservations taken during the year. The per reservation cost is multiplied times the number of reservations taken for a particular tour during the month and the monthly figures are then added up to determine the reservations cost for each tour.

On the tour financial accounting report, all income and all expenses will be identified, and either a profit or a loss on the tour will be shown. This report gives management a clear understanding of tour profitability. Executives can rapidly identify which tours are more profitable, which are less profitable, and which are unprofitable.

Post-Tour Marketing

Because of the large potential for repeat clients, tour companies spend considerable time and money to market to repeat clients. Marketing often starts toward the end of the tour. Marketing efforts usually are intensified after the tour is over. Usually during the farewell dinner on a lengthy tour or as the bus is returning on a short bus tour, the tour manager makes a speech in which tour members are thanked for coming, are recognized for their contributions to the tour, and are invited to take another tour soon. Some companies have tour managers go through a listing of the dates of future tours. They may ask for a show of hands of those people who are interested in specific destination areas and will distribute brochures on tours run by the company to those destinations. Most tour companies conduct their marketing at this stage in a relatively low-key manner.

Shortly after the tour is over, tour members are mailed information on future tours accompanied by a letter inviting them to sign up. Some companies have telemarketers call tour members a few weeks after the tour and attempt to sell them a future tour by phone.

Many of the older and more affluent tour companies hold "reunions." These are held in conjunction with travel agencies. All who have attended tours with the company are invited. It is normally a social function where there is perhaps wine and cheese. Previous tour members are given a review of upcoming tours. Sometimes there are slides or short film presentations on a destination the tour company may be pushing for the next season. Tour companies also market heavily by direct mail, sometimes sending a newsletter or a brochure to past tour participants as often as once a month. Tour companies are aware that a satisfied client is the best potential future client. They spend considerable effort and money to encourage past tour participants to be future tour participants.

Summary

After the tour is over, several reports need to be completed and marketing for future tours starts. The tour manager post-tour trip report is both an accounting for monies that were spent during the tour and a reaction survey identifying the opinions of the tour manager regarding the services rendered and the products provided by vendors.

Tour members are asked to complete an evaluation of the tour. They also evaluate vendors, but their evaluations will usually also include opinions regarding the sites visited, the tour manager, and other facets of the tour.

After the tour is over, an accounting of the tour will be conducted. This involves balancing all expenses for the tour against all income for the tour and identifying the profit made (or loss incurred) on the tour.

Post-tour marketing starts before the tour is over. The tour manager encourages tour members to take future tours. This is usually followed up with direct mail. Sometimes, company telemarketers encourage them to sign up for a future tour. Some of the more affluent companies will hold "reunions" in cities throughout the country.

DISCUSSION QUESTIONS

These questions may be discussed by two or more students outside of class as a fun way of reviewing this chapter or they may be discussed by everyone during class for a more wide-ranging discussion.

1. What do most tour companies that have been in business for some time require tour managers to do at the end of each completed tour?

2. What purpose is served by holding a tour company "reunion?"

3. The end of the tour establishes a beginning point for those working in which division of the tour company?

4. How might you identify a monthly cost per reservation?

5. How soon after a tour is over do most tour companies expect the post-tour report to be filed?

6. The tour manager is expected to submit a report which balances all monies received at the beginning of the tour to two figures. One of these figures is the total amount on the expenses line. What is the other figure considered in the calculation?

7. A transcription of what section frequently accompanies a post-tour report so that those evaluating and considering changes will have additional documentation on which to base change recommendations?

8. Can vendor evaluation reports be computer-generated?

9. What kind of evaluation pattern relating to sites, vendors, or any other facet of the tour is considered important?

10. One of the two purposes of tour member evaluations is to remind the tour member how enjoyable the trip was. In this subtle way, the evaluations encourage the tour member to sign up for a future tour with the company. What is the other purpose for which tour member evaluations are intended?

ROLE PLAY EXERCISES

1. Two students may participate in this role play either out of class as a fun way to review the chapter or as an in-class exercise. One plays the role of a tour manager and the other plays the role of a tour company President. Please read the script and then pick up the conversation in your own words.

   TOUR MANAGER: I appreciate the offer you extended to work for you and I am looking forward to leading tours for your company.

   TOUR COMPANY PRESIDENT: We've wanted you to join our ranks for some time. We'll do whatever possible to try to make you happy with our company. I know your association with us will be mutually beneficial.

   TOUR MANAGER: I'm not sure what you are looking for when it comes to end-of-tour reports. The companies I have worked for before are pretty informal and do not require any written reports. What does your company expect?

   TOUR COMPANY PRESIDENT: We have a very formal process. It provides feedback on all aspects of the tour and gives us the ability to continually upgrade the quality of our tours. In addition, the financial accounting provides us with an ability to know exactly where our profits are coming from. These are generalities, however. Our specific requirements are that . . .

CONTINUE ON YOUR OWN

2. Two students may participate in this role play either out of class as a fun way to review the chapter or as an in-class exercise. One plays the role of a tour member (client) and the other plays the role of the tour manager who is leading the tour. Please read the script and then pick up the conversation in your own words.

TOUR MEMBER: I've been on some tours where when the tour was over the company forgot about us. I understand your tour company keeps in touch. Is that right?

TOUR MANAGER: That's correct. We consider past tour participants to be members of our tour company family and we keep in touch regularly. Before this tour is over, I will brief you and your fellow tour members on upcoming tours but, in addition to that, we will . . .

CONTINUE ON YOUR OWN

3. Two students may participate in this role play either out of class as a fun way to review the chapter or as an in-class exercise. One plays the role of a tour planner and the other plays the role of a tour manager. They both work for the same company. Please read the script and then pick up the conversation in your own words.

TOUR PLANNER: It looks like you had some problems when you went to the Grungy Gremlins Museum the last time you took out the "Greater Grungy" tour. I see in the tour report that you are recommending dropping the museum from the tour altogether. It has been a highlight in the past. Tell me about the problems.

TOUR MANAGER: It seemed like they started as soon as we drove up. The first thing we encountered was . . .

CONTINUE ON YOUR OWN

GROUP DISCUSSION SITUATION: MACHO TOURS MUSSELS MISTAKE

"I think we made a mistake," commented Leesa Leer, the Operations Manager for Marvelous Macho Tours. "After reviewing our tour member evaluation reports you terminated Mark Mussels."

"That's right," responded Tim Tinee, Tour Guide Manager for the company. "We received three very negative evaluations from people on Mark's last two tours and all three indicated that Mark seemed to give more attention to one or two of the women in the tour group than to all of the others. As you know, we must have tour managers who treat tour members equally."

"I understand that," agreed Leesa, "but perhaps you will remember that I pointed out the three comments might be from disgruntled constant complainers. One of them, Griss Grunt, has had complaints about every tour manager on every tour she has taken and yet she still comes back and takes tours with us year after year. I urged you to reconsider since the other two might be similar constant complainers."

"I know you urged reconsideration," interrupted Tim. "Mark also pointed out that these were simply a few of the passengers who never seem to get along with anyone. He said they made up their minds to get even with him since he was trying to enforce the nondrinking in bus bathrooms rule. All three of these people like to gather in the bus restroom and drink together, according to Mark. He was pretty stringent about enforcing the rule on the first tour. On the second one, when they started to do it again, he threatened to kick them off the tour."

"Why did you fire him then," questioned Leesa Leer.

"Frankly, I didn't believe Mark," Tim Tinee sternly observed. "And I still don't."

"You and Mark did not seem to get on very well from the beginning," Leesa reflected. "However, I think you now have a problem. The owner of our tour company, Bigg Bucks, passed me in the hall yesterday and asked me what had happened to Mark Mussels. I told him about Griss Grunt's complaint and the other complaints and I told him that's why Mark was fired. Bucks told me we had better get him back.

It seems 12 travel agencies have called during the last week asking to book Mark's next tour. When we tell them that Mark is no longer with us, they refuse to book any other tour and all of them have said that they are going to try to contact him and find out where he will be working next year. If we keep losing business like this each week, the significant profit we earned last year, will dwindle substantially. I suggest you find Mark right away and get him to come back to the company."

Turning green, Tim meekly responded, "When he left, I told Mark never to show his face here again. He said he had two other standing offers and would be working with a competitor within two days."

Tim has decided to face the issue head on, but is concerned about bringing Mark back. He is still not sure he should bring him back and if he decides to make an effort to get Mark, he is not certain what it will take to convince Mark to return. He has, therefore, called a meeting of the other tour managers to discuss the matter.

You are the other tour managers working for Marvelous Macho Tours. Consider the situation. What should Tim do? Decide among yourselves how you would handle the situation if you were in Tim's place. Discuss the situation among yourselves. Be prepared to present your suggestions in a paper that will be no longer than three pages in length. Also make sure the paper is double spaced and typed. Be prepared to present your suggestions verbally in class if your instructor suggests that you do so.

EXERCISE

Break into groups of no more than three students working together. Yours will probably be the same group that has been working together in the development of a one-day tour since the beginning of the course.

Review the sample end-of-tour client evaluation form provided in this chapter and draw up an end-of-trip client evaluation form for your one-day tour. Make sure it is typed and spaced appropriately and make sure that it includes all information you as a tour company marketing and management executive would want to receive from the members on your tour.

CHAPTER 16

The Financial/Accounting Aspects of the Tour Business

OBJECTIVES

Upon completion of this chapter the student will be able to:

1. Define "float" as the term is used in the tour business.
2. Develop a chart of accounts to be used in accounting for receipts and disbursements for a one-day tour.
3. Identify the financial reports which are customarily completed and maintained for tour companies.
4. Discuss reasons why profit is sometimes neglected by tour companies.

Introduction

In considering the financial aspects of the tour business, you should be concerned primarily with profits. This chapter will concentrate on profit attainment. Float is one of the major profit sources. This chapter will address the importance of *float* and it will describe the techniques and processes used by tour companies to maximize *float income*.

The financial management of any business normally starts with the accounting processes. Much of the emphasis of this chapter will be on accounting and financial management processes. Charts of accounts, fixed and variable costs, and financial reports (both standard reports and those reports that are unique to the tour industry) will be considered.

The Importance of Profit

The purpose of most businesses is to make a profit for those who invested in and are owners of the business. Many who start tour companies, however, especially those who run tours on a part-time basis, give less consideration to profit than they might.

Profit can be neglected for a number of reasons. Two of the major ones are fear and structural direction. Many who start running tours from their home are aware of the statistics relating to the inability of most small businesses to make a profit during the first year or two of business. Many books and educators advise new business persons that a profit should not be expected during the first or second year.

Some new tour company owners decide, therefore, that to give them a price competition edge against potential or real competitors, they must price their tours at an unprofitably low level. This seldom has merit. Unfortunately, some have difficulty ever costing tours at a profitable level. However, any delay in profit pricing due to fear, is usually a delay that is unjustified. Make every effort to price tours at a level that will include a profit as early in the business history as possible. It is recommended that the very first tour be priced at a profit level. You'll often find that profits will result and you'll need never run an unprofitable tour.

Another reason why profits may be less than they could be is that the concentration on profits may well structure the business in a direction that the owner(s) do not wish to take.

For example, an adventure tour company owner who started the company from scratch running short, one-day rock climbs in Colorado out of Denver expanded and within three years was running rafting trips in South America, mountain climbs in Nepal, bicycle trips through Switzerland, safaris in Africa, and other exciting, interesting trips all over the world. When the company started making less money than investors expected, he was forced to conduct a tour-by-tour analysis of profits. He found that the one-day rock climbs provided the greatest percentage of profit per person of any of the trips run. Many of the exotic, interesting international trips were losing money, being subsidized by the comparatively duller, mundane, more routine domestic trips. While he still wanted to run the exciting international trips, the company investors pushed to concentrate on domestic trips. Ultimately, the founder of the company sold his stock in the company because he did not want to be structured into having to run so many domestic (profitable) trips. He found employment as a tour manager for a competitor which ran international adventure travel trips while the purchasers of his stock reoriented his company so that it was far less exciting, but far more profitable.

When entering the business, you should decide where your priorities are. If profits are important, as they are in most businesses, structure the company so that only trips that are profitable or can expect to be profitable in a short period of time are conducted. The financial and accounting processes and paperwork should flag potential sources of unprofitability and should be designed to identify sources of strong profitability. In this way, the tour company will steadily move to a position of constantly increasing profitability.

The Importance of Float

Float is earned interest. It accumulates by putting tour deposits into interest-bearing, but secure bank or other financial institution accounts. These monies are left in the accounts until the tour operator needs to pay tour vendors either deposits or final payments. When a tour company is able to obtain payment for tours from clients several weeks or, ideally, several months prior to a tour and when deposits for vendor services are not required until several weeks or, preferably, several months after receipt of the tour member deposits, a substantial amount of money can accumulate in interest.

Since many tour companies do not pay the bulk of their vendors until after the service has been rendered, these tour companies are able to realize a substantial float income. Some tour companies make more money from float than from any other source of income. The late R. W. (Bert) Hemphill, founder and President of Hemphill Tours (later Hemphill/Harris Tours) advised that he earned over $100,000 in the initial year he invested deposit income in order to obtain float.

Basic Tour Company Accounting Processes

Tour companies have most of the same accounting and financial management needs that other small businesses have but, in addition, they have accounting and financial management needs and processes unique unto themselves. While they stock no inventory other than brochures, tour companies still have accounts payable and account receivable—the records for which must be maintained on a regular, systematic basis. These are records of the monies that are owed to the tour company (accounts receivables) and the monies the tour company owes to its suppliers and vendors (accounts payables). The accounts receivables and the accounts payables normally are recorded on reports prepared monthly, quarterly, and annually. Some tour companies have these reports prepared on a weekly or even a daily basis.

Unlike most other companies, tour companies have substantial amounts of deposits and final payments made by clients, the records of which must be kept accurately and maintained consistently at all times. Deposits and final payments are recorded by tour. A *weekly tour status* report must be prepared.

Status reports reflect the financial and the nonfinancial status of each tour. The number of deposits received during the week are noted. The number of deposits received for each tour on a year-to-date basis or (more often) a total-to-date basis are shown. The amount of final payments received last week are compared to year-to-date or total-to-date receipts. And a total of all deposits and receipts received for each tour is provided.

The tour company financial planner gathers this data for all tours. A comprehensive weekly report on deposits and full payments received for all tours during the past week and either year-to-date or total-to-date basis is then compiled.

Because tour deposits can be substantial, clients and vendors sometimes fear incurring substantial losses if the tour company declares bankruptcy. To alleviate these fears, many tour companies place deposits and other tour payments into "escrow" accounts. These are interest-earning accounts, but they block the usage of funds for any expenditures other than for the tour itself until all tour vendor payments are made and the tour is over.

Monthly financial statements tend to be based on two standard financial documents. These are the *income statement* and the *balance sheet*. The income statement identifies all income received during the month by category of income or type of income and all expenditures made during the month by type of expenditure or category of expenditure. The type or category of income or expenditure is classified through a *chart of accounts system* (see Figure 16-1). Tour

```
    * * *        TRENTWAY TOURS        * * *        3090    COMMISSIONS
                                                    30902   COMMISSIONS
              G/L CHART OF ACCOUNTS  11/01/91       3115    TAXIS
                                                    31152   TAXIS
GLNO          DESCRIPTION                           3120    TOUR SUPPLIES
                                                    31202   TOUR SUPPLIES
                                                    3125    CONTINGENCY FOR BUS
1000   PETTY CASH                                   31252   CONTINGENCY FOR BUS
1005   CASH ON HAND
1006   CREDIT CARD ADVANCES
1010   BANK-GENERAL
1011   BANK-TRUST                                   3135    EXCHANGE
1012   BANK-US                                      31352   EXCHANGE
1020   SHORT-TERM INVESTMENTS                       62012   SALARIES & WAGES REALLOCATED
1025   ACCOUNTS RECEIVABLE                          62202   EMPLOYEE BENEFITS
1027   ALLOWANCE FOR DOUBTFUL ACCOUNTS              62402   INSURANCE
1035   MISCELLANEOUS RECEIVABLE                     62422   LEASED EQUIPMENT
1040   INCOME TAXES RECOVERABLE                     62702   TELEPHONE
1045   ADVANCES TO EMPLOYEES-TRAVEL                 62823   BANK CHARGES
1046   ADVANCES TO EMPLOYEES-OTHER                  62882   INTEREST - OTHER THAN BANK
1050   RETURNED ITEMS                               62912   PROFESSIONAL FEES
1055   PREPAID ACCOMODATIONS                        62932   TAXES - BUSINESS & CAPITAL
1057   PREPAID TICKETS & ATTRACTIONS                62942   INCOME TAX PROVISION
1059   PREPAID EXPENSES-OTHER                       68002   SALARIES & WAGES
1061   PREPAID TAXES                                68162   SALARIES & WAGES   - PART-TIME
1201   ADVANCES/FROM TRENTWAY-WAGAR (PROPERTIES) INC  68202  EMPLOYEE BENEFITS
1203   ADVANCES TO/FROM TRENTWAY-WAGAR LEASING INC  68222   AUTO EXPENSE
1204   ADVANCES TO/FROM TRENTWAY-WAGAR INC.         68262   COMPUTER EXPENSE-LEASE PAYMENT
1205   ADVANCES TO/FROM GRAY COACH LINES LTD        68272   COMPUTER EXPENSE-SUPPLIES & SOFTWARE
1430   LEASEHOLD IMPROVEMENTS                       68302   DEPRECIATION
1445   FURNITURE & FIXTURES                         68402   INSURANCE
1530   ACCUMULATED DEPRECIATION-LEASEHOLD IMPROVEMENTS  68422  LEASED EQUIPMENT
1545   ACCUMULATED DEPRECIATION-FURNITURE & FIXTURES  68442  MEETINGS EXPENSE & CONVENTIONS
1605   GOODWILL                                     68452   OFFICE EXPENSE
1615   ACCUMULATED AMORTIZATION                     68462   STATIONARY & FORMS
1700   ACCOUNTS PAYABLE-TRADE                       68472   POSTAGE
1705   ACCRUED LIABILITIES                          68502   RENT
1706   ACCRUED VACATION PAY                         68552   REPAIRS & MAINTENANCE
1707   ACCRUED WAGES                                68582   FEES , DUES, SUBSCRIPTIONS
1708   PAGODA MOTEL ACCRUAL                         68652   ADVERTISING - CONSUMER
1715   CUSTOMER ADVANCES-TRUST                      68662   ADVERTISING - TRADE
1725   PAYROLL CLEARING                             68702   TELEPHONE,TELEX,ETC
1730   EMPLOYEE INCOME TAX PAYABLE                  68712   TRAVEL & ENTERTAINMENT
1735   UNEMPLOYMENT INSURANCE PREMIUMS PAYABLE      68772   MISCELLANEOUS
1740   CANADA PENSION PLAN PREMIUMS PAYABLE         68912   AMORTIZATION OF GOODWILL
1745   OHIP PREMIUMS PAYABLE                        68922   BANK INTEREST & CHARGES
1746   PENSION PAYABLE-MUTUAL LIFE                  68932   BAD DEBT EXPENSE
1747   MISC PAYROLL DEDUCTIONS                      68982   INTEREST - OTHER THAN BANK
1751   GOODS & SERVICES TAX PAYABLE                 68902   MANAGEMENT FEES
1757   REFUNDS PAYABLE                              7000    ADVERTISING-TRADE
1765   GARNISHEES                                   7005    ADVERTISING-CONSUMER
1780   CORPORATIONS TAX PAYABLE-FEDERAL             7010    ADVERTISING-OTHER
1785   CORPORATIONS TAX PAYABLE-ONTARIO             7015    AUTOMOBILE EXPENSE
1855   NOTES PAYABLE-OTHER                          7020    AUTOMOBILE LEASING
1860   BANK LOANS                                   7035    BAD DEBT EXPENSE
1880   DEFERRED INCOME TAXES                        7040    BANK INTEREST & CHARGES
1900   CAPITAL STOCK-COMMON                         7045    BROCHURES
1905   CAPITAL STOCK-FIRST PREFERRED                7050    COMPUTER EXPENSE
1980   RETAINED EARNINGS                            7060    DEPRECIATION
1990   DIVIDENDS DECLARED                           7061    EMPLOYEE BENEFITS
2100   GROUP TOUR REVENUE                           7062    DONATIONS
21002  GROUP TOUR REVENUE                           7065    EXCHANGE
2110   REFUNDS                                      7070    FEES & DUES & SUBSCRIPTIONS
21102  REFUNDS
2140   DAY TOUR REVENUE                             GLNO    DESCRIPTION
21402  DAY TOUR REVENUE
2141   DAY TOUR - ORMOND BEACH                      7075    INSURANCE
21412  DAY TOUR - ORMOND BEACH                      7074    INTEREST-OTHER THAN BANK
2510   INCOME FROM CANCELLATION PROTECTION          7085    LEASED EQUIPMENT
25102  INCOME FROM CANCELLATION PROTECTION          7090    MANAGEMENT FEES
2520   COMMISSION INCOME                            7091    CONVENTION & MEETINGS EXPENSE
25202  COMMISSION INCOME                            7095    OFFICE EXPENSE
2525   TRAVEL INSURANCE                             7100    POSTAGE
25252  TRAVEL INSURANCE                             7103    PROFESSIONAL FEES
3020   WAGES - ESCORTS                              7110    PROFIT & LOSS ON DISPOSAL OF FIXED ASSETS
30202  WAGES - ESCORTS                              7115    RENT
3040   BENEFITS - ESCORTS                           7120    REPAIRS & MAINTENANCE
30402  BENEFITS - ESCORTS                           7125    SALARIES & WAGES
3045   BUS CHARGES-T-W INC                          7126    SALARIES & WAGES-PART-TIME
                                                    7127    SALARIES & WAGES REALLOCATED
GLNO          DESCRIPTION                           7130    STATIONARY & FORMS
                                                    7135    TAXES-BUSINESS & CAPITAL
30452  BUS CHARGES-TW INC                           7140    TELEPHONE, TELEX, ETC
3050   EQUIPMENT RENTAL - BUS                       7145    TRAVEL & ENTERTAINMENT
30502  EQUIPMENT RENTAL - BUS                       7160    INCOME TAX PROVISION
3070   ESCORT TRAVEL EXPENSES                       7165    MISCELLANEOUS
30702  ESCORT TRAVEL EXPENSES                       7175    AMORTIZATION OF GOODWILL
3075   AIR TRAVEL                                   74002   WAGES
30752  AIR TRAVEL                                   74012   SALARIES & WAGES REALLOCATED
3080   ACCOMMODATIONS                               74202   EMPLOYEE BENEFITS
30802  ACCOMMODATIONS                               74442   MEETINGS EXPENSE & CONVENTIONS
3085   ATTRACTION TICKETS                           74682   BROCHURES
30852  ATTRACTION TICKETS                           74712   TRAVEL & ENTERTAINMENT
                                                    74772   MISCELLANEOUS
```

FIGURE 16-1 SAMPLE CHART OF ACCOUNTS SYSTEM

Reproduced with permission from Trentway Tours, Peterborough, Ontario, Canada.

company charts of accounts allow them to always record income and expenditures in exactly the same way.

The same chart of accounts is followed when preparing both the income statement (often called a *profit and/or loss statement*) and the balance sheet. The income statement shows a profit or a loss for each month and for the year-to-date (see Figure 16-2). The balance sheet reflects the overall financial picture of the tour company at the end of each month (see Figure 16-3).

Most tour companies go beyond these documents by developing daily and financial profitability analyses. Many prepare daily financial status reports (see Figure 16-4). Some prepare a profitability analysis by tour and by type of tour. An increasing number of tour companies are developing and using profitability analyses on a tour-by-tour, month-by-month, quarterly, and annual basis. These profitability analyses allow tour company executives to design their inventory of tours for increasing levels of profitability.

Budgeting

Just as individual tours have both fixed and variable costs, the company itself also has both fixed and variable costs. To control costs, it is necessary to analyze both fixed and variable costs and to project both as accurately as possible.

In addition to projecting costs, however, the financial manager must also project income. Sometimes this is more difficult. By looking at historical data and evaluating plans, it should be possible to project a budget that will be accurate within a 10 percent level in both income and expenditures. This takes work. By careful analysis, realistic projections, and constant comparisons between actual income/expenditures and budgeted income/expenditures, many tour companies are able to reach a point of profitability within a few years of starting the business. Most are able to maintain a reasonable degree of profitability on a continuous basis.

Summary

Those who manage the financial matters of tour companies need to consider earning float income. They should also develop financial reports. Float income can add substantially to the profits of a tour company, but financial reports can provide the executives of a tour company with the instruments needed to evaluate both individual tours and the company as a whole. By studying financial reports, it is possible to determine where expenses need to be cut and which tours have the potential of providing the best profits.

The financial reports considered in this chapter are income statements and balance sheets. End-of-tour reports are also important.

FIGURE 16-2

TRENTWAY TOURS LIMITED

COMPARATIVE PROFIT OR LOSS STATEMENT

	For the Period				Year to Date			
	July 01, 19___ to		July 31, 19___		January 01, 19___ to		July 31, 19___	
	Actual	Pctg	Budget	Pctg	Actual	Pctg	Budget	Pctg
SELLING & ADMINI- STRATIVE EXP.								
SALARIES & BENEFITS								
ADVERTISING								
AUTO LEASING & EXPENSE								
BAD DEBT EXPENSE								
BROCHURES								
COMPUTER EXPENSE								
DEPRECIATION								
DONATIONS								
FEES, DUES, SUBSCRIPT.								
INSURANCE								
LEASED EQUIPMENT								
MANAGEMENT FEES								
MEETING & BUSINESS REGISTR								
OFFICE								
POSTAGE								
PROFESSIONAL FEES								
RENT								
REPAIRS & MAINTENANCE								
TAXES - CAPITAL								
TELEPHONE								
TRAVEL & ENTERTAINMENT								
MISCELLANEOUS								
TOTAL OVERHEAD								
NET INCOME FROM OPERATIONS								
PROFIT ON SALE OF F/A								
AMORT 'N OF GOODWILL								

Reproduced with permission from Trentway Tours, Peterborough, Ontario, Canada.

	For the Period				Year to Date			
	July 01, 19___ to		July 31, 19___		January 01, 19___ to		July 31, 19___	
	Actual	Pctg	Budget	Pctg	Actual	Pctg	Budget	Pctg
NET INCOME BEFORE TAXES								
INCOME TAX - CURRENT								
NET INCOME FOR PERIOD								
REVENUE								
GROUP TOURS								
DAY TOURS								
OTHER REVENUE								
TOTAL REVENUE								
DIRECT EXPENSES								
ESCORT WAGES & BENEFITS								
COACH RENTAL								
CONTINGENCY FOR TRANSPORT								
AIR TRANSPORTATION								
ESCORT TRAVEL								
ACCOMMODATIONS								
ATTRACTIONS								
COMMISSIONS								
TAXIS								
TOUR SUPPLIES								
EXCHANGE								
TOTAL DIRECT EXPENSES								
GROSS PROFIT								

FIGURE 16-2 (cont'd)

FIGURE 16-3
✳ ✳ ✳ TRENTWAY TOURS LIMITED ✳ ✳ ✳
BALANCE SHEET
JULY 31, 1991

Liabilities & Shareholders' Equity

CURRENT LIABILITIES
  ACCTS PAYABLE & ACCRUED LIAB
  PAGODA INN ACCRUAL
  CUSTOMER ADVANCES
  EMPLOYEE DEDUCTIONS PAYABLE
  MISCELLANEOUS PAYABLES
  CORPORATION TAX PAYABLE

TOTAL CURRENT LIABILITIES

LONG-TERM INDEBTEDNESS
  NOTES PAYABLE
  BANK LOANS
TOTAL LONG-TERM

DEFERRED INCOME TAXES

SHAREHOLDERS' EQUITY
  CAPITAL STOCK-COMMON
  CAPITAL STOCK-PREFERRED
  RETAINED EARNINGS-BEGINNING
  NET INCOME FOR PERIOD

  DIVIDENDS DECLARED

RETAINED EARNINGS - END

TOTAL SHAREHOLDERS' EQUITY

TOTAL LIAB. & SHAREHOLDERS' EQUITY

Current Assets

  CASH & BANK
  ACCOUNTS RECEIVABLE-TRADE
  OTHER REFUNDABLE AMOUNTS
  PREPAID EXPENSES
TOTAL CURRENT ASSETS

DUE TO/FROM ASSOCIATED COMPANY

FIXED ASSETS
  FURNITURE, EQUIPMENT & IMPROVE

  LESS: ACCUM. DEPRECIATION

TOTAL FIXED ASSETS

OTHER ASSETS
  GOODWILL

TOTAL ASSETS

Reproduced with permission of Trentway Tours, Peterborough, Ontario, Canada.

```
----------------------------------------------------------------------------
DAILY REPORT
----------------------------------------------------------------------------

DAY_____    DATE:_____/_____/_____     TAX 1                    $_____
(attach Z tape)
                                             TAX 2                    $_____
RECEIVED ON ACCOUNT........$_____
                                             VISA/MC                  $_____
_____
                                             20% TAXABLE COMMISSIONS ON:
_____
                                             MT. BIKING               $_____
PAID OUT..................$_____
                                             RAFTING                  $_____
_____
                                             CUMBRES TOLTEC           $_____
_____
TOTAL CASH REGISTERED  ....$_____        10% TAXABLE COMMISSIONS ON:
(item CD on tape)
                                             HORSEBACKRIDING          $_____
ACTUAL CASH IN DRAWER......$_____
(less bank)                                  AYH                      $_____
DIFFERENCE (if any)        $_____
(SHORT) (OVER)                               MISC. TAXABLE _____%      $_____

DEPOSIT...................$_____         TOTAL TAXABLE COMMISSIONS $_____
----------------------------------------------------------------------------
```

FIGURE 16-4 SAMPLE DAILY FINANCIAL STATUS REPORT
Reproduced with permission from Rojo Tours, Santa Fe, NM.

This chapter stresses the importance of profit and points out that tour companies can be oriented toward building profits. If they are oriented toward building profits, they will run tours that will be profitable although these tours may be less romantic and less interesting to run than other tours. By identifying the most profitable tours and by preparing budgets for those tours, it is possible for the tour company to analyze both variable and fixed costs and study both total costs and total income in a continuing effort to increase profits.

DISCUSSION QUESTIONS

These questions may be discussed by two or more students outside of class as a fun way of reviewing this chapter or they may be discussed by everyone during class for a more wide-ranging discussion.

1. In considering the financial aspects of the tour business, with what should you be concerned primarily?
2. The budget is a projection of two financial factors. One of these is income. What is the other?
3. The financial management of any business normally starts with what?
4. Tour companies have two types of costs. One of them is fixed costs. What is the other?
5. What is the purpose of most businesses?

6. What type of analyses allow tour company management to design their inventory of tours so that they should move into a consistent pattern of profitability?

7. Two of the major reasons why profit is neglected in some companies are provided in this chapter. One of them is for structural direction. What is the other?

8. Tour company monthly financial statements tend to be based on two standard financial documents. One of these is the income statement. What is the other?

9. How is "float" accumulated?

10. Since tour companies stock no inventory other than brochures, do they still have accounts payables and accounts receivables?

ROLE PLAY EXERCISES

1. Two students may participate in this role play either out of class as a fun way to review the chapter or as an in-class exercise. One plays the role of a new bookkeeper and the other plays the role of an experienced tour company accountant. Please read the script and then pick up the conversation in your own words.

   NEW BOOKKEEPER: I don't understand which financial reports are prepared for tour companies. I've kept books for companies in several different industries and find that the types of required reports vary considerably from industry to industry.

   EXPERIENCED TOUR COMPANY ACCOUNTANT: You won't find a great deal of difference between the reports that are required in a tour company as compared with other companies. The reports that we maintain on a weekly, monthly, quarterly, and annual basis are . . .

   CONTINUE ON YOUR OWN

2. Two students may participate in this role play either out of class as a fun way to review the chapter or as an in-class exercise. One plays the role of a new bookkeeper and the other plays the role of an experienced tour company accountant. Please read the script and then pick up the conversation in your own words.

   NEW BOOKKEEPER: I've never encountered "float" before. What is it and how does it apply in the tour industry?

   EXPERIENCED TOUR COMPANY ACCOUNTANT: Float is very important. Let me first explain to you what it is and then why it is important. Basically, float is . . .

   CONTINUE ON YOUR OWN

3. Two students may participate in this role play either out of class as a fun way to review the chapter or as an in-class exercise. One plays the role of a new bookkeeper and the other plays the role of an experienced tour company accountant. Please read the script and then pick up the conversation in your own words.

NEW BOOKKEEPER: I keep hearing you talk about companies in the business that don't make a profit and it doesn't seem to bother them.

EXPERIENCED TOUR COMPANY ACCOUNTANT: That's right. There are some companies that don't make a profit and don't get disturbed about it.

NEW BOOKKEEPER: I've never run across that before in business. Why would a company not expect to or plan to make a profit?

EXPERIENCED TOUR COMPANY ACCOUNTANT: It seems strange to me too. However, there are several reasons. Some tour companies . . .

CONTINUE ON YOUR OWN

GROUP DISCUSSION SITUATION: FLUSTER'S BLUBBER BLUNDER

Last year, Flippy Fluster of Fluster Tours, Inc. discovered an untapped market. Flippy has been conducting adventure tours quite successfully for several years and has consistently made a good profit. However, she had not really broken into a market she always felt would be a very good one—the 50- to 70-year-old overweight, sedentary executive and spouse market. These were people who she considered to be couch potatoes. They watch TV most of the time, have little activity, and are constantly going on unsuccessful diets. Although she had felt for a long time that these people, especially those who had substantial incomes, constituted a large untapped market for adventure tours, Flippy Fluster had been frustrated by trying for years to find a way to tap the market and had been unsuccessful.

However, last year in talking with several local bicycle retailers, Flippy learned that bicycle retailers periodically receive telephone calls from overweight, sedentary people who seem to be exactly in the target market Flippy wanted to capture. These periodic calls were to find out about bicycle tours for overweight people. They wanted easy tours that were predominantly on level surfaces or downhill only. They wanted short bicycle tours with the potential to increase to multi-day tours over a period of time.

Flippy was amazed at the level of interest expressed by bicycle retailers and without exception, the retailers pointed out that they had nothing to recommend to such callers. No one marketed such tours.

Flippy nearly flipped out in her excitement in finding a way to market to this previously untapped target group. She immediately got together with her bookkeeper, Fanny Fenny, and together they designed and budgeted a series of tours strictly for this market. They set up a new fully owned subsidiary called Fluster Blubber Bicycle Tours and funded it with $50,000 of initial capital. Flippy found a delightful woman in the target market group to run the subsidiary. She just bubbled over with excitement about the prospect of tours for those weighing three hundred pounds and over. The company has been formed and has been running now for several months.

However, a problem seems to have arisen. This morning, Fanny Fenny pointed out that a problem in broken bicycles had not been considered. Twelve bicycles have been broken in the last two weeks because the weight of the riders is simply too great for the bikes. In addition, the insurance company, having discovered the broken bicycle problem has increased the liability insurance premium and threatened to withdraw the insurance altogether. It seems that they are afraid that a bicycle seat will break and the tubing holding up the seat will skewer the rider. This, they believe, will result in considerable lack of comfort for the skewered overweight bicyclist, but having a metal rod sticking through the client's body lengthwise may very well result in ultimate death. Finally, Fanny raised a concern about the consumption of food by tour members. The budget had called for a 10 percent in price over that which is budgeted for most adventure tour members, but these people are eating three times what the average adventure tour member eats on tour.

"We've sold out for the season because the tours are so popular, but if we continue to break bicycles at this rate, feed tour members this generously, and pay inflated insurance premiums, not only will Fluster Blubber Bicycle Tours go broke, but our parent company, Fluster Tours Inc. will go broke as well," fumed the frustrated Fanny Fenny.

Flippy Fluster has gathered her Board of Directors together and has presented you with the problem. Consider the situation. What should Flippy Fluster do? Decide among yourselves how you would handle the situation if you were in Flippy's place. Discuss the situation among yourselves. Be prepared to present your suggestions in a paper that will be no longer than three pages in length. Also make sure the paper is double spaced and typed. Be prepared to also present your suggestions verbally in class if your instructor suggests that you do so.

EXERCISE

1. Break into groups of no more than three students working together. Yours will probably be the same group that has been working together in the development of a one-day tour since the beginning of the course.

Study the line items on the comparative Profit or Loss Statement in this chapter. Also study the chart of accounts numbering system in Figure 16-1. Consider these to constitute a chart of accounts for your tour. Review the income and cost budget for your one-day tour and prepare a chart of accounts and a blank Profit or Loss Statement tailored to meet your needs as it relates to your one day tour. Keep in mind that all expense items of a similar nature should be categorized into the same Profit or Loss Statement line item. Also keep in mind that all income receipts of a similar nature should appear on the appropriate Profit or Loss Statement line. Instead of preparing a Profit or Loss Statement for a one-month period, your Profit or Loss Statement should cover your one-day tour and should show either a profit or a loss for that tour. Note: The Comparative Profit or Loss Statement used as an example in this chapter is the equivalent to an "Income" Statement or a "Receipts and Disbursements" Statement used by other tour companies. All three terms are used in common practice. Keep in mind that your Profit or Loss Statement may be prepared as a separate document from your Chart of Accounts. Alternatively, you may elect to show the chart of accounts number to the left of each line on your Profit or Loss Statement and hand in only the one page Profit or Loss Statement (including chart of accounts numbers). The choice is yours.

CHAPTER 17
Professionalism

OBJECTIVES

Upon completion of this chapter the student will be able to:

1. List five tour associations serving the tour industry.
2. Prepare an individual development plan which will concentrate on the development of professionalism in the tour industry.
3. Identify the major areas of ethical concern and discuss ethical issues in each area.
4. Group tour associations by location categories, audience served categories, and specialization categories.

Introduction

Professionalism in the tourism industry is marked by joining and working with the industry associations, maintaining a strong sense of ethics, taking advantage of educational opportunities, subscribing to the trade press, and acting in a professional manner in business dealings. Each of these segments of professionalism will be discussed in this chapter with suggestions as to the directions students may wish to take depending upon their tour specialty emphasis.

The Tour Associations

There are many tour associations serving the tour industry today. These can be broken down into various categories of type of association. For example, one category type is service area. There are both domestic and international associations. Another category type relates to the audience served. There are associations for those who work in the guiding field (tour guides, tour leaders, and tour managers) and there are associations for tour company executives. Tour associations can also be categorized by specialization. There are associations serving each of the following tour industry specializations:

• incentive tour operators;
• inbound tour operators;
• adventure tour operators; and
• destination management firms.

The Tour Operator Associations

The tour operator associations are those associations which serve tour companies. Their memberships are corporate, not individual. Top executives of tour company members attend the meetings of these associations. If an executive moves to another company, the membership does not go with him. It stays with the business. There are two major associations in this category. These are the National Tour Association and the United States Tour Operators' Association.

The larger (in number of member companies) of these two associations is the National Tour Association (Box 3071, Lexington, Kentucky 40596, Phone: 606-253-1036). It is made up of tour companies of all types and sizes. Many member services are offered. Educational services predominate. In addition, it maintains a lobbying effort and it funds and administers the National Tour Foundation, a non-profit educational institution designed to provide scholarships, encourage academic endeavors, and offer internships in the tour field. NTA also has a certification program and offers its members group buying benefits for purchases such as liability insurance.

The United States Tour Operators' Association

The United States Tour Operators' Association (USTOA) (211 East 51st Street, Suite 12B, New York City, New York 10022, Phone: 212-944-5727) is a much smaller association of tour companies, but the companies which belong tend to be large international air tour companies. One of the major programs of the United States Tour Operators' Association is a self-insurance bonding program which offers travel agencies and their clients protection in case of the bankruptcy of one or more of its member tour companies.

Basically, the program offers tour members who have paid deposits or full payments for a tour either a refund on the tour or an ability to transfer the equivalent payments to another USTOA member in case the member tour companies with which the traveler is booked files for bankruptcy after the deposit or final payment is made. This guarantee encourages travel agencies to book tours with USTOA member companies. However, the membership fee and the self-bonding fee are expensive. It is partially for this reason that comparatively few tour companies are members of USTOA. The United States Tour Operators' Association also lobbies on behalf of its member tour companies and maintains a strong educational program for both its members and its travel agency clients.

The Tour Guide/Manager's Associations

There are two associations for tour guides and tour managers. These are the Professional Guides Association of America (2416 South Eads Street, Arlington, Virginia 22202, Phone: 703-892-5757) and the International Association of Tour Managers (297 Walworth Road, London SE. 17, England, Phone: 01-703-9154). Both are individual membership associations made up of those working in the guiding field.

The Professional Guides Association of America has local chapters throughout the United States. These chapters hold monthly meetings which tend to be educational and social in nature. They provide the guide member with an opportunity to exchange viewpoints, learn from speakers and other members, and find out about guiding opportunities with local and out-of-state tour companies. PGAA has a certification program and it is working on offering a liability insurance program for its members. One of PGAA's major services to its members is a computerized listing of tour guide specializations and languages. Tour operators access the computerized list to find specialized guides throughout the United States. The service is free to tour companies and it has assisted in boosting the income levels of many PGAA members.

The International Association of Tour Managers

The International Association of Tour Managers is considered by many to be the elite of associations for those working in the guiding field. It does not accept a guide into membership unless the guide qualifies for the Silver Badge of Tour Management. In order to qualify, a guide must have a minimum of five years of full-time experience.

The association offers recognition of greater professional expertise in the form of the gold badge of tour management. In this case, a minimum of 10 years of experience as a full-time tour manager is required. IATM members are the better paid professional guides. Many make incomes in excess of $80,000 per year. The bulk of the members are European and are based in Europe, but membership is composed of professional guides working in all major tourist countries of the world.

The Inbound Travel Association—TIAA

The Travel Industry Association of America (1899 L Street, N.W. Washington, D.C.) has as its membership primarily state tourist boards. Affiliated members include tour operators, inbound operators, and sightseeing companies. Although the Travel Industry Association of America provides many standard association benefits for its members, its major function is the annual Pow Wow held in a different U.S. city each year.

Over 2,000 tour operators from countries outside the United States are invited to this conference. These tour operators meet U.S.-based inbound tour company executives, hoteliers, sightseeing executives, and others interested in obtaining their business while their tours are in America. Meetings are 15 minutes each and they are scheduled over a four-day period. Some U.S.-based tour companies find they can sell virtually all of their tours to tour operators who are putting together trips from their countries to the United States. While booth space is expensive, participation in the Pow Wow by U.S. tour companies and other U.S. travel suppliers is strong. Over a billion dollars of contracts are written each year at the Pow Wow.

Three associations will be of interest to those with specialized tour interests. These are:

1. The International Reception Operators (8530 Wilshire boulevard, Beverly Hills, California 90211, Phone: 213-278-0745);
2. the Society of Incentive Travel Operators (21 West 38th Street, Tenth Floor, New York City, New York, 10018, Phone: 212-575-0910); and
3. the International Destination Management Association (IDMA Mauerkircherstrasse 4, 8000 Munich 80, Germany, Phone: 089-98-8835).

Industry Ethics

Ethical considerations exist in many industries. Tour companies need to be especially watchful to make sure that strong ethical standards are maintained in four directions. These relate to:

1. dealings with clients;
2. interrelationships with suppliers;
3. other tour companies; and
4. tour guides and tour managers.

For clients, it is especially important to identify clearly what is included and what is not included on a tour. Some brochures and tour company literature read in such a misleading way that many tour members believe that the tour will offer more than it does. While the brochure should not grossly undersell the features of the tour, brochure wording should be precise and exact with the goal in mind that there will be as little confusion as possible regarding what is and what is not included.

A second factor relating to dealings with clients concerns refunds of deposits or full payments. While most tour companies have clear refund policies, some have policies that are confusing and a few have written policies but ignore them when it comes time to make a refund. The refunds are either delayed or, in some cases, not forthcoming without legal action. Most consider this to be unethical. Tour executives should consider the ramifications of their cancellation and refund policies and be prepared to follow the policies they adopt.

Interrelationships with suppliers also have the potential for exhibiting either a strong sense or a lack of ethics. The three areas complained about most by suppliers relate to delays in payments, blaming the supplier when the mistake is really that of the tour company, and not cancelling when arrangements are changed. Payment schedules are usually identified in a contract with suppliers. Frequently, a final payment is made after the tour group has completed the tour. Some tour companies delay the final payment by a month or more in order to take advantage of the float earnings potential. While suppliers may need the tour company's money and, therefore, will sometimes accept this situation, they nevertheless consider it unethical. They rightfully believe that if the tour company expects to hold on to money for a longer time than the contracted payment date, the tour company should be up front about that when the contract is developed. Much of the time the vendor will go ahead and accept the later date if it is requested at the time that the contract is negotiated.

Both tour company executives and guides have found that blaming the vendor for mistakes that are their own can help get them off the hook with tour members. This is usually short sighted, though. Tour members still hold the tour company responsible for the delivery of all services described in the brochure. Most tour members will accept it if the tour company is up front about stating that it is the tour company's or the tour guide's fault. They can be especially receptive if the company or the guide takes steps to correct the mistake or to make up for it.

Ethical responsibilities extend to other tour companies as well. Professionals do not speak badly or in a derogatory manner about their competitors. In selling, marketing, and making comparisons between companies, it is considered more professional to discuss the strengths of one's company while avoiding a discussion of the weaknesses or the failings of competitors. In addition, it is considered unethical to copy the tours, manuals, or brochures of other tour companies. While it is difficult for a tour company to obtain total copyright protection for tours and competitors can easily copy the major itinerary, brochure, and document information, to do so is clearly unethical.

Ethics are also involved in the treatment of tour guides and tour managers. Guides should be compensated in a timely manner and in a manner consistent with the way described verbally and in the company's literature. Tour company executives should publicly back up the decisions of their guides. It is considered unethical to speak badly about guides in public, even when an unfortunate incident may have occurred in relationship to the guide(s). If the company has a policy regarding guide assignments to tours, that policy should be followed uniformly. Executives should strive to avoid showing favoritism.

While ethics in the tour industry is generally thought to be stronger than in many segments in the travel industry, establishing and maintaining strong ethics is the responsibility of everyone in the field. It behooves the executives of tour companies to be especially concerned about ethics and to set high ethical standards. It is these executives who establish an ethical pattern which sets a tone for the industry as a whole.

Ongoing Educational Opportunities

Relatively few ongoing educational opportunities exist for those in the tour industry to increase their technical knowledge of the field. There are few technical books relating to tour operations, only a very few college courses in the field, and relatively few continuing education programs regarding tour planning, tour development, and tour marketing. However, the ongoing educational opportunities today are better than they have ever been in the past and they are increasing at a rapid pace. Many educational opportunities are centered with trade associations. Certification programs are now available and both short seminars offered by the associations and annual convention presentations offer those wishing to increase their professional expertise a growing opportunity for participation.

Several books have been produced in tour management and in tour conducting and while there are still few college-based programs, the number of such programs is growing steadily. You may need to search to find educational opportunities in specific tour development areas, but it is usually possible to find what you need. Professionals stay updated and those seeking to maintain high personal professional standards spend considerable time and money seeking out and participating in ongoing continuing education. Some who strive for excellence develop individual development programs for themselves and corporate professional development plans for their companies. Travel educators, especially those trained in human resource development and some industry consultants can lend quality assistance in preparing individual and corporate development programs/plans.

The Trade Press

Other than association newsletters and other publications, there are few trade publications for those working in the tour industry. However, several of the travel industry trade publications provide an emphasis in the tour field. Primary among these is *Tour and Travel News*. Both *Travel Weekly* and *Travel Agent* emphasize the retail travel industry, but both publications provide some information regarding the wholesale tour industry as well.

Summary

Five areas of professionalism were considered in this chapter. They are:

1. industry association membership;
2. the maintenance of strong ethics;
3. continuing one's education;
4. subscribing to trade publications; and
5. acting in a professional manner.

Five associations were discussed in detail and contact information for other associations was provided. The chapter also discussed four areas of industry ethics. These are ethics dealing with:

1. clients;
2. suppliers;
3. other tour companies; and
4. tour guides and tour managers.

It was noted that relatively few educational opportunities are available on a continuing education basis in the tour field. However, the opportunities are increasing rapidly. Professionals in the industry make an effort to find the educational opportunities available and to participate in them.

Trade publications were listed. It is recommended that professionals read those publications that have strong relevance to the tour industry and read them on a regular basis.

DISCUSSION QUESTIONS

These questions may be discussed by two or more students outside of class as a fun way of reviewing this chapter or they may be discussed by everyone during class for a more wide-ranging discussion.

1. What are the names of five tour associations which were discussed in this chapter?
2. What are some of the trade publications to which a professional in the tour industry might wish to subscribe?
3. Three approaches to categorizing or breaking down associations into types were suggested in this chapter. One of them is by specialization. Another is by location. What is the third way in which you might categorize tour associations?

4. Where might you find the majority of educational opportunities for professionals in the tour industry who wish to take advantage of continuing education opportunities?

5. Two associations were discussed in this chapter which are associations designed to serve tour companies. One of them is the National Tour Association. What is the other?

6. The National Tour Foundation is a nonprofit educational institution which is closely associated with which association?

7. Are ethics in the tour industry generally thought to be stronger or weaker than in many segments of the travel industry?

8. There are two major associations which serve tour guides and tour managers. What are these two associations?

9. Is it considered ethical to center a sales presentation on a discussion of the weaknesses or failings of competitors?

10. What are the two badges awarded by the International Association of Tour Managers?

ROLE PLAY EXERCISES

1. Two students may participate in this role play either out of class as a fun way to review the chapter or as an in-class exercise. One plays the role of a new tour company executive and the other plays the role of an experienced tour company executive. Please read the script and then pick up the conversation in your own words.

   NEW TOUR COMPANY EXECUTIVE: There seem to be so many associations in the industry. I don't know which ones to join.

   EXPERIENCED TOUR COMPANY EXECUTIVE: It is wise to join one or more of the associations that will help you to become more professional.

   NEW TOUR COMPANY EXECUTIVE: I want to do that and I also want to be active in the associations to which I belong. However, I do have a limited budget and a limited amount of time. Which would be the best association for me?

   EXPERIENCED TOUR COMPANY EXECUTIVE: That all depends. There are advantages and disadvantages in joining each of the associations. Let me run down the list of associations for you and explain why you might wish to join or not join each of them. The first association is . . .

   CONTINUE ON YOUR OWN

2. Two students may participate in this role play either out of class as a fun way to review the chapter or as an in-class exercise. One plays the role of a new tour company executive and the other plays the role of an experienced tour

company executive. Please read the script and then pick up the conversation in your own words.

NEW TOUR COMPANY EXECUTIVE: The last company I worked for had a very poor sense of ethics. They seemed to take the attitude that more money could be made if they ignored ethics. In spite of that, they still made relatively little.

EXPERIENCED TOUR COMPANY EXECUTIVE: That sense of ethics is probably one of the main reasons why you left the company, isn't it?

NEW TOUR COMPANY EXECUTIVE: Yes, but it gave me a jaundiced view of the industry. What are the industry ethical concerns and what kind of standards should I be aiming for in my dealings with others?

EXPERIENCED TOUR COMPANY EXECUTIVE: Our company wants us to maintain high ethical standards in our dealings with clients, suppliers, other tour companies, and our tour guides and tour managers. Let me explain exactly what they are looking for as it relates to each of these groups. Let's start with . . .

CONTINUE ON YOUR OWN

3. Two students may participate in this role play either out of class as a fun way to review the chapter or as an in-class exercise. One plays the role of a new tour company executive and the other plays the role of an experienced tour company executive. Please read the script and then pick up the conversation in your own words.

NEW TOUR COMPANY EXECUTIVE: I graduated with a degree in travel and tourism. I feel that gives me an edge, but I want to make myself as professional as possible.

EXPERIENCED TOUR COMPANY EXECUTIVE: That's a commendable goal. What do you plan to do?

NEW TOUR COMPANY EXECUTIVE: I was hoping you could help me in preparing an ongoing educational plan. What would you recommend?

EXPERIENCED TOUR COMPANY EXECUTIVE: Ongoing education is important, but it is sometimes a challenge finding what one needs at any particular point in time. I would suggest that you . . .

CONTINUE ON YOUR OWN

GROUP DISCUSSION SITUATION: CHUBBY CHOCKY CHOPS CHUNKY CHOCOLATE

The Chunky Chocolate Tour Company has been running chocolate tours for several years and has consistently made a good profit. One of their most popular tours is to Chocolate, Iowa where they stay at the Chocolate House Inn and visit the Chocoholics' Museum. They have a full day at leisure at Chocolate

Land with admission tickets included in the price of the tour. This allows all tour members to ride all of the Chocolate Land rides and participate in all of the Chocolate Land activities without having to pay anything out of pocket. The tours are always scheduled for the first weekend of each month during the summer since the first Saturday evening of each summer month the city government of Chocolate, Iowa holds its spectacular Chocolate Night Parade. At least three meals are included at the Double Chocolate Restaurant and when tour participants leave Chocolate, Iowa to return home, the tour company always purchases chocolate sweaters and a box of chocolate chocolate candy as souvenir gifts for each tour member.

The Chocolate, Iowa tours are always sold out well in advance and for many years this tour has been the most profitable tour Chunky Chocolate Tour Company has run. However, it has become even more profitable in recent months since Leach Miser became the Corporate Comptroller. He instituted several cost cutting moves and several profit-gaining changes. Although the tour evaluations have not been drastically critical, their raving praise of the tour has been considerably more muted after some of the more recent tours. There have even been some negative evaluations received. These appear to directly relate to the cost cutting moves implemented by Leach.

The Chunky Chocolate Tour Company Board of Directors is well aware of the additional income resulting from Leach Miser's cost cutting moves and additional profit-gaining changes. They are also aware that the evaluations have reflected at least some of these changes. There was some discussion at the last weekly board meeting regarding reducing Leach's ability to manipulate the tours since it was generally agreed that if he were given total power to manipulate them, the tours would become far less popular and the excellent reputation the company has enjoyed in the industry with both suppliers and travel agency clients might begin to be reduced.

Of special concern at the last meeting was Leach's new policy of not paying suppliers until 90 days after payment due dates. It is not a matter of the money not being there. He has invested the money and is earning more interest for the company. Although the additional income is appreciated by the board, several of the board members are very concerned about the complaints received from suppliers. They pointed out that relationships with suppliers have been excellent over the years and this move on the part of Leach has begun to jeopardize those good relationships. Taking action on this is the number one agenda item for today's board meeting.

However, this action item has become even more important with the receipt of a letter from the Executive Director of the Chocolate House Inn, Chubby Chocky. The letter was received two hours ago. Chubby's letter advised that due to the lack of receipt of payment for rooms provided for the last two Chunky Chocolate tours, due to the fact that he had sent four letters directly to Leach Miser requesting payment, and since payment had not yet been received, he (Chubby) had now released all contracted rooms for the next tour (departing next Friday) and all future tour bookings and has sold the rooms to another tour

company. Chubby's letter went on to state that in view of the lengthy good relationship with Chunky Chocolate Tours, he regretted having to take this move.
However, he noted that Leach Miser had been advised twice that the release of
rooms would be made if payment was not received immediately. Chubby Chocky
noted that he hoped Chunky Chocolate Tour Company would take corrective
action and start paying suppliers on time. If such a history can be identified, his
letter noted, he would again sell rooms to Chunky Chocolate Tours. However, in
the future all rooms would have to be totally prepaid.

This matter and Chubby Chocky's letter have been presented to you, the
Board of Directors as you meet for this week's Board of Directors' meeting. Consider the situation. What should your company do? Decide among yourselves
how you will handle the situation. Discuss the situation among yourselves. Be
prepared to present your suggestions in a paper that will be no longer than
three pages in length. Also make sure the paper is double spaced and typed. Be
prepared to also present your suggestions verbally in class if your instructor suggests that you do so.

EXERCISE

1. For this exercise take on the role of a professional tour industry consultant. Your "client," a person who was recently promoted into a supervisory
position with a large tour company, asks you to assist her in the preparation of
an individual development plan so that she can obtain a high degree of professionalism and so that she can move into a top executive position with the company. Prepare a one-page description of your recommendations for her. Identify
what you suggest that she do to upgrade her level of industry professionalism
and to increase her ability to meet the qualifications that can be expected from
a top executive in a tour company. Include in your recommendations ongoing
educational opportunities, reading and publication subscription suggestions,
and association memberships. In your recommendation, include other suggestions which you feel are appropriate. Attempt to bring uniqueness into your list
of recommendations in an effort to make your client stand out as a candidate for
an executive position.

Since budget is always a concern and a consideration, identify potential
costs for each of your development recommendations. You may have to undertake some research to identify these costs.

Make certain that your recommendations are professionally presented to
your client. The paper should be typed and it should be double spaced.

APPENDIX
Tour Manual Sample Pages

Anniversaries and Birthdays

We do not provide champagne, cakes, or any other gifts to persons celebrating anniversaries, birthdays, or other personal events while on tour. Be cautious. You might have several tour members have events they may expect to celebrate on a single tour. If you overlook someone, they will be upset. If the tour members as a group wish to celebrate, the company has no objection to a cake, champagne, flowers, etc. if this is funded on a pass-the-hat basis. Be sensitive to a potentially embarrassing situation if one or more tour members are "pressured" into participating in a "Dutch Treat" party.

Baggage Count Forms

Each escort will be provided with a supply of pre-printed baggage count forms. These identify the exact number of bags to be handled for each tour member. As you know, especially on long tours, one or more tour members may decide to purchase an additional bag in which to carry purchased gifts or a tour member may decide to handle her make up case rather than have you do so. These additions and deletions of baggage to be handled by you can cause lost luggage and miscounts unless the baggage count forms are updated each time a change is made. On most tours there are few or no additions or deletions of baggage. However, whenever a change occurs you are expected to log in the change on your master baggage count form *and on all other copies of the baggage count form.* Keep in mind also that we tip based on the total number of pieces of luggage handled. Make number changes in your tip records as well. Accounting will expect to be able to balance luggage tips paid out with baggage count form copies.

Escort Tips

Our tour managers NEVER solicit a tip for themselves. While we allow voluntary tipping by tour members and while it is customary on our tours for tour members to tip tour managers, the solicitation of a tip either directly or indirectly is considered justification for terminating the employment of a tour manager. Most of our tour groups tip generously. There is a strong correlation, however, between the demeanor of the tour manager and the tip received. If the tour manager has handled himself/herself in a conservative, professional manner throughout the tour, the tip received is usually larger than it is when the tour manager was less conservative or less professional. If you receive a tip, be appreciative and gracious no matter how much or how little the amount of the tip.

Death Enroute

While we may not want to think about it, tour members occasionally die while on tour. Even if the deceased tour member is accompanied on the tour by a friend or a relative, the immediate family of the deceased must be contacted immediately. Advise our headquarters office by telephone or telex. Urge the family to make funeral arrangements through their personal "family" undertaker. Professional undertakers are accustomed to handling funeral arrangements for those who pass away while away from home. By having the home town undertaker handle the arrangements from the beginning the family will save money (they will avoid paying a duplication of costs) and will avoid confusion. Remember that your time is limited. Contact the transportation official (if the death occurred while enroute) or the hotel manager (if death occurred at the hotel). These individuals are familiar with how to handle guests who die and they can normally handle all arrangements quite well. Make sure that all of the deceased's valuables are inventoried with at least two witnesses present. Ask the family contact person to whom valuables should be sent and arrange for immediate air shipping, insuring all valuables at a "reasonable" full value. Keep receipts and shipping documents and turn these in with your tour report. Console other tour members, but get the tour on schedule as rapidly as possible.

Personal Entertainment Costs

Itinerary "free time" is often your free time too. Often tour members will invite you to accompany them. The invitation may or it may not be at the expense of the person(s) extending the invitation. We allocate $30 per week for your expenses to cover your costs when the pressures are such that you feel it would be rude to say, "no". However, any additional cost for such entertainment will have to be paid for by you, personally. In most cases you will be able to politely decline the invitation, if you choose to do so. Participation is not "required" by the company and any entertainment functions you attend during "free time" will not be considered "duty" time for financial compensation purposes. Be sensitive to "cliquishness" among tour members and if you accept invitations for free time entertainment, try to vary the person(s) or tour member groups you accompany during free time activities.

Index